Rethinking
Professional Issues
in Special Education

Rethinking Professional Issues in Special Education

Edited by James L. Paul, Carolyn D. Lavely,
Ann Cranston-Gingras, and Ella L. Taylor

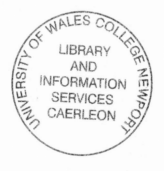

**Contemporary Studies in Social and Policy Issues in
Education: The David C. Anchin Center Series**
Kathryn M. Borman, Series Editor

Ablex Publishing
Westport, Connecticut • London

Library of Congress Cataloging-in-Publication Data

Rethinking professional issues in special education / edited by James L. Paul ... [et al.].
   p. cm.—(Contemporary studies in social and policy issues in education)
   ISBN 1-56750-626-7 (alk. paper)—ISBN 1-56750-627-5 (pbk. : alk. paper)
   1. Teachers of handicapped children—Training of—United States.
  2. Handicapped students—Education—United States. I. Paul, James L. II. Series.
LC4019.8.R48 2002
371.9′0973—dc21   2001053297

British Library Cataloguing in Publication Data is available.

Library of Congress Catalog Card Number: 2001053297
ISBN: 1-56750-626-7
    1-56750-627-5 (pbk.)

First published in 2002

Ablex Publishing, 88 Post Road West, Westport, CT 06881
An imprint of Greenwood Publishing Group, Inc.
www.ablexbooks.com

Printed in the United States of America

The paper used in this book complies with the
Permanent Paper Standard issued by the National
Information Standards Organization (Z39.48-1984).

10 9 8 7 6 5 4 3 2 1

Copyright Acknowledgment

Chapter 16, "Ethics and Special Education," originally appeared in *Focus on Exceptional Children*, V. 34 no. 1 (September 2001). Reprinted with permission of Love Publishing.

Contents

Preface

James L. Paul and Ann Cranston-Gingras

PROFESSIONAL CHALLENGES AT THE BEGINNING
OF THE TWENTY-FIRST CENTURY

The modern field of special education began around the middle of the twentieth century. Since that time there have been significant gains in special education services and quantum leaps in public policies supporting educational and related services for children with disabilities. These include, for example, dramatic changes in educational service delivery philosophy, a valued voice for families, extensive development of special education teacher education programs, doctoral programs to prepare teacher educators, the development of a knowledge base of evidence-based practices, and a law mandating appropriate educational services for all children in the least restrictive environment. At the same time, the professional issues for special educators have never been greater. For example, full funding for special education services continues to be challenged by some political leaders and members of the public media who charge inadequate benefits to justify the escalating costs of services. The philosophy of special education services continues to be debated, special educators are swamped with paperwork, and definitions and labels of disability continue to vary among states. Students served in programs for children with emotional and behavior disorders are more likely to be poor, lacking community supports, academically far behind their age-peers, and minorities, especially African American males. Resources to support the implementation of adequately designed studies, including longitudinal research, to address these and other issues are not available. In addition, a critical shortage of special education teachers continues to exist.

During the last half of the twentieth century, several useful books describing the professional issues facing special educators were published. Each reflected the author's views of the challenges in the social, political, professional, and economic contexts at the time. At the beginning of the twenty-first century, these contexts have changed in significant ways. For example, the emphasis on outcome accountability has reached new heights in the school reform movement, and professionals continue to be divided on the justification for full inclusion. The jobs of directors of special education in school districts are being expanded so that they cover more programs, or they are being diminished and consolidated with other areas. Categorical teacher certifications are being replaced, in many instances, by noncategorical or cross-categorical certification. Departments of special education in many universities are being dismantled and faculty members reassigned to other departments. Partnerships between universities and public schools are being developed and strengthened in ways that are transforming the special education curriculum, pedagogy, and structure of special education teacher education programs. The philosophy of educational research is being rethought to include support for nonpositivist approaches.

These changes are so dynamic that it is difficult to project the eventualities of the next few years. What is clear, however, is that the work of all special educators is changing and is likely to continue changing in significant ways in the foreseeable future. With this in mind, the editors planned this text to provide an analysis of significant professional issues in the education of teachers in special education at the beginning of the twenty-first century. The work was shaped by a decade of research and program development at the University of South Florida. A brief description of that work follows.

CONTEXT OF THE DESIGN AND PREPARATION OF THIS TEXT

For the past decade, faculty in the Department of Special Education at the University of South Florida have been pursuing a line of inquiry regarding substantive and methodological issues in teacher education in special education. Our research and development interests have centered on school reform, special education reform, inclusion, university-school partnerships, the nature of knowledge informing policy and practice, and ethics. Four of our initiatives have shaped the focus of the book: (1) research and development initiatives aimed at restructuring the Department of Special Education and university-public school relationships; (2) a scholarly project to examine the relationship between discipline-based knowledge and the knowledge base of special education policy and practice; (3) a study of ethics and school-based decisions about children with disabilities; and (4) a national Delphi study of the perceptions of special education researchers, teacher educators, parents, school administrators, and policymakers of the most significant challenges facing the field of special education. Each of the first three of these initiatives was funded and the data on implementations shared in books, articles, and at professional conferences by special education faculty at the University of South Florida (USF).

Restructuring University–Public School Relationships

The first major project brought together studies of school reform in public schools and related work in restructuring the mission and work of faculty in education at USF, with specific attention to changes in the teacher education program in special education. This work involved, and was the product of, changing the culture and curriculum in the university-based program and the program's relationships with schools.

Our work originated in collaborative research groups (CRGs) with varied interests—for example, special education reform, diversity, special education teacher education, and ethical decision making in schools. The CRG focusing on special education reform and the CRG on teacher education generated several different relationships between the department, other departments in the College of Education, and public school systems. The relationships were structured to address a major problem of out-of-field teachers, in one district, to develop a co-teach program to facilitate inclusion in a second, and to develop a professional development school to integrate research and teacher education in a school. Also, a funded study of school-based decision making about students with disabilities was implemented to help us understand more about the complexities of inclusion schools and the empirical and ethical rationales associated with policy decisions. These and other programs are shared in *Integrating School Restructuring and Special Education Reform* (Paul, Rosselli, & Evans, 1995).

Discipline-Based Knowledge in Special Education

One aspect of this work involved our interest in the relationship between knowledge bases in special education and knowledge bases in core disciplines. Our belief was that, since the beginning of the modern era of special education and support for doctoral programs, researchers in special education have increasingly relied on the emerging knowledge bases in special education and less on knowledge bases in disciplines such as psychology. This has implications for the history and scope of research interests and for theorizing about problems—for example, atypical development, learning, behavior management, and teaching.

The faculty initiated a study that resulted in two publications. The first (Paul et al., 1997a) included discussions of selected areas of scholarship in the social and neurosciences and humanities including psychology, anthropology, neurology, and ethics. Leading scholars from different disciplines contributed chapters, including, for example, Ed Ziegler, Urie Bronfenbrenner, Howard Gardner, Richard Lerner, Sonia Nieto, Nel Noddings, and Kenneth Howe. The primary knowledge bases currently guiding special education—child development, systems theory, and behavioral theory—were also described and placed in the context of discipline-based knowledge by scholars in special education.

The second publication (Paul et al., 1997b), building on the first, articulated the current state of knowledge in specific areas of practice such as assessment, work with families, technology, and teacher education. These chapters were contributed by leading scholars and researchers in special education and were processed through a dialogue conference with policymakers, administrators, and parents to validate the focus and import of the work.

These two volumes provide a fresh examination of some of the foundational knowledge in the social sciences, neurosciences, and humanities as bases for reflection on the nature of knowledge guiding special education practice and policy development. The primary goals were to bring more coherence to the discourse on knowledge and special education practice and to contribute to the substantive curriculum in doctoral education.

Ethics and School-Based Decision Making

Another project (Paul, Berger, Osner & Martinez, 1997) grew out of the work of a CRG on ethics and special education. The research interest of the group focused on ethical decision making in schools, with particular focus on how the needs of children with exceptionalities are understood and represented in the political and policy forums of local schools involved in reform. We were especially interested in how the interests of students with disabilities were interpreted and the voices of parents represented in the construction of ethical arguments to support inclusion or pullout programs.

The study of school advisory committees informed the development of an ethical perspective that can be used as the basis for an ethics curriculum to be used by local school policy bodies. This perspective has been useful in our thinking about our work in local schools.

Another interest of the CRG was the ethical content of doctoral programs in special education. A national survey of the curricula in doctoral programs in special education initiated by the group found that there is little specific attention to ethics except as ethical issues emerge in doctoral seminars. One of the outcomes of the work of this CRG and the examination of our doctoral program was to plan and implement a doctoral seminar in Ethics and Special Education that focused on ethics in research, policy, intervention, and teacher education.

Perceptions of Issues Facing the Field

We were interested in what special educators, teacher educators, policy-makers, and parents considered to be the most pressing issues facing the field. We conducted a national Delphi study with a limited sample of these different groups who have vested interests in special education and experience the challenges in their work and/or personal lives.

The categorical issues that emerged in the study were: (1) accountability and assessment; (2) technology; (3) research; (4) ethics; (5) curriculum; (6) service delivery; (7) interagency collaboration; (8) policy; and (9) philosophy and theory. Specific issues were included within each of these categories. A summary of major issues included the following:

1. Ensuring that students with disabilities have access to high-quality curricula and educational programs, and establishing systems to monitor and evaluate these programs. [Accountability and Assessment]
2. Ensuring the availability of appropriately qualified personnel willing and able to teach children with disabilities and providing them with a background in approaches to educating exceptional student populations. This includes developing and disseminating effective practices and establishing funding to provide intensive, personalized instruction and supervision in teacher preparation programs. [Teacher Education/Policy]
3. Developing collaborative relationships that effectively link special education, regular education, parents, and other community services (e.g., health and social welfare). [Interagency Collaboration]
4. Developing intensive prevention and early intervention programs for unidentified high-risk children throughout the preschool years. [Service Delivery]
5. Improving special education services, including curricula, for children with disabilities from diverse racial, ethnic, and linguistic backgrounds, and those from rural and inner-city settings. [Service Delivery/Curriculum]
6. Developing a credible response to attacks on the cost of special education and sustaining adequate financial support in an era of budget reduction and negative public perception. [Policy]
7. Bridging the gap between research and practice, including the efficacy of various instructional methods. [Research]
8. Maintaining support for a continuum of services, while implementing inclusive policies that do not compromise the quality of education. [Service Delivery]

9. Determining the desired outcomes of special education. [Theory/Philosophy]
10. Increasing awareness of ethical issues in special education teaching and research and addressing ethical quandaries facing special educators. [Ethics]
11. Integrating technology that is cost-effective and meaningful into classrooms, schools, and teacher education, and improving accessibility for minorities and students from low SES environments. [Technology]
12. Placing more emphasis on improving the organizational structure and culture of schools. [Service Delivery]

Although the present text is focused primarily on the education of teachers of students with disabilities, the selection of chapter topics and the content were shaped by two general considerations. The first was the perceptions of national leaders in special education as indicated in the Delphi study. The second was what we learned and came to believe as a result of the three major initiatives that guided much of the work of the department through almost a decade.

Guided by this work, our next step involved focusing our attention on the intellectual, ethical, and professional challenges facing the field of special education in the future. From the social science that grounds classroom practice to the moral, legal, and professional codes that legitimate special education policies, what are the issues that matter most and must be anticipated and addressed at all levels of preparation—undergraduate through doctoral—in special education?

We knew that arguments about professional challenges in the future must be informed by some projection of the populations to be served. We commissioned a demographer, Harold Hodgkinson, to project an analysis of the demographic context in which special educators will be working in the year 2020. His paper is included in the text.

The guiding principles for the work presented here came largely from the values, experiences, and constructions of an academic community as well as the specific data collected. The following section, therefore, makes explicit our own perceptions and values with respect to the intellectual, ethical, and professional challenges in special education.

OUR VALUES AND PERCEPTIONS OF ISSUES IMPACTING SPECIAL EDUCATION

The faculty in special education at the University of South Florida has attempted to function as a learning community. Most of the research generated by faculty and doctoral students during the past ten years has come from collaborative research groups. Within the context of the academic culture of the department, values or perceptions emerged that shaped our construction of issues. Following is a list of some of those perceptions that most influenced the development of this text.

- At its best, special education as a professional area of education accesses, integrates, and contributes to the scholarship of multiple disciplines. More commonly, however, the use of knowledge to support practice is fragmented with selected perspectives being privileged without explicit moral or philosophical defense.
- The knowledge bases relevant to special education practice and policy development have become more complex as they have, in some instances, made quantum advances. Instructional technology, multiple intelligence research, and behavioral pharmacology are examples.
- The large mainstream body of special education research is framed within a positivist, primarily behavioral, epistemology. The rest of the research in special education is "scattered," often with loose epistemological mooring and lack of systematic linkage with theory or explicit philosophical connectivity with other work.
- A commitment is needed to reconnect practices and policies with the knowledge bases of disciplines and to nurture a pluralistic epistemological discourse among researchers in special education. Such a commitment will create challenges for practitioners, policymakers, researchers, and teacher educators. It will involve a more concerted effort to educate teachers and teacher educators in the nature of knowledge and the forms of inquiry necessary to support the facilitation of learning in the classroom. It will also require a more dedicated focus on the part of researchers to understand and seek to address the challenges of practitioners and policymakers.
- Special education has been drawn into a political and social vacuum of socializing and providing basic care for students who are victims of poverty, abuse, and social displacement. "At riskness" has become a euphemism for students who fit neither the traditional disability criteria nor the normative standards for acceptable behavior in the general education classroom. Special education programs are, in many instances, serving a different population than those for whom special education programs were designed. Many students in special education programs today would have been expelled and on the streets, or in a residential facility, twenty-five years ago. They were not in school except in closed institutional contexts. Some of these students are homeless, and many present problems such as violence and drug abuse, for which special education, as traditionally conceived, has no answers. There is a serious mismatch between mission, technology, methods, training programs, and research on the one hand, and the challenges facing special educators, especially in urban areas, on the other.

- Reform in the structures and finance of education has challenged the heretofore unexamined assumptions about how special education programs should be administered and how services should be provided. The metacritique of special education by general educators at all levels of administration, in the classroom, and in teacher education programs, is that special education has deep pockets that should be accessed to support needed programs for children who do not have disabilities but who are nonetheless equally worthy. This view is beginning to be reflected in administrative restructuring and changing funding formulas.

- Special educators struggle among themselves over the moral mission of their work, where the children with exceptionalities will be educated, the philosophical adequacy of behavioral interventions, the sufficiency of "empirically-validated practices," and the nature and extent of family participation in special education programs. With so much local variation in approaches to these issues, the question of how special education teachers should be educated and trained for their work is one of the most pressing.

- The definition of special education has, from the beginning, been a subject of controversy because it exists in so many different constructions—in law, professional practice, political agenda, and in the moral consciousness of those who advocate for children with disabilities. The purpose may be less clear today than ever before because the advocacy and caretaking agendas are being so rethought with respect to public financial support. The next crisis in special education will most likely come when the bear market returns.

- The deep attacks on the value and cost-benefit of special education have not been sufficient to dismantle it. Reasoned and empirically supported arguments have challenged the integrity of what is viewed by some as a well-funded racist program in public education. One can view the continued public support for special education to be a function of the rationality and data supporting the counterarguments. Equally compelling as an explanation for continued support is that, with the provision that all children have a right to a free, appropriate public education in the least restrictive environment, special education is filling a need to provide some form of care for students who are not acceptable to, and are believed not to be educable in, regular education classrooms. The innocent assumption is that these students are those with disabilities. The elastic definitional boundary of emotional and behavioral disorders may suggest otherwise.

The perspective and content of the text reflect a decade of work of a diverse academic community in special education at the University of South Florida. Collaborative work creates the context for productivity; it does not require, nor even necessarily seek, consensus. The chapters here, therefore, do not follow a script or seek to advance a single point of view. They do reflect the outcomes, for the most part, of extended deliberations informed by studies of several issues.

The text is also informed by a national Delphi study of the perceptions regarding significant challenges facing the field of forty-five individuals associated with family leadership and disability advocacy groups and university faculty in special education, social foundations of education, and ethics. The views reflected in the work of the local academic community are, therefore, balanced by the views of a sample of national leaders.

All but five of the chapters were written by individuals who are, or have been, members of the local academic community. We were strongly motivated to garner perspectives on issues not typically developed in the special education literature.

Nel Noddings, Lee L. Jacks Professor of Child Education at Stanford, was asked to examine the issue of high-stakes testing and the implications for students with disabilities. Again, the analytic tools of a philosopher do not necessarily lead to the same conclusions as those of us with vested interests in the field of special education. However, Professor Noddings was asked to write the chapter not only because she is a philosopher but because she has a strong vested interest in the agenda of care in schools.

Historian Sherman Dorn, on the social foundations faculty at USF, was asked to examine the history of the field of special education from the perspective of an historian. The histories of special education have been written, typically, by special educators who write from inside the field and without necessarily having the tools of historiography.

Ann Turnbull and H. R. Turnbull, both professors at the University of Kansas, have provided national leadership in revisioning families with children with disabilities. Their research and positive perspective counter the deep and long-standing misunderstandings and negative constructions of families in clinical and educational communities. Their work is helping reshape the images of families and persons with disabilities.

Harold Hodgkinson is widely recognized for his work as a demographer. We knew from the beginning that it would be necessary to contextualize our identification and analysis of professional issues in the changing demography of schools. Professor Hodgkinson provides useful statistical data to inform our considerations of the challenges yet to face special educators.

James Gallagher, a psychologist, special educator, and Kenan Professor of Education at the University of North Carolina, was asked to write the chapter on research on interventions and the implications for special education policy. Professor Gallagher has a distinguished career in linking research and policy and is widely respected for his balanced and mature perspective for over four decades. Given policy challenges in the current context of differences of opinion about fundamental issues, and of poor communication in a cost-sensitive political environment, Gallagher offers ballast to a ship given to listing in the storms of controversy.

In addition to these scholars contributing chapters, Professor Peter French shared authorship of the chapter on ethics. French, Chair of the Department of Philosophy at USF and holder of the Cole Chair in Ethics, is well known for his scholarship in ethics. He participated directly in some of the academic community's studies of ethical decision making in local schools.

The collaborations of the academic community and the work of the scholars named here produced the content of the text.

REFERENCES

Paul, J. L., Churton, M., Morse, W., Duchnowski, A., Epanchin, B., Osnes, P., & Smith, L. (Eds.). (1997b). *Special education practice: Applying the knowledge, affirming the values and creating the future.* Pacific Grove, CA: Brooks/Cole Publishing Co.

Paul, J. L., Churton, M., Rosselli, H., Morse, W., Marfo, K., Lavely, C., & Thomas, D. (Eds.). (1997a). *Foundations of special education: Some of the knowledge informing research and practice in special education.* Pacific Grove, CA: Brooks/Cole Publishing Co.

Paul, J. L., Berger, N., Osnes, P., & Martinez, Y. (1997). *Ethics and decision making in local schools: Inclusion, policy, and reform.* Baltimore: Paul Brookes Publishing Co.

Paul, J. L., Rosselli, H., & Evans, D. (1995). *Integrating school restructuring and special education reform.* Fort Worth, TX: Harcourt Brace.

To Improve or Reconstruct Special Education: Issues Facing the Field

James L. Paul and Ann Cranston-Gingras

A GROUND-LEVEL VIEW OF ISSUES FACING SPECIAL EDUCATORS

Mary Johnson lives alone, and most days begin with a hot cup of coffee, a bagel with cream cheese, and the morning paper. This morning a headline on the editorial page in the Monday edition of the *Daily Record* catches her eye: "The Scandal of Special Education." She skims the article, and terms like "the road to hell," "bureaucrazy," "gross inequities," and the "unjustifiable costs of special education" catch her attention.

Her heart sinks; she is a teacher of students identified as having severe emotional disturbance (SED) at Northridge High School. She knows what is ahead of her today and wonders if the writer had any idea of the challenges in educating students like those in her class. Sure, he probably had visited schools and found that nothing in many special education classes looked like school as he remembered it. As his article indicated, he had read some published reports on costs and benefits. He knew some of the "facts" easily accessible from many sources distant from the lives of children with disabilities and their teachers. He knew the "facts"; he didn't know the story.

She pours herself another cup of coffee for the road, a forty-five-minute drive through heavy traffic in her suburban community to an overcrowded high school. Jermaine and Billy, two of her fourteen students, were arrested at the end of last week, one for aggravated battery and the other for larceny. She knows her class, usually high on Monday morning, will be wound tight from the events of last week. Her students have serious behavior problems, and all but one are at least four grade levels behind in their reading skills.

She faces challenges every day, sometimes centered on Wayne, a scapegoat in the class, and, at other times, involving relationships among the students: Jay is accused of knocking over Anita's desk, Oscar is accused of writing in Barry's book, and Mario explodes and attacks Joseph because he called him a name. This is a typical morning as Mary attempts to mediate among her students, teach them problem-solving skills, and, as possible, get through the reading lesson. Mary's anxiety about control of her students rises as lunchtime approaches. At least in her classroom, she has a manageable environment and social dynamics. When her students go to the lunchroom, the noise and the social stimulation create a situation where control of her students' behavior becomes the dominant issue. Other teachers watch her and, she believes, expect her to be the expert and control her students; after all, her class is much smaller than theirs and she has special training in behavior management. Because her day is so full and her "breaks" are virtually nonexistent, she has been able to develop a positive collegial relationship with only one other teacher and the school social worker who visits her classroom a few times a week and seems to have an affinity for her students. Together, they talk about the hope of positive outcomes for her students, but she notices that there are a lot of "only ifs" in their conversations.

As the day draws on, she is grateful that she has not had to break up a fight. The boys are bigger than she is, and sometimes she has been the only one with bruises when the fight stopped. At 3:00 P.M. the students leave the class, one of them to a home where the only parent works until 11:00 P.M., another to a home where the father was recently arrested for public drunkenness and spousal abuse. No one in her ethnically diverse class of adolescent boys returns to Pleasantville.

Mary's days in the classroom vary in intensity, with quiet seatwork more the exception than the rule. Keeping up with the students is psychologically exhausting. She is constantly making decisions that involve some thought about her students' individual needs and dynamics, not personalizing the verbal abuse she gets from Oscar and Mario, recognizing the discontinuity of her own history as a white, middle-class woman with eight of the students in her classroom who are African American males from low-income families, and attempting to focus on building a positive classroom culture. She wonders if there is something she should know or be able to do that would improve positive learning opportunities for her students. She often has doubts that she is a competent teacher. Her rewards as a teacher are minimal.

After school, Mary is free to meet with Ms. Adams, Wayne's mother, who is angry that the other students are picking on him. Wayne is withdrawn and has serious academic deficiencies. He is one of six children and helps around the house but falls apart when he is forced to leave to go to school. Ms. Adams lives alone with her children and works until 6:00 P.M. She does not have the time to assist Wayne with his homework.

Mary hears Ms. Adams' concerns and assures her that she will be more diligent in protecting Wayne from the abuse of other students and in teaching him skills to reduce his vulnerability. She also assists her in thinking about strategies to help Wayne complete his homework. After forty-five minutes in conference with Ms. Adams, Mary is ready to start on the paperwork she will need for Barry's IEP meeting on Wednesday.

After that, and an additional hour preparing for Tuesday, Mary leaves and drives home in her 1991 Sentra. Thinking about the "scandal of special education," she stops on the way at the grocery store to pick up some food for dinner, which she eats at 8:00 P.M. as she watches *Who Wants to Be a Millionaire*. She didn't feel like calling her mother tonight, so she takes a shower and climbs into bed with *The Crossing*, which she hopes to finish tonight. Tomorrow morning begins another day, coffee, a bagel. . . .

Friday, Mary has an appointment with her doctor. Her symptoms, she believes, are stress-related, but she doesn't see any way to get enough support at the school to reduce the stress. She has thought often during the past couple years of other professions, but she feels that she would be leaving students who need her. She feels responsible for the welfare of these students, and her own sense of responsibility is one of many ethical issues she thinks about on her often stalled drives to and from the school. Although she is not sure what, if anything, she accomplishes with some of her students, at least she is there, trying to teach them and, in many instances, support them through crises in their lives.

A teacher who was taking one of my classes (first author) commented recently, "I cried as I saw Raymond leaving the building in his wheelchair. He was leaving me and going to another school and I don't know if they will take care of him." Teachers often enter the profession with a romantic idealism about the role they can play in the lives of children with disabilities. Unfortunately, cultural realities and utilitarian policies of schools can defeat interest in individualizing instruction for students, and the bureaucracies of public education can create an environment that places the individualized care agenda in jeopardy and ultimately defeats the idealism. Some teachers leave; some lower their expectations to save their sanity and stay.

Thousands of special education teachers in this country leave home each new day to face many different circumstances in schools. Some of them are well prepared by training; some are teaching out-of-field and without credentials for teaching children with disabilities. Policies governing the special education services in each school vary widely, ranging from including all children in the regular classroom to pullout and special classes. Assessment philosophies and procedures vary from one school district to another. Special education departments in universities and colleges have different approaches to the education of teachers, ranging from applied behavior analysis to humanistic curricula. Special educators, general educators, parents, and policymakers disagree about whether students with disabilities should be educated in general education classrooms or in pullout programs. Professionals disagree about the goals of special education, whether the emphasis should be more on academic skills or on social skills. Researchers disagree about the kind of research needed to improve practice, and their debates occur far from the sites of need.

Yet, we have come a long way in this country in making educational provisions for children with disabilities. Mary Johnson is teaching fourteen students who thirty years ago would probably not have reached high school. They would have been suspended, some would have dropped out, and some of them would have had encounters with the juvenile justice system. They would have had little or no opportunity to stay in school and learn academic and positive social skills. It is unlikely that all fourteen of Mary's students will become successful after leaving school, and some may get into trouble with the legal system. However, without her and the opportunities provided by special education programs, most, if not all, would have had little chance of success. In 1987, Eugene Edgar reported that special education students appeared not to be benefiting from secondary programs. He cited high unemployment, meager wages among individuals who were employed, and poor community adjustment among former special education students (Edgar, 1987). More recent studies (Frank & Sitlington, 2000; Blackorby & Wagner, 1996), however, indicate that special education programs in collaboration with adult service providers are contributing to better outcomes for students with disabilities.

DEVELOPMENT OF MODERN DAY SPECIAL EDUCATION SERVICES

The modern day field of special education dates back to the middle of the twentieth century. It was developed in the wake of the civil rights movement, and advances, though uneven, occurred on several fronts. There were heroic efforts on the part of advocacy groups such as the National Association for Retarded Citizens, the United Cerebral Palsy Association, the Epilepsy Foundation of America, and the National Society for Autistic Children. Alliances between these advocacy organizations, political leaders, and professionals were successful in effecting major national policy changes and reforming the system of education for students with disabilities. Section 504 of the Vocational Rehabilitation Act in 1973 guaranteed the civil rights of individuals with disabilities and prohibited discrimination against them in education, employment, or any other activities. PL 94-142, Part B of the Education of the Handicapped Act, passed in 1975, provided for a free appropriate education for all children in the least restrictive environment. The Americans with Disabilities Act (ADA) in 1990 extended 504 protections to all programs and activities, not just those receiving federal funding. These plus other national legal and policy changes supporting the interests of individuals with disabilities, including children and their families during the last half of the twentieth century, have functioned as channel markers keeping the disability movement from running aground on issues of cost, rights, or public apathy.

Professional leadership has helped steer the advances in special education. Individuals such as Nicholas Hobbs, William Cruickshank, Sam Kirk, James Gallagher, Francis Connors, and other university-based leaders, worked alongside advocates like Elizabeth Boggs (NARC), Elsie Helsel (UCP), Eunice Shriver, and state and federal leaders in government and in the Congress in improving special education services. The vision was clear: Children with disabilities were being excluded from educational opportunities, and without special education services, they would fail and have no place in public schools. The vision prevailed.

When I (first author) first started working as the children's consultant in a state Department of Mental Health in 1967, most children identified as having severe emotional disorders were in psychiatric institutions, many of them on adult wards or treated in mental health centers or child guidance clinics. During the same time period, children like the second author's younger brother, who was then a five-year-old child who had a physical disability, were routinely excluded from school on the grounds that their inability to walk posed a "fire hazard." For the most part, cases like these no longer exist. Reforms in the mental health system focusing on normalization and the reduction of institutional dependency have led to the development of community-based services. Reforms in public education reflect a similar vision of normalization and integration of children with disabilities into the educational mainstream. Mental health and education policies have increasingly focused on more integrated and "normalized" services for over three decades.

An important part of the development of public policy over this period has been integration between as well as within services. As children are moved increasingly into the regular classroom with instructional supports, education and mental health services have recognized the need for better articulation between the services. With roots in mental health legislation passed in the 1960s, the move toward comprehensive community services included ideas of a "single portal of entry" into human services, and several models involving professional liaisons working between systems. Over time this same commitment to a better-coordinated system became "wrap-around services" and, most recently, a systems approach to mental health services.

A fundamental feature of the change in education and mental health policies relates to the attitude toward parents and families. Once viewed as the source of the problems that educators and mental health professionals were trying to solve in working with children, families are now understood to be allies who are part of the solutions and who have the final say in education and treatment decisions about their children. Attitudes about disability change at glacial speed; worldviews and community norms are reinforced through generations.

In bringing about major changes in law and public policy over the past three decades, parents, allied with some professional leaders and politicians, challenged the arrogance of exclusive public policies and practices of professionals that silenced their voice as a price of services for their children.

CHALLENGES AT THE BEGINNING OF THE TWENTY-FIRST CENTURY

Now, however, things are changing. Special education teachers, once held in high regard, are now being challenged to do what other teachers cannot do, and to do it under conditions of inadequate support (Miller, Brownell, & Smith, 1999). Adequately prepared special education teachers are in short supply (Boe, Cook, Kauffman, & Danielson, 1996; Boe, Cook, & Bobbitt, 1998; OSEP, 1996). Those who are well prepared and, especially those who are not, are facing difficult and, in some instances, impossible challenges in the classroom. Students who are victims of poverty and lacking social supports are often found in special education classes with labels of emotionally disturbed or behavior disordered. African American males continue to be placed disproportionately in special classes, and the teaching force continues to be primarily white female. Caring teachers often find themselves defeated by the ethos of high-stakes tests, excessive accountability-focused paperwork, lack of administrative support, and lack of success as a teacher.

The public media have carried articles that represent special education as ineffective and too costly. Some have presented the other side of the story. The *New York Times Magazine* (September 21, 1997) captured the spirit of the debate in an article titled "Special Education Is Not a Scandal." The author, Brent Staples, pointed out that prior to Congress intervening, schooling for children with disabilities ranged from very poor to barbaric.

There continue to be major policy challenges in providing the "most appropriate" education and services to children and their families that provide a continuity of care, and the issues facing the field are complex and pervasive. Teacher educators, researchers, teachers, supervisors, administrators, and policymakers, with their various responsibilities for the education of children with disabilities, all face mounting challenges. They range from countering negative criticism in the public media, to planning and conducting research to improve special education services, to finding ways to improve the quality of teacher preparation, to teaching children with disabilities. Three general professional issues that affect all special educators and all special education programs are discussed here: (1) the identity, philosophy, and ethics of special education, (2) the discontinuities among the different discourse communities in special education; and (3) the unsettling and often contentious context within which special educators function.

IDENTITY, PHILOSOPHY, AND ETHICS OF SPECIAL EDUCATION

Special education has always labored under the structuralist burden of categories of disability. It is recognized that the medical and psychological categories have little, if any, educational meaning. The presumption of homogeneity notwithstanding, the differences among children with emotional and behavioral disorders, for example, and children with learning disabilities are greater than the differences between them. Definitional disputes and debates are a part of the legacy of special education. The general defense of categories of disability has been that there seems to be no better way of drawing down funds to support children with disabilities. Rapprochement has been reached by expediency, not by a resolution of the conceptual and empirical issues associated with the language employed.

Advances have been made in the field of learning disabilities, for example, since the mid-1960s when the professionals and parents gave support to this label in place of forty-two other, mostly medical, labels such as brain damaged, Strauss syndrome, and brain injured. Although there continues to be debate about the definition of learning disabilities as well as other categories, significant gains have been made in identifying and developing educational interventions to address the learning difficulties of children.

Similarly, with the labels "emotional disturbance" and "behavior disorder," the definition is far from satisfactory and the labels and the definitions vary from state to state. Substantial advances have been made, however, in managing the disruptive behavior of children in the classroom.

The definitional problems have created difficulties in identifying children with disabilities. Screening and assessment tools are developed with a particular understanding of the issues and specific indicators of the problem(s). The epidemiology of groups of children identified for special education services continues to be an inexact science and results in a wide variation of estimates.

Fortunately, there are now strength-based approaches to assessment (Epstein & Sharma, 1998) that reflect a different view of disabilities. Still, approaches to assessment continue to be mired in conceptual, definitional, measurement, and ethical issues. Although the conceptual frameworks within which disabilities are understood have changed over the past three decades, some perspectives have remained relatively stable. For example, debates about different theories of emotional disturbance stimulated by publications from the Child Variance Project (1972–1975) were resolved as a practical matter by most teachers opting for a behavioral view. Although that view has been challenged by individuals on humanistic grounds, it has generally prevailed.

Similarly, when learning disabilities was accepted as the most relevant for educational purposes, special educators generally took the lead suggested by Barbara Bateman (1965), which built on the perspective of William Cruickshank (1961) and others in pursuing a behavioral perspective.

The conversation about theories changed over the past thirty years. Although behavioral theory continues to be the view of choice of many, if not most, issues have been raised about the applications and about the science (see next section). Importantly, there have been major advances in the behavioral philosophy and technologies, including positive behavior support and functional assessment (Sugai et al., 2000). There is more appreciation for the child's different environments and the role families can play as allies in treatment programs.

Another issue that is raised periodically has to do with the "specialness" of special education. "Isn't special education just good education?" Some have argued forcefully that the task ought to be focusing on the general education classroom and promoting the empirical validation of instructional practices and assisting in the implementation of these practices. Others have argued that the sociology and politics of education make this a daunting, if not impossible, task. Children with "mild disabilities," it is argued, may be appropriately served in the regular classroom, but children with severe disabilities, especially those with severe emotional disturbance, cannot (Hallenbeck, Kauffman, & Lloyd, 1993). The social ecology of schools functions in ways to marginalize and ultimately to segregate and stigmatize children who violate expectation as well as behavioral norms. This dynamic held minority children "in place" until revolutionary interventions, especially legal, forced schools to change. In this context it is noteworthy that African American males continue to be disproportionately placed in segregated classrooms for children with emotional and behavioral disorders (Harry & Anderson, 1994).

Perhaps the most basic issue in the philosophy of special education has to do with the definition and philosophy of education. Here the conversation extends to a discussion of the purpose of education in a liberal democracy. Basic ethical questions of the meaning of equity, free choice, and desert are raised. Paul, French, and Cranston-Gingras discuss these issues at some length in chapter 16 of this text.

Not surprisingly, there are different views of what needs to change and how it should change in the reform of education. Andrews and others (2000) distinguished between those who seek incremental improvements and those who advocate more substantial reconceptualization of the field. Fuchs and Fuchs (1991) distinguished the idealists, or abolitionists, and the pragmatists, or conservationists. The underlying issue is whether or not special education services are improving over time, or whether the education of children with disabilities needs to be substantially rethought. Although there are good reasons supporting both views, leaders in the field are divided on this matter and their division is reflected in the literature.

DISCONTINUITIES AMONG DISCOURSE COMMUNITIES IN SPECIAL EDUCATION

The categorical foundations of special education have created different discourse communities. Individuals associate themselves and their research and teaching with mental retardation, for example, or some other category of disability. Although the move during the last decade has been increasingly toward cross-categorical programming, and a focus on degrees of disability (mild, moderate, and severe) rather than the traditional categories, and a considerable literature now exists reflecting that move, there continue to be categorical certification courses, and journals that serve to maintain categorical discourse communities.

Some strongly oppose the cross-categorical approach because, they argue, so much of the content—history, philosophy, characteristics, and approaches—associated with specific categories is lost. Those supporting cross-categorical approaches argue that the methods for educating children with different labels are very similar and that different methods courses in teacher education programs are not needed.

CONTENTIOUS CONTEXT OF SPECIAL EDUCATION

Special education is a subsystem of the general education system. Created to meet the educational needs of children whose needs could not be met in the general education curriculum, special education took on a life of its own. It has been evaluated as less effective than the general education system for many children and, at the same time, advocated as the only viable educational solution by many others.

The independent variables of interest have ranged from the curriculum and methods to the competencies, or preparation, of teachers and the location of the service. The dependent variables have also varied widely and included academic achievement and behavior. Notwithstanding significant gains in developing a knowledge base of empirically validated practices, measurement problems, and, because of ethical issues, constraints on implementing experimental designs have kept the issues of "best practices" a much debated topic.

Special education has become increasingly complex over the past thirty years. Schools have become more diverse, parents have become more involved, accountability for the academic gains of students has increased, the philosophy of service delivery has become a larger policy issue, and funda-mental questions about the traditional philosophy of research have been raised. At the same time, special education teachers have become more burdened by paper, and more special education programs are staffed with out-of-field teachers. Special education teacher educators are being drawn into mergers with academic departments that do not necessarily support their work, being viewed as accountable for former students who are unsuccessful in their work as teachers, and needing to spend more time in liaisons between the university and public schools.

Special education researchers are being challenged by the limited success of traditional research to guide practice and by critiques of the positivist epistemology of most special education research. They find themselves caught in a dilemma of having the effectiveness of empirically validated practices challenged when, in fact, they have never been widely implemented.

The complexity has required professional special educators to reflect and take stock of research, policy, and practice issues. Several professional special educators have assessed the issues and shared their assessments in books (e.g., Jones & MacMillan, 1974; Schmid, Moneypenny, & Johnson, 1977; Schmid & Nagata, 1983; Benner, 1988; Lloyd, Singh, & Repp, 1991; Ysseldyke, Algozzine, & Thurlow, 2000). The assessments have been the perceptions of individuals based on their experiences, values, and the research available to them at the time. The issues have included basic topics such as theories, definitions, assessment, placement, instruction, transitions, technol-ogy, early intervention, school reform, inclusion, ethics, and law. General topics in the 1990s have included, among other things, the nature of the knowledge guiding the practice (Paul, Churton, Roselli et al., 1997); the philosophical nature of the system of special education (Skrtic, 1991); the challenges of postmodern thought (Benner, 1998); and critiques of special education in the context of a democracy (Skrtic, 1991; Danforth, 1997).

OVERVIEW OF THE TEXT

We have elected to focus on critical issues facing special education that, in the context of the beginning of the twenty-first century, may need to be rethought. Answers to questions about practice raised in the 1960s or 1970s may be inappropriate for the present time. Even the questions may need to be reframed. We have organized our discussion of what we consider to be among the most significant professional issues in special education today around fifteen general questions.

- *Who Will Need the Services?* In his chapter on the demographics of special education, Harold Hodgkinson summarizes changes in the de-mographics of American youth with projections to 2020. He discusses the literature on special education and shows the relationship between demographic variations and shifts in the special education population.

- *What Are the Policy Implications of Intervention Research with Students at Risk and Those with Disabilities?* James Gallagher, in his chapter on research regarding interventions and children with special needs, describes representative studies involving direct and indirect interventions with populations of students at risk and those with disabilities. He discusses the findings of these studies and their implications for policy in the field.
- *How Is High-Stakes Testing Distorting the Care Agenda in Schools and What Are the Implications for Special Education?* Nel Noddings, in her chapter on high-stakes testing and the distortion of care, examines the inherent threats high-stakes testing poses to care in schools. She discusses how the reduction of accountability in public schools to outcome measures of academic achievement presents a serious challenge to a competing curriculum designed to understand and respond to the holistic learning needs of children and how issues of poverty and disability predispose many children to an uneven playing field with respect to academic outcomes.
- *How Will We View and Understand the Service Needs of Families?* In their chapter on the old and new pagadigm of disability and families, Ann and H. R. Turnbull discuss the old paradigm of disability with its emphasis on power-over relationships between professionals and mothers. The new paradigm of disability and families is then presented as having power-through relationships where families and professionals work together in a synergistic way.
- *How Is Violence in the Home, School, and Community Impacting Children with Disabilities?* Zena Rudo, Vestena Robbins, and Denise Smith address the impact of violence in the home (domestic abuse), in the community (gangs), and in the schools (fights, weapons) on the learning of children with disabilities. They address professional issues including the emotional and behavioral effects of violence leading to placement in special education classes, the impact of violence on students' learning, skills teachers need to work with students who have been traumatized, working with the families of children who have been abused, collaborating with the community regarding the violence that occurs within the child's environment, and developing systems of care that include the schools, families, social services, community and medical systems.
- *What About the Voice of Persons with Disabilities in Special Education Policy and Services?* Ann Cranston-Gingras and Crystal Ladwig write about the area of disability studies that has become a focus of scholarly literature. They discuss how the perspectives of individuals with disabil-

ities and their families are informing professional issues in special education and present implications for teacher preparation.

- *Who Will Teach the Students?* Calling upon memories teachers have of their own former teachers, Jim Paul and Patricia Parrish discuss how experiences with their teachers contribute to a moral vision of teaching, their values and sense of social justice in the classroom, and their construction of power and privilege. They discuss the importance of these factors especially with regard to the education of students with exceptionalities and provide illustrative narratives written by teachers.

- *What Is the Role of Self in Education and How Can It Be a Part of the Teacher Education Curriculum?* Pat Fagan and Ella Taylor discuss the challenges faculty members face in rethinking the perspective they bring to understanding their relationships with students preparing to be teachers and in helping students learn self-reflective skills. They describe components of a teacher education program designed to help develop practitioners who will have the skills to create reflective, ethical environments in their classrooms.

- *How Can the Demographics of the Teaching Force Be Made More Culturally Valid?* Brenda Townsend and Karen Harris describe a university-school professional development initiative that recruits and prepares African American men to teach learners with special needs. Their chapter includes a discussion of lessons learned in developing successful teaching strategies for urban children and youth.

- *How Can Schools and Universities Work Together in Improving the Education of Teachers for Urban Special Education Environments?* In their chapter on collaborative professional development partnerships, Karen Colucci, Betty Epanchin, and Kathy Laframboise describe the development of a partnership designed to simultaneously meet the needs of two school districts and a university to prepare teacher candidates for work with diverse learners and to retain master teachers in the fields of general and special education. Assumptions on which the partnership has been established, challenges faced, and lessons learned through the partnerships are presented.

- *How Can Educational Technology and Assistive Devices Improve the Education of Students with Disabilities?* In her chapter, Barbara Loeding examines the range of educational technology and assistive devices now available for students with disabilities and makes projections for the future regarding potential developments. She explores issues related to pre-service training such as selection of appropriate assistive technology and provision of training for students and their families with an emphasis on the impact of the family's culture and first language.

- *How Can Distance Learning and Technology Help Meet the Needs of Students with Disabilities?* In their chapter on distance learning and technology, Michael Churton examines how distance learning technologies can be used to provide access to information and learning for children with disabilities in nontraditional settings.

- *What Is the Status and Future of Charter Schools in Serving Students with Disabilities?* Myrrha Pammer, Carolyn Lavely, and Cathy Wooley-Brown, in their chapter on charter schools and children with disabilities, provide an overview of the charter schools movement, present a summary of the most recent research related to charter schools and children with disabilities, and discuss the major special education issues currently facing charter schools. The authors provide recommendations to charter schools for serving students with disabilities.

- *What is Special Education and What Will It Be?* Sherman Dorn identifies six common themes from the special education literature for what authors say has influenced special education in the past: individuals, ideas, cultural values, social movements, structural conflict in society, and organizational development. He discusses how these themes cut across how authors evaluate the ethics of special education practices, and how they can help orient readers to the subtler issues at stake in the professional literature.

- *What Are the Moral Dilemmas in Special Education and How Can They Be Addressed?* In our chapter on ethics and special education, we, along with Peter French, examine the moral and political narrative of special education. We explore the theory of character morality as a complement to the more familiar choice morality as a way to think about ethical dilemmas in the field and discuss special education in the context of a liberal democracy. We also discuss the need to develop an ethical basis for discourse on the nature and representation of knowledge.

REFERENCES

Andrews, J., et al. (2000). Bridging the special education divide. *Remedial and Special Education*, 21 (5), 258–260.

Bateman, B. (1965). An educator's view of a diagnostic approach to learning disorders. In J. Hellmuth (Ed), *Learning disorders*. Seattle: Special Child Publications.

Benner, S. (1998). *Special education issues within the context of American society*. Belmont, CA: Wadsworth.

Blackorby, J., & Wagner, M. (1996). Longitudinal postschool outcomes of youth with disabilities: Findings from the National Longitudinal Transition Study. *Exceptional Children, 62*, 399–413.

Boe, E., Cook, L., and Bobbitt, S. (1998). The shortage of fully certified teachers in special and general education. *Teacher Education and Special Education, 21*, 1–21.

Boe, E., Cook, L., Kauffman, M. J., and Danielson, L. (1996). Special and general education teachers in public schools: Source of supply in a national perspective. *Teacher Education and Special Education, 19*, 1–16.

Cruickshank, W. M., Bentzen, F. A., Ratzeburg, F. H. & Tannhauser, M. T. (1961). *A teaching method for brain-injured and hyperactive children*. Syracuse, NY: Syracuse University Press.

Danforth, S. (1997). Postmodernism, narrative and hope in special education. In J. Paul, M. Churton, H. Rosselli, W. Morse, K. Marfo, C. Lavely, D. Thomas (Eds.), *Foundations of Special Education* Pacific Grove, CA: Brooks/Cole Publishing Co.

Edgar, E. (1987). Secondary programs in special education: Are many of them justifiable? *Exceptional Children, 53*, 555–561.

Epstein, M. H., & Sharma, J. (1998). *Behavioral and emotional rating scale: A strength-based approach to assessment*. Austin, TX: PRO-ED.

Frank, A., & Sitlington, P. (2000). Young adults with mental disabilities—does transition planning make a difference? *Education and Training in Mental Retardation and Developmental Disabilities, 35*, 119–134.

Fuchs, D., & Fuchs, L. S. (1991). Framing the REI debate: Abolitionists versus conservationists. In J. Lloyd, N. Singh & A. Repp (Eds.), *The Regular Education Initiative: Alternative Perspectives on Concepts, Issues and Models* (pp. 241–255). Sycamore, IL: Sycamore Publishing Co.

Hallenbeck, B. A., Kauffman, J. M., & Lloyd, J. W. (1993). When, how, and why educational placement decisions are made: Two case studies. *Journal of Emotional and Behavioral Disorders, 1*, 109–117.

Harry, B., & Anderson, M. G. (1994). The disproportionate placement of African American males in special education programs: A critique of the process. *Journal of Negro Education, 63*, 115–149.

Jones, R., & MacMillan, D. (1974). *Special education in transition*. Boston: Allyn and Bacon.

Lloyd, J. W., Singh, N. N. & Repp, A. C. (1991). *The Regular Education Initiative: Alternative Perspectives on Concepts, Issues and Models*. Sycamore, IL: Sycamore Publishing Co.

Miller, M. D., Brownell, M. T. & Smith, S. (1999). Factors that predict teachers staying in, leaving or transferring from the special education classroom. *Exceptional Children, 65*, (2), 201–18.

Office of Special Education Programs (OSEP). (1996). *Eighteenth Annual Report to Congress on the Implementation of the Education of the Handicapped Act.* Washington: U.S. Department of Education.

Paul, J., Churton, M., Rosselli, H., Morse, W., Marfo, K., Lavely, C., & Thomas, D. (Eds.). (1997). *Foundations of special education: Some of the knowledge informing research and practice in special education*. Pacific Grove, CA: Brooks/Cole Publishing Co.

Schmid, R., Moneypenny, J., & Johnson, R. (1977). *Contemporary issues in special education*. New York: McGraw Hill.

Schmid, R., & Nagata, L. (1983). *Contemporary issues in special education*. New York: McGraw Hill.

Skrtic, T. (1991). *Behind special education*. Denver: Love Publishing Co.

Sugai, G., Horner, R. H., Dunlap, G., Hieneman, M., Lewis, T. J., Nelson, C. M., Scott, T., Liaupsin, C., Sailor, W., Turnbull, A. P., Turnbull, H. R., Wickman, D., Wilcox, B. & Ruef, M. (2000). Applying positive behavior support and functional behavioral assessment in schools. *Journal of Positive Behavior Interventions, 2*, 10.

Ysseldyke, J., Algozzine, B., & Thurlow, M. (2000). *Critical issues in special education* (3rd ed.). Boston: Houghton Mifflin Co.

2

The Demographics of Special Education

Harold Hodgkinson

CHANGES IN YOUTH DEMOGRAPHICS, 1990–2020

History: Boom to Bust to Boomlet

Between 1946 and 1964, 70 million children were born, virtually doubling the number of children in that eighteen-year period. We call this the Baby Boom. Births then began declining, from 4.2 million per year down to 3.1 million by 1974 (the so-called "Baby Bust"). By 1976, baby boomers started to have their own children, and things started up again, but never attained the numbers at the boom's peak. Around 1990, the numbers started down, but very gradually, and now seem to be stable at 3.8 million births a year (see Figure 2-1). Remember that the trough after the boom went down to about 3 million, whereas the current situation is a stable group of 3.8 million per year, a long-term increase of 800,000 children born per year. (If you add the children of immigrants coming every year, we are at a "floor" of about a million children a year over the previous bottom of 3.1 million.)

State Differences

Nothing is distributed evenly in the United States, because people are not distributed evenly. While most states have seen small increases, about half of the nation's growth has been in only three states—California, Texas, and

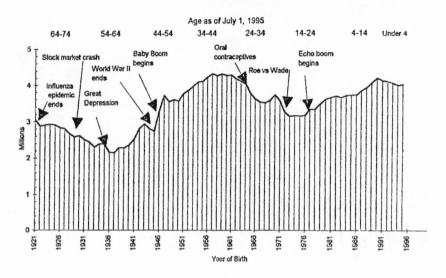

Figure 2-1. Boom to bust to boomlet (*Source:* U.S. Public Health Service, *Vital Statistics of the U.S.*, 1921–1995).

Florida. The increases in these states have been heavily "minority." (California, Texas, and Florida also led in *total* population increases, thereby picking up fourteen seats in the U.S. House of Representatives (distributed by population rank), seats given up by New York (three), Pennsylvania, Michigan, Illinois, and Ohio losing two each. These five states made two classic mistakes: (1) They neglected to have children, and (2) no one with children moved in. Many mid-Atlantic, New England, and "Heartland" states are becoming old by default, because movers are younger and more educated than "stayers." The 2000 census will show these trends continuing (Figure 2-2). As young people moved out of these states, they were not replaced, leaving a "net" of an increasingly aging population. The Southeast and Southwest (including most mountain states) gained in youth population while the northern half of the states lost youth or stayed even. The northern half is extremely white, whereas the southern half, showing the maximum growth of youth, is ethnically very diverse.

Between 2000 and 2010, the U.S. population under age 18 goes from 71 to 73 million, but the increase is far from uniform. All the New England states, New York, and Pennsylvania decline in 0–18 year olds, as do Ohio, Indiana, Illinois, Michigan, Wisconsin, Minnesota, Iowa, Missouri, North Dakota, Nebraska, Kentucky, and Mississippi. In fact, California alone goes from 9.7 million under age 18 to 11 million. Virtually half of the nation's growth in youth will be in the single state of California! Add Texas and Washington

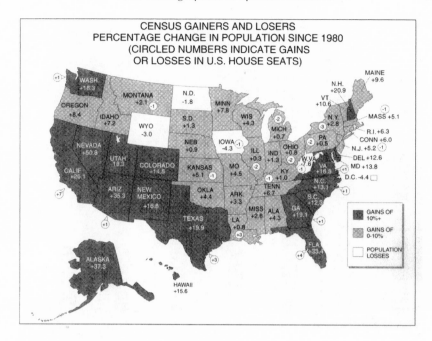

Figure 2-2. Census gainers and losers.

state and you almost have the nation's entire gain in youth. The rest of the "growth" states have very small increases indeed. The "teacher shortage" will certainly not be spread evenly across the nation, if there is any shortage at all. (There's always been a shortage of special education teachers, bilingual teachers, and teachers in inner city schools, but good suburban districts still have twenty applicants per opening, more or less.) Almost nothing is distributed evenly across the United States.

Fertility and Transiency

White fertility (in the United States and in the world) is either at replacement level or beginning to decline. Of the 5.6 billion people on the planet in 1995, only 17 percent were white, dropping to 9 percent white by 2010. White people represent one of the smallest ethnic groups in the world, which is why "minority" is put in quotes. The most diverse sector of Americans is our youngest children. Virtually everywhere in the world, the number of children produced over the lifetime of a white female is below the replacement level (see Figure 2-3): 2.1 children per female will allow a population to "stay even," but the current white fertility rate in the United States is 1.7 children

AVERAGE BIRTHS PER WOMAN							
	1963	1993	% fall		1963	1993	% fall
Thailand	6.4	2.1	67%	Brazil	6.1	2.9	53%
Columbia	6.7	2.7	60%	Mexico	6.7	3.2	53%
Dominican Rep.	7.3	3.1	58%	Lebanon	6.5	3.1	51%
Kuwait	7.3	3.1	58%	Peru	6.8	3.4	50%
Tunisia	7.1	3.1	56%	Venezuela	6.6	3.3	50%
Costa Rica	6.8	3.1	54%	United Stated	3.2	2.1	34%

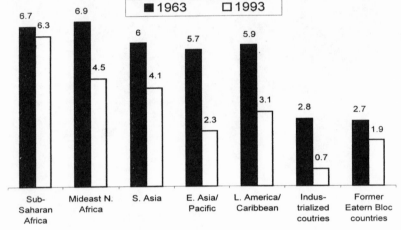

Figure 2-3. World fertility.

over the lifetime of the mother (Utah is a major exception). Except for a couple of mountain states, those with the largest gain of youth under age 18 have been in the Southeast and Southwest, and the gains have been significantly nonwhite.

In addition to fertility differences, more than half of this increased population and diversity in the south is due to people leaving northern states and moving south (Figure 2-4). In one recent five-year period, 103 million Americans changed addresses! That's almost half of our 160 million total. No other nation has this rate of movement. But if you look at the moves made, about 70 million people were still in the same state, and 34 percent were still in the same county. However, to a third grader moving from one school district to another in the same county, the move might as well have been across the nation: new school, new friends, new teachers, new curriculum, and so on. Transiency is almost never addressed as a major school problem in the United States, but virtually anywhere in the nation you can find teachers with twenty-three students in September, twenty-three the following June, but twenty-one of the twenty-three will be a different person.

Even with transiency we find vast differences. In Pennsylvania, about 80 percent of the people who live there were born there. In Nevada, less than 30 percent of the residents were born there. Rapidly growing states obviously have the most transient populations. With transiency generally go high crime rates, lack of social cohesion and consensus, difficult child rearing, unstable families, and difficult home/school communications, as well as a "temporary" attitude toward life, creating many educational problems that stable (or declining) areas do not have.

Ethnicity

As of 1993, 34 percent of U.S. school-age children were non-White, 16.6 percent Black, 12.7 percent Hispanic, 3.6 percent Asian, and 1 percent American Indian. (One tricky thing is that "Hispanic" is not a census racial category but an "ethnic group," often double-counted as white—every Hispanic must also choose a "race" on the census form.) As of 1993, the NEA reported that less than 12 percent of public school teachers were "minority," declining to about 3 percent in about fifteen years when more than 40 percent of the students will be "minority"! As of 1997, public school teaching is not seen as a desirable career choice by most college non-White youth. By 2010,

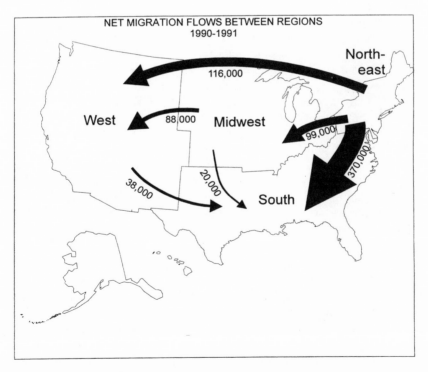

Figure 2-4. Net migration flows between regions (Source: U.S. Bureau of the Census, *Current Population Reports* P-20. No. 463 [October 1992]).

the "Hispanic" and "Black" populations will be of equal size (Meetings of NAACP and LaRaza to see who represents "colored people" should begin immediately, but probably will not. The last thing the nation needs would be a contest between those two key organizations.) Shortly after 2020, most U.S. children will be "minority" (at which time we will need a new word for a population that is half or more of the total), and by 2050, half of all the U.S. people will be diverse.

The issue of defining this increasing diversity of our people will be resolved (for good or ill) by the 2000 census. In no previous censuses (required by our Constitution every ten years to redistribute the government based on changes in the population) have the same categories been used. (The 1990 Census listed four races—White, Black, Asian, and Native American—and one "ethnic group"—Hispanic. In addition, many nations could be checked as well, particularly nations in South and Central America and Asia.) What was *not* allowed—and never has been—is a mixed race category. Some studies indicate that as many as 60 percent of Americans would check such a box if it were available. Any changes in these categories would have serious consequences for schools, in reporting and in eligibility for federal funds, some of which are targeted to specific racial/ethnic/national origin groups.

It is clear today that minority no longer means "poor." Twenty percent of black households have incomes higher than the white average, and the "over $80,000 a year income" category is the most rapidly increasing among Hispanics. Except for American Indians, every minority group has a rapidly expanding middle class, usually living in the suburbs. Although there are many minorities in severe poverty, in 1997, minorities have spread across as broad an economic range as whites. Although ethnicity is no longer a universally handicapping condition, poverty is. There is no person who is better off in poverty than out of poverty, particularly our children. While there are hundreds of places in which Blacks, Whites, Hispanics, Asians, and Native Americans live together in peace and harmony, there are few if any places in which rich and poor live next door in peace and contentment. We are far more segregated by wealth in the United States today than we are by ethnicity.

Youth Poverty and the Elderly

As of 1994, the census reports that 21.2 percent of children under age 18 (17.4 million children) were below the poverty line. Statistics show that 16.3 percent of white children, 43.3 percent of black children, and 41 percent of Hispanic children were poor—that's 8.8 million White, 4.7 million Black, and 3.9 million Hispanic children below the poverty line. Children were in poverty more often than any other age group: while 21.2 percent of children were in poverty, only 14.5 percent of all people were; 11.7 percent of all

Whites were poor, but 16.3 percent of White children were; 30.6 percent of all blacks were poor, but 43.3 percent of Black children; 30.7 percent of all Hispanics were poor, but 41.1 percent of Hispanic children. The largest number of poor kids are White, but the highest percentage of children in poverty are Black and Hispanic. (No data for Asian and Native American children are provided in the 1996 *Statistical Abstract of the US*, although other sources show Native American children with the highest poverty levels of any group.) In 1994, 21.2 percent of all children were poor, and only 11.4 percent of America's over-65 population were. (In 1970, 14.9 percent of all children were poor, and 24.6 percent of those over age 65 were—the situation has almost exactly reversed.) Whereas it is good that fewer older citizens are in poverty today, it was accomplished on the backs of our youngest and most dependent people, which is not so good.

There is a curious lack of concern for the plight of young children in poverty in America—they are the future work force/parents/taxpayers (we are all dependent on the generation that comes behind us to take care of us in our old age), yet we ignore the issues of youth poverty. One of the reasons for this tendency to ignore youth can now be explained: The average American has little or no daily contact with a child. Only one household in four has a child of public school age. Older people seldom support school bond issues out of sheer self-interest. School leaders must begin to see older persons as a resource in order to try to turn this attitude around. Older persons vote far more often than people in their twenties, making their political clout even stronger. We will, by 2025, have twenty-seven "Floridas" in the nation—20 percent of Floridians are over 65 today; twenty-seven states reach that level by 2025 (Figure 2-5). Most of the twenty-seven are states from which young people have fled without being replaced by other young people. Less of these states' income will come from wages (taxable) and more will come through the mailbox—Social Security, Medicare, stock dividend checks, annuities, and pension funds. A mailbox economy is very hard to tax until the older person spends the money. Like income segregation, age segregation is a major force keeping us apart. (There are many condo developments in which children are legally not allowed to live. There are very many places in which low-income people are not able to live, because there is no low-income housing there. There are no places in which minorities are legally not allowed to live.)

"SuperCities," Metro Development, and Population Density

Most of the migration that we have already described occurred as people left small towns and rural areas, especially in the Heartland and "Rust Bowl" states, and moved to the suburban areas around our 320 SMSAs—Standard Metropolitan Statistical Areas (Figure 2-6). Each one has a core city of 50,000 or more and clearly defined suburban areas. Just a little more than half the

U.S. population lives in suburbs, one quarter in core cities, and one quarter in rural areas. (Of our 60 million rural residents, only 2 million have any connection with farming.) Some major changes have taken place in metro areas since 1980 (Figure 2-7).

- A majority of good jobs have been created in the suburbs.
- Income of city workers has steadily declined compared to suburban workers.
- The typical commute today is from a suburban home to a suburban job. Only a quarter of commuters are going from a suburban home to a "downtown" job.
- Because they can't buy their way out to the suburbs, cities are more segregated by income than by race. (Two of our most economically segregated states are Wisconsin and Minnesota, because of very small populations of middle-income [suburban] minorities.)
- If you win the suburbs, you win any national election.
- Mostly because suburbanites are wealthier and better educated, their schools have higher scores on standardized tests and a higher percentage

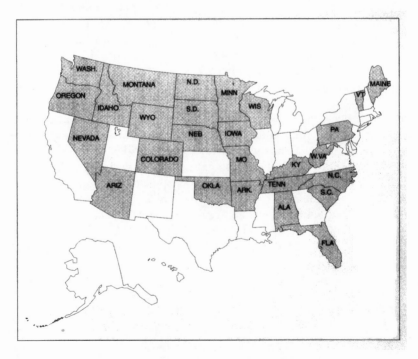

Figure 2-5. Twenty-seven Floridas by 2025: States where at least 20 percent of the population will be elderly (*Source:* U.S. Census Bureau, U.S. Department of Commerce, PPL-47).

A Metro Area is...

...in the minds of most people, a big city and its suburbs. But the Census Bureau,

which counts 284 metro areas, uses a more formal definition:

- A metro area is built around one or more central counties containing an urban area of at least 50,000
  people. It also includes outlying counties with close ties —economic and social— to the central
  counties. To be considered part of the metro area, the outlying counties must meet certain criteria,
  including number of commuters, population density and growth, and urban population.

- In New England, metro areas are composed of cities and towns rather than whole counties.

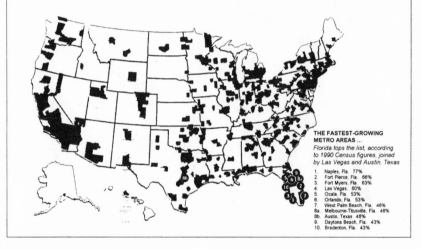

THE FASTEST-GROWING
METRO AREAS ...
*Florida tops the list, according
to 1990 Census figures, joined
by Las Vegas and Austin, Texas*

1. Naples, Fla. 77%
2. Fort Pierce, Fla. 66%
3. Fort Myers, Fla. 63%
4. Las Vegas 60%
5. Ocala, Fla. 53%
6. Orlando, Fla. 53%
7. West Palm Beach, Fla. 46%
8a. Melbourne-Titusville, Fla. 46%
8b. Austin, Texas 46%
9. Daytona Beach, Fla. 43%
10. Bradenton, Fla. 43%

Figure 2-6. How metro areas compare to the rest of the country (1990 census results).

of college preparatory students than core city schools. The "general curriculum" (neither college nor job related) is mostly in inner-city high schools.

- "Edge Cities" like Dearborn Michigan, are increasing. These suburbs have become completely autonomous, having cut the umbilical cord with their core city. (In some cases, people brag about their having not visited "downtown" in six months.) Everything they could want—from jobs to restaurants to theaters—is in their edge city.

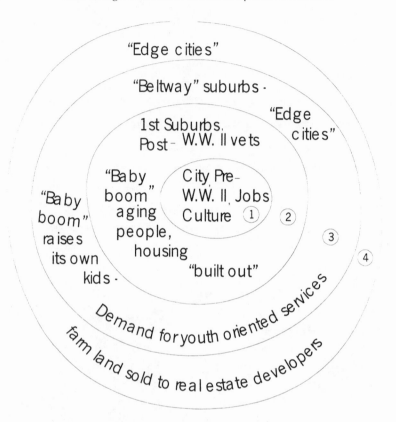

Figure 2-7. Metropolitan changes over time.

- Edge Cities exhibit total disregard of the large city that made them possible in the first place. Big questions are just beginning to be asked: What do cities and their suburbs owe each other? If the core city dies, how can the suburbs thrive?
- Rural children have almost the same poverty rate as urban children, but with a much smaller base of support services in rural areas. In hundreds of rural school districts, the total student body K through 12 is under 100 students. (If the senior class is only six students, it's very hard to hire a physics teacher.) It is very hard to bring political pressure to bear in low-density areas. Six votes per square mile is easy to ignore if you're running for office. In addition, services are more expensive per delivery in rural areas. In a New Jersey apartment house, you can deliver twenty Meals on Wheels for the elderly in twenty minutes. In southern Utah, it would take all day—it's eight miles between stops. Rural people and their needs are politically invisible.

Eastern core cities have thicker walls between city and suburb, because land is so expensive and because annexation of neighboring areas is virtually impossible. As you move west, metros are less often concentric circles and more often grids, which are much more flexible and spread jobs, college graduates, as well as poverty, more evenly across the entire metro area. So far, anywhere in the nation, suburban public schools will be superior, on almost any measure, to inner-city schools. There is no evidence that suburban kids are inherently superior, but they are usually advantaged. Just as small rural schools in Kentucky and other states have sued because of the advantage of wealthy districts in their state, court cases will be brought by inner-city districts against suburban districts on the same grounds—inability to provide a thorough and efficient education as mandated by state law. We have done a rather good job at reducing ethnic segregation in schools. The next task may be the reduction of economic segregation between city and suburb—a much more difficult task.

Immigration—The Creator of Tomorrow

According to the census, virtually all the population growth in the United States up to 2040 will be from immigrants and their descendents (Figure 2-8). While European immigrants have been the mainstay of the United States for most of our history, during the period 1980–1995 European immigrants were only 15 percent of the total, while South and Central America and Asia were responsible for 85 percent. (The dominant nation now is Mexico, with 1.3 million immigrants arriving just between 1991 and 1993, out of 3.7 million total arrivals from sixty-seven nations during that brief period. In general, the closer the geographical proximity to the United States, the larger the immigrant flow. Also, people from far away come to the United States knowing that they will not return often; and Puerto Ricans are more likely to feel like "dual citizens."

Immigrants come to a small number of states. Of the 804,000 admitted in 1994, New York accepted 144,000; Florida 58,000; Texas 56,000; California 208,000; Illinois 42,000; and New Jersey 44,000—or 550,000 of the total. This is because of the Ports of Entry (POE), which were the major ways into the country, particularly New York City, Chicago, and Newark. Today, you would have to add Dallas/Fort Worth, Miami, Los Angeles, and San Francisco to the POE list, representing the shift from European immigration to South/Central America and Asia. Some have suggested that the Statue of Liberty be set on ball bearings so that she could move 360 degrees and face the newly arrived, wherever in the world they were coming from. At present, she only beckons toward Europe.

Although today there is much criticism of immigrants, in Germany and France as well as the United States, the evidence suggests that at least in the United States, today's immigrants are doing about as well as previous groups.

IMMIGRATION: LEADING NATIONS	
1820-1945:	**1991-2000:**
GERMANY	MEXICO
ITALY	PHILIPPINES
IRELAND	KOREA
U.K.	CHINA-TAIWAN
U.S.S.R.	INDIA
CANADA	CUBA
SWEDEN	DOMINICAN REPUBLIC
	JAMAICA
	CANADA
	VIETNAM
	U.K.
	IRAN

Figure 2-8. Immigration: Leading nations.

They buy houses at the same rate (almost at the U.S. average if the immigrant has been in the United States ten years or more), their children learn English at the same rate (fourteen years to fluent English for an Italian immigrant at the turn of the twentieth century; fourteen years today for a Korean child, born in the United States). If the immigrant child's mother reads to the child regularly—in any language—the child learns English much more rapidly, even if the mother was reading to him/her in Korean! Ironically, just as the research is showing that bilingual programs are very effective, the nation is losing interest in them.

There is considerable argument as to whether or not immigrants take jobs away from native Americans. The majority of evidence suggests that this is not the case, because immigrants generally take jobs that cannot be filled by citizens, and they also start small businesses in droves, hiring citizens in the process. Basically, diversity in America is an advantage, as new groups move through the mobility system and into the middle class, creating new jobs and wage levels as they go. Over 20 percent of the members of the U.S. Senate have immigrant grandparents, a statement that cannot be made by any other nation. The best college students in the 1960s and 1970s were the children and grandchildren of Jewish immigrants; today the high scorers are children and grandchildren of Asian immigrants. There are some school problems with language and cultural differences to be sure, but in the main, immigrants have added a vitality to American life that is unmatched.

Changes in the Family

Between the 1980 and the 1990 census, only one family type declined: married couples with children, down 1 percent. Married couples without children was up 17 percent, single parent families up 35 percent, persons living alone up 25 percent, and persons living with nonrelatives (the base of every *Seinfeld* plot) up an amazing 46 percent. *Leave It to Beaver* would seem like science fiction to most of today's TV audience. The family father who worked outside the home, the homemaker mom, and their two+ children is actually an aberration, lasting only thirty years. As women entered the work force, usually because of economic necessity, everything changed. Day care became an essential, but many working mothers could not afford it. For single mothers, the poverty rate of their children is at least three times higher than for two-parent families, in White, Black and Hispanic households. It is also important to note that among single mothers, there are now as many never-married mothers as there are divorcees. Marriage is now separated from procreation for about one out of five children in the nation. (Although we feel this is uniquely American, the percentage of births to unmarried women is almost the same in the United States as in France and the United Kingdom: 30 percent; in Denmark, 46 percent of births are to unmarried women.)

There has been a major change in the trajectory of women's lives. Since the 1930s, women have been educated, then almost immediately got married, had children in their early twenties, and perhaps thought of a job twenty years later when the nest emptied. Today's woman (more than half) gets educated, then immediately gets a job, delaying marriage a number of years and in many cases never marries at all, delays children until her thirties or has no children at all even though married. This has made for smaller families, looser super-vision, and less "quality time" between parents and children. When several generations of a family lived together, even if the mother was working, there was a "spare adult" around when the kids got home from school or other activities. With today's nuclear family, there are few "spare adults" around, leaving the children to fend for themselves. This has major consequences: If a child is home alone for eleven hours a week or more, the chances of that child becoming involved with illegal drugs (including tobacco and alcohol as well as cocaine, marijuana, uppers, downers, ice, hosing, etc.) doubles, regardless of income or educational level of parents.

Although the economic difficulties of being a single parent are spread across all ethnic categories, the degree of poverty experienced by the children is often greater in minority single-parent households (Figure 2-9). (Most children of single mothers are White, but the highest percentage of children with single mothers is Black.) Again, Americans take a peculiar view of these major problems for families and children—which is to avoid them whenever possible. Visitors to the United States are often surprised that we neglect our youth as a national resource—they often say that we are "eating our seed corn," and they are undoubtedly correct.

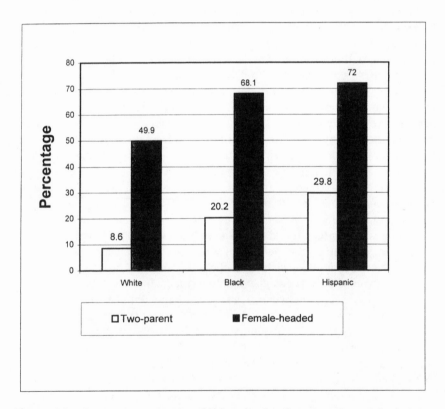

Figure 2-9. Poverty rates among children by family type, race, and ethnicity, 1990 (*Source: Beyond Rhetoric: A New American Agenda for Children and Families* [National Commission on Children, 1991. p. 25); *Statistical Source: Statistical Abstract of the United States* [Bureau of the Census, 1992, Table #719]).

Prevention

Before attacking the special education literature, a word needs to be said about what we have learned about young people who enter school at risk of failure from a variety of sources: poverty, single parents, bad neighborhoods, neglect, pregnancy, violence, and so on. That knowledge can be contained in a single phrase: *Prevention works.* It is much cheaper and more effective to prevent bad things from happening to young people than it is to wait until after the bad thing(s) have happened and then try to patch them up. The earlier you intervene, the better the results. Recent research has illuminated the importance of the preschool years, in which we learn over 60 percent of our lifetime total. Getting every child vaccinated, detecting signs of hearing loss, making sure that kids don't go hungry, ensuring high-quality day care when one or both parents work, all are clearly in the national interest.

As one example, consider that over 70 percent of prisoners are high school dropouts (Figure 2-10). Each prisoner is now costing the taxpayer over $26,000 a year just to maintain, enough cash to send two or three students to the state university tuition-free! (It is twice as expensive to have a person in the state pen than to have one in Penn State.) In fact, it is more likely that a

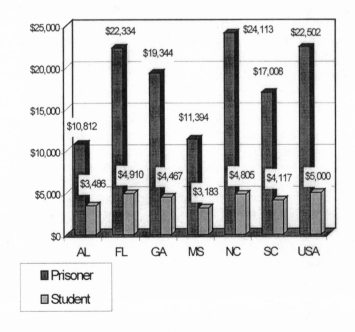

Figure 2-10. Average annual cost per prisoner versus student (1991–1992) (Source: U.S. Bureau of the Census, 1991).

high school dropout will become a prisoner than that a heavy smoker will get lung cancer. The latter we see as a national emergency; the former is totally ignored. Even universities need to understand that the most crucial years of development have already happened by the time the child knocks on the kindergarten door for the first time. Generally, prevention gets about 15 percent of our total social program money, even though it's about 75 percent effective. The longer we wait, the more it costs, and the less likely we are to succeed.

THE DEMOGRAPHICS OF SPECIAL EDUCATION

If the followers and supporters of special education have a zeal and commitment that seems almost too high for some, there is a good reason. Before 1973, any principal or superintendent in the nation could exclude any child from attending any public school by simply pronouncing them "uneducable." Appeals were not useful in most cases, so over 1 million children had no schooling, or in a few cases were educated in private facilities, at extraordinary cost to the parents. It was as easy to deny public schooling for having a disability as for being Black in the 1960s.

Two landmark court decisions changed everything. *Brown v. Board of Education* in Topeka outlawed racial segregation in schools. *Mills v. Board of Education* in 1973 entitled every disabled youth to "a free, appropriate public education in the least restrictive environment, regardless of disability," under the Equal Protection Clause. Just as racial desegregation laws had to be clearly and aggressively enforced because of more than a century of segregation, so too the 1975 Education for all Handicapped Children Act had to be written with equal clarity as PL 94-142, now (with revisions) called the Individuals with Disabilities Education Act, or IDEA. It clearly spelled out (1) who was eligible for special education services, (2) parental rights, (3) the necessity of IEPs, or Individual Education Plans, for each special education student, (4) "least restrictive environment," and (5) the need to provide related (noneducational) services such as transportation.

Although states had been gearing up for special education programs for a decade before the Mills decision, something like 94-142 was necessary before concerted activity could proceed. Over the twenty years since passage of 94-142, the numbers of students served and teachers certified in special education has expanded at a rate greater than any national student increases; definitions of categories of disability have changed; arguments about "mainstreaming" and "inclusion" have occurred; total funding has soared to a current $32 billion from all sources; local, state, and federal responsibilities have been clarified; and the programs have become a part of virtually all public school districts. However, in this author's opinion, there has been a dearth of any outcome measures, at least until 1992 and 1993, when the first reports from SRI International—*What Makes a Difference?* and *What Happens Next?*—were published. Although both are sample studies from the National Longitudinal Transition Study (NLTS), they are more comprehensive than anything else, including many measures of self-sufficiency, integration into the community, and aspiration. In 1996, the David and Lucile Packard Foundation produced *Special Education for Students with Disabilities*, an excellent summary in their series, The Future of Children. The 17th and 18th reports from the Office of Special Education Programs (or OSEP) to Congress for 1995 and 1996 round out the comprehensive reports that combine issues and data presentations. Much more needs to be done, but this is a start.

Defining Disability

The categories have shifted somewhat during the lifetime of the program, as might be expected, but these thirteen would cover most of the cases: specific learning disability, speech or language impairment, mental retardation, serious emotional disturbances, multiple disabilities, hearing impairment, deafness, orthopedic impairment, other health impairment, visual impairment or blindness, autism, traumatic brain injury, and deaf-blindness. NOT covered are consequences of AIDS, those born with cocaine in their veins, low birth weight and (most important) attention deficit hyperactivity disorder (ADHD), which affects over 2 million children and has caused a fourfold increase in the production of Ritalin (Packard, p.129). These were grouped in the SRI study into "Mildly Impaired" (learning disability, speech impairment, serious emotional disturbance, or mild mental retardation), "Sensory Disabilities" (hard of hearing, visually impaired, or deaf), "Physical Disabilities" (orthopedic and other health impairments), and "Severe Disabilities"(deaf-blindness, multiple disabilities, moderate/ severe mental retardation).

Although these categories sound precise, there is considerable ambiguity in their use, as the discipline of the evaluator can make a very large difference, as can the individual state itself. (Massachusetts, for example, uses only one category for all special education children, but estimates the numbers in each subcategory.) If a person is evaluated by several experts from different disciplines, there is a greater possibility that the person evaluated will be deemed disabled, as each discipline adds criteria. (An earlier study from the University of Minnesota established that half of the adult population in the nation would be declared disabled under one of the many definitions.)

Each state implements these categories differently. As of 1992, Massachusetts leads with 16 percent of all its K through 12 students in special education, Hawaii has only 7 percent. In Connecticut, 19 percent of special education students are emotionally disturbed; in Idaho, it's 2 percent. To be fair, conditions change with time. (For example, there was a "boom" of deaf children, the increased numbers being caused by a maternal rubella epidemic.

Deafness and measles have long gone together, which is why 90 percent of deaf children have hearing parents. Get rid of measles, premature births, and severe colds, vaccinate all the kids, and deafness could be reduced to a tiny fraction of today's total.) It's even possible that heredity-related problems may shift with changes in the environment. It's often said that one thing that determines your chance of being in special education is the state that you're from.

HOW MANY KIDS? HOW MUCH MONEY?

According to the 1996 OSEP *Report to Congress,* 5.5 million children were receiving OSEP services. One of the reasons the number has jumped since 1993 is that the 1994 Improving America's Schools Act eliminated disability programs for children funded under Chapter One, the largest anti-poverty program in DOE, and those children and programs are now handled by OSEP, which explains the one-year jump in OSEP children from 4.9 million in 1994 to the 5.5 million just mentioned.

Although the percentages vary somewhat depending on the source, the categories of disability are as follows, with the percentage of all K through 12 students in each category:

Learning disabilities as the primary disability: 51%
Speech or language impairments: 22%
Mental retardation: 11%
Serious emotional disturbances: 9%
All other: 7%

(The 13, or 15, subcategories mentioned earlier are nested within these five.) Of these, learning disability (LD) is not only half the special education population, but 5 percent of *all* public school students. Most LD stedents have disabilities in reading, language, and mathematics, or in combination. (Many also have social/emotional behavior disorders as well.) Most have deficits in basic reading skills, particularly due to phonologic problems, like not being able to relate sounds (speech) to symbols (writing). Diagnosing these problems is relatively simple, cheap, and reliable, and it can be done by kindergarten if not earlier. A major problem is the lack of teachers equipped to work with problems of language development and reading, an issue for schools of education as well as in-service programs and certification for this special field. Early diagnosis is easy, cheap, and crucial for the child's educational success. As the Packard report states: "The longer children with LD in basic reading skills, at any level of severity, go without identification and intervention, the more difficult the task of remediation and the lower the rate of success." There seems to be absolutely no disagreement with this statement.

However, many other kinds of LD are very difficult to diagnose and treat. Speech and language impairments also benefit from early diagnosis and treatment, whereas the other categories may not be so easy to diagnose and treatment strategies may vary within the profession.

Cost estimates run around $30 to $32 billion from all funding sources. Although the federal government has been authorized to cover up to 40 percent of all costs, they actually provide only about 8 percent. Fifty-six percent comes from state sources, the remainder comes from local and other sources. Although individual cases will vary widely, it costs 2.3 times as much to educate a special education student as it does the other 90 percent (Figure 2-11). There is little doubt that in at least two thirds of the states, funding patterns have rewarded school districts for assigning students to special education programs, in that they can get several times as much state/federal aid for that student compared to a normal placement. In a few cases, costs for transporting a student to a special school and paying for a special education program there can easily be ten times the normal student cost. Cost of a

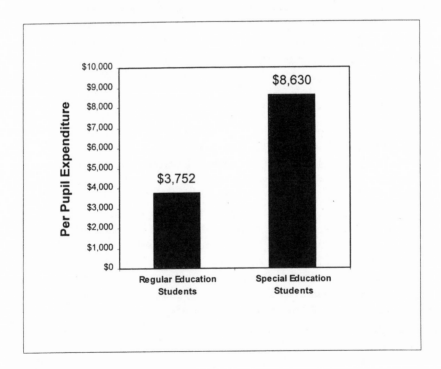

Figure 2-11. Approximate pupil cost for regular education students and special education students, 1988–1989 (*Source:* Robinson & Brandon, *Perceptions About American Education: Are They Based on Facts?* 1992, p. 9; *Statistical Source:* U.S. Department of Education).

treatment for a special education student cannot be used to justify denying that treatment to that student. However, if there are several appropriate treatments, cost can be used in the decision. In addition, states have lured school districts into "mainstreaming" students or to keeping them in separate classrooms, varying with the state. Texas, for example, was paying districts ten times more for teaching special education students in separate classrooms than in regular classes. As a result, only 5 percent of special education student in Texas were "mainstreamed" in the early 1990s. In North Dakota, 72 percent of special education students were in regular classes, whereas in South Dakota (with an almost identical population) only 8 percent were in regular classes (as of 1992)! Money made all the difference. In preschool special education, as of 1994, 48 percent of the students were in regular classes, 31 percent were in separate classes, 9 percent in separate schools, and the rest in residential facilities, home, or hospitals. There are few if any funding rewards at this level.

Partly as a result of these problems, there is now a move to fund districts based on their census count of all children in the district, assuming that a constant percentage of them will be special ed. (This author feels that ethnicity and poverty rates should be added. As we will see, Blacks, inner-city, LEP, and low-income students are far more likely to be included in special education populations than the average.)

Personnel

Considering the comparatively short duration of special education programs, the recruitment of special education teachers has gone well, although there are still major shortages in some areas. (Particularly needed are teachers who are bilingual, and familiar with inner-city and minority students.) As of 1994, 331,392 special education teachers were employed to work with students of school age (6 to 21 years old). As of 1994, over 90 percent of special education teachers were fully certified, according to the OSEP 18th report to Congress. There are no data on the number of teachers in subject fields who are working with special education kids in "inclusion" or mainstreamed" classes, but this may become a key special education issue in the future. It is important to understand that in addition to the 331,000 special education teachers in 1994, an additional 331,000 non teaching but paid persons were employed in special education programs, including rehabilitation counselors, interpreters, teacher aides, and the like. In fact, 20,104 FTE psychologists, 18,884 nonprofessional staff, and 18,053 "other professionals" were used (OSEP 18th Report, p. 26). It is worth noting that the ratio of special education teachers to "support staff" was 1 to 1 as of 1994, perhaps justifiable in terms of the complexity of the problems, perhaps not. No data could be found on the ethnicity, age, or years of service for the special education teaching force.

Ethnicity, Class, and Urbanicity

These are the three factors that significantly increase the chances that a student will be in special education. The 1992 OCR survey indicated that Blacks were 16 percent of all U.S. students in public schools, but they were 35 percent of the educable mentally retarded, 27 percent of the trainable mentally retarded, and 27 percent of those with serious emotional disturbances. (The diagnosis of Blacks in the mentally retarded categories, compared with Whites, indicates that it is twice as likely that a Black student will be diagnosed as mentally retarded as a White.) Although there are some differences by category and state, Hispanics are 10 percent of all students in the nation and about 10 percent of all disabled students. Asians are less often found in special education than in the overall student population—3 percent of all students and 0 to 2 percent of special education (However, Whites seem to be placed in learning disability categories more often.)

Although ethnicity systematically affects special education membership, Wagner and others using OCR and NLTS (National Longitudinal Transition Study) data have shown that poverty is the primary predictor, although being black increases chances of mental retardation diagnosis independently of class. (Even a wealthy black child is more likely to be classed as mentally retarded than any other wealthy child.) But across special education, the percentage of ethnic groups in special education decreases as income rises, and above $40,000 the percentages are almost equal, with the one exception we have noted. Another interesting discriminator is gender. Although not mentioned in the 18th Report to Congress in their 255 tables in the Appendix, males are almost twice as likely to be in special education as females, according to *What Makes a Difference?* (pp. 3–14); and among learning disabled and emotionally disturbed, males are three times as likely to be included. Given the large body of research on developmental differences by gender, this seems a striking deficiency in the congressional report from OSEP. We should also mention that only 1 to 12 percent of fourteen-year-olds and older in special education are declassified per year, meaning that the label is with you for your entire educational career.

Transiency is a double problem for special education students, as a move to a different state, even a different district, may put into place a very different set of rules, rewards, and sanctions. It is usually crucial that the new teacher understand the nature of the special education student's disability, what progress has been made, recommendations for program, and the like; yet the information may not follow the student to the new site. In 1994, according to the GAO, 8.4 percent of special education students moved to another district or state. Students with severe emotional disturbances moved the most—16.4 percent, the highest rate of any special education category. They also drop out of school most frequently. In most inner-city schools, poverty, transiency, minority differences, and limited

English proficiency mix in such a way that it's hard to tell which factor
is responsible for what outcome.

Results

Although it is obvious that special education students are better off than
the 1 million children denied admission to any public education before 1972,
it is important to ask the final questions of this report: What does the taxpayer
get for his/her $32 billion? First, we look at retention to high school gradua-
tion. While the Packard Report indicates that 30 percent of special education
students do not complete high school (and, interestingly, 9 percent drop out
before the 9th grade, when dropout studies usually start counting), the 18th
Report to Congress indicates a 25 percent dropout figure for the disabled in
1994, compared to 40 percent for that group in 1986. High school graduation
rates for the disabled are 30 percent in 1994, 31 percent in 1986. A big
improvement was shown for the disabled with some college: 15 percent in
1986 and 28 percent in 1994, while those with a four-year degree improved
slightly from 14 percent in 1986 to 16 percent in 1994. In addition, the
American Council on Education reported in 1992 that college freshmen with
disabilities increased from 2.6 percent of full-time freshmen in 1978 to 8.8
percent. (It is hard to understand the increase in those with some college when
the high school graduation rate remained stable.) Certainly these data look
optimistic. But in OSEP's compendious 18th Report to Congress, "Educational Attainment" is only given one paragraph in total—there's no analysis.
From *What Makes a Difference?* we learn that for the learning disabled and
seriously emotionally disturbed, of those who made it to 9th grade, 48 percent
dropped out. There are apparently major dropout differences by disability
category, but this is seldom discussed. It is also worth mentioning that special
education students who enter high school are usually one year older than their
peers in the general population. That may mean that they have been held back
a year, a factor known to increase chances of dropping out in the general
population, or that they entered K through 12 a year late (Packard).

A number of key factors occur after leaving high school, during the
transition to work, college, or both. Those who had taken a series of vocational education courses in high school (arranged around a core, like auto
mechanics) did much better in achieving employment, and made more money.
Those whose parents had expectations for them to get a job or go to college
or vocational school tended to do so. Unexpected by parents was probably
the fact that three to five years out of education, 41 percent of disabled women
had become parents, compared to 28 percent for females in general. About
one third of these mothers with disabilities were single mothers. Again, there
is little analysis in the literature about the results. If a disabled person drops
out of high school, the chances are low that the person will return, but not
impossible. In the general population, 60 percent of dropouts were re-enrolled

or doing GEDs within two years of dropping out. Thirteen percent of special education dropouts were also back in education, but after five years of dropping out, special education youth were up to 27 percent finishing their high school, a significant improvement. Finishing high school for special education dropouts is difficult, but dropping out is not irrevocable *(What Happens Next?* p. s-5). There are major differences by disability in the life after public school. Speech impaired youth look very much like their peers in the general population, and did much better than other disabled categories—58 percent had jobs three to five years out, and 20 percent were more likely to go to some postsecondary education than learning disabled; severely emotionally disturbed had much trouble moving into adult life. But in general, effects seemed to strengthen through the three to five years after high school—increased numbers are in postsecondary education, and those with jobs increase (as with the general population).

But along with increased jobs, and jobs that pay well, increased postsecondary education, increase in living independently, in marriage, in community involvement, goes an increase in arrest rates from 19.3 percent in the first two years out of high school to 29.5 percent after three to five years! (From *What Makes a Difference?* p. 6-3). There is no indication in any report consulted for this chapter as to what crimes the arrests were for, how many convictions resulted, what percent were high school dropouts, which disability categories were responsible, and so on. It is hard to derive normal numbers to compare with this one, but there are few groups one can identify in which 30 percent have been arrested three to five years after leaving high school. In general, those who were on a positive trajectory when they left high school continued to improve in most dimensions, those on a downward trajectory continued downward. Although there were large differences by disability category, most special education students continued to improve on many dimensions after leaving secondary school. One question for OSEP now might be—How could the positive trajectories be increased? Is special education, as practiced today, the best way to improve the potential of students with special needs? These young people are as vulnerable to social forces as the general population, and usually more so: Being in poverty, having a single mother, being Black, living in the core city can serve as a "double deficit"—the normal deficit that every person in these categories shares, plus the second deficit of disability. We need to consider what we expect from people with special needs—as the Packard report says, "No intervention eliminates the impact of having a disability."

Remaining Issues for Schools

There have been several efforts, parallel to racial segregation, to "desegregate" special needs youth. First came "mainstreaming," in which special education students were simply allowed to attend regular classes, without altering the nature of that class in content, instructional design, pacing, attention span, and the like. At present, the "inclusion" movement insists that the nature of the class be changed because of the special needs students. Although successes can be found in every placement strategy, there is no compelling research support for any one. In academic classes, some special education students thrive, others are more likely to fail and therefore to drop out of school. Many models that showed the greatest success for special education students are not easily transferable to the (academic) regular classroom. Many teachers of academic subjects who are excellent instructors for academically oriented students may not have the skills needed for special education students. Many of these teachers resent having students who have the potential for disrupting the learning of others in their class, and find their normal disciplinary repertoire reduced almost to zero. (Even bringing a gun into class does not always allow the disabled student to be sent home. Drug use, violent behavior, even physically hurting other students does not allow any disciplinary action, in almost all cases.)

Many national education organizations disagree on inclusion. The *ERIC* Review for Fall, 1996 quotes one: "The AFT denounces the appalling administrative practices that have accompanied the inclusion movement. This includes placing too many children with disabilities in general education classrooms without services, professional development, or paraprofessional assistance." On the other hand, there are many instances in which including special education students has been good for everyone, including the general students who may learn a great deal positively from contact with special education students. (Generally, the benefits are more visible in the early grades. In high school, when subject matter content increases in importance, the conflicts increase.)

The Public Agenda 1997 report called *Getting By* finds that 80 percent of teachers, 82 percent of high school students, and 73 percent of the U.S. public agrees that "disruptive students should be removed from regular classes so that other students can learn." Even though special education students are often included in general classes, they are very often excluded from statewide assessment programs, in that funding is usually based on mean score results. Sixteen states exclude 10 percent of special education, three states exclude 10 to 24 percent, nine exclude 25 to 49 percent, seven exclude 50 to 74 percent, six exclude 75 to 90 percent, and one state excludes 100 percent of special education students from statewide assessments, according to the Packard study (p. 164). Two contradictory values are at play in this conflict: (1) Each student is a unique, complex individual who learns in his/her own way, at his/her own pace; (2) All students must be held to the same high standards if we are to be number one in education. It is extremely likely that any state that includes all of its special education students in statewide testing will not do as well as another state that excludes them all. (The same is true for districts.)

As this is being written, President Clinton and others have begun pushing for a national series of exams, perhaps like NAEP. (This homogenizing effort will again make our schools more like those of Japan, whose schools are greatly admired by U.S. leaders, at the very time that Japanese school leaders are rethinking their schools to make them more like ours, with more individualization, innovation, and a tendency to reject one of the previous values of Japan: "The nail that sticks out gets hammered down.") There is no point in comparing all states on achievement unless you plan to reward them on their median scores. Special education could easily get caught in the middle. Some in special education have argued that the IEPs can be used for evaluation—if a student fulfills the requirements of the IEP, that should be the equivalent of passing the statewide tests. It is doubtful that this argument will win the day, as the nations we compete with do not include disabled students in their teams, and we seek "world class schools."

There also should be some concern about charter schools, probably the hottest idea around in 1997. Although recent research indicates that the several hundred such schools that exist now are quite diverse by ethnicity and (to some extent) by income, programs (and schools) for those with disabilities are in very short supply. In fact, a GAO study could only find one charter school designed to work with hearing impaired or deaf students. In addition, almost all charter schools, whatever their special focus, have no policy for including disabled students. Because they are, in a minimal sense, "private," they seem to be immune from the strict rules of 94-142 and IDEA. If they continue to expand rapidly, the number of students in "private schools" could jump from 11 percent to 15 percent or more. Some parents of nondisabled students could send their children to a private school in order to avoid the responsibility for special education and seek "high quality academics." No one knows how many parents of nondisabled students are taking their students out of public schools just for that reason, but the number will undoubtedly increase as the best colleges and universities become even more selective given the increase in youth. The public schools must continue to be attractive for all students—regardless of their abilities. A "brain drain" exodus of the brightest teachers and students out of public schools would be good for no one. As students get older, and subject matter increases in importance, demands for inclusion seem to decline, although the legal, political, and ethical mandates for it remain. There are many ambiguities here to be sorted out.

CONCLUDING COMMENTS

The more one investigates special education, the less comfortable one is with generalities, but we end here with a few. Certainly the nation is better off with 4 million young people being able to increase their knowledge, skills, and commitment to our nation. Special education and OSEP have come a very long way in a short time. Much of the news about special education programs is very positive concerning the outcomes, at least up to three to five years after high school in educational and vocational advancement. Virtually all special education teachers are certified. Funding from federal and state sources seems assured. The questions that must be raised are new: (1) What should Americans expect for a $30 billion investment in this area? (2) Should special education students be included in all statewide (and national) testing? (3) What would be a reasonable way to finance special education? (4) What changes are needed in special education programs? (5) How do we wrestle with the equity issues of spending 2.5 times as much on a special education student as average, while we spend less than average on the Black rural poor as well as inner-city students in poverty, even though they also have "special needs"? (6) If "mainstreaming" and "inclusion" are steps along a path, what's next? (7) Why are the striking high rates of arrest among special education students, as well as the very high rates of female single parents, completely avoided in all the research publications? (8) Poverty, ethnicity, urbanicity and transiency are disproportionately found among special education students, as they are in general populations. Special education students have a "double dose"—these environmental factors plus their disability. What should be government's responsibility to these two kinds of debilitating factors?

DISCUSSION QUESTIONS

1. Discuss the implications for the recruitment and retention of teachers for the increasing diversity of our student population.
2. Approximately 22 percent of all children in the United States live in poverty, and in many areas of our country that percentage is much higher. Given that poverty is one of the best predictors of academic failure, how can we increase the probability of academic success for children who live in such adverse conditions, especially those in rural areas and in the inner city in large urban areas?
3. Discuss how we can improve the percentage of dropouts among the special education student population.
4. Discuss the pros and cons of including special education students in statewide assessment programs.
5. Discuss why the demand for inclusive settings for special education students appears to decline among older students.

REFERENCES

Charter Schools and Students with Disabilities: Issue Brief. Alexandria, VA: Center for Policy Research on the Impact of General and Special Education Reform, September, 1996.

Eighteenth Annual Report to Congress on the Implementation of the Individuals with Disabilities Education Act. Washington: USDOE, 1996.

Inclusion. Washington: *ERIC Review,* v.4, #3 (Fall, 1996).

Lewis, Rena, and Doorlag, Donald, *Teaching Special Students in the Mainstream,* (4th ed.). Englewood Cliffs, NJ: Merrill, 1995.

Seventeenth Annual Report to Congress on the Implementation of the Individuals with Disabilities Education Act. Washington: USDOE, 1995.

Special Education for Students with Disabilities. Los Altos, CA: David and Lucile Packard Foundation, 1996.

Statistical Abstract of the United States: 1996. Washington: Department of Commerce, Bureau of the Census, 1996.

What Happens Next? Menlo Park, CA: SRI International, 1992.

What Makes a Difference? Menlo Park, CA: SRI International, 1992. (Both reports prepared for Office of Special Education Programs, USDOE.)

What Will It Take? Standards-based Reform for All Students. Alexandria, VA: Center for Policy Research on the Impact of General and Special Education Reform, September, 1996.

Women, Minorities, and Persons with Disabilities in Science and Engineering: Washington: National Science Foundation, September, 1996.

Youth Indicators, 1996: Trends in the Well-Being of American Youth. Washington: National Center for Education Statistics, USDOE. 1996.

3

Interventions and Children with Special Needs

James J. Gallagher

There is probably no more popular topic in the field of children with special needs than intervention findings. Intervention signifies our attempt to make things better for children and families and symbolizes the American belief that things can and should get better. We are so interested in the results of intervention that we often wish to skip the often boring methodological issues and get right to the "meat of the matter" or "cut to the chase" or look at "the bottom line," or whatever cliché suits our purpose.

However understandable these feelings are, it is a bad mistake to try to interpret findings without first considering the methods by which data are collected when these methods have often shaped and determined the breadth and scope of the outcomes. Accordingly, this chapter begins with a discussion of a series of factors that have a major impact on the findings reported later in this chapter.

THE METHODOLOGY OF INTERVENTION RESEARCH

Definitions

One ugly question we might ask ourselves is: Have we been intervening before we knew precisely what it was that we were trying to change? We need operational definitions for the key concepts we will be reviewing. Take intelligence, for example. We have been intervening to try to improve "children's intelligence" for decades through programs such as Head Start (Zigler & Styfco, 1994) and a wide variety of programs for children with special needs (Casto, 1987). But if our operational definition of the construct of "intelligence" was what was being measured on our tests of intelligence, we ran the risk of a very narrow effort and limited result.

If the operational definition of intelligence, for example, does not include the executive function (Gallagher, 1994; Sternberg, 1997), the ability that allows us to make decisions, to direct attention, and to determine response modes, then how complete has been the measurement of our intervention? If our view of intelligence was limited to verbal and mathematical abilities and did not include the multiple dimensions proposed by Gardner (Ramos-Ford & Gardner, 1997), then how complete could the measurement of such intellectual intervention be?

One can ask the same question about attempted modifications of social behavior or personality. If our operational definition of the child's personality is only a self-concept scale, then how effective can our assessment of intervention be? There is a case to be made that we are so impatient to make things better that we have done the equivalent of starting off on a trip with only a vague notion as to where we are going, but eager to get going nevertheless.

Changing Definitions

We need to remind ourselves, also, of the continually changing definitions that we may be using for categories such as "children with mental retardation" or "children with emotional disturbance." A child who might have been termed mentally retarded two decades ago may now be called "high risk," so the previous findings from intervention studies on children with mental retardation will have to be viewed with that changed definition in mind. Also, Bryant and Maxwell (1997) point out, intervention programs must now deal with higher levels of violence, substance abuse, fear, and despair than might have been present in earlier decades. In other words, the current environment might be less helpful to the developmental progress of these children through intervention than had previously been the case. Limited results from such interventions might have to do with those environmental factors rather than a difference in the type of treatment chosen.

What Is an Intervention?

Intervention in the life of a child means inserting a different set of conditions into the life space of that child in the hopes that some aspect of that child's development or adaptation is improved. It can be done directly as in remedial reading exercises or play therapy with the child or indirectly through changing the environmental envelope of the child, as in parental counseling or finding appropriate community resources. These interventions may differ in being direct or indirect or in the specific target behavior being addressed (cognitive skills, educational achievement, social skills, etc.). There have also been two major target groups that have served as samples: children in poverty and children with disabilities, because it has been assumed that the early development of each group was less than desirable so that intervention could be assumed to bring some tangible benefits.

Significance?

One of the terms that has been causing substantial confusion in communication between the professional community and policymakers and the general public is the word "significance." The professional tends to use this term as a statistical one referring to "statistical significance." This can mean that intervention with a sample of children with special needs has increased IQ scores or improved social behavior to a point where the likelihood that such a change took place by chance is minimal. In other words, the intervention had some recognizable effect.

This statistical significance can be obtained with a modest gain in IQ scores or behavior changes. If, under stimulation, a sample of children with moderate retardation gains from a mean of 50 IQ to 55 IQ over time, that gain would almost be sure to be a "statistically significant" difference. However when such results are reported to policymakers who are accustomed to the more general meaning of the term "significance," meaning a major change from the current state to a different one, they will be disappointed by these changes. These children with moderate retardation will not look very different from one time to another, particularly if you were not in a position to observe them daily. We might even say that the change was not "functionally significant" even if "statistically significant."

Because such a five-point IQ shift is unlikely to meaningfully improve the child's likelihood of academic success, or later employment, the public and the decision-makers may feel that the professionals have given them misleading or inaccurate information. It is also within the realm of possibility that some professionals could be well aware of the different uses of the term "significance" and are using it, knowing that there may be a public misinterpretation in their favor, and still able to feel protected by being able to fall back on the technical correctness of the term.

TREATMENT INTEGRITY

One of the often overlooked problems in intervention research is treatment integrity or treatment fidelity. This means that the intervention is, in fact, being presented as advertised. When someone announces that "applied behavior analysis" is being used in an intervention study, then we should demonstrate that it is truly "applied behavior analysis" as the experts in that field would recognize. This is particularly important in view of the reports of "treatment drift" from programs of "new math" to "nondirective counseling."

One field that has paid some attention to this topic is learning disabilities (Gresham, MacMillan, Beebe-Frankenberger & Bocian, 2000). A review of the articles published in that field has caused the authors to suggest that we have data on the implementation of the intervention in less than 20 percent of the published articles. Nor are they alone in that omission. The "applied behavior analysis" literature with children reported that only 16 percent of published articles provide evidence at determining treatment integrity (Gresham, Gansle & Noell, 1993).

If "cooperative learning" is not being properly applied or "problem-based learning" is being misinterpreted by the teachers who are providing that intervention, then how should we judge the evaluation results coming from such studies? We are surely underestimating the power of the intervention just as if we watered down an antibiotic and then tried to measure its effect on children's illnesses.

There are a wide variety of methods to ensure such integrity including teacher journals, periodic observations, videotaping, and the like. It should be clear that one aspect of a review of any potential article on intervention should be to require that the authors need to show their attempts and their results on treatment integrity as one aspect of proper review.

Intervention Power?

Are we using the most powerful interventions that we can conceptualize or merely the interventions over which we have control? As Gallagher (1991) pointed out, "It was unlikely that investigators would have been given the power or authority to bulldoze an entire section of a major urban area so that they could experimentally try a new and more responsive environment." So, we designed lessons for young children and interviews with the family that were within our reach. It is those "within reach" interventions that we are evaluating, not what might be possible given a broader mandate for societal change.

While we have been struggling with our direct efforts to move cognitive abilities to greater levels of efficiency, we can see that major shifts in measured cognitive ability do take place apparently under the influence of large cultural factors changing. Flynn (1999), reviewing the performance of large samples of students from one time to another on IQ tests, reports a continued increase in measured intellectual ability over time for these large samples of children, changes often of a greater level than we have been able to produce with our direct or indirect intervention efforts.

What is it in our theories of human development or social ecology that gives us the confidence that we can, through careful intervention with specific program elements, cause a demonstrable positive effect? One other assumption is that the earlier we intervene, the less effort and resources will be necessary to make such a desirable change. To make those assumptions, we must presuppose a good deal of malleability in the human being, and of course, we need to have a powerful enough intervention to also make a difference. This does not mean that there is a definitive age line beyond which the child in trouble is lost forever. There are enough individual vignettes of adolescents and adults shifting life courses to make us aware that there is always a combination of circumstances that, coming together, can cause the individual to change course (Bailey, Bauer, Symons & Lichtman, 2001)

More than a decade ago a volume of multidisciplinary contributors (Gallagher & Ramey, 1987) asked the question, "How malleable are children?" The consensus of these multidisciplinary investigators seemed to be "somewhat." Not as malleable as we who deal with children in trouble might hope for, but demonstrably better than the status quo. Such findings have importance for the design of public policy. As Gallagher (1987) noted, "High malleability favors remediation; low malleability favors prevention."

How much money and scarce personnel resources are we willing to spend to move a child from the first percentile to the third percentile in intelligence or achievement? How much money and scarce personnel resources are we willing to spend to move a child from a future of a totally dependent adult to a partially dependent adult? These are cost-benefit and more questions of the type that concerns public decision-makers, such as legislators or governors or presidents (Barnett, 1991).

In addition to the economics of the situation, there is also a moral position that it "is right and just" that we help those who are less fortunate than ourselves. This is the vertical equity argument (the unequal treatment of unequals in order to make them more equal!). Such decisions are based on morality rather than cost-benefit, but the amount of resources we commit to that goal remains a powerful policy question.

What Is Success?

We should have a clear vision before starting an intervention project as to just how we can define success so that we do not become unrealistic about what can be expected and, therefore, run the risk of downgrading the actual accomplishments because they failed to meet some unrealistic level of expectation. If we are helping a child with cerebral palsy become mobile, is our concept of success his ability to run the 100-yard dash? For that matter, what do we mean by a "significant advance" for the child and family?

Hopes and Expectations

What do we expect to change as a result of early intervention? Federal legislation in 1986 (PL 99-457) underlying the infant-toddler program for disabilities specified four goals:

1. Enhancing children's development and reducing potential delay
2. Reducing the need for subsequent special education and related services
3. Minimizing the likelihood of institutionalization and maximizing independence
4. Supporting the capacity of families to meet their child's needs (Gallagher, Clifford, & Trohanis, 1989)

Two assumptions underlie the major thrust for early intervention in the United States. These are (1) that the early years provide an unusually receptive opportunity to have a significant and lasting impact on the lives of children, and (2) that the identification of a child with a disability has profound implications for families and warrants special efforts to assure family support (Bailey, 1997).

Meisels (1990), in discussing early intervention, makes a useful distinction between four questions that help to sharpen the discussion about intervention: What is the underlying developmental model that allows one to assume success in intervention? What is the nature of the intervention? How is change measured? What is measured? And finally, what is the nature of the sample of children (families) that are receiving the intervention? These are all relevant questions that need to be revisited by anyone seriously reviewing this literature.

Guralnick (1997) supported the general proposition that early intervention programs are effective, producing average effect sizes falling in the range of ½ to ¾ of a standard deviation. This represents a meaningful change developmentally but still would represent, for example, in intelligence test scores, 8 to 12 IQ points. Nevertheless, Guralnick urges a focus on second-generation research that would identify specific program features that were associated with optimal outcomes for children and families (p. 13).

Although a gain in IQ scores of about 8 to 12 points is not to be shrugged off, we are reminded that change indicates our sample of students after intervention are now producing IQ scores of about 80. So, a group of students that had been scoring well below average is now scoring still considerably below average on measures of intelligence. It is unlikely that external observers would see much of a difference in this group of students and unlikely to think that they were observing a scientific or educational miracle such as is described in the sensitive story *Flowers for Algernon* (Keyes, 1966), which catalogues the movement of a man with mental retardation to genius-level intelligence with the aid of a new drug only to have the drug gradually wear off and the man return to his previous level of low intelligence. No, we can't do that, or anything like it, with our current interventions.

An extensive review of meta-analyses, a meta-analysis of meta-analyses, completed by Lipsey and Wilson (1993) more or less confirms the point made by Guralnick. They reviewed all known interventions into the human condition from early intervention to remedial reading, to psychoanalysis, to counseling, and so on, and reached the general conclusion that intervention can be counted upon to make a difference in favor of the experimental group of about ½ to ¾ a standard deviation. Though it is encouraging to find that one can document improvement through intervention, it is also worth reflecting about what the level of that gain translates to be in practical circumstances.

Before we become too critical about the limited cognitive gains made by the children in the intervention programs, we need to review just what level of intellectual growth would have to be obtained in order to help the child with a 70 IQ to become average in ability over a two-year period. Consider Jeanie, a 10-year-old girl with an IQ of 70, and therefore, a developmental age of 7 years. By the age of 12, in order to become average in measured ability, Jeanie would have to have gained five years in developmental age (reaching a DA of 12 at Life Age of 12) in the elapsed two years. In other words Jeanie would have to operate during that two-year period like a child with an IQ of 250! Is that a likely outcome? Indeed, in order to gain just 10 IQ points the child would have to have been operating at a developmental level of over 100 for two years.

THE RESULTS OF INTERVENTIONS

The goal of this chapter is not to intensively review every piece of intervention available—this has been done very well by others (Guralnick & Neville, 1997; Lipsey & Wilson, 1993; Bryant & Maxwell, 1997)—but to use some studies as illustrations of the general findings and to reflect on the overall policy and instructional implications of this body of research. What have been the results of these well-meaning efforts to improve the lot of the child with special needs?

At-Risk Populations—Direct Intervention

Although there have been many lists of "at-risk" factors compiled, it is important to distinguish between moderate-risk and high-risk students (Farmer, Quinn, Hussey, & Holahan, 2001). Some of the risk factors for behavioral disorders that have been generally agreed upon are

- academic problems
- low academic motivation
- peer relations problems
- association with deviant peers
- history of aggression
- attention problems
- hyperactivity
- family difficulties

Children deemed as moderate risk may have only one or two of these risks. Pete has been showing evidence of physical aggression in the classroom and on the playground. But his academic record is acceptable, and he has supportive parents. In such an instance a plan to support the positive aspects of Pete's life situation may help keep him from getting into trouble in other dimensions of his school life.

A different situation faces George, who has multiple risk factors—difficulties at home and in school including being behind in his academic work. In such a situation a change in educational environment to a structured alternative educational program would seem to be called for. Students treated in such settings have shown a reduction in problem behavior and an improvement in academic performance (Stage & Quiroz, 1997). Such intense problems have to be met with an intense and coordinated therapeutic program designed to meet the multiple problem areas that George has shown.

The largest number of intervention studies have involved low-income youngsters who are perceived to have substantial environmental disadvantage or risk in their early years of development. The interventions were designed to compensate for these early deprivations by providing enriched experiences, such as increased language stimulation. Lazar and Darlington (1982) produced one of the most well-known reports of the influence of these early intervention programs. This publication synthesized the results of a consortium of investigators each of whom followed their early intervention program for their economically deprived children with follow-up data in later childhood. The results of this consortium set the pattern for results that would come from later intervention studies.

First of all, the treated preschool children were superior to comparison groups in IQ gains but lost their advantage in IQ scores over the comparison samples with the passage of time. Second, the efficiency with which the intervened students used their abilities in an academic setting did improve, and that improvement remained over time. One indication of that improvement was that fewer children from the experimental groups were referred for special education services or were retained at their current grade level. Finally, the students who had been in the special programs tended to have higher self-concepts than students who had not participated.

The Carolina Abecedarian Study used a randomized experimental control group design and began intervention (an eight-hour child care program) shortly after birth for youngsters considered high risk from environmental circumstances (Ramey & Ramey, 1998). They obtained the same general findings of the Cornell Consortium (Lazar & Darlington, 1982) with early gains in measures of intelligence during the preschool periods for the experimental group, which subsequently leveled off. However, the increased academic efficiency remained through the school years for the intervention children.

LONG-TERM EFFECTS OF INTERVENTION

The long-term effects of intervention have been speculated about but rarely studied. The Perry Preschool project reported on a follow-up of their preschool program when the participants were between 19 and 24 years of age and then again eight years later (Berrueta-Clement, Schweinhart, Barnett, Epstein, & Weikart, 1984). In comparing the preschool group with the control sample of students, the percentage of children in the preschool group that were charged with a crime were significantly lower. The mean number of arrests was also lower as were instances of violent crimes. These differences continued into adulthood (Schweinhart, & Weikart, 1993). These findings are central to the cost-benefit analyses conducted by Schweinhart & Weikart (1993) reporting much societal economic saving through the intervention of preschool programs, because the cost of incarceration is extremely high.

The rationale for these differences was speculated to be that the preschool program increased the child's self-confidence and self-control, two characteristics that could be a buffer against an unfriendly school and neighborhood environment.

However, another study with a similar population, the Abecedarian project, in which the intervention program began slightly after birth and consisted of an eight-hour day-care program, failed to find any difference in arrests or crimes between the experimental population and a randomly selected control group at age 19 (Clarke & Campbell, 1998) with about 40 percent of each group charged with some offense by age 19. The incidence of 40 percent compared well with the overall figures from the Perry Preschool follow-up (39 percent). The mechanisms by which the young child may be protected from a life of delinquency or misbehavior remain mysterious.

The one intervention study that reported substantially different reports from the others is referred to as the Milwaukee Study (Garber, 1987). This early intervention study provided home care for the first eighteen months and then a center-based care program for the small number of high-risk children involved. Garber reported that the students under treatment scored average or above in intellectual ability not only at the end of the preschool but also at the age of 10 years. However, other social and behavioral data were not as favorable; Garber reported, "Their school behavior was poor, quite similar to the control children's deportment in school." As other investigators have also found, even a strong preschool program is unable to inoculate children against unfavorable environments in school and community at later ages.

Zigler & Styfco (1994) have been quite clear in pointing out that changes in intelligence in programs such as Head Start have *not* been a primary goal. In this Head Start program, there are a number of objectives such as increased indicators of overall health (such as freedom from disease), ability to cooperate with others, to be socially empathic, and so on. If the parents become more interested in their own education or more active in the community, this would also be seen as a positive outcome. There has been some reflection after three decades of work on the poor decision-making that resulted in trying to change intellectual development as a major goal in child development programs when cognitive development has proven to be the most resistant-to-change developmental quality in young children.

Gallagher (1991) proposed to save government policymakers, interested in conducting similar intervention programs, large sums of money by announcing in advance what the findings would be of such a multiyear intervention program. They would be:

- The treatment group, as opposed to the untreated or comparison group, would demonstrate modest gains.
- A small number of youngsters may gain appreciably in IQ and achievement scores.
- A small number of children will show no effect from the intervention at all.
- If nothing is done to follow up on the program, many of the gains will be lost.
- The real advantage may be that such educational intervention programs mainly lie in the spirit of new optimism and encouragement within the family of the child in question.

In short, we don't need any more of these kinds of expensive intervention studies to discover again what we already know.

At-Risk Populations—Behavior Change

The programs that have tried to modify the unacceptable social behavior of children have focused upon early intervention with some tangible results. Yoshikawa (1994) reviewed programs for their effect on the eventual behavior of children considered at risk and came to two main conclusions:

1. The programs that demonstrated long-term effects on crime and antisocial behavior tended to be those that combined early childhood education and family support services.
2. Those programs that were designed primarily to serve adults tend to benefit adults more than children, and those designed primarily to serve children tend to benefit children more than adults (p. 59).

One of the limitations of the "cost benefit" model is that it does not take into account that small differences in child and family may result in large functional differences. For example, a small amount of gain in parental stress reduction may result in the cancellation of divorce plans, which, in turn, could, if carried out, have catastrophic financial and personal implications for the family.

Small developmental gains in the child may reverse a decision to institutionalize the child, which, in turn, would have major financial consequences for the state or the family. It is the inability to translate minor shifts in stress and growth into these larger implications that is one cause of the apparent dysjunction between small gains and large parental satisfaction.

One of the limitations of many of the early intervention projects is that they were atheoretical, basing their intervention strategies on presumed advancement of developmental channels through direct and specific remedial lessons on language, social skills, and the like. If the new emphasis on the importance of transactions between child and family and between teacher and child is correct, then a good deal more than direct lessons with the child would seem to be needed for maximum effect (Sameroff & Fiese, 1990).

Werner (Werner & Smith, 1982) particularly noted the impact of the environmental context in her study of vulnerable children on the island of Kauai. She found that when children with prenatal complications were raised in a positive cultural and family environment, they became indistinguishable from children without such complications. However, in less favorable family contexts, the earlier problems predicted later developmental problems.

Sameroff and colleagues (Sameroff, Seifer, Baldwin, & Baldwin, 1993) identified ten environmental risk factors that put a child at developmental risk and concluded from a study of 215 four-year-old children that it was the number of risk factors present, rather than the specific nature of a risk factor, that determines the degree of effect such factors were having on the children. These factors included such diverse dimensions as mother-child interaction, minority status, parental occupation, and anxiety. Because of this diversity of problems, a question surfaces as to where to focus useful interventions.

One of the recent topics involving "at-risk" children is intervention programs for those who have been born with low birth weight (LBW) (under 2500 grams) or very low birth weight (VLBW) (under 1500 grams). A major multisite study was undertaken to measure the effects of early intervention for LBW and VLBW children (Infant Health and Development, 1990). The combination of environmental disadvantage and LBW appears to create a greater likelihood for the appearance of later disability conditions. When a well-organized child-care program from age 1 to 3 is provided, combined with parental counseling, the negative impact on LBW children is much less. This positive interaction involved 377 infants randomly assigned to experimental and control groups in multiple sites and resulted in positive findings on intellectual growth and social behavior, particularly for those youngsters between 2001 grams and 2500 grams at birth (Infant Health and Development, 1990).

Blair and Ramey (1997), reviewing the literature on low birth weight in general, concluded that comprehensive intensive early interventions that begin early are most likely to be effective: "Given the effectiveness of both more intense center-based and less intense home-based interventions for

LBW infants, a continued focus on parents and an emphasis on the importance of educational and intersectional routines at home would be warranted" (p. 93).

This work with LBW infants is one more indication of the potential positive impact of early intervention on young children, if the intervention is intense enough and long enough.

At Risk Populations—Indirect Intervention

An indirect treatment is one that attempts to achieve gains in the target child by working with the family or caretakers of that child. One of the indirect intervention treatments designed to improve the lot of families in poverty that has received considerable attention is the case manager approach, as an intervention. The case manager provides access to a wide variety of services and resources based upon a particular family's need. The assumption is that services will be more effective if they are broadly focused on the family as a whole, rather than just on mothers or just on children. The Administration for Children, Youth and Families undertook a huge study to test the effectiveness of the case manager approach (St. Pierre, Layzer, Goodson, & Bernstein, 1997). Using a randomized "exper-imental-control" design and twenty-two separate sites, they tried to assess (with health and performance measures on the mother, and ability and performance measures on the child) the effectiveness of the case manage-ment approach. The results were startlingly negative. The investigators reached the following conclusions:

- The Child Care Development Program (CCDP) did not produce any important positive effects on participating families.
- Five years after the program began, CCDP had no statistically signifi-cant impacts on the economic self-sufficiency of participating mothers, nor on their parenting skills.
- Five years after the program began, CCDP had no meaningful impacts on the cognitive or social-emotional development of participating chil-dren (p. 83).

To add to the disappointment, this proved to be one of the more expensive forms of intervention.

Sameroff and Fiese (1990) suggested that it is important to look at the role that cultural codes (e.g., "We Irish always discipline our children this way") and family codes (e.g., "It is a Johnson family tradition to have family conversation at the dinner table") are playing in determining parental reac-tions to children with special needs. When the child is identified as having special needs, these cultural and family codes of behavior become modified in some ways that may not be productive. The family may interact with the child less because of assumptions that the child will not develop normally anyway, and such assumptions will influence the nature and amount of adult-child transactions in the foreseeable future, with potentially unfavorable consequences.

Part of an intervention program might well be designed to help parents redefine the child's potential and the child's behavior. For example, the mother may be convinced that the child's crying is not evidence of the child's hostility to her but merely the result of the child being wet or hungry. Such redefinition frees the mother to engage in more and more positive transactions than previously.

Unfortunately even when we have "family intervention" as an intervention principle, we often have very little notion as to what the precise nature of that family intervention turns out to be. We don't know whether it amounts to aiding the family to get food stamps or fuel for the winter, or whether it is addressing some of the cultural codes and family codes that turn out to be developmentally nonproductive for this child in this family. We also need clarification on the length and intensity of the intervention because both of these factors seem to be important to the outcome.

Children with Disabilities—Direct Intervention

One of the earliest attempts at intervention for children with disabilities was carried out by Kirk (1958) who intervened over a multiyear period with an experimental-control sample of institutionalized and noninstitutionalized young children with mental retardation. He discovered the now familiar pattern of initial cognitive growth related to the intervention, which tended to lessen over time for both institutional and noninstitutional populations. His findings also included data suggesting that intervention was less effective with children who had identifiable organic injuries.

Gallagher (1960) followed up the Kirk study with a four-year intervention program tutoring institutionalized children with brain injury and mental retardation. He also found modest gains in cognition and behavior made under one-on-one tutoring. These gains decayed over time and also confirmed that the gains were less evident with the organically injured population than with the more "at-risk" population and that gains were more difficult the older the child.

Casto (1987) reviewed the intervention data from seventy-four studies available on children with disabilities at the time and reached the general conclusion that short-term benefits were clearly available in terms of positive effect sizes largely in cognition, motor, and language development. Few results were available on children with sensory handicaps or on social competency or self-concept. He reminded readers that there is an interaction between the effects of intervention and the severity of the disability that needs to be taken into account, with the more severely impaired being less likely to respond on developmental measures.

In response to Guralnick's call for second generation research on intervention (i.e., testing types of interventions against one another rather than exploring the impact of intervention itself), a study included a group of 141 at-risk children who participated in two quite different preschool intervention programs (Millis, Dale, Cole, & Jenkins, 1995). One group focused on direct instruction based on an extensive task analysis and systematic academic skills and was used as a basis for teaching systematic academic skills.

The second group stressed mediated learning, which emphasized the development of generalizations of cognitive processes using comparison, classification, perspective changing, and sequencing. All children in this program received two hours of instruction per day until they entered the first grade.

There was a definite aptitude-by-treatment interaction with students with higher aptitudes in the direct-instruction program, and students with lower aptitudes in the mediated learning program learned better at post-test relative to their contrast program counterparts. There was a suggestion that the mediated learning had relatively consistent influence across ability levels. Such findings should increase the investigations on the impact of specific instructional strategies because these influences spanned a three-year period of time.

The Early Intervention Research Institute at Utah State University carried out a series of intervention experiments testing the effectiveness of various types of intervention on children with disabilities between birth and age 4 (see special issue of *Early Education and Development*, October 1993). In each study, the samples were randomized, and a battery of instruments measuring child functioning and family functioning measured the outcomes from more versus less intense treatments. The samples of children involved were medically fragile, children with visual impairments, and a variety of children with developmental delays. In each instance, it appeared that the more intense treatment did *not* result in major improvements and that increasing parental participation did not help either.

These results have been criticized by Telzrow (1993), who was concerned that the measuring instruments were not linked to the treatments and questioned whether the treatments themselves were true treatments. Nevertheless, such findings make it more relevant to conduct carefully designed second-generation studies as requested by Guralnick (1997) so that the actual gains can be documented and cost-benefits identified. It is quite likely that severely impaired children may have a limited potential for increased developmental gains regardless of the intervention, but the intervention could still have a meaningful impact on the family.

There have been several attempts to track and improve the development of young Down syndrome children. Casey, Jones, Kugler, and Watkins (1988) compared a small group of Down syndrome children where half the sample attended general nursery and primary school and half the sample attended segregated special schools. There was some indication over twenty-four months that the Down syndrome children who had been mainstreamed had moderately higher scores in comprehension and in mental age gain than did the children from the special schools group. Gibson and Harris (1988) reported a meta-analysis of twenty-one early intervention programs that featured Down syndrome children and reported short-term benefits in fine motor and adaptive skills but with lesser improvements in language, cognition, and gross motor skills.

Children with autism and related disorders have been receiving greater attention during the last decade. A large number of programs with different theoretical models and treatment strategies have been claiming substantial success (Dawson & Osterling, 1997). While clinical reports of these intense treatments (20+ hours a week) have been encouraging (one half of the children being integrated into a general classroom), Dawson and Osterling commented: "To date, there have been no true experimental studies that would require at minimum, random assignment to different intervention groups and outcome assessments conducted by people naïve with regard to intervention status" (p. 314).

A recent report from the National Academy of Sciences has called for a series of carefully designed studies that would document the claims of many advocates who have developed special treatment programs for children with autism. The costs of many of these intense interventions have created serious tensions between parents and schools (Lord, 2001).

Children with sensory handicaps (visual and auditory) have few studies illustrating the results of intervention. There is a practical problem in terms of the limited number of subjects available, because these are both low-incidence conditions. The field of deaf education has actually been referred to as "pre-scientific" (Calderon & Greenberg, 1997). The two areas of recent attention appear to be attempts to assess the effectiveness of cochlear implants and mother-child interactions. Although there appears to be increased speech intelligibility in the children with the cochlear implants, the short- and long-term effects of these implants are unclear. Jameson and Pederson (1993) investigated the maternal style of communication with deaf and hearing five-year-olds. The dyad that had the most communication difficulty was the hearing mother and the deaf child, more so than deaf mother and deaf child. Some special areas of instruction for the hearing mother-deaf child dyad seemed to be called for.

In children with visual problems, the number of research or evaluation projects is also quite limited (Davidson & Harrison, 1997). Some of the earlier work by Frieberg looking at infants with congenital blindness found impressive delays in many gross motor milestones, clearly calling for a targeted early intervention program. Sonksen, Petrie, and Drew (1991) reported an intervention program for infants in which a program for general development of the children and a program for visual development, specifically helping infants with orientation, tracking, and spatial awareness, were compared. The children who received both the general development and the specific program for visual development seemed to be more advanced developmentally than those children receiving only the development program.

A carefully done intervention for infants and toddlers with visual impairment compared a high-intensity intervention (children and families received weekly, home-based parent-infant sessions in which primary caregivers and their children received services tailored to the needs of the family and the child) and a low-intensity intervention (parents were invited to group meetings held twelve times a year to discuss, in general, the effects of visual impairment on development). Measures of child development, adaptive behavior, parent stress, and so on, were taken after one and two years.

There were few differences found between the two groups of children with visual disorders over time, nor of family functioning. The authors (Behl, White, & Escobar, 1993) caution that different interventions could result in different results, but they also pointed out that the high-intensity program costs over $7,000 per family, and the low-intensity program costs $1,000 per family.

In both the visual and auditory areas, there needs to be substantial stimulation from the scientific and evaluation communities noting the importance of these target groups. Otherwise, needed funding for investigations will unlikely take place.

Children with Disabilities—Behavior

Webster-Stratton (1997) has pointed out that there is an appalling lack of comprehensive treatment programs for preschoolers with behavioral problems: "These children are spending large amounts of time with untrained caretakers in the least adequate facilities where the child-to-caregiver ratios make it impossible to provide the degree of attention, affections, and emotional support required to meet the psychological needs of these children" (p. 477).

By far the number of treatment programs for conduct problem children are parent training programs, and these have proven successful, in part. By successful we mean that the child has changed in the mother-child interaction domain, even though such changes rarely carry over into child-care or school settings (Webster-Stratton, 1997). Such training obviously has to be inclusive of the child caretakers in school and child-care settings if we expect substantial carryover from the home to larger social settings.

One of the samples of children at risk for emotional and developmental problems is children who have been subjected to persistent child abuse. Over a million victims of maltreatment have been identified, and the reported cases have been steadily increasing (Barnett, 1991). These samples, of course, represent only the reported cases of abuse. There are concerns that such abuse interferes with the social and emotional development of the child and even has an impact on the development of the child's cognitive abilities.

Consequently, various therapeutic day-treatment programs have been established, and, in some cases, evaluations of their effectiveness have been conducted. After nine months' attendance in these programs, children showed significant gains in developmental areas such as cognition and language; motor, social, and emotional development; scoring higher than a control sample of children drawn from a waiting list for these programs (Culp, Little, Letts, & Lawrence, 1991).

One of the educational strategies that have been employed by teachers working with children with emotional and behavioral disorders has been cooperative learning. This approach organizes classrooms into small groups of four students working together for mutual benefit. This cooperative work is designed to help the social and personal adjustments of the child with special needs with his/her peers.

A literature review of projects using cooperative learning by Sutherland, Wehby, & Gunter (2000) for E/BD students has reported that the effectiveness of the method is uncertain, although there were some indications that there may be some improvements in social skills and on-task behavior. There was some concern that the treatment fidelity (were the principles of cooperative learning really being followed?) in many of the studies was dubious.

Children with Disabilities—Social Skills

It has been increasingly apparent that the future adult adjustment of the child with disabilities depends not only on the cognitive skills needed to hold a job, but also on the social skills necessary to get along with coworkers and to adapt in the community. One of the advantages of the extensive attention to cognition has been that there was an easily available measuring instrument, the IQ test, to assess the level of development of the child.

Now in the field of social competence there are not only the Vineland Adaptive Behavior Scales (Sparrow, Balla, & Cicchetti, 1984) but scales such as An Assessment of Peer Relations (Guralnick, 1992), and the Preschool Socioaffective Profile (LaFreniere, Dumas, Capuano, & Debeau, 1992). Even though the relationship between cognitive development and social competence is only modest (see Quay & Jarrett, 1984), there is still the hope that improvement in social competence may lead to improvement in the cognitive realm, and vice versa.

As is true in cognitive development, early problems in social development appear to predict later social adjustment problems, and that fact increases the importance of early intervention designed to develop social skills. Also the consistency of social problems over time enhances the importance of early intervention designed to strengthen the attachment relationship between the primary caretaker and the child. This attachment relationship seems linked to social development and positive orientation to other children. It is related to global social competence ratings at age 3, with fewer behavior problems and greater emotional health being noted (Guralnick & Neville, 1997).

The general assumption is that the social skills learned in the earlier positive parent-child attachment and the positive sense of self that such attachment generates are carried over into peer relationships. The import-ance of parental warmth and moderate parental control can hardly be overestimated. Similarly, children with behavior problems have been noted as having poor earlier attachment and more negative input from their caretakers. One should be careful here to not assign causality from parent to child in this situation when what may be happening may well be the result of a complex interaction factor. That is, difficult children are less responsive to the mother, and this stirs up angry and intrusive behavior on the part of the mother, which in turn results in weaker attachment, and so on. A downward spiral of child misbehavior, parental negative response, and more child misbehavior is a cycle that professionals want to break before it becomes an ingrained family pattern.

Intervention for social competence apparently requires more than just modifying specific behaviors (Don't hit Kenny!). It involves the teaching of shared understandings (Guralnick, 1992) to young children or the design of scripts that lay out appropriate social behavior in recurring situations: the lunch table, circle time, joint sandbox play, and the like. The direct training in common scripts appears to be effective, especially when followed up with caretaker prompts in subsequent interactions (Goldstein, Wickstrom, Hoyson, Jamieson, & Odom, 1988).

Another illustration of the importance of both duration and intensity in our attempts to modify behavior of young children is illustrated in a project that involved the identification of children at-risk for behavior and emotional problems by kindergarten teachers and then the formation of Parent-Teacher Action Research (PTAR) teams. These teams consisted of the first or second grade teacher, one or more parents, and a parent liaison recruited from the local community. These teams worked together as equal partners to develop a portrait of the child's strengths and problems and established mutual parent-teacher goals. They agreed on how each would collect data to deter-mine whether the goals were met or not. In addition, to a random "matched pair" of control subjects, all the students participating in this study received social skills instruction (McConaughy, Kay, & Fitzgerald, 2000).

Much more significant improvements in children's problems and compe-tencies compared to their control pairs were found at the end of year two than at the end of year one, indicating the importance of maintaining an interven-tion effort over an extended period of time in order to modify children's behavioral patterns. The importance of beginning early in the school career of the youngsters was also noted in this study.

Once the goal of social competence is recognized as a major interaction goal, then specific intervention strategies and techniques can be formulated. It is necessary to recognize that social competence will not emerge as a natural by-product of cognitive instruction. It needs to be planned for, in its own right, with social techniques introduced and practiced in social situations in order for it to be effective.

Children with Disabilities—Indirect Intervention

Given the modest results that have emerged from the attempts to directly stimulate cognitive development and problem-solving processes in children with special needs, it is not surprising that attempts have been made to improve the status of the child through attempts to improve the family's status, or by directing attention to the child's social skills development.

One strategy has been to introduce more social support for the family attempting to cope with the child with special needs (Dunst, Trivette, & Jodry, 1997). Social support refers to information or material aid or assistance to the family and can be accomplished through either informal social supports (kin, friends, neighbors, etc.) or through a formal support system (professionals or social agencies). The provision of such social supports can be viewed as one type of early intervention.

The studies that have compared informal and formal social supports seem to favor the informal social supports as having the best chance of changing family adjustment (Trivette, Dunst, & Jodry, 1997; Innocenti, Hollinger, Escobar, & White, 1993). These findings are complicated by the reports of Affleck, Tennan, Allen, and Gershman (1986), who conclude that the treatment is effective only when the family is in a condition of perceived need. Unless the family feels the need for help, they are not likely to respond to help that is available. Additionally, the treatment intervention will have its best effect upon the family member most affected, which in most instances is the mother, and the effect on the child will be less conspicuous.

A variation of the social support notion is parent-child interaction intervention (McCollum & Hemmeter, 1997). In this instance parent-child interaction behaviors that were desired were "quality of affect" and interactive behaviors such as "game playing." Child behaviors were determined by ratings of affect and various measures of development. In the ten studies reviewed by McCollum and Hemmeter (1997), they found clear evidence of change in parent behavior in the direction of the parent training. The results on the children, however, were not so clear. Some studies seem to show modest gains in child cognitive ability and some positive changes in the child behavior within the mother-child dyad but little evidence of behavior generalization to other settings.

Dunst, Trivette, and Jodry (1997) reported a unique contribution to the intervention literature with a study that randomly divided thirty families participating in an early intervention program into two different treatment groups. One group received formal supports involving respite care with a trained provider, while another group received informal supports by a staff member who identified a range of community-based child-care options. Parents participating in the informal support approach demonstrated the greatest positive changes across time. When parents were asked where they had received the most important support, they often mentioned relatives, friends, and neighbors before members of the helping professions. This might well mean that the professionals might better spend their time organizing these friends-and-neighbors networks rather than providing direct therapeutic support.

Dunst, Trivette, and Jodry (1997) concluded, "Social support provided by informal personal network members had the greatest positive effect on behavioral functioning, and the more components and dimensions of social support relationships that were considered, the greater the percentage of variance accounted for in the outcomes by social support" (p. 516)

Although by far the number of treatment programs for conduct problem children are parent-training programs and these have proven successful. That is, the child has changed in the mother-child interaction domain—such changes rarely carry over into child-care or school settings. Such training obviously has to include the child's caretakers in school and child-care settings if we expect substantial carryover from the home to larger social settings.

A DESIGN FOR ACTION

What is one to make of this mass of information? How can it inform policy and practice? We must first agree on the major threads of the findings.

1. Interventions that are intensive and extensive result in modest gains (0.50 to 0.75σ) in cognitive and social adaptation.
2. Although cognition gains tend to erode over time, evidence of increased educational efficiency remains.
3. Indirect treatments (e.g., family case management) result in little or no child gains, unless combined with other treatments.
4. Informal social supports (friends and neighbors) seem to be more influential than formal (professional) supports in their impact on families.
5. Antisocial behavior in young children does not go away over time and needs early attention.
6. We need to pay more attention to design and interpretation issues (What does "significance" mean?).

One of the most difficult assumptions for many educators and interventionists to accept is that it is inordinately hard to modify the developmental trajectories of children or adults once they have been set. From the educators' standpoint, it is not of great moment if the reason for this limited malleability lies in the constitutional makeup of the individual or in the early interaction of environment and heredity. The bald truth is that such resistance to change has to be confronted regardless. Despite bushels full of data indicating that change for either child or family is hard and requires much intense and continuing effort, there remains a tendency to hope for a magic bullet that will allow us to apply a treatment without much individual effort and have it transform the child or adult without the necessity for professional follow-up or staying the course over extended time. It is clear that there is recognition of the importance of intensity and length of treatment.

Effective Interventions

One of the questions is: How can we make interventions more efficient? One strategy would be to make the intervention goals more targeted. Instead of saying that we wish to improve "intelligence," we could say that we wish to target the executive function and help the child with attention and decision-making. Instead of proclaiming that we wish to improve the child's "social skills," we can say that we want to improve his "initiation of social contact with others." A further implication is that we need to support research and theoretical formulation about development in order to discover more specifics about social adaptation and cognition. The more targeted the intervention, the more likely we can demonstrate change.

Such specificity can narrow and focus the intervention to the point where some specific skills can be mastered or special knowledge learned that can help the child adapt more effectively. This requires a better understanding of what lies beneath general concepts such as intelligence and social skills. It is the assessment of skills mastered and knowledge acquired that should help evaluate the utility of the intervention, not some global measure of development, such as the IQ test, that is far distant from the specifics of the teaching or the intervention.

For example, the needs of children with Fragile X syndrome are rather specific and call for a specific remedial strategy. Their specific needs include academic adaptations, behavior management, attention deficit hyperactivity disorder, and a variety of autistic-like characteristics. (Hatton, Bailey, Jr., Roberts, Skinner, Mayhew, Clark, Waring, & Roberts (2000). Therefore the intervention program needs a focus on such problems and the needed intervention research should be directly related to the needs of these particular children. Just as the needs of children with specific disorders need specialized therapies, so should the intervention research design and measurement fit these special conditions.

Multidisciplinary Interventions

Another way to strengthen interventions is to organize our service delivery systems for multidisciplinary interventions. If the child with disabilities is merely the core of an interacting set of concentric circles representing family, peers, school, and so on (Bronfenbrenner, 1989), then actions need to be taken to try to improve the child's linkage to all these factors by working with those persons involved with the child, as well as working directly with the child. Because many of these children with special needs may need the help of pediatricians, audiologists, early interventionists, psychologists, and other professionals, a more comprehensive IEP or IFSP would be required that reflected goals that only can be achieved through the teamwork of professionals from many disciplines. The provision for such community agencies that encompass many disciplines is much needed (Comer, 1988).

Instrument Development

If science advances on the wings of its measuring instruments, then we should pay more attention as to how our instruments are developed. Although we have improved somewhat our measures of cognition and social adaptation over the years, we can still use, and are in need of, more appropriate measurement development on a regular and consistent basis. So far, agencies and foundations supporting research have paid little attention to developing measurement instruments, which in reality takes a half decade or more plus substantial personnel and financial resources. Waiting passively for someone to come up with a new test of "self-concept" is probably not going to help us very much. We will be forced to continue to curse our current measures as poor tools but still use them because they are the best that are available. We have established enough centers and institutes now that could take responsibility for measuring development in their area of expertise, if given the appropriate amount of multiyear resources and a mandate to develop a better instrument for cognition, social adaptation, or whatever.

Consequences of Small Gains

Finally we have to come to grips with the clearly observable fact that our interventions will make only small increments of change within the child and family. We should point out that those small increments can sometimes have large consequences. Schneidman (1985) has pointed out, for instance, that a Just Noticeable Difference in the lives of disturbed youths can make the difference between suicide or not. Those working with families know that a small improvement in the life of a family with children with special needs can sometimes head off a pending divorce. An improvement in social interaction can help a person keep a job instead of being totally dependent. And the list goes on.

These are individual triumphs that can incrementally improve our clients and our society. If those scientists who discover new life-saving drugs are the glamorous "air force" of the helping professions, then we, in special education, must be the unglamorous but very necessary infantry of the helping professions, making progress one step or one hill at a time. We might not make the cover of *Parade* or be *Time*'s Person of the Year, but there are families everywhere who are grateful for what we have done for their members.

DISCUSSION QUESTIONS

1. How have evolving definitions of special education categories (e.g., intelligence, mental retardation, at-risk) shaped intervention strategies?
2. How effective have direct and indirect interventions been?
3. How can the information presented in this chapter help to inform policy for individuals with exceptionalities?

REFERENCES

Affleck, G., Tennan, H., Allen, D., & Gershman, G. (1986). Perceived social support and maternal adaptation during the transition from hospital to home care of high risk infants. *Infant Mental Health Journal, 7*, 6–18.

Bailey, D. (1997). Evaluating the effectiveness of curriculum alternatives for infants and preschoolers at high risk. In M. Guralnick (Ed.), *The effectiveness of early intervention*. Baltimore: Paul H. Brookes.

Bailey, D. Bruer. J., Symons, F., & Lichtman, J. (2001). *Critical Thinking About Critical Periods*. Baltimore: Paul H. Brookes.

Barnett, W. (1991). Long-term effects of early childhood programs on cognitive and school outcomes. In *The future of children: Long-term outcomes of early childhood programs, 5*(3). Los Altos, CA: The Center for the Future of Children.

Behl, D., White, K., & Escobar, C. (1993). New Orleans early intervention study of children with visual impairments. *Early Education and Development, 4*(4), 256–274.

Berrueta-Clement, J., Schweinhart, L., Barnett, W., Epstein, A., & Weikart, D. (1984). *Changed lives: The effects of the Perry Preschool Program on youths through age 19*. Ypsilanti, MI: High/Scope Press.

Blair, C., & Ramey, C. (1997). Early intervention for low-birth-weight infants in the path to second generation research. In M. Guralnick (Ed.), *The effectiveness of early intervention* (pp. 77–98). Baltimore: Paul H. Brookes.

Bronfenbrenner, U. (1989). Ecological systems theory. *Annals of Child Development, 6*, 187–249.

Bryant, D., & Maxwell, K. (1997). The effectiveness of early intervention for disadvantaged children. In M. Guralnick (Ed.), *The effectiveness of early intervention* (pp. 23–46). Baltimore: Paul H. Brookes.

Cairns, R., & Cairns, B. (1994). *Lifelines and risks: Pathways of youth over time*. New York: Harvester Wheatsheaf.

Calderon, R., & Greenberg, M. (1997). The effectiveness of early intervention for deaf children and children with hearing loss. In M. J. Guralnick (Ed.), *The effectiveness of early intervention* (pp. 455–483). Baltimore: Paul H. Brookes.

Campbell, F. A., Ramey, C. T., Pungello, E. P., Sparling, J., & Miller-Johnson, S. (In press). Early childhood education: Young adult outcomes from the Abecedarian Project. *Applied Developmental Science*.

Casey, W., Jones, D., Kugler, B., & Watkins, B. (1988). Integration of Down's syndrome children in the primary school: A longitudinal study of cognitive development and academic attainments. *British Journal of Educational Psychology, 58*, 279–286.

Casto, G. (1987). Plasticity and the handicapped child: A review of efficacy research. In J. Gallagher & C. Ramey (Eds.), *The malleability of children*. Baltimore: Paul H. Brookes.

Clarke, S., & Campbell, F. (1998) Can intervention early prevent crime later? The Abecedarian project compared with other programs. *Early Childhood Research Quarterly 13* (2), 319–343.

Comer, T. (1988). Educating poor minority children. *Scientific American, 254*, 42–48.

Culp, R., Little, V., Letts, D., & Lawrence, H. (1991). Maltreated children's self-concept: Effects of a comprehensive treatment program. *American Journal of Orthopsychiatry, 61*, 114–121.

Davidson, P., & Harrison, G. (1997). The effectiveness of early intervention for children with visual impairments. In M. Guralnick (Ed.), *The effectiveness of early intervention* (pp. 483–499). Baltimore: Paul H. Brookes.

Dawson, G., & Osterling, J. (1997). Early intervention in autism. In M. Guralnick (Ed.), *The effectiveness of early intervention* (pp. 307–326). Baltimore: Paul H. Brookes.

Dunst, C., Trivette, C., & Jodry, W. (1997). Influence of social support on children with disabilities and their families. In M. Guralnick (Ed.), *The effectiveness of early intervention* (pp. 499–523). Baltimore: Paul H. Brookes.

Early Education and Development (October 1993).

Farmer, T., Quinn, M., Hussey, W., & Holahan, T. (2001). The development of disruptive behavioral disorders and correlated constraints: Implications for intervention. *Behavior Disorders, 26*(2), 117–130.

Flynn J. (1999). Searching for justice: The discovery of IQ gains over time. *American Psychologist, 54*(1), 5–20.

Gallagher, J. (1960). *The tutoring of brain injured, mentally retarded children*. Springfield, IL: Charles C. Thomas.

Gallagher, J. (1987). Public policy and the malleability of children. In J. Gallagher & C. Ramey (Eds.), *The malleability of children*. Baltimore: Paul H. Brookes.

Gallagher, J. (1991). Longitudinal intervention: Virtues and limitations. *American Behavioral Scientist, 34*(4), 431–439.

Gallagher, J. (1994). Policy designed for diversity: New initiatives for children with disabilities. In D. Bryant & M. Graham (Eds.), *Implementing early intervention*, (pp. 336–350). New York: Guilford Publications.

Gallagher, J., Clifford, R., Trohanis, P., (1989). *Policy Implementation and P.L. 99–457*. Baltimore: Paul H. Brookes.

Gallagher J., & Ramey, C. (Eds.). (1987). *The malleability of children*. Baltimore: Paul H. Brookes.

Garber, H. (1987). *The Milwaukee Project: Prevention of mental retardation in children at risk*. Washington: American Association on Mental Retardation.

Gibson, D., & Harris, A. (1988). Aggregated early intervention effects for Down's syndrome persons: Patterning and longevity of benefits. *Journal of Mental Deficiency Research, 32*, 1–17.

Goldstein, H., Wickstrom, S., Hoyson, M., Jamieson, B., & Odom, S. (1988). Effects of script training on social and communicative interactions. *Education and Treatment of Children, 11*, 97–177.

Gresham, F., Gansle, K., & Noell, G. , (1993). Treatment integrity in applied behavior analysis with children. *School Psychology Review, 18*, 37–50.

Gresham, F., MacMillan, D., Beebe-Frankenberger, M., & Bocian, K. (2000). *Learning Disabilities Research & Practice, 15*(4), 198–205.

Guralnick, J., and Neville, B. (1997). Designing early intervention programs to promote children's social competence. In M. Guralnick (Ed.), *The effectiveness of early intervention* (pp. 459–611). Baltimore: Paul H. Brookes.

Guralnick, M. (Ed.). (1992). A hierarchical model for understanding children's peer-related social competence. In S. Odom, S. McConnell, & M. McEvoy (Eds.), *Social competence of young children with disabilities: Issues and strategies for intervention* (pp. 37–64). Baltimore: Paul H. Brookes, Publishing Co.

Guralnick, M. (1997). Second-generation research in the field of early intervention. In M. J. Guralnick (Ed.), *The effectiveness of early intervention* (pp. 3–23). Baltimore: Paul H. Brookes.

Hatton, D., Bailey, Jr., D., Roberts, J., Skinner, M., Mayhew, L., Clark, R., Waring, E., & Roberts, J. Early intervention services for young boys with Fragile X syndrome. *Journal of Early Intervention. 23*, (4), 235–251.

Infant Health and Development Program (IHDP). (1990). Enhancing the outcomes of low birth weight, premature infants. *Journal of the American Medical Association, 263*, 3035–3042.

Innocenti, M., Hollinger, P., Escobar, C., & White, K. (1993). The cost effectiveness of adding one type of parent involvement to an early intervention program. *Early Education and Development, 4*(4), 306–345.

Jameson, J., & Pederson, E. (1993). Deafness and mother-child interaction: Scaffolded instruction and the learning of problem-solving skills. *Early Development and Parenting, 3*, 51–60.

Keyes, D. (1966). *Flowers for Algernon.* New York: Harcourt Brace & World.

Kirk, S. (1958). *The early education of the mentally retarded.* Urbana, IL: University of Illinois Press.

LaFreniere, P., Dumas, J., Capuano, E., & Dubeau, D. (1992). The development and validation of the Preschool Socioaffective Profile. *Psychological Assessment: A Journal of Consulting and Clinical Psychology, 4*, 442–450.

Lazar, I., & Darlington, R. (1982). Lasting effects of early education. *Monographs of the Society of Research in Child Development, 47*(2–3, Serial No. 195).

Lipsey, M., & Wilson, D. (1993). The efficacy of psychological, educational and behavioral treatment. *American Psychologist, 48*(2), 1181–1209.

Lord, C. (2001). *Education of Children with Autism.* Washington: National Academy of Sciences.

McCollum, J., and Hemmeter, M. (1997). Parent-child interaction intervention when children have disabilities. In M. Guralnick (Ed.), *The effectiveness of early intervention* (pp. 549–579). Baltimore: Paul H. Brookes.

McConaughy, S., Kay, P., & Fitzgerald, M. (2000). How long is long enough? Outcomes for a school-based prevention program. *Exceptional Children, 67*(1), 21–34.

Ramey, C., & Ramey, S. (1998). Early intervention and early experience. *American Psychologist, 53*(2), 109–120.

Ramey, C. T., Campbell, F. A., Burchinal, M., Skinner, M. L., Gardner, D. M., & Ramey, S. L. (2000). Persistent effects of early intervention on high-risk children and their mothers. *Applied Developmental Science, 4*, 2-14.

Ramos-Ford, V., & Gardner, H. (1997). Giftedness from a multiple intelligences perspective. In N. Colangelo & G. Davis (Eds.), *Handbook of Gifted Education.* Boston: Allyn and Bacon.

Sameroff, A., & Fiese, B. (1990). Transactional regulation and early intervention. In S. Meisels and J. Shonkoff (Eds.), *Handbook of early childhood intervention* (pp. 119–149). New York: Cambridge University Press.

Sameroff, A., Seifer, R., Baldwin, A., & Baldwin, C. (1993). Stability of intelligence from preschool to adolescence: The influence of social and family risk factors. *Child Development, 64,* 80–97.

Schneidman, E. (1985). *Definition of suicide.* New York: Wiley.

Schweinhart, L. & Weikart, D. (1997) *Lasting differences: The High/Scope preschool comparison study through age 23.* Ypsilanti, MI: High/Scope Press.

Schweinhart, L., & Weikart, D. (1993, November). Success by empowerment: The High/Scope Perry Preschool Study through age 27. *Young Children, 49 (1),* 54–58.

Sonksen, P., Petrie, A., & Drew, K. (1991). Promotion of visual development of severely impaired babies: Evaluation of a developmentally based program. *Developmental Medicine and Child Neurology, 33,* 320–335.

Sparrow, S., Balla, D., & Cicchetti, D. (1984). *Vineland adaptive behavior scales (VABS).* Circle Ines, MN: American Guidance Service.

St. Pierre, R., Layzer, J., Goodson, B., & Bernstein, L. (1997). *The effectiveness of comprehensive case management interventions: Findings from the nation evaluation of the Comprehensive Child Development Program.* Cambridge, MA: Abt Associates.

Stage, S., & Quiroz, D. (1997). A meta-analysis of interventions to decrease disruptive classroom behavior in public education settings. *School Psychology Review, 26,* 333–368.

Sternberg, S. (1997). A triarchic view of giftedness: Theory and practice. In N. Bolangelo & G. Davis (Eds.), *Handbook of Gifted Education.* 3rd Edition. Boston: Allyn & Bacon, p. 43–53.

Sutherland, K., Wehby, J., & Gunter, P. (2000) The effectivness of cooperative learning with students with emotional and behaviorial disorders: A literature review. *Behavioral Disorders.* 25, #3, 225–238.

Telzrow, C. (1993). Commentary on comparative evaluation of early intervention alternatives. *Early Education and Development, 4*(4), 359–365.

Webster-Stratton, C. (1997). Early intervention for families of preschool children with conduct problems. In M. Guralnick (Ed.), *The effectiveness of early intervention* (pp. 429–455). Baltimore: Paul H. Brookes.

Werner, E., & Smith, R. (1982). *Vulnerable but invincible: A longitudinal study of resilient children and youth.* New York: McGraw Hill.

Yoshikawa, H. (1994). Prevention as cumulative protection: Effects of early family support and education on chronic delinquency and its risks. *Psychological Bulletin, 115,* 28–54.

Zigler, E., & Styfco, S. (1994). Head Start: Criticisms in a constructive context. *American Psychologist, 49*(2), 127–132.

4

High-Stakes Testing and the Distortion of Care

Nel Noddings

The current reform movement promotes many of its recommendations as ways of caring for children. Generous-sounding slogans such as "All children can learn" are hard to argue against and make it difficult to question either the philosophy underlying them or the tactics supported in their name. In this chapter, I examine one of the most troubling features of the current standards movement—high-stakes testing. First, I look at the reason most often offered for such testing: that high standards require it. Second, because this reason appears inadequate, I look at the view of motivation that seems to be operating even though it is rarely confessed. Third, I try to show how the concentration on test scores tends to distract us from the real needs of many children. Finally, I say something about care theory and how it might guide a more effective and thoughtful policy.

STANDARDS AND TESTING

It is reasonably argued that standards imply some method of evaluating whether or not they have been reached. For example, Diane Ravitch (1995) writes: "Every meaningful standard offers a realistic prospect of evaluation; if there were no way to know whether anyone was actually meeting the standard, it would have no value or meaning" (p. 9). But, with some thought, one can see that the need for evaluation of some kind does not imply high-stakes testing; indeed, in itself, the need for evaluation does not imply testing (of the usual paper and pencil sort) at all.

I want to work backwards here from the most obvious questions that arise in response to Ravitch's claim to deeper questions about the whole process of setting standards. Setting a particular standard for, say, fourth graders in mathematics does not commit us to testing all fourth graders to find out "how we are doing." We could, instead, test by sampling, as we do with NAEP. Such testing seems reasonable when standards are new and are themselves untested; that is, if we are unsure how teachers and students will handle a particular standard, it makes sense to test it in ways that will harm neither students nor teachers. Testing all students suggests that we are not simply trying to find out "how we are doing," but how each and every child is doing with the new standards. There is the clear implication that if kids and teachers are working hard enough, every child should pass. I come back to this in a discussion of the theory of motivation that seems to underlie this claim.

It seems reasonable to direct evaluation/research at the standards themselves before we subject students to high-stakes testing (if we ever make such a move). Are we absolutely sure that every fourth grader should be able to meet Standard X? Is Standard X demonstrably important? Is it crucial that X be met in fourth grade? Why? As we ask such questions, we can spot deplorable gaps in our research knowledge. What has been the experience of teachers with X? of students? In addition to the results of random testing, we need the sort of information that careful qualitative studies can give us (McNeil, 2000). If teachers feel, for example, that they are sacrificing valuable elements of the teaching-learning process to meet trivial standards, that is important information. Either such standards should be abandoned or there should be a massive re-education of teachers to help them understand the importance of the standards they reject.

There are three different senses of "standard" involved. "Standard" often refers to content; it specifies what should be taught. But it also refers to performance; that is, it sets a level or score that will be considered passable. Finally, it suggests standardization. Not only are content and performance level specified (by someone for some students), but the requirement is to apply uniformly to everyone at a particular age or grade. Thus curriculum is standardized, testing is standardized, and the expectations are universal; they too are standardized. But how far should we go in specifying what everyone should know or be able to do?

In today's highly complex society, educated people differ from one another more than ever. Twelve reasonably successful people (of, let's say, the same age) from very different occupations will reflect very different bodies of knowledge. What is essential for one may not even be useful for another. The old notion of an ideal of the educated person must give way to a multiplicity of ideals. What do they all know, and what can they all do? Surely, they can all read well enough to acquire essential information, write well enough to convey a message, and use numbers and graphs well enough to make decisions; they probably know how to make at least minimal use of technology; they almost certainly know something about their rights and obligations as citizens; and they probably have some common knowledge about health and fitness. Beyond this, they know a tremendous amount, but the commonalties become fewer as specialization increases. If I am right on this, we should focus far more narrowly on what everyone must know (Berkson, 1997; Noddings, 1997b) and, beyond that, open the educational world to a vast variety of possibilities.

The argument for uniformity or standardization is often made in the name of fairness. Some members of our society have been cheated of fair opportunities. Confessing that this has happened, the proposed remedy is now to give everyone exactly the same education at least through high school (Adler, 1982), but this decision may well miss the point and actually make things worse. Of course it is wrong to allow students to graduate from high school unable to read, but the appropriate response to that dereliction is to teach them to read, not to require them to pass an array of tests on nonessential facts.

Teachers have agonized over this problem for years. When I was a high school mathematics teacher in the 1960s, several of my colleagues in social studies regularly gave oral tests to some of their students. In response to my challenge (even then I thought something was wrong with this approach), they answered, "Well, they are nonreaders, and we want to give them a chance." A chance at what? To graduate without being able to read! My response was always: Teach them to read. Surely, you can find something related to social studies that will fit with a more important reading lesson. To make matters worse, the facts crammed in for response to test questions were quickly forgotten; the inability to read was lasting. The kids lost on almost every reasonable criterion, but their teachers could not be faulted on their good intentions. Today, when policymakers declare that high-stakes testing will give poor and minority children better chances at further education and good jobs, we should raise similar questions. Suppose the result, despite the best of intentions, is that more poor children fail and drop out? It will take courage to fight back against people who insist that their program will benefit poor, minority, and handicapped students.

The errors in thinking go far deeper than supposing that "standards" require standardized testing. As I have suggested, the proposed standards themselves need evaluation. Not only do educators need time to try out new content to see "how it goes," but they need also to ask fundamental questions about the material to be incorporated in the standards. Knowledge and skills demonstrably needed by everyone are almost certainly narrower and fewer than current recommendations suggest. It has probably been a mistake to ask subject matter specialists to define basic knowledge and skills. Unable to control their passions for the subjects they love, such experts quickly go beyond what everyone needs to an elaborate list that captures what *they* know or would like to have learned when they were children.

I do not mean to suggest that subject matter experts have nothing to contribute to the construction of content and performance standards. The work of groups such as the National Council of Teachers of Mathematics (NCTM) has often been very useful. When a course labeled "algebra" is offered, it should be constructed, taught, and evaluated under the guidance of specialists. But we also need the Socrates-like thinker who will raise the more fundamental questions: Should we teach algebra? Must all students take algebra? Why? And must everyone learn exactly the same material in algebra? Can there be legitimate variations? Why must every student who wants to go to college pass two or three years of academic mathematics in high school? Subject matter experts are not the people who should answer these questions, although they may contribute to the discussion.

To illustrate my point, consider NCTM's (1998) statement of "The Equity Principle":

> An emphasis on "mathematics for all" is important because of the role that mathematics has historically played in educational inequity. A student's mathematical proficiency is often used as a basis for decisions regarding further schooling and job opportunities. Furthermore, mathematics has been one of the subjects frequently associated with "tracking," a practice in which students are sorted into different instructional sequences that often results in inequitable opportunities and outcomes for students. (p. 23)

The generous mathematics educators involved in this discussion, although they clearly wanted good things for all students, did not even consider the possibility that mathematics should simply not be used as a gateway to all future education and job opportunities. It should be used, of course, where it is directly relevant to a student's goals and purposes, but why should it stand as a narrow gate to all higher education? Similarly, like so many other educators properly concerned with the inequities associated with tracking, math educators simply advocate abandoning tracking instead of reforming it. But different tracks could be wonderful. Students should be able to choose proudly among a variety of courses of study, all of which are rigorous, well taught, and relevant to an identifiable set of student interests. That such courses can be valuable in promoting both specialized knowledge and cultural breadth has been convincingly demonstrated (McNeil, 2000; Rose, 1995).

Is it more in keeping with democratic principles to provide rich and interesting courses compatible with the interests and abilities of individual students or merely to assume that everyone can do (and will want to do) whatever we once required of a few? Sometimes the argument is made that adolescents are too young to make the kind of choices that will eventually be open to them in a liberal society. Therefore, coercion at the precollegiate level is justified. A youngster who at the present believes she will never touch math may change her mind and then be sorry that she did not study it in high school. But this is not a good educational argument. People forced to study certain subjects often fail to learn them well; they acquire a credential of sorts but no real learning. Many young people are in this predicament today and find themselves in need of remediation at the college level. It is plausible to argue that when people change their minds about what they want to do, they will be in a better position to learn the new material if they have acquired the habits of mind that are often generated by working with material they have chosen. This may be an especially important lesson in today's complex world; many people change their minds and occupations even in middle age, and those who make the easiest transitions are those best prepared by past success in learning.

It is clear that new and/or higher standards do not require high-stakes testing to evaluate whether schools are, in general, meeting them. Indeed, current standards—construed as specified content and prescribed performance levels—need evaluation themselves, and I have suggested that researchers study in some depth the experience of teachers and students with these new standards. Finally, if we interpret standards as a means to standardization, we miss the whole point of vital and creative learning. It makes sense to identify the skills and knowledge that students must acquire for further learning, but beyond that standardization of content and performance is almost certainly detrimental to education. Why, then, do policymakers continue to push such programs?

MOTIVATION

High-stakes testing by its very name carries with it penalties for those who do not measure up. The object is said to be "leaving no child behind"—that is, teaching so well, working so hard that every child will meet the standards set. We all know that this goal will not be achieved. Indeed, policymakers would not allow it to be achieved. If such a result threatened, the tests would be made harder. There would be a clamor to "raise the bar." It is interesting, by the way, to note that the slogan "Leave no child behind" was borrowed from the Children's Defense Fund, but people at the Fund were not talking about raising the test scores of poor children; they were pressing for social reforms that would remove the worst overall effects of poverty.

Although policymakers know that not all children will pass the tests (and, if the tests are norm-referenced, failure for some is built in), the intention seems to be a move in this direction—to push students and teachers to take school work seriously and increase learning. Why is it, then, that although most of us agree that more learning is a fine goal, many of us disagree strenuously on the current recommendations to accomplish it? The answer may lie in different views of human motivation. Advocates of more homework, longer school days, and high-stakes testing seem to believe that people have to be pushed into learning and teaching. Unless they are threatened with real, unpleasant consequences, they will not be motivated. Others of us find this view of motivation pernicious. We believe that human beings are naturally motivated (Noddings, 1997a; Purkey and Novak, 1996). Indeed, life would simply end were there no motivation. But this view does not commit us to a permissive "let 'em do as they please" educational philosophy. We, too, want to encourage more and better learning.

As early as 1913, John Dewey (1975/1913) laid out the problem and argued that neither coercion nor permissiveness would be successful in exercising student motivation. When students are forced to learn for an external end such as a test, they are not fully engaged. They may learn enough to respond accurately to test questions, but the learning is likely to be shallow and temporary. At the opposite extreme, when students are allowed to do whatever they want, they may simply follow impulses and move from one activity to another in a restless and unproductive quest for some undefined form of fulfillment. The psychologically sound approach is to identify natural motivation and guide it toward worthwhile ends—ends that are chosen freely by the student and approved as academically sound by the teacher. Certainly the Deweyan approach is much harder work than just leaving students alone. (I return to the issue of teacher motivation a bit later.)

First, let's consider what follows when we assume that students must be controlled by punishments and rewards if they are to learn. The classroom becomes a place where all sorts of minor rewards—stars on papers, free time, even candies—are given out for compliant behavior, and penalties are assessed for negligence or failure. What should be one of life's great joys—learning—is turned into wage labor (Kohn, 1993). While teachers struggle to make lessons interesting (and sometimes succeed), students learn to work for extrinsic rewards.

It is often said that if we expect more from students, they will achieve more. There is an important nugget of truth in this. But what should we expect from them? Discussion of this issue is largely missing from educational debate today, and the idea is reduced to slogans. Thomas Lickona (1991) describes with approval a classroom poster whose first rule was: "Always do your best in everything" (p. 215). No creative, happy, productive adult would ever adopt such a slogan, and I have myself warned brilliant graduate students away from such nonsense. Do an adequate job on everything you're forced to do, I advise, and save your best for those things in which you are passionately interested. A sure way to mediocrity is to slave away at every trivial task and feel somehow equally satisfied with every item checked off the to-do list. Yet evidence is mounting that exactly this sort of behavior is increasingly encouraged in schools (Kohn, 2000; McNeil, 2000), and many bright, compliant students are deeply unhappy (Pope, 2001).

To have high expectations for each child does not mean that we must hold the same expectations for all children. We should expect that all children will find some commendable interests, learn to persist in tasks they find worthwhile, have wonderful ideas at least occasionally, make satisfying friendships, contribute positively to the social and physical environment, find something deeply satisfying in the world of ideas. (Duckworth, 1987; Harcombe, 2001; Meier, 1995). But wise teachers and parents know that children will meet these expectations in very different ways and at different times. Moreover, teachers need to believe that it is legitimate to spend time trying to encourage these expectations. In contrast to the expectations teachers are told to have—high expectations for students to do things they are often not motivated to do—the expectations I just listed are usually shared by students, parents, and teachers.

But perhaps policymakers who insist on high-stakes testing just want to be sure that youngsters are adequately prepared for each new phase of schooling. They do not want students to be at risk of failing fifth or sixth grade because they did not learn the material offered in fourth grade. But if this is the case (and I share a concern about "cumulative ignorance"), they would not suggest retention as a remedy (Darling-Hammond & Falk, 1997). Fear of failing a grade is one of childhood's great terrors, and retention inflicts humiliation. If a lack of skills is making it impossible for students to succeed, then special efforts should be made to help them acquire these skills. This does not mean removing children from classes in the arts, from problem-solving and critical thinking, from participation in school governance and other extra-curricular activities (Paul et al., 1997). In my earlier example, the well-intentioned social studies teachers could have found material of some significance in social studies that might also be used to teach reading. They would sacrifice only a set of facts likely to be forgotten anyway. Nor does teaching essential skills mean pressing relentlessly for school-based skills at the loss of students' own cultural knowledge and pride (Valenzuela, 1999). It means providing a culturally rich and sensitive environment in which natural motivation can be guided to the acquisition of necessary skills. However, I want to emphasize again that educators should be careful in identifying "necessary" skills. The needs we define for students are often very different from those expressed by the students themselves. We cannot help students effectively without attending to both sets of needs. In the next section, I say more about the issues involved in defining and meeting needs.

Before turning to that discussion, we should say a bit more about the issue of motivation. The view that seems to prevail in schools today applies not only to students but to teachers and administrators as well. Policymakers express the view that educators will not do an adequate job unless they are held "accountable." But this view is at least questionable and may actually be counterproductive. Just as students respond more positively when they are trusted and encouraged to follow their own legitimate interests, teachers also respond to encouragement, helpful advice, and administrative modeling of the positive behaviors endorsed (Beck, 1994). It may even be harmful to insist that all teachers agree with a set of methods or one particular philosophy so long as all agree that "we are here for the kids" (Lyman, 2000). Teachers, like students, need encouragement to do the best possible job in ways that are congruent with their own justifiable beliefs and personal aptitudes (Noddings, 1986).

If we believe this, if we trust teachers, students, and administrators, we will certainly put a stop to the present practice of pitting student against student, teacher against teacher, school against school, district against district, state against state, the United States against the world. We can find better ways to find out how we are doing and how to do better.

NEEDS

It is useful in both ethics and educational theory to make a distinction between those needs that arise within the one expressing them and those that arise externally. I call the first "expressed" needs and the second "inferred" needs (Noddings, 2002). Expressed needs include basic biological needs that are not necessarily expressed by voice but are universally expressed by bodies. All human beings need food, water, shelter, and protection from harm. We might argue that all people also need care in ways appropriate to their age, status, and immediate conditions. Infants need total care in order to live. Young children need psychological care in order to thrive. Successful adults need care in the form of positive response to their efforts and overtures.

In contrast to expressed needs, inferred needs are those that people in authority posit for those in their power. It is adults who decide that children need vaccinations, dental work, and schooling. Caring adults approach inferred needs sensitively, hoping that if they have identified truly significant needs, these needs will eventually become expressed needs; that is, that children will internalize the needs and seek to satisfy them without coercion. If the need is not merely instrumental (e.g., vaccinations and dental work) but something thought worth valuing for itself (e.g., reading), adults are even more careful in how they press such needs on children. Those of us who love to read and to learn feel enormous sadness when we read accounts of teenagers whose pursuit of excellence in school is totally instrumental—a constant drive for high grades without regard for what might be learned (Pope, 2001).

Ethical systems have rarely emphasized needs. It has been more common to stress virtues, principles, and rights. Indeed, there is no term for one-who-needs that carries anything like the dignity of "rights-bearer." To be needy is to be somehow deficient, and yet we all have needs. One great strength of an ethic of care—a needs-based ethic—is that it recognizes the contribution of both carer and cared-for. In mature relationships, people fill both positions;

they alternate as carers and cared-fors. But even in unequal relations, where the cared-for cannot possibly fill the role of carer, he or she contributes importantly. The ways in which needs are expressed and the responses to their satisfaction are significant in sustaining (or discouraging) the carer. We all know how much easier it is to work with cheerful, responsive children than with those who are sullen and withdrawn.

When teachers have time to establish relations of care and trust with students, they gain opportunities to hear their expressed needs, and responding to these needs deepens the relationship. This does not mean, of course, that every want or desire is satisfied. Children express many wants that do not rise to the level of needs, and part of an adequate education is learning how to distinguish fleeting (and perhaps unhealthy) wants from genuine needs. We might use criteria such as the following to decide when a want should be warranted as a need: The want is fairly stable over a considerable period of time and/or it is intense; the want is demonstrably connected to some desirable end or, at least, to one that is not harmful; the want is in the power (within the means) of those addressed to grant it; and the one wanting is willing and able to contribute to the satisfaction of the want. When these criteria are met, most of us acknowledge the want as an expressed need.

What I am calling "expressed needs" are not always actually expressed. Many children have difficulty expressing their deepest needs, and children in special education often suffer this difficulty. One of my favorite stories involves two contrasting approaches to this problem. A youngster storms into his classroom and, in rage or despair, sweeps all the books off his teacher's desk. In one account, the teacher, using an approved technique of behavior modification, leads the boy to an established spot for time-out and tells him to stay there until he feels better and can behave in an acceptable fashion. She does not try to find out what need is being expressed by the behavior. In the second scenario, the teacher asks another adult in the room to work with the other children while he goes into an adjoining office with the offender. There he listens to the boy's story. It is horrendous; it is just heartbreaking. The teacher sweeps a stack of books onto the floor; the boy does, too. They litter the floor with books, and then teacher and student sit down and cry together. Eventually, the teacher laughs a little and says, "Now we have to pick the damn things up," and they do.

One might argue that the second teacher has reinforced a bad way to respond to unhappiness. Well, maybe. But no object or person was hurt, and the temporary chaos was repaired. More than anything else, the boy learned that his rage was justified and that someone cared enough to share his hurt. A very deep need was satisfied even though the original problem (which was beyond the control of both student and teacher) remained.

In today's schools, we too often avoid deep expressed needs. We establish long lists of inferred needs, even including the memorization of facts long forgotten by most intelligent adults. In this whole process, we often justify our coercion in terms of "rights" because it is so much more impressive than "needs" in an individualistic society. The children are said to have a right to the satisfaction of needs that we have imposed on them. One influential book is even entitled "The Right to Learn" (Darling-Hammond, 1997), and the rights-language does capture something important—that all children have the right to resources that make it possible for them to learn. But if the right to learn is translated into a "right" to be coerced to learn mountains of material for which a child sees no need, and his/her real needs remain unmet, the language becomes a form of "newspeak." It does not, then, capture what we usually mean by a "right."

To treat needs with care requires time. There are no formulas to tell us when an expressed need should be encouraged or when an inferred need should be discarded (although I have offered some criteria). The same is true of the desires, wants, and initial interests of children. Dewey (1966/1916) said it well:

> Realization that life is growth protects us from that so-called idealizing of childhood which in effect is nothing but lazy indulgence. Life is not to be identified with every superficial act and interest. Even though it is not always easy to tell whether what appears to be mere surface fooling is a sign of some nascent as yet untrained power, we must remember that manifestations are not to be accepted as ends in themselves. They are signs of possible growth. They are to be turned into means of development, of carrying power forward, not indulged or cultivated for their own sake. (1966/1916, pp. 51-52)

Dewey finishes this paragraph with lines from Emerson. Working this way, Emerson warned, "involves at once, immense claims on the time, the thought, on the life of the teacher. It requires time, use, insight, event . . . and only to think of using it implies character and profoundness" (in Dewey, 1966/1916, p. 52).

Talk of immense claims on time, thought, and insight returns us to another great concern about the current standards/testing movement. Policymakers and taxpayers are often unwilling to fund the resources necessary for teachers to work closely and continuously with students. Instead, they seize on measures of accountability that will, they hope, produce desirable results with less cost in both money and effort. Thus, if we are convinced that poor children can learn as well as rich ones, we need not concern ourselves with poverty. We are distracted from the real needs of poor children. We simply "expect" both teachers and students to do better. Careful attention to needs, however, would direct us to do something about the poverty, homelessness, poor parenting, decaying neighborhoods, lack of adequate health care, and the host of problems associated with deficient resources. In schools, instead of concentrating relentlessly on basic skills, we would try harder to provide conditions that are known to sustain curiosity and broaden interests. The closing section moves us in this direction.

CARE THEORY AND SOCIAL POLICY

The great strength of care theory is its emphasis not just on caring as a virtue but on caring as a desirable attribute of relations. When we look at caring as a kind of relation, we are forced to consider the role and response of the cared-for; it is not sufficient to note the virtues exhibited by carers. We all know people who have done dreadful things in the name of caring, and they often feel justified in insisting that the miseries they have inflicted were done for the sake of the those cared for (Miller, 1983; Noddings, 2002). In care theory, therefore, we insist that there be some form of acknowledgment from the cared-for that caring has been received. Moreover, we recognize that the cared-for *qua* cared-for contributes something significant to the relationship. From the smiles and wriggles of the healthy infant to the light of recognition in the eyes of an elderly patient (or a hand squeezed in appreciation or a sigh of relief), the positive responses of our cared-fors "keep us going."

It seems obvious, then, that we have a double reason for discerning and responding to expressed needs. In doing so, we not only contribute to the growth and well-being of the cared-for, but we also strengthen the relation of which we are part. Our work as teachers or parents is thus facilitated by establishing and maintaining relations of care.

Can we claim to impose high-stakes testing on children "because we care"? The only way such a claim could be justified is through a move I have already rejected. We would have to claim that such testing is in the best interests of children. The evidence is reasonably clear that this is not the case—not for present learning, and not for long-term and continued learning. Moreover, the practice makes many children miserable; fear and anxiety destroy the quality of present experience and make learning into labor.

I have heard people say that even special education students should be forced to take the current tests. If they are excluded, the argument goes, they will feel left out! One has trouble imagining this result, but, if it occurs, care theory would suggest that children be invited to try the tests if they'd like—no high stakes attached. The horrified rebuttal to this might be that the results would be hard to interpret—some children taking the tests, some not—and that we need to report on all special kids. Then, clearly, the aim is not to care for kids but to check on performance. Underlying this reaction is, again, a dim view of human motivation. If we exclude special education students from the tests, critics fear, more and more children will likely be classified as "special" so that scores will seem higher than they really are. Further, we have to be sure that teachers are making a genuine effort to teach all children the standard curriculum.

It may be true that some educators would classify children just to improve their school's test scores, but this is not a reason to inflict tests on everyone. It is another good reason to eliminate the high-stakes aspect of testing and concentrate on diagnostic purposes. Similarly, it is surely right to monitor what teachers do with their special education students, but we need not (and almost certainly should not) insist that those students—"special needs" kids—receive exactly the same curriculum as all other students.

Part of the strong aversion to high-stakes testing comes directly from our concern with needs. Educating, as Dewey pointed out, is hard, time-consuming work. It requires, among other things, a continual effort at balancing expressed and inferred needs. When we move too far in the direction of inferred needs, we are using what political philosophers refer to as a "positive" conception of liberty. In contrast to a negative sense that promotes the rights of individuals to become whatever they can and want to be, a positive view says that people should have the liberty to become what they should become. Of this view, Isaiah Berlin (1969) wrote:

> Once I take this view, I am in a position to ignore the actual wishes of men or societies, to bully, oppress, torture them in the name, and on behalf, of their "real" selves, in the secure knowledge that whatever is the true goal of man (happiness, performance of duty, wisdom, a just society, self-fulfillment) must be identical with his freedom—the free choice of his "true," albeit often submerged and inarticulate self. (p. 133)

Reading this passage, we are reminded of all the totalitarian regimes in history that have taken precisely this view of human freedom. But we also know, and Berlin is careful to acknowledge, that we all share something of the positive view, particularly with respect to children. We want our children to be good, not bad; to be well-informed, not ignorant; to be pleasant companions, not boors; to be interested and zestful, not lackadaisical; to be involved as citizens, not alienated; to be spiritually alive and sensitive, not dead to the wonders of the universe. But, again, to fill out this loosely outlined positive view, we have to achieve an exquisite balance between addressing the needs we infer and those expressed by our children and students.

We are losing something we almost had a grip on. Think what we have accomplished. The twentieth century was marked by an increasing humanization of schooling. Many states have abandoned corporal punishment in schools, and even in states that allow it, many districts forbid it. We try harder to keep kids in school. We are ashamed of past patterns of racial segregation and are still struggling to overcome its effects. We encourage young women in math and science. We provide education for youngsters once labeled "trainable" or not schooled at all. We send more students to higher education than any nation in history. We feed hungry children breakfast and lunch. In many districts, we provide preschool education for three- and four-year-olds. We reject the notion that some kids are slated from the start for manual labor and others for professional work. We have even flirted with the idea that education should promote something called "self-actualization."

The question arises: Why do we periodically reject the most democratic and liberating ideas and retain the most restrictive and controlling? Education can be considerate of students, and teaching can follow and guide the natural motivation of students without being permissive or intellectually deficient. In the footsteps of Froebel, Pestalozzi, Dewey, Jane Addams, Maria Montessori, David Hawkins, Frances Hawkins, Caleb Gattegno, and so many others who have had faith in children and taken delight in them, we can improve our schools without high-stakes testing. It requires imagination, industry, sensitivity, trust, faith, and yes, love.

DISCUSSION QUESTIONS

1. How would you answer the author's question about why we "reject the most democratic and liberating ideas and retain the most restrictive and controlling"?
2. What "standards" does the author support?
3. The author states, "To have high expectations for each child does not mean that we must hold the same expectations for all children." What does she mean by this? What ramifications would such a philosophy have for education?

REFERENCES

Adler, M. J. (1982). *The paideia proposal*. New York: Macmillan.
Beck, L. G. (1994). *Reclaiming educational administration as a caring profession*. New York: Teachers College Press.
Berkson, W. (1997). "A place to stand": Breaking the impasse over standards. *Phi Delta Kappan, 79*, 207–211.
Berlin, I. (1969). *Four essays on liberty*. Oxford, U.K.: Oxford University Press.
Darling-Hammond, L. (1997). *The right to learn*. San Francisco: Jossey-Bass.
Darling-Hammond, L., & Falk, B. (1997). Using standards and assessments to support learning. *Phi Delta Kappan, 79*, 190–199.
Dewey, J. (1966). *Democracy and education*. New York: Macmillan. (Original work published in 1916).
———. (1975). *Interest and effort in education*. Carbondale & Edwardsville: Southern Illinois University Press. (Original work published in 1913).
Duckworth, E. (1987). *"The having of wonderful ideas" and other essays on teaching and learning*. New York: Teachers College Press.
Harcombe, E. (2001). *Dare to learn: Science teachers accept the challenge*. New York: Teachers College Press.
Kohn, A. (1993). *Punished by rewards: The trouble with gold stars, incentive plans, A's, praise, and other bribes*. Boston: Houghton Mifflin.
———. (2000). *The case against standardized testing*. Portsmouth, NH: Heinemann.
Lickona, T. (1991). *Educating for character*. New York: Bantam Books.
Lyman, L. L. (2000). *How do they know you care?* New York: Teachers College Press.
McNeil, L. M. (2000). *Contradictions of reform*. New York: Routledge.
Meier, D. (1995). *The power of their ideas*. Boston: Beacon Press.

Miller, A. (1983). *For your own good*. Translated by H. & H. Hannun. New York: Farrar, Strauss, Giroux.

National Council of Teachers of Mathematics. (1998). *Principles and standards for school mathematics: Discussion draft*. Reston, VA: NCTM.

Noddings, N. (1984). *Caring*. Berkeley: University of California Press.

———. (1986). Fidelity in teaching, teacher education, and research on teaching. *Harvard Educational Review, 56*(4), 496–510.

———. (1997a). Must we motivate? In N. C. Burbules & D. T. Hansen (Eds.), *Teaching and its predicaments* (pp. 29–44). Boulder, CO: Westview Press.

———. (1997b). Thinking about standards. *Phi Delta Kappan, 79*, 184–189.

———. (2002). *Starting at home: Care theory and social policy*. Berkeley: University of California Press.

Paul, J. L., Churton, M., Rosselli-Kostoryz, H., Morse, W. C., Marfo, K., Lavely, C., & Thomas, D. (Eds.), (1997). *Foundations of special education*. Pacific Grove, CA: Brooks/Cole.

Pope, D. C. (In press). *"Doing school."* New Haven: Yale University Press.

Purkey, W. W., & Novak, J. M. (1996). *Inviting school success*. Belmont, CA: Wadsworth.

Ravitch, D. (1995). *National standards in American education*. Washington: Brookings Institution Press.

Rose, M. (1995). *Possible lives: The promise of public education in America*. Boston: Houghton Mifflin.

Valenzuela, A. (1999). *Subtractive schooling*. Albany: State University of New York Press.

5

From the Old to the New Paradigm of Disability and Families: Research to Enhance Family Quality of Life Outcomes

Ann P. Turnbull and H. R. Turnbull

The new paradigm of disability is contextual and societal: A person has an impairment that becomes a disability as a result of the interaction between the individual and the natural, built, cultural, and social environments. Accordingly, research into the natural, cultural, and social environments is warranted and is targeted at enhancing enablement and preventing disablement.

We take as a fact that one of the natural environments affecting individuals with disabilities is their family. A person with a disability affects and is affected by the person's family; families are systems in which an event that affects primarily one person (e.g., a child with a disability) also affects all other members (Turnbull & Turnbull, 2001; Whitechurch & Constantine, 1993). The converse is true as well (particularly as it concerns families who have children with disabilities): Whatever happens to the family affects the child. A leading family therapist describes the reverberating impact of family members on each other analogous to a mobile:

> In a mobile all the pieces, no matter what size or shape, can be grouped together and balanced by shortening or lengthening the strings attached or rearranging the distance between the pieces. So it is with the family. None of the family members is identical to any others; they are all different and at different levels of growth. As in a mobile, you can't arrange one without thinking of the other. (Satir, 1972, p. 119-120)

It follows, then, that family research is wholly consistent with the new paradigm.

Upon this fact we rest certain assertions. These are as follows:

1. Families are integral to society.
2. Their empowerment and quality of life are the *sine qua non* of research on families.
3. Whatever research is conducted on and on behalf of families should have the consequence of advancing the empowerment and quality of life of the individual with a disability.
4. Research on and on behalf of the individual (especially when the individual is a child—defined as a person who is legally a minor) should also benefit the family's empowerment and quality of life.

In this chapter, we trace the history of family research over the past half-century. We show how it was premised originally on a psychotherapy model; how it moved from that model to a parent training model; and then how it left that model for a parent involvement model. We argue that these three models together constitute an old paradigm of research on, and on behalf of, families.

We then focus on the two elements of the new paradigm. These are a family-centered model of research and a family empowerment/family quality-of-life model. In a nutshell, we assert that the new paradigm must involve family research and that the only type of family research that is tolerable under the new paradigm is that which has empowerment and quality of life as the outcomes for families, including members with disabilities. We suggest a research program and teacher education program consistent with this new paradigm vision.

THE OLD PARADIGM OF
DISABILITY AND FAMILIES

The old paradigm characterizes disability as a deficit within the individual resulting in functional impairments associated with daily activities. Thus, the old paradigm service system primarily focuses on "fixing" the individual's functional impairments as contrasted to providing environmental accommodations.

Just as the old paradigm influences individuals with disabilities, so it also influences families of children and youth with disabilities. Three examples of the old paradigm's service and research models targeted on families include (a) the psychotherapy model, (b) the parent training model, and (c) the parent involvement model (Turnbull, Turbiville, & Turnbull, 2000). We now analyze these three old paradigm models.

Psychotherapy Model

The psychotherapy model, most prevalent in the 1950s to 1960s, regarded the birth of a child with a disability as a "tragic crisis" that could best be dealt with by providing psychotherapy to the child's parents in order to help them overcome their grief and cope with the unexpected and presumptively unwanted fact of disability (Bowlby, 1960; Goshen, 1963; Mandelbaum & Wheeler, 1967; Solnit & Stark, 1961; Wolfensberger, 1967). In the case of some disabilities, such as autism and asthma, parents were considered to be the cause of their child's disability (Akerley, 1985; Warren, 1985; Gallagher & Gallagher, 1985). Accordingly, psychoanalysis was aimed at "fixing" the parents so that they, in turn, could "fix" their child. This view is described by Ruth Sullivan, a parent of a son with autism, who experienced the brunt of this old paradigm.

> Parents who were not around in the 1950s, 60s, and even 70s trying to get a diagnosis for their (usually) beautiful young child with extremely difficult and inexplicable behavior might have a hard time understanding the oppressive and guilt-provoking dogma of most mental health professionals at that time. For some parents that I knew then, *each* time they took their child for an evaluation, they were told that they (especially the mother) had caused the autism. Families who could afford it went into psychotherapy or psychoanalysis. No assistance was given to the parents in handling the day-to-day worrisome behavior of their child. The theory, acted upon as fact, was that once the parents recognized and confronted their repressed and deep-seated anger (which caused their child to withdraw) they would then be fit to raise their otherwise normal child.
>
> Bruno Bettelheim, the most articulate proponent of this mindset, was a skillful and much published writer. . . . In Bettelheim's book, *The Empty Fortress*, he compares the homes of autistic children to Nazi concentration camps (where, as an Austrian Jew, he was once a prisoner). (Turnbull, Turnbull, Shank, & Leal, 1999, p. 413)

In the psychotherapy model, parents frequently became the "cases" to receive "treatment" from the "experts" who had the decision-making power to define "normalcy." The "treatment" was to "fix" mothers' personal pathologies so that they could be an adequate parent of their child. Almost no attention was given to changing or supporting the family's environment, enabling it to build on the family's or child's strengths and to address needs so as to best support the child's development and self-determination and the family's integrity and wholeness.

The psychotherapy model reflects a power-over relationship (Table 5-1) in which professionals exerted decision-making control over parents through their socially awarded higher status, their trained competence, and their insistence on having control of outcomes of their relationships with families and the child. Professionals possessed the power to "diagnose" and to prescribe "treatment" that, if not followed, would suggest that the parents were "dysfunctional." Figure 5-1 summarizes key elements of the psychotherapy model.

Although the psychotherapy model was particularly prevalent in the 1950s to 1960s, there are still applications of it today. It probably is more prevalent in the area of emotional disability than in other types of disability professional-family interaction.

Parent Training Model

Beginning in the 1970s and proceeding to the 1980s, the primary emphasis shifted from psychotherapy to parent training. Largely influenced by President Johnson's Great Society programs and the emergence of the Head Start model (Hunt, 1972; Zigler & Valentine, 1979), the parent training model also presumed parental deficits. It suggested that parents needed to be "fixed" by expanding their knowledge and skills. The assumption was that knowledge and skill needed to be provided by professionals to families in a unidirectional fashion, with almost no recognition being given to the value of parents sharing their knowledge and skills with other parents (Turnbull, Blue-Banning, Turbiville, & Park, 1999).

With Head Start as the precursor, Congress authorized the 1968 Handicapped Children's Early Education Program for children birth to age 8. The program's major goal was to enhance the development of preschoolers with disabilities ("fix" their functional impairments) (Harvey, 1977). A major strategy for developmental gain was enlisting parents as early intervention allies, as the Chairman of the Select Committee on Education, Congressman Dominick V. Daniels, made clear:

> Few parents are prepared to take care of a child who looks different, behaves in grossly unacceptable ways or fails to respond even to the sound of a mother's voice. Parents of handicapped children have fears and are often frustrated and bewildered. They need help in understanding their child's disability. They need help in working with their handicapped child.
>
> This bill will bring us into a new era of educating handicapped children. In addition, it is anticipated that this legislation will enlist the help of the parents as allies and associates of educators to provide a total program. (Lavor & Krivit, 1969, p. 381)

Major emphasis was placed on teaching skills to mothers so that they in turn could and would teach their child at home. The ultimate goal was to "fix" the child with the disability by "fixing" the parents' competence. Once again, professionals maintained a power-over relationship with parents as they instructed them and guided them in skill acquisition.

TABLE 5-1.
Overview of Old and New Paradigm of Disability and Families

Service/Research Emphasis	Type of Power	Type of Decision-Making	Participants	Anticipated Outcome
Parent psychotherapy; parent training; parent involvement	Power-over	Exerting control	Professionals and mothers	"Fixing" deficits of mothers as conduit of "fixing" child
Family-centered services	Power-with	Collaborating	Families and professionals	Addressing families' priorities
Family empowerment/ family quality of life	Power-through	Synergizing	Families, friends, community citizens, and professionals	Strengthening empowerment; enhancing family quality of life

Prepared for: Meisels, S. J., & Shonkoff, J. P. (Eds.). (in press). *Handbook of early intervention*. New York: Cambridge University Press.

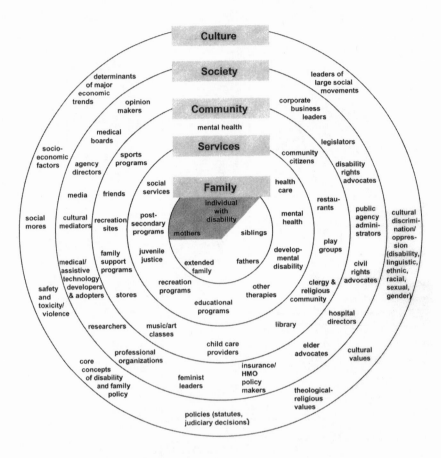

Figure 5-1. Emphasis on "fixing" individuals with disabilities and their mothers. Shaded area represents target of "fix-up" efforts.

Parents who actively participated in this parent training model report on the profound implications it had on their relationship with their child. Martha Blue-Banning, a parent of a now 22-year-old son with a developmental disability, describes the impact of the parent training model on her relationship with her son.

> The message to me as a mother that was pervasive in early intervention's emphasis on developmental milestones was that we needed to "fix" James. The harder I worked, the more he would achieve. And achievement was the name of the game. "Developmental milestones"—how I learned to hate those words. They were the gold medals for the winners of the "fix it" set.
>   I readily became James' teacher. His playtime at home became "learning time"—actually *all* his time was learning time. Any free time we had was to be

spent on his therapy or to be spent feeling guilty that we weren't doing his therapy. I remember one developmental milestone that he never achieved—stacking three blocks. He had finally achieved stacking two blocks; the next milestone was stacking three. I modeled for him, prompted him, and finally held his hand while we did it together. Inevitably, when left to attempt it on his own, James would pick up the blocks and throw them. He found this hysterically funny. His early intervention teacher thought he was noncompliant. James obviously didn't get the fact that his ticket to acceptance rested heavily on stacking those blocks. (Turnbull, Blue-Banning, Turbiville, & Park, 1999, p. 165)

Parent Involvement Model

The parent involvement model received a major impetus when IDEA was first implemented in 1975. IDEA specified active roles for parents in educational decision-making. The most prominent and most frequent role is involvement in the IEP conference. Over twenty years later, parent involvement is still primarily actualized in elementary, middle, and secondary schools by parents attending IEP conferences. Although the IEP process was intended to provide a context for equal decision-making among parents and professionals, the power-over approach has clearly been prevalent. Extensive reviews of research on parent involvement in IEP conferences reveal that schools try to comply with the letter (but not the spirit) of legal mandates; however, there is scant evidence that the IEP process has empowering outcomes for students, parents, or educators (Smith, 1990; Turnbull & Turnbull, in press). Interestingly, almost no research has focused on the outcomes of the IEP process, but rather research has addressed issues such as teacher, parent, and student roles; topics discussed at meetings; the length of meetings; and the content addressed (Espin, Denot, & Albayrak-Kaymak, 1998; Farel, Shackelford, & Hurth, 1997; Gerber, Banbury, Miller, & Griffin, 1986; Getzel & deFur, 1997; Goldstein & Turnbull, 1982; Lewis, Busch, Proger, & Juska, 1981; Lynch & Stein, 1982; Nadler & Shore, 1980; Pyecha, Cox, Dewitt, Drummond, Jaffe, Kalt, Lane, & Pelosi, 1980; Salembier & Furney, 1998; Smith & Simpson, 1989).

Moreover, parent involvement in educational decision-making has occurred primarily through the involvement of mothers (Able-Boone, 1993; Campbell, Strickland, & La Forme, 1992; Turnbull & Turnbull, 2001). Only limited attention has been given to the involvement of children and youth with disabilities and other family members (Morningstar, Turnbull, & Turnbull, 1995; Shellady, Hendrickson, Reisen, Sampson, & Vance, 1994; Van Reusen & Bos, 1994). Parent reports clearly document limited decision-making influence in IEP conferences, mediation, and due process hearings (National Council on Disability, 1995; Turnbull & Turnbull, in press).

A power-over approach associated with parent involvement in educational decision-making is particularly problematic for families from culturally and linguistically diverse backgrounds (Harry & Kalyanpur, 1999; Kalyanpur & Harry, 1999). Researchers have described a conflict of culture between the bureaucratic special education culture, operationalized through IDEA, and the culture of families from culturally and linguistically diverse backgrounds that relies more on relationships rather than legal procedures:

> The combination of the "direct," informal manner of American professionals, with their assumptions of the validity of detached, scientific information (Wright et al., 1983), can be alienating rather than reassuring for people accustomed to a slower pace, more personal yet more generalized approach. . . . The bureaucratic structure of schools, and, certainly of the special education system, with its formal procedures and systems, presents people from such cultures with a formidable challenge. When these systems are implemented without regard for the need for personalized information, and, as has been emphasized earlier, without opportunity for dialogue, the result is often confusion and alienation on the part of parents and increasing impatience on the part of professionals. When they are implemented in a vein of compliance rather than communication the results can be disastrous. (Harry, 1992b; Harry & Kalyanpur, 1994, p. 160)

A second group of parents who have been particularly frustrated by the power-over approach of the parent involvement model are activist parents who have a strong empowerment orientation. The perspectives of many of these parents were set out in the National Council on Disability hearings on IDEA conducted in 1994. The Council's report is replete with testimony characterizing the high level of frustration experienced by families who have attempted to be empowered decision-makers (National Council on Disability, 1995):

> I have come to call myself Bonnie, the bitch, because of what I've had to become to fight the system for the handicapped child, and yet I have contacted multiple state offices. I have followed through with every lead that anybody has ever given me. I have talked with the Governor's office here in the state. I've gone so far as to call the White House. . . . I guess my feeling at this point is, "Is there anybody out there who really cares?" I don't know what more to do. I, as a parent, have pursued every option. (Testimony by Bonnie Weninger, in National Council on Disability, 1996, p. 123)

> When you have to advocate for your child, you pay a high price for that in many ways. It's very stressful on the family. . . . Because of the kind of advocacy work that I've had to do. . . . I'm not able to teach anywhere locally. I actually teach school in Texas, which is a 30-mile drive in the time difference away from my home. . . . My son suffers from bipolar disorder and numerous other difficulties. That illness itself is stressful, but when you have a vindictive,

harassing, retaliatory school district to deal with, it makes your life completely miserable . . . . That's what I've had to deal with. (Edris Klucher, Albuquerque, NM) (National Council on Disability, 1995, p. 124)

Summary

Key themes characterizing the old paradigm of services and research related to families of children and youth with disabilities include the following:

1. Children with disabilities and their mothers were viewed as needing to be "fixed." (We limit this comment to children with disabilities because there is almost no emphasis in old paradigm literature about youth with disabilities. Likewise, there is almost no emphasis on any family members other than mothers.)
2. "Fixing" the mothers was viewed as a conduit for "fixing" the child.
3. Professionals were "experts" and parents were "cases," "clients," "patients," and/or "trainees."
4. IDEA's authorized equal-decision making between professionals and parents resulted primarily in power-over relationships between professionals and mothers.
5. The almost sole focus of special education has been to "fix" the student's developmental deficits, with little attention to self-determination of students and/or their parents.
6. Negligible attention was given to any environmental accommodations.
7. The literature is absent of any descriptions related to outcomes from service-delivery or research such as family empowerment and/or enhancement of family quality of life.

NEW PARADIGM OF DISABILITY AND FAMILIES

Family services and research have been in transition from the old to the new paradigm. One of the bridges between the old and new paradigm has been an emphasis on family-centered services and research. Once that bridge is crossed, the emerging model for family research emphasizes a family empowerment/family quality of life model (Turnbull & Turnbull, 2001; Turnbull, Turbiville, & Turnbull, 2000).

Family-Centered Model

The family-centered model was introduced in the 1980s in early intervention and early childhood services and research. The family-centered model has many definitions; but among these many definitions, there are three central characteristics—family choice, family strengths perspective, and family as the unit of support (Allen & Petr, 1996).

First, the family-centered model primarily attempted to honor family choice by changing the power relationship between professionals and families, moving from a power-over approach to a power-with approach (see Table 5-1). A major emphasis is encouraging families to take the lead in stating their priorities and having professionals respond to those priorities (Dunst, Johnson, Trivette, & Hamby, 1991; McBride, Brotherson, Joanning, Whiddon, & Demmitt, 1993; Turnbull, Turbiville, & Turnbull, in press).

Second, the family-centered model abandoned a pathology orientation and adopted a strengths orientation (Bailey & McWilliam, 1993; Dunst, Trivette, & Deal, 1988; Saleebey, 1996). This approach is evident in IDEA, Part C, which requires the identification of family priorities, resources, and concerns as part of the process to develop the individual family services plan (this legislation uses the term resources, rather than strengths).

Third, the entire family is the unit of support, not just the child with a disability and the child's mother. An outgrowth of this approach has been an emphasis on conducting research and providing support to fathers (Ainge, Colvin, & Baker, 1998; Frey, Fewell, & Vadasy, 1989; Meyer, 1995; Levine, Murphy, & Wilson, 1993), siblings (Heller, Gallagher, & Fredrick, 1999; McHale & Gamble, 1989; Meyer & Vadasy, 1994; Powell & Gallagher, 1993; Stoneman & Waldman-Berman, 1993), and extended family (Able-Boone, Sandall, Stevens, & Frederick, 1992; Meyer & Vadasy, 1986; Mirfin-Veitch, Bray, & Watson, 1997). It is disconcerting that the family member who is most neglected in family research is the individual with the disability.

Currently, the family-centered model is considered the prevalent one in early intervention and early childhood services for young children with disabilities (McWilliam, Lang, Vandiviere, Angel, Collins, & Underdown, 1995; Murphy, Lee, Turnbull, & Turbiville, 1995; Wehman, 1998). Research indicates, however, that the family-centered philosophy is stronger than its actual implementation (Katz & Scarpati, 1995; McBride, Patterson, Joanning, Whiddlen, & Demmit, 1993; Menke, 1991).

At the elementary, middle, and secondary school levels, the bridge from the old to the new paradigm is not as strong as it is during the early years. The emphasis is still much more on parent involvement in IEP conferences and parent attendance at school events than on a family-centered model and on a shift in the power relationship from a power-over to a power-with orientation (Turnbull & Turnbull, 2001).

Family Empowerment/Family Quality-of-Life Model

The family empowerment/family quality-of-life model emphasizes empowerment as the process and family quality of life as the outcome of research and professional services. This model emphasizes a participatory action research approach as part of the new paradigm.

Family quality of life as outcome. Within all human service areas, there is a contemporary emphasis on conceptualizing and measuring outcomes. As stated by Schorr (1997):

> A new attention to results [outcomes] signals a profound shift, because it moves us from the technocratic concerns with procedural protections to focus on the purpose of what we choose to pursue. If we as a nation are serious about efforts to strengthen children, families, and depleted neighborhoods, we must know the outcomes we are after and we must be continually able to monitor progress—and face up to failures as well. (p. 116)

There appears to be general agreement that a positive family quality of life should be an appropriate outcome of policies and services (Bailey et al., 1998; Osher, 1998; The Accreditation Council, 1995; Turnbull & Brunk, 1997; Turnbull, Blue-Banning, Turbiville, & Park, 1999; Turnbull, et al., in preparation). Research in conceptualizing and measuring the quality of life of individuals with disabilities has far exceeded comparable work focusing on the family quality of life (Brown, Brown, & Bayer, 1994; Cummins, 1997; Felce & Perry, 1997; Gardner, Nudler, & Chapman, 1997; Keith, Heal, & Schalock, 1996; Schalock, 1997). The research literature has not yet conceptualized and developed a taxonomy and corresponding measurement system for family quality-of-life domains and indicators; however, a research agenda for such work is described in this chapter.

Empowerment as process. Although definitions of empowerment vary across disciplines, the central definitional element of empowerment is taking action to get what one wants and needs (Akey, Marquis, & Ross, in press; Benett, DeLuca, & Allen, 1996; Cochran, 1992; Dempsey, 1996; Dunst, Trivette, & Deal, 1985; Gutiérrez & Nurius, 1994; Heflinger, Bickman, Northrup, & Sonnichshen, 1997; Koren, DeChillo, & Friesen, 1992; Man, 1998, 1999; Pinderhughs, 1994; Rappaport, 1981; Turnbull, Turbiville, & Turnbull, 2000; Turnbull & Turnbull, 2001).

The type of power characterizing an empowering process is a power-through approach (see Table 5-1) in which synergy is created leading to the collective empowerment of all participants (Bond & Keys, 1993; Katz, 1984; Senge, 1990). Synergy is a combustible catalyst for collective empowerment of all partners as they collaborate to make environmental accommodations.

Key components of an empowering process are (a) participation of key stakeholders and (b) commitment to changing community ecology to enable families to enhance their quality of life. In terms of participation, all family members are key decision-makers in terms of sharing visions, preferences, and preferred modes for problem-solving. An empowering process strongly encourages self-determination of children and youth with disabilities, from the earliest ages, in developing motivation and knowledge/skills to direct their own lives (Turnbull & Turnbull, 2001; Wehmeyer, Agran, & Hughes, 1998; Wehmeyer & Sands, 1998). Thus, a critically important element for family roles is to support the evolving self-determination of the child or youth with a disability in ensuring power-through support rather than power-over parental and/or professional control.

The emphasis on changing the community ecology is a pervading theme of an empowerment process. Figure 5-1 illustrates five environmental levels that are patterned after Bronfenbrenner's (1979) model of ecological systems as they apply to families of children and youth with disabilities. The shaded portion of the family level includes the child with the disability and parents. This is the portion that the old paradigm emphasizes—"fixing" the parents so that they can, in turn, "fix" the child. Alternatively, the new paradigm, as characterized in the family empowerment/family quality-of-life model, emphasizes the entire environment in terms of what accommodations are needed (through an empowerment change process) so that the family can experience the quality of life that is important to them, as depicted in Figure 5-2. The family empowerment/family quality-of-life process that permeates this approach is characterized as follows:

- regarding the child as an authentic member of the family's and community's ecological environments
- taking stock of what is important for the family in terms of quality of life across all five systems
- determining what is in place that is consistent with family priorities
- determining what accommodations are needed to create a better match between what is important and what exists in the family members' lives
- providing supports and services to all key stakeholders to create preferred quality-of-life enhancements

In this new paradigm, the major shift is in "fixing" the multiple environments in which the family desires authentic participation rather than "fixing" the child and parents. Thus, the emphasis is on transformed services, communities, societies, and cultures within which families, including children and youth with disabilities, can flourish in their development as they interact with responsive contexts (Turnbull, Blue-Banning, Turbiville, & Park, 1999).

Participatory action research. Participatory action research refers to research that is conducted jointly by families and researchers as they collaboratively set the research agenda, implement it, and assure that the fruits of knowledge derived from the research are disseminated to families, administrators, service providers, and policymakers (Turnbull, Friesen, & Ramirez, 1998).

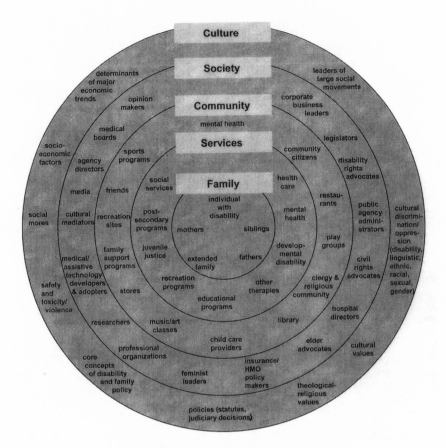

Figure 5-2. New paradigm: Emphasis on supporting and accommodating individuals with disabilities and their families across all environments. Shaded area represents target of "fix-up" efforts.

Participatory action research reflects, in at least four ways, a fundamental change of research procedures: (a) Families are and should be stakeholders in new paradigm research intended to benefit families; (b) their role should be as valued participants with the researchers and other beneficiaries; (c) at least three different kinds of research inquiries are valid when families and the new paradigm are concerned, namely, qualitative, quantitative, and legal/policy; and, (d) families and researchers should be in a *"power through"* relationship. Figure 5-3 illustrates a continuum of family participation in research. Levels 4 to 6 in Figure 5-3 constitute the nature of partnerships that are necessary for participatory action research.

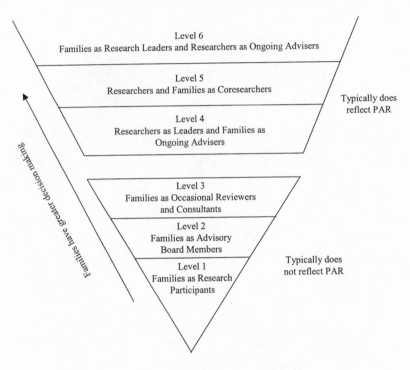

Figure 5-3. Continuum of family participation in research. *From:* Turnbull, A. P., Friesen, B. J., & Ramirez, C. (1998). Participatory action research as a model for conducting family research. *Journal for the Association for Persons with Severe Handicaps, 23*(3), 178–188.

Summary of New Paradigm

Key themes characterizing the new paradigm of services and research related to families of children and youth with disabilities include the following:

1. Particularly at the early childhood level there is an increased emphasis on family-centered services and research characterized by family choice, a family strengths perspective, and family as the unit of support.
2. A family-centered model has served as a bridge between the old and new paradigm.
3. A family empowerment/family quality-of-life model exemplifies the new paradigm of disability and family. The key theme is "fixing" the broad environment (from macro to micro levels) so that all of society, including families of children and youth with disabilities, take action to ensure quality of life outcomes.

4. A transformed ecology is necessary in order to enhance family quality-of-life outcomes.

5. A participatory action research approach is consistent with the new paradigm research model emphasizing family empowerment/family quality of life.

NEW PARADIGM ANALYTICAL FRAMEWORK FOR ENHANCING FAMILY QUALITY OF LIFE

Building on the foundation of understanding the evolution from the old paradigm to the new paradigm related to disability and families, we now turn our attention to an analytical framework aimed at illuminating the connections between policy, services, and family quality-of-life outcomes. Figure 5-4 is an analytical framework that is currently guiding our new paradigm family research at the Beach Center. This analytical framework has four major components. In this section we describe those components and relate them to key literature. The four components are (a) core concepts, (b) policy, (c) services, and (d) family quality-of-life outcomes.

The first component of the analytical framework is the core concepts of disability policy. These core concepts reflect fundamental values—values that advance the quality of life for citizens with disabilities and their families, values that are widely recognized as necessary for the pursuit of life, liberty, and happiness (Brakel, Parry, & Weiner, 1985; Levy & Rubenstein, 1996; Minow, 1990; Silverstein, 1998; Turnbull, 1990). Relating back to Figure 5-1 and Figure 5-2 depicting the five environmental levels, core concepts of disability and family policy occur at the culture level and pervasively influence not only the policy level but the other three levels as well. Table 5-2 includes the core concepts of disability policy as they have currently been identified by our Beach Center policy research. The process of identification has been (a) a systematic review of federal statutes and case law and (b) focus groups of nationally recognized family advocacy organization leaders, policy leaders at the federal/state levels, and senior policy and family researchers in the disability field.

The second component of the analytical framework is public policy. The disability policy core concepts should be infused into policy and services at federal, state, and local levels (vertical implementation). Disability policy core concepts should also be infused across the strands of education, human and social services, and health care (horizontal implementation.)

The third component of the analytical framework is service delivery. Within the delineation of environmental levels (Figure 5-1 and Figure 5-2), services at the state and local levels are typically at the services and community levels. In addition to the usual emphasis on the vertical coherence of policies and services, we are especially interested in horizontal coherence that leads to

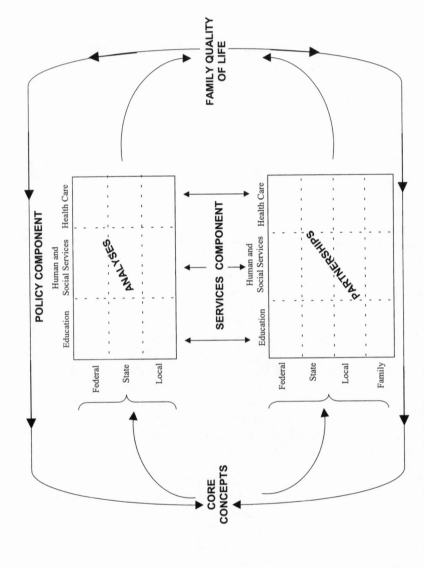

Figure 5-4. New paradigm analytical framework for enhancing family quality of life.

TABLE 5-2
Definitions of Core Concepts

Anti-discrimination	Under various statues generally known as "civil rights acts," it is illegal to discriminate against a person with a disability solely by reason of the person's disability.
Autonomy	This term refers to the right of a person with a disability or the person's family to consent, refuse to consent, withdraw consent, or otherwise control or exercise choice or control over what happens to him or her.
Empowerment/ Participatory Decision-Making	Empowerment involves the means by which a person or family or their duly appointed surrogate secure what they want from a service provider system; the means is through their participation with the system in consenting (see "autonomy") or otherwise participating in the decision-making processes by which the services that they will receive are planned, developed, implemented, and evaluated.
Privacy and Confidentiality	Privacy refers to protection against unwarranted governmental interference in decision making that affects private interests.
Liberty	A person has the right to be free from unwarranted physical or other confinement by a government.
Protection against Harm	A person has the right to be free from harm while in state custody or in the care of such private individuals as family members or other caregivers.
Individualized & Appropriate Services	These services are specially tailored to meet the needs and choices of persons with disabilities and their families.
Capacity-Based Services	Capacity-based services evaluate the unique strengths and needs of a person with a disability or the person's family.
Classification	Classification includes processes (ways) and the standards (criteria) by which a person with a disability or the person's family qualifies (becomes eligible) to benefit from certain laws (anti-discrimination or other rights or entitlements).
Productivity and Contribution	Productivity refers to engagement in income-producing work or in other unpaid work that contributes to a household or community.
Integration	A person with a disability has the right to not be segregated, solely on the basis of disability, from persons who do not have disabilities and to not be barred from participation in services that serve persons who do not have disabilities or to be limited to participation in services that serve only persons with disabilities.

TABLE 5-2 continued

Family Integrity and Unity	Policy presumes in favor of preserving and strengthening the family as the core unit of society.
Family-Centeredness: Services to Whole Family	These services respond to the needs of the entire family of a person with a disability in an individualized and appropriate manner.
Service Coordination & Collaboration	These activities assist individuals with disabilities or their families to access and benefit from services from more than one provider system (inter-agency) or within a single provider system (intra-agency).
Cultural Responsiveness	These services respond to the beliefs, values, interpersonal styles, attitudes, cultural, ethnic, linguistic, or other socioeconomic traits of the person or family and thereby have a great likelihood of ensuring maximum participation of and benefit to the person or family.
Accountability	This term refers to various methods of achieving the specified outcomes of services.
Prevention	Prevention services seek primary, secondary, and tertiary prevention of disability.
Professional Capacity	A service system should have the capacity to implement any one or more concepts, as appropriate for that system.

systems of care and service integration (Adelman & Taylor, 1997; Burns & Goldman, 1999; Calfee, Wittwer & Meredith, 1998; Dryfoos, 1997, 1998; Sailor, in press; Stroul, 1996). We believe that a service integration approach characterized by empowering partnerships at the family-professional, intra-agency, and interagency levels will particularly benefit families, especially those who face multiple challenges.

In terms of multiple challenges, family demographic research has identified economic status and family structure as two critically important variables that must be addressed in new paradigm research. These services must be delivered through empowering partnerships at the family-service level, intra-agency level, and interagency level. Regarding economic status, children whose families have low income are 1.4 times more likely than children from other families to have chronic health conditions; they are 1.9 times more likely to have limitations in major activities; and they are 2 times more likely to be completely unable to carry out a major activity for their age (LaPlante & Carlson, 1999; Fujiura & Yamaki, 1997; Newacheck & Halfon, 1998). Regarding family structure, single parenthood is a significant predictor of poverty (Fujiura & Yamki, 1997; Sherman, 1994; U.S. Census Bureau, 1996). In 1996, 59 percent of children under age 6 who lived in female-household families were living below the poverty line (Forum on Child and Family Studies, 1998).

Many families who live with complex and multiple challenges, including those associated with economic status and family structure, have needs not only within the vertical strands of education, human and social services, and health care, but also across horizontal strands. Paradoxically, the service system typically responds to horizontal problems by crafting vertical semi-solutions (Toffler, 1990). Policies and systems deal with only segments of families in children's lives; a comprehensive, integrated service delivery approach to families and children is elusive. Families need policies and service systems characterized by intrastrand and interstrand partnerships and service integration.

The fourth component of our analytical framework is family quality of life, which we have previously discussed. The theory of change leading to enhanced family quality-of-life outcomes inherent in this analytical framework is as follows:

1. Core concepts should shape policy (statutes, regulations, and court cases) (a) at the federal, state, and local levels and (b) across the three strands of education, social services, and health care.
2. Policy shapes service delivery structures and processes (a) at the federal, state, local, governmental, and family levels and (b) across the three strands of education, human and social services, and health care.
3. Enhanced family quality of life results when policies and services are (a) infused with the core concepts and (b) delivered through partnerships.
4. Family quality-of-life domains/indicators should influence and be integral to core concepts, so that, in turn, the core concepts' impact on policies and services will advance and enhance family quality of life.
5. Accordingly, there should be an unbroken loop in the relationship among (a) core concepts, (b) policies, (c) services, and (d) family quality-of-life outcomes.

RESEARCH DIRECTIONS EMANATING FROM NEW PARADIGM ANALYTICAL FRAMEWORK

This analytical framework (see Figure 5-4) generates a comprehensive, long-term research program whose ultimate aim is to enhance family quality of life. We describe research directions in terms of (a) development of measurement tools and (b) an overview of a programmatic research agenda (see http://www.beachcenter.org).

Development of Measurement Tools

The new paradigm analytical framework requires new measurement tools. Three of these measurement tools include the following:

1. A disability policy core concepts matrix for policy analysis is needed to assess specific statutes/regulations regarding core concepts.

2. A family quality-of-life scale is needed to assess the outcomes of policies and services on families. In order to develop such a measure, a starting point is the development of a taxonomy of family quality-of-life domains and indicators. Figure 5-5 outlines the sequential process of combining qualitative and quantitative research methods to ensure that the family quality-of-life scale is grounded in the perspectives of families while simultaneously possessing rigorous psychometric properties.

3. Partnership scales are needed to measure partnerships in delivering services at the levels of family-service provider, intra-agency, and interagency. These scales will measure the third component of the analytical framework. They, too, require the combination of qualitative and quantitative methodologies depicted in Figure 5-5.

Overview of Programmatic Research Agenda

These measurement tools will be used to accomplish research agenda focusing on three levels: (a) policy analysis, (b) explanatory research, and (c) program evaluation and quality enhancement.

Policy analysis. Policy analysis research is needed to analyze federal and state statutes and their respective regulations to determine the degree to which they incorporate one or more of the disability policy core concepts and family quality-of-life domains (see Table 5-2). Two levels of analysis are needed: (a) the extent to which it is appropriate for statutes/regulations to reflect specific disability policy core concepts and family quality-of-life domains, and (b) the extent to which statutes/regulations reflect coherence with disability policy core concepts and family quality-of-life domains.

Because statutes have different purposes, it is not appropriate for every disability policy core concept to be incorporated into every statute/regulation. For example, it arguably is more appropriate for IDEA to reflect the disability policy core concept of productivity than it is for the Developmental Disabilities Assistance and Bill of Rights Act to do so. This is so because IDEA has the explicit affirmative purpose of providing an appropriate education so that the student will secure employment after leaving school. By contrast, the DD Act creates statewide systems-change opportunities, only some of which are related to productivity. Thus, a first task for policy analysis is to establish a reliable rating of appropriateness.

An analysis is also needed of the extent to which statutes/regulations are coherent with respect to core concepts and family quality-of-life domains. Coherence addresses the consistency with which the statute and regulations incorporate the disability core concepts and family quality-of-life domains throughout all of its parts.

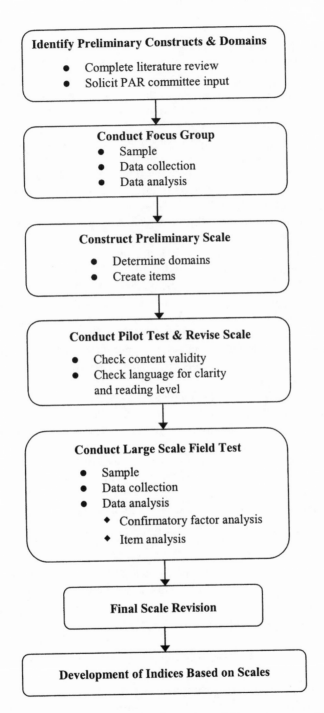

Figure 5-5. Steps in constructing family quality-of-life and partnership scales.

Based on policy analysis, it will be possible to develop a "Disability Policy Grade Card" for key statutes/regulations to communicate to interested stakeholders the extent to which policy advances the disability policy core concepts. More importantly, the policy analysis research can serve as a basis for policy enhancement through (a) the legislative route (e.g., amendments to existing statutes and enactment of new laws) and/or (b) the executive agency route (e.g., amendments to existing regulations, promulgation of new regulations, adoption of guidelines governing the content of competitive contracts, grants, and cooperative agreements). Technical assistance priority should be given to working on statutes/regulations that are deemed to be highly appropriate for incorporation of disability core concepts but currently have low coherence.

For many years, family-and-disability research has seemed to be unconnected to research involving families whose children do not have disabilities. The practice of separate-but-equal research agendas—one for families and disability, another for families and nondisability—has at least two significant limitations. One limitation is that many families who have children with disabilities also have children who do not have disabilities; their concerns, so far as research and its dissemination and utilization are concerned, are therefore about not just disability but also about family policy generally. A second limitation is that a disability-only approach fosters the segregation that many families and individuals with disabilities find anathema and that federal policy condemns.

Fortunately, the new paradigm recognizes that families affected by disability, just like individuals affected by disability, are nested within and are strongly influenced by and strongly influence policy, practice, and research as they affect all families. Accordingly, the new paradigm calls for merging two separate lines of research—the line that is disability only and the line that is not-at-all disability. At the Beach Center, this merger—this honoring of the new paradigm—is underway as we conduct research on the core concepts of disability policy and link that research to our work on the core concepts of family policy. Moreover, this merger is also underway as we include families whose children do not have disabilities into our research on family quality of life.

The underlying premise—one that can hardly be disputed, no matter what policy perspectives one may have about families and given the new paradigm—is that families are, and for more than a decade have been, legitimate foci of NIDRR research and of the new paradigm.

Explanatory research. There is a need for research to examine statistically the relationship between the core concepts of disability policy, service provision offered through partnership arrangements, and family quality-of-life outcomes. Based on the analytical framework, a structural model can be hypothesized that (a) a family's perceived quality of life is positively related to the services a family receives and that (b) the processes through which the services are delivered (incorporation of core concepts based on authorizing policies and empowering partnerships at the family-service provider, intra-agency, and interagency levels) will mediate the relationship between the services and the family quality of life. This structural model can be tested separately for each of the three service strands of education, human and social services, and health. It can also be tested in programs that are explicitly aimed at service integration. Figure 5-6 is a structural model that is based on the analytical framework.

In addition to investigating the mediating facts of this structural model, the relationship among the various factors can also be investigated in light of the family's structure, cultural and linguistic diversity characteristics, and socio-economic level. As we stated earlier, these are the variables that have been found to place families of children with disabilities at highest risk.

An explanatory research strand of research is particularly important in adding to the state-of-the-art knowledge base given that policy and service variables impacting family quality of life have not been systematically inves-tigated previously. Furthermore, this research will provide a framework for quality enhancement to improve outcomes for families in a variety of service settings.

Program evaluation and quality enhancement. In order for policy analysis and explanatory research to benefit families (including children and youth with disabilities), the third stage in the research process is conducting thor-ough program evaluation and quality enhancement processes within strand-specific programs, as well as programs reflecting state-of-the-art service integration. The Council on Quality and Leadership in Supports for People with Disabilities (The Council) has taken a leadership role in combining principles of total quality management, re-engineering, and disability state-of-the-art concepts (Gardner & Nudler, 1999). Their process has focused on personal outcomes for adults with developmental disabilities; an extension of this work is needed to focus on outcomes for families of children and youth with disabilities. Special emphasis is needed on the needs of families who are most at risk, including families with single-parent status and lower socioeco-nomic income.

Research associated with a state-of-the-art quality enhancement process should focus on (a) increasing the incorporation of disability core concepts into services, (b) infusing an empowering process into the family-service provider, intra-agency, and interagency partnerships, and (c) ultimately in-creasing family quality-of-life outcomes. A research methodology appropri-ate for this type of program evaluation and quality enhancement research is a multiple case study design that allows for the analysis of individual cases as sub-units as well as cross-case analyses designed to identify patterns (Yin, 1994). Thus, case study methodology fits within the core of these scientific

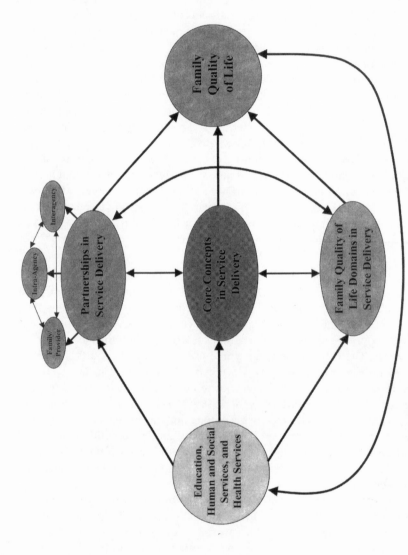

Figure 5-6. Structural model for explanatory research.

methods as a valuable means for exploring the impact and process related to quality enhancement (Campbell, 1994). Table 5-3 outlines possible phases of a quality enhancement process that incorporates case study data as a guide to technical assistance and training.

TEACHER EDUCATION DIRECTIONS EMANATING FROM NEW PARADIGM ANALYTICAL FRAMEWORK

The analytical framework (see Figure 5-4) and the comprehensive, long-term research program that we have just described have major implications for teacher education. We see that we have a responsibility to translate theory and research into teacher education preservice and in-service instructional materials. The way that we have approached that responsibility is to prepare a textbook that is entitled *Families, Professionals, and Exceptionality: Col-*

TABLE 5-3
Quality Enhancement Process

1. A quality enhancement team comprised of individuals with disabilities, parents, service providers, and community representatives administer measurement tools to administrators, service providers, and families in the service agency.

2. The quality enhancement team presents the results of the measurement process to all stakeholder groups.

3. The quality enhancement team facilitates the service agency staff in an agency analysis. Each family quality of life domain is examined from a perspective of the agency's mission, task, process, structure, and personnel.

4. The quality enhancement team, working with agency stakeholders, develops a quality enhancement plan for agency. The quality enhancement team analyzes the linkages between and among the various organizational systems to ensure all systems are aligned to promote outcomes.

5. The quality enhancement team and agency staff, in collaboration with agency stakeholders, implement the quality enhancement plan.

6. The quality enhancement team re-administers the measurement tools on a periodic basis to monitor progress and refine the agency enhancement plan.

laborating for Empowerment (Turnbull & Turnbull, 2001). This book is published by Merrill/ Prentice Hall; outlines of the chapters can be found on their Web site (http://www.prenhall.com/turnbull/). The book is currently in its 4th edition; and as we complete research based on the new paradigm approach, we will continue to prepare new editions to incorporate this research so that the textbook will reflect the latest and best knowledge that we have. We will briefly describe this textbook in terms of its organization and key features.

Text Organization

Families, Professionals, and Exceptionality is organized into three parts:

1. Part I: "Understanding Empowerment"— describes the concept of empowerment historically and currently.
2. Part II: "Understanding Families"—describes families as interactive systems and enables students to understand the unique and idiosyncratic characteristics of families and how they relate to the families' perspectives on what constitutes quality of life for them.
3. Part III: "Collaborating for Empowerment"— explains how professionals and families can collaborate to take action to address seven opportunities for partnerships. These seven opportunities for partnerships are:

- Communicating among reliable allies
- Meeting families' basic needs
- Referring and evaluating for special education
- Individualizing for appropriate education
- Extending learning into home and community
- Attending and volunteering at school
- Advocating for systems improvement

We emphasize that *what* families and professionals do in their partnerships, such as the previous seven opportunities for partnerships, is a very important part of the empowerment equation, but it is not all of it. It is equally important in *how* they carry out these activities. We describe partnerships as reliable alliances, and we underscore the necessity of infusing the following eight obligations for reliable alliances into every partnership:

- Knowing yourself
- Knowing families
- Honoring cultural diversity
- Affirming family strengths
- Promoting family choices
- Envisioning great expectations

- Communicating positively
- Warranting trust and respect

We place emphasis on how teams can create reliable alliances (a) to identify barriers that are standing in the way of quality of life and (b) to move forward in decisively removing those barriers to enhance family quality of life.

Text Features

In seeking to be consistent with a family-centered approach, we have put families at the center of the book by starting each of the fifteen chapters with a vignette about a real family who is experiencing real challenges in real communities. These family vignettes are told as family stories; and we believe that they enrich, inform, and enliven the research and best practice information that is found throughout the book. In fact, we believe that part of the new paradigm is to bring together the very best of firsthand, anecdotal, qualitative insight about families with current research and best practice findings. We reject the notion that information has to be dichotomized in "one camp" (quantitative research) or the "other camp" (family stories) in terms of how knowledge is verified. We seek the best of all worlds in merging knowledge so that readers perceive that the information that they are reading in the book "reeks with reality." In addition to vignettes that open and close each chapter, we also include other first person accounts such as:

- "My Voice Boxes"—feature parents, individuals with a disability, brothers and sisters, teachers, administrators, related service providers, and community citizens who share their personal convictions about various issues.
- "Making a Difference Boxes"—feature individuals and teams who embrace complexity, act courageously, and make a difference in infusing supports and services throughout all environmental levels.
- "Into Practice Boxes"—feature state-of-the-art strategies for translating research into everyday practice.

Throughout all the boxes, families and professionals speak with many dialects and accents because they represent a broad spectrum of American life. They show how people of every economic and social stratum; of every color, race, and ethnic origin; in every part of this country can empower themselves and each other to enhance quality of life.

SUMMARY

In this chapter, we assert that family research must be part of the new paradigm because families are among the natural environments that affect and are affected by a person who has an impairment. Knowledge is power. That much, we all know. And the world of disability is contextual. That, too, we all know. The challenge is to rebalance the power relationships between researchers and families so that the knowledge that comes from research will change the world of those affected by disability. To do that, we must recognize that the research community is itself one of those cultural and social environments that has limited—but need not continue to limit—the life opportunities of people with disabilities and their family members.

In describing the old and the new paradigms, we emphasize the relationship between professionals on the one hand and families on the other. That relationship involves certain degrees of power. We argue that, under the old paradigm, professionals had power over families. The psychotherapy, parent training, and parent involvement models located power within professionals and outside of families.

Under the family-centered model, however, power shifted. Theoretically, it no longer should be the case that professionals have power over families. Now, it should be the case that families and professionals will collaborate to address the priority needs of families as the families themselves identify those needs. Here, power-with obtains.

Under the emerging family empowerment/family quality-of-life model for which we advocate here, the relationship changes yet again. No longer is power-with sufficient. Now, power-through occurs. Here, synergy obtains. Here, families, friends, community citizens, and professionals collaborate to "fix" environments at multiple levels (family, services, community, society, culture). We offer an analytical framework that leads to a new paradigm research approach incorporating policy analysis, explanatory research, and program evaluation and quality enhancement. Then, we offer a way to organize information for teacher education programs through our textbook that incorporates the new paradigm research—*Families, Professionals, and Exceptionality: Collaborating for Empowerment*. We are highly enthusiastic about the ultimate outcomes for families, including children and youth with disabilities, when new paradigm research leads to new paradigm teacher education, which, in turn, leads to new paradigm supports, services, and, ultimately, outcomes.

DISCUSSION QUESTIONS

1. Compare and contrast the roles of families in the old and new paradigms.
2. Stand in the shoes of a parent of a teenager with Down syndrome who is graduating from high school and transitioning to adulthood. How might the application of the new paradigm make a meaningful difference in enabling you and your family to experience success with this transition?

3. Identify at least five domains of family quality of life and give an example of something that you might do as a professional to support a family in each of those domains.
4. Identify at least five core concepts of disability policy. What could you do as a practicing professional to ensure that each of those core concepts is incorporated into how you form partnerships with families?

REFERENCES

The Accreditation Council on Services for People with Disabilities. (1995). *Outcome measures for early childhood intervention services.* Towson, MD: Author.

Able-Boone, H., Sandall, S. R., Stevens, E., & Frederick, L. (1992). Family support resources and needs: How early intervention can make a difference. *Infant-Toddler Intervention, 2*(2), 93–102.

Able-Boone, H. (1993). Family participation in the IFSP process: Family or professional driven? *Infant-Toddler Intervention, 3*(1), 63–71.

Adelman, H. S., & Taylor, L. (1997). Addressing barriers to learning: Beyond school-linked services and full-service schools. *American Journal of Orthopsychiatry, 67*(3), 408–419.

Ainge, D., Covin, G., & Baker, S. (1998). Analysis of perceptions of parents who have children with intellectual disabilities: Implications for service providers. *Education and Training in Mental Retardation and Developmental Disabilities, 33*(4), 331–341.

Akerley, M. S. (1985). False gods and angry prophets. In H. R. Turnbull & A. P. Turnbull (Eds.), *Parents speak out then and now* (pp. 23–31). Columbus: Merrill.

Akey, T. M., Marquis, J. G., & Ross, M. E. (in press). Validation of scores on the psychological empowerment scale: A measure of empowerment for parents of children with a disability. *Educational and Psychological Measurement.*

Allen, R. I., & Petr, C. G. (1996). Toward developing standards and measurements for family-centered practice in family support programs. In G.H.S. Singer, L. E. Powers, & A. L. Olson (Eds.). *Redefining family support: Innovations in public-private partnerships* (pp. 57–86). Baltimore: Brookes.

Bailey, D. B., & McWilliam, P. J. (1993) The search for quality indicators. In P. J. McWilliam & D. B. Bailey (Eds.), *Working together with children and families* (pp.3–20). Baltimore: Brookes.

Bailey, D. B., McWilliam, R. A., Darkes, L. A., Hebbeler, K., Simeonsson, R. J., Spiker, D., & Wagner, M. (1998). Family outcomes in early intervention: A framework for program evaluation and efficacy research. *Exceptional Children, 64,* 313–328.

Bennett, T., DeLuca, D. A., & Allen, R. W. (1996). Families of children with disabilities: Positive adaptation across the life cycle. *Social Work in Education, 18*(1), 31–44.

Bond, M., & Keys, C. (1993). Empowerment, diversity, and collaboration: Promoting synergy on community boards. *American Journal of Community Psychology, 21*(1), 37–57.

Bowlby, J. (1960). Grief and mourning in infancy and early childhood. *Psychoanalytic Study of the Child, 15,* 1–9.

Brakel, S. J., Parry, J., & Weiner, B. A. (1985). *The mentally disabled and the law.* Chicago: American Bar Association.

Bronfenbrenner, U. (1979). *The ecology of human development: Experiments by nature and design.* Cambridge, MA: Harvard University Press.

Brown, R. I., Brown, P. M., & Bayer, M. B. (1994). A quality of life model: New challenges arising from a six year study. In D. A. Goode (Ed.), *Quality of life for persons with disabilities: International perspectives and issues* (pp. 39–56). Cambridge, MA: Brookline Books.

Burns, B. J., & Goldman, S. K. (Eds.). (1999). *Systems of care: Promising practices in children's mental health.* Washington: Center for Effective Collaboration and Practice, American Institutes for Research.

Calfee, C., Wittwer, F., & Meredith, M. (1998). Why build a full-service school? In C. Calfee, F. Wittwer, & M. Meredith (Eds.), *Building a full-service school* (pp. 6–24). San Francisco: Jossey-Bass Publishers.

Campbell, D. T. (1994). Forward. In R. K. Yin, *Case study research: Design and methods* (2nd ed.). Thousand Oaks, CA: Sage.

Campbell, P. H., Strickland, B., & La Forme, C. (1992). Enhancing parent participation in the individualized family service plan. *Topics in Early Childhood Special Education, 11*(4), 112–124.

Cochran, M. (1992). Parent empowerment: Developing a conceptual framework. *Family Science Review, 5*(1 & 2), 3–21.

Cummins, R. A. (1997a). Assessing quality of life. In R. I. Brown (Ed.), *Quality of life for people with disabilities: Model, research and practice* (pp. 116–150). Cheltenham, U.K.: Stanley Thornes (Publishers) Ltd.

Cummins, R. A. (1997b). *Comprehensive quality of life scale: Adult* (5th ed). Melbourne, Australia: Deakin University.

Cummins, R. A. (1997c). *Comprehensive quality of life scale: Intellectual/cognitive disability* (ComQol-15) (5th ed.). Melbourne, Australia: Deakin University, School of Psychology.

Cummins, R. A. (1997d). *Comprehensive quality of life scale: School version: Grades 7–12* (ComQol-S5, 5th ed.). Melbourne, Australia: Deakin University, School of Psychology.

Cummins, R. A. (1997e). Measuring quality of life for people with an intellectual disability: A review of the scales. *Journal of Applied Research in Intellectual Disabilities.*

Dempsey, I. (1996). Facilitating empowerment in families with a member with a disability *Developmental Disabilities Bulletin, 24*(2), 1–19.

Dryfoos, J. G. (1997). Adolescents at risk: Shaping programs to fit the need. *Journal of Negro Education, 65*(1), 5–18.

Dryfoos, J. (1998). *Safe passage: Making it through adolescence in a risky society.* New York: Oxford University Press.

Dunst, C. J., Johnson, C., Trivette, C., & Hamby, D. (1991, October–November). Family-oriented early intervention policies and practices: Family-centered or not? *Exceptional Children, 58*(2), 115–126.

Dunst, C. J., Trivette, C., & Deal, A. (1988). *Enabling & empowering families: Principles and guidelines for practice.* Cambridge, MA: Brookline.

Espin, C. A., Denot, S. L., & Albayrak-Kaymak, D. (1998). Individualized education programs in resource and inclusive settings: How "individualized" are they? *The Journal of Special Education, 32*(3), 164–174.

Farel, A. M., Shackelford, J., & Hurth, J. L. (1997). Perceptions regarding the IFSP process in a statewide interagency service coordination program. *Topics in Early Childhood Special Education, 17*(2), 234–249.

Felce, D., & Perry, J. (1997). Quality of life: The scope of the term and its breadth of measurement. In R. I. Brown (Ed.), *Quality of life for people with disabilities: Models, research and practice* (2nd ed., pp. 56–71). Cheltenham, U.K.: Stanley Thornes.

Forum on Child and Family Statistics. (1998). *America's children: Key national indicators of well-being 1998* [On-line]. Available: http://www.childstats. gov/ac1998/highlite.htm.

Frey, K. S., Fewell, R. R., & Vadasy, P. F. (1989). Parental adjustment and changes in child outcome among families of young handicapped children. *Topics in Early Childhood Special Education, 8*(4), 38–57.

Fujiura, G. T., & Yamaki, K. (1997). Analysis of ethnic variations in developmental disability prevalence and household economic status. *Mental Retardation, 35* (4) 286–294.

Gallagher, J. J. & Gallagher, G. G. (1985). Family adaptation to a handicapped child and assorted professionals. In H. R. Turnbull & A. P. Turnbull (Eds.), *Parents speak out then and now* (pp. 233–242). Columbus, OH: Merrill.

Gardner, J. F., & Nudler, S. (Eds.). (1999). *Quality performance in human services: Leadership, values, and vision.* Baltimore: Brookes.

Gardner, J. F., Nudler, S., & Chapman, M. S. (1997). Personal outcomes as measures of quality. *Mental Retardation, 35*, 295–305.

Gerber, P. J., Banbury, M. M., Miller, J. H., & Griffin, H. D. (1986). Special educators' perceptions of parental participation in the individual education plan process. *Psychology in the Schools*, 23, 158–163.

Getzel, E. E., & deFur, S. (1997). Transition planning for students with significant disabilities: Implications for student-centered planning. *Focus on Autism and Other Developmental Disabilities, 12*(1), 39–48.

Goldstein, S., & Turnbull, A. P. (1982). The use of two strategies to increase parent participation in IEP conferences. *Exceptional Children*, 46(4), 360–361.

Goshen, C. E. (1963). Mental retardation and neurotic maternal attitudes: A research report. *Archive of General Psychiatry, 9*, 168–174.

Guitiérres, L., & Nurius, P. (Eds). *Education and research for empowerment practice* (Monograph No. 7). Seattle: University of Washington, School of Social Work, Center for Policy and Practice Research.

Harry, B., & Kalyanpur, M. (1994). Cultural underpinnings of special education: Implications for professional interactions with culturally diverse families. *Disability and Society, 9*(2), 145–165.

Harvey, J. (1977). The enabling legislation: How did it all begin? In J. B. Jordan, A. H. Hayden, M. B. Karnes, & M. M. Wood (Eds.), *Early childhood education for exceptional children: A handbook for ideas and exemplary practices.* Reston, VA: Council for Exceptional Children.

Heflinger, C. A., Bickman, L., Northrup, D., & Sinnichsen, S. (1997). A theory-driven intervention and evaluation to explore family caregiver empowerment. *Journal of Emotional and Behavioral Disorders, 5*(3), 184–191.

Heller, K. (1990). Social and community interventions. *Annual Review of Psychology, 41*, 141–168.

Hunt, J. (Ed.). (1972). *Human intelligence.* New Brunswick, NJ: Transaction Books.

Kalyanpur, M., & Harry, B. (1999). *Culture in special education.* Baltimore: Brookes.

Katz, L., & Scarpati, S. (1995). A cultural interpretation of early intervention teams and the IFSP: Parent and professional perceptions of roles and responsibilities. *Infant-Toddler Intervention, 5*(2), 177–192.

Katz, R. (1984). Empowerment and synergy: Expanding the community's healing resources. *Prevention in Human Services, 3*(2 & 3), 201–226.

Keith, K. D., Heal, L. W., & Schalock, R. L. (1996). Cross-cultural measurement of critical quality of life concepts. *Journal of Intellectual and Developmental Disability, 21*(4), 273–293.

Koren, P. E., DeChillo, N., & Friesen, B. (1992). Measuring empowerment in families whose children have emotional disabilities: A brief questionnaire. *Rehabilitation Psychology, 37*, 305–321.

LaPlante, M. P., & Carlson, D. (1996). [National Health Interview Survey data]. San Francisco: University of California, Institute for Health and Aging, Disability Statistics Research and Training Center.

LaPlante, M. P., Carlson, D., Kaye, H. S., & Bradsher, J. E. (1996). *Families with disabilities in the United States* (Disability Statistics Report 8). Washington: U.S. Department of Education, National Institute on Disability and Rehabilitation Research.

Lavor, M., & Krivit, D. (1969). The Handicapped Children's Early Education Assistance Act, Public Law 90–538. *Exceptional Children, 35*, 379–383.

Levine, J. A., Murphy, D. T., & Wilson, S. (1993). *Getting men involved: Strategies for early childhood programs*. New York: Scholastic.

Levy, R. M., & Rubenstein, L. S. (1996). *The rights of people with mental disabilities: The authoritative ACLU guide to the rights of people with mental illness and mental retardation* (Rev. ed.). Carbondale: Southern Illinois University Press.

Lewis, C. L., Busch, J. P., Proger, B. B., & Juska, P. J. (1981). Parents' perspectives concerning the IEP process. *Education Unlimited, 3*(3), 18–22.

Lynch, E. W., & Stein, R. (1982). Perspectives on parent participation in special education. *Exceptional Children, 3*(2), 56–63.

Man, D. W. K. (1998). The empowering of Hong Kong Chinese families with a brain damaged member: Its investigation and measurement. *Brain Injury, 12*(3), 245–254.

Man, D. (1999). Community-based empowerment programme for families with a brain injured survivor: An outcome study. *Brain Injury, 13*(6), 433–445.

Mandelbaum, A., & Wheeler, M. E. (1960). The meaning of a defective child to parents. *Social Casework, 43*, 360–367.

McBride, S. L., Brotherson, M. J., Joanning, H., Whiddon, D., & Demmitt, A. (1993). Implementation of family-centered services: Perceptions of families and professionals. *Journal of Early Intervention, 17*(4), 414–430.

McHale, S. M., & Gamble, W. C. (1989). Sibling relationships of children with disabled and nondisabled brothers and sisters. *Developmental Psychology, 25*(3), 421–429.

McWilliam, R. A., Lang, L., Vandiviere, P., Angell, R., Collins, L., & Underdown, G. (1995). Satisfaction and struggles: Family perceptions of early intervention services. *Journal of Early Intervention, 19*(1), 43–60.

Menke, K. (1991). The development of individualized family service plans in three early intervention programs: A data-based construction. *Dissertation Abstracts International, 52*(06), 2077A. (University Microfilms No. 9134817)

Meyer, D. J. (Ed.). (1995). *Uncommon fathers*. Bethesda, MD: Woodbine House.

Meyer, D. J., & Vadasy, P. F. (1986). *Grandparent workshops: How to organize workshops for grandparents of children with handicaps*. Seattle: University of Washington Press.

Meyer, D. J., & Vadasy, P. F. (1994). *Sibshops: Workshops for siblings of children with special needs*. Baltimore: Brookes.

Minow, M. (1990). *Making all the difference: Inclusion, exclusion, and American law*. Ithaca, NY: Cornell University Press.

Mirfin-Veitch, B., Bray, A., & Watson, M. (1997). We're just that sort of family: Intergenerational relationships in families including children with disabilities. *Family Relations, 46*(3), 305–311.

Morningstar, M. E., Turnbull, A. P., & Turnbull, H. R. (1995). What do students with disabilities tell us about the importance of family involvement in the transition from school to adult life? *Exceptional Children, 62*(3), 249–260.

Murphy, D. L., Lee, I. M., Turnbull, A. P., & Turbiville, V. (1995). The family-centered program rating scale: An instrument for program evaluation and change. *Journal of Early Intervention, 19*(1), 24–42.

Nadler, B., & Shore, K. (1980). Individualized Education Programs: A look at realities. *Education Unlimited, 2,* 30–34.

National Council on Disability (1995, May). *Improving the implementation of the Individuals with Disabilities Education Act: Making schools work for all of America's children.* Washington.

Newacheck, P. W., & Halfon, N. (1998). Prevalence and impact of disabling chronic conditions in childhood. *American Journal of Public Health, 88,* 610–617.

Osher, T. W. (1998). Outcomes and accountability from a family perspective. *Journal of Behavioral Health Services & Research, 25*(2), 230–232.

Pinderhughs, E. (1994). Empowerment as an intervention goal: Early ideas. In L. Gutierrez & P. Nurius (Eds.), *Education and research for empowerment practice* (pp. 17–30). Seattle: University of Washington, School of Social Work, Center for Policy and Practice Research.

Powell, T. H., & Gallagher, P. A. (1993). *Brothers and sisters: A special part of exceptional families* (2nd ed.). Baltimore: Brookes.

Pyecha, J. N., Cox, J. L., Dewitt, D., Drummond, D., Jaffe, J., Kalt, M., Lane, C., & Pelosi, J. (1980). *A national survey of Individualized Education Programs (IEPs) for handicapped children* (5 vols.). Durham, NC: Research Triangle Institute. (ERIC Document Reproduction Service Nos. ED 199 970–974)

Rappaport, J. (1981). In praise of paradox: A social policy of empowerment over prevention. *American Journal of Community Psychology, 9*(1), 1–25.

Sailor, W. (in press). Devolution, school/community/family partnerships, and inclusive education. In W. Sailor (Ed.), *Inclusive education and school/community partnerships* . New York: Teachers College Press.

Saleebey, D. (1996). The strengths perspective in social work practice: Extensions and cautions. *Social Work, 41*(3), 296–306.

Salembier, G., & Furney, K. S. (1994). Promoting self-advocacy and family participation in IEP and transition planning. *Journal for Vocational Special Needs Education, 17*(1), 12–17.

Satir, V. (1972). *Peoplemaking.* Palo Alto, CA: Science and Behavior Books.

Schalock, R. L. (1997). Can the concept of quality of life make a difference? In R. L. Schalock (Ed.), *Quality of life: Vol. 2: Application to persons with disabilities* (pp. 245–267). Washington: American Association on Mental Retardation.

Schorr, L. B. (1997). *Common purpose.* New York: Anchor Books Doubleday.

Senge, P. M. (1990). *The fifth discipline: The art and practice of the learning organization.* New York: Doubleday.

Sherman, A. (1994). *Wasting America's future: The Children's Defense Fund report on the costs of child poverty.* Boston: Beacon Press.

Silverstein, R. (1998). *Core concepts of our nation's disability policy.* Unpublished manuscript, George Washington University Medical Center, Center for the Study and Advancement of Disability Policy.

Smith, S. W., & Simpson, R. L. (1989). An analysis of Individualized Education Programs (IEPs) of students with behavioral disorders. *Behavioral Disorders, 14,* 107–116.

Smith, S. W. (1990, September). Individualized Education Programs (IEPs) in special education: From intent to acquiescence. *Exceptional Children,* 6–14.

Solnit, A. J., & Stark, M. H. (1961). Mourning and the birth of a defective child. *Psychoanalytic Study of the Child, 16*, 523–537.

Stoneman, Z., & Waldman-Berman, P. (Eds.). (1993). *The effects of mental retardation, disability, and illness.* Baltimore: Brookes.

Stroul, B. A. (1996). *Children's mental health: Creating systems of care in a changing society.* Baltimore: Brookes.

Toffler, A. (1990). *Powershift.* New York: Bantam.

Turnbull, A. P., Blue-Banning, M., Turbiville, V., & Park, J. (1999). From parent education to partnership education: A call for a transformed focus. *Topics in Early Childhood Special Education, 19*(3), 164–171.

Turnbull, A. P., Brown, I., & Turnbull, H.R. (in preparation). *Family quality of life: An international perspective.* Washington: American Association on Mental Retardation.

Turnbull, A. P., Friesen, B. J., & Ramirez, C. (1998). Participatory action research as a model for conducting family research. *Journal of the Association for Persons with Severe Handicaps, 23*(3), 178–188.

Turnbull, A. P., Turbiville, V., & Turnbull, H. R. (2000). Evolution of family-professional partnership models: Collective empowerment as the model for the early 21st century. In S. J. Meisels & J. P. Shonkoff (Eds.), *Handbook of early intervention* (pp. 630–650). New York: Cambridge University Press.

Turnbull, A. P., & Turnbull, H. R. (2001). *Families, professionals, and exceptionality: Collaborating for empowerment* (4th ed.). Upper Saddle River, NJ: Merrill/Prentice Hall.

Turnbull, A. P., Turnbull, H. R., Shank, M., & Leal, D. (1999). *Exceptional lives: Special education in today's schools* (2nd ed.). Englewood Cliffs, NJ: Merrill/Prentice-Hall.

Turnbull, H. R. (1990). *The Supreme Court and disability law.* Lawrence: University of Kansas, Beach Center on Families and Disability.

Turnbull, H. R., & Brunk, G. L. (1997). Quality of life and public policy. In R. L. Schalock (Ed.), *Quality of life: Vol. 2. Application for persons with disabilities* (pp. 201–210). Washington: American Association on Mental Retardation.

U. S. Census Bureau. (1996, September). Almost half of the nation's chronic poor are children. *Census and You, 31*(9), 1.

Van Reusen, A. K., & Bos, C. S. (1994). Facilitating student participation in Individualized Education Programs through motivation strategy instruction. *Exceptional Children, 60*(5), 466–475.

Warren, F. (1985). A society that is going to kill our children. In H. R. Turnbull & A. P. Turnbull (Eds.), *Parents speak out then and now* (pp. 201–219). Columbus, OH: Merrill.

Wehman, T. (1998). Family-centered early intervention services: Factors contributing to increased parent involvement and participation. *Focus on Autism and Other Developmental Disabilities, 13*(2), 80–86.

Wehmeyer, M. L., Agran, M., & Hughes, C. (1998). *Teaching self-determination to students with disabilities: Basic skills for successful transition.* Baltimore: Brookes.

Wehmeyer, M. L., & Sands, D. J. (1998). *Making it happen: Student involvement in education planning, decision making, and instruction.* Baltimore: Brookes.

Whitechurch, G. G., & Constantine, L. L. (1993). Systems theory. In P. G. Boss, W. J. Boherty, R. LaRossa, W. R. Schumm, & S. K. Steinmetz (Eds.), *Sourcebook of family theories and methods: A contextual approach* (pp. 325–352). New York: Plenum.

Wolfensberger, W. (1967). Counseling the parents of the retarded. In A. A. Baumeister (Ed.), *Mental retardation: Appraisal, education, and rehabilitation* (pp. 329–400). Chicago: Aldine.

Wright, R., Saleeby, D., Watts, T. D., & Lecca, P. J. (1983). *Transcultural perspectives in the human services: Organizational issues and trends*. Springfield, IL: Thomas.

Yin, R. K. (1994). *Case study research: Design and methods* (2nd ed.). Thousand Oaks, CA: Sage.

Zigler, E., & Valentine, J. (Eds.). (1979). *Project Head Start: A legacy of the war on poverty*. New York: Free Press.

6

Addressing Home, School, and Community Violence for Children with Disabilities

Zena H. Rudo, Vestena Robbins, and Denise Smith

Nine-tenths of mankind are more afraid of violence than of anything else.
Walter Bagehot, 1880 (as cited in Murphy, 1981)

CURRENT PROBLEM

A wave of violence has swept the United States, taking a toll on children from all cultures and backgrounds. For centuries, violence has elicited enormous fear in society but has only recently been acknowledged as a predominant societal problem necessitating increased understanding of its complexity and demanding practical solutions. In their homes, schools, and communities and through the entertainment and news media, children are exposed to violence at an alarming rate. Whether a witness, victim, or perpetrator, violence invades their daily lives, impeding their ability to learn.

In urban, suburban, and rural communities, the proliferation of problems such as schoolyard shootings, child abuse and neglect, partner abuse, drive-by killings, and gang wars has added to the public's fears that the safety of many children in their homes, schools, and neighborhoods is in jeopardy. For children with disabilities, these problems can be even more exacerbated. These children often have multiple problems and needs that encompass all, or many, of the service systems. However, the various systems helping these children and their families have experienced added burdens and are often not equipped to undertake the problem singularly. It is necessary for special educators to play a significant role in forming collaborative partnerships between the home, school, and community to find solutions to enhance their students' success.

A number of questions are often asked in relation to the impact of violence on children with disabilities. "Does the child's disability lead to greater violence perpetrated by the child?" "Does the child's disability lead to greater victimization of the child?" "Does exposure to violence as the victim or observer lead to a child's disability?" There are no standard answers to these questions. However, it is clear that prevention and intervention efforts to decrease the violence children encounter in their homes, schools, and communities rely on the limited knowledge that currently exists.

Although encompassing a wide array of circumstances and consequences, violence is defined in this chapter as any act or threat of physical or verbal force with the intent to inflict pain on or harm the well-being of another person. More specifically, violence in the home refers to child maltreatment—that is, the physical, sexual, and psychological abuse and neglect of a child under the age of 18 perpetrated by a parent or caregiver. It also includes partner abuse between two adults in the home in which the child either witnesses or is a victim of the violent interactions. School violence refers to acts such as physical aggression, bullying, harassment, and school shootings or the use of any weapon against another student or school personnel on school grounds perpetrated by school-age children. Community violence refers to physical altercations, drive-by and other shootings, the use of any form of weaponry against another, and drug- and gang-related incidents that occur outside the home and school environment.

Given the need to broaden and integrate what is presently known, the focus of this chapter is on the systemic interrelationship of home, school, and community violence and its impact on the educational process for children with disabilities. Following a historical overview of home, school, and community violence, a framework integrating multiple theories is proposed as a basis for understanding the interrelationship between the systems in which violence occurs. Working from this framework, subsequent sections of this chapter describe psychosocial factors contributing to violence, its impact on children, and strategies and best practices for special educators.

HISTORICAL OVERVIEW OF HOME, SCHOOL, AND COMMUNITY VIOLENCE

Violence in the Home

Many children encounter violence within the four walls of their homes. All too often these children are physically, sexually, and/or psychologically abused by their parent, sibling, or another household member or they are a witness to partner violence. Although child abuse was only formally recognized by the medical profession and general public in 1961 as the "battered child syndrome," it has been a serious problem for children, families, and society since recorded human history (Kempe & Helfer, 1980).

Centuries ago, infanticide was not only condoned, but all too frequently it was mandatory. An infant who was weak, premature, or had any type of deformity was likely to be disposed of with little shame or remorse. Aristotle recommended a law prohibiting children with any disability to be reared. This freedom for parents to kill their child with a disability was upheld in a number of European societies well into the nineteenth century (Kempe & Helfer, 1980). Children with mental retardation were especially vulnerable to violence perpetrated by family members, often resulting in serious injury or death. Children were also brutalized as laborers, and in some locales this problem still exists. Sexual defloration rites, mishandling, and rape were among the various types of sexual violence against children commonly practiced and accepted prior to the twentieth century.

By 1905, 400 societies to prevent physical cruelty to children and to intervene protectively had been established in the United States. Protective services for battered children have changed from the early 1900s to the present, and the number of children referred for services has drastically risen. According to the *Third National Incidence Study on Child Abuse and Neglect* (NIS-3; Sedlak & Broadhurst, 1996), a comprehensive source of information about the current incidence of child abuse and neglect in America, reports of child maltreatment increased 18 percent between 1990 and 1996, with the greatest increase in reports of seriously injured children and of endangered children.

It is believed that many cases of child abuse never come to the attention of authorities, with perhaps as few as one in seven cases of children receiving a physical injury being reported (Schene, 1987). Gelles and Straus (1990) found in a national survey of two-parent households that in one year an estimated 6.9 million children were assaulted by their parents—that is, kicked, beat, punched, bit, choked, and injured by weapons. Further, it is believed that children with disabilities are maltreated physically and sexually at a higher rate than the overall child population—with rates reported between 3 percent and 61 percent for disabled populations (Botash & Church, 1999).

One of the difficulties in obtaining accurate prevalence rates is the varied definitions and conceptualizations of child abuse. There is no universal standard or federal definition for child abuse. Instead, child abuse is defined by state mandate, often reflecting the administration's philosophy related to children and families and the fiscal constraints of the child protection system. By 1969, every state had adopted a child abuse reporting law requiring professionals to report any suspicion of child abuse or neglect to the local authority (Kempe & Helfer, 1980). Under most state laws, the domain of physical child abuse is defined as a child, up to 18 years old, who has sustained an intentional physical injury at the hands of his/her parent, legal guardian, or temporary custodian/caretaker, including, but not limited to, burns, bites, bruises, broken bones, battering, abrasions or cuts, marks or scars, contusions, cortical damage, gunshot wounds, and suffocation.

Cultural differences in child-rearing beliefs and practices may also play a role in how child abuse is defined and reported. For example, the traditional Vietnamese practice of "cao gio" (coin rubbing), in which heated coins are firmly pressed on the child's body, often leaving bruises, is believed to reduce fever, chills, and headaches (Yeatman, Shaw, Barlow, & Bartlett, 1976). Even though bruises are inflicted, physical abuse may not be considered because of cultural beliefs.

A look at the statewide statistics on child abuse and neglect further exemplifies the magnitude of the problem of violence in the home for children in the United States. In 1998, state Child Protective Services (CPS) investigated child maltreatment reports involving 3 million children, fifty times more than when national statistics were first reported in 1978 (U.S. Department of Health and Human Services, 2000). Of these children, 59 percent were neglected, 23 percent were physically abused, and 12 percent were sexually abused. Twenty-five percent of the children were reported to be victims of other types of maltreatment, including "abandonment," "threats of harm to the child," and "congenital drug addiction." Only 6 percent of the children were classified as emotionally maltreated, but this may reflect the lack of laws nationally regarding psychological child abuse and the difficulty in documenting this type of abuse.[1] The most disturbing of these national data is an estimated 1,087 children known by CPS to have died as a result of child maltreatment in 1998, as reported by forty-nine states. Although disabilities are not regularly identified in abuse cases, it is estimated that 9 percent to 40 percent of children served by CPS have a developmental disability.

School Violence

The horrific nature of the recent string of school shootings across the nation has shocked the American public and brought to the forefront a focus on school violence and safety. Although school violence is clearly not a new phenomenon, the type, frequency, and degree have changed dramatically over the years. The extreme changes in the incidence and nature of school violence are clearly reflected in survey data trends found from the 1940s to the present (Warner, Weist, & Krulak, 1999). For example, a 1949 survey of high school principals indicated an absence of problems with interpersonal violence or property destruction on school grounds. In fact, the most serious problems noted were lying and disrespect. However, in 1956, a study by the National Education Association revealed that violence was beginning to become a problem in our schools, particularly violent acts against teachers in inner-city settings. This trend continued into the 1960s with increases in racially motivated interpersonal violence, likely due to the racial integration of school systems. School violence continued to increase during the 1970s with discipline reported as the primary problem facing educators. Interestingly, and for reasons not well understood, there appeared to be a leveling off of school violence in the 1980s.

Reports of school violence in the 1990s paint quite a different picture. Whereas the seriousness and lethality of acts committed on school grounds have increased, reports indicate conflicting results as to the level of school violence. Some surveys have reported increases in school violence or the seriousness of the violent acts (National School Boards Association [NBSA], 1993; Petersen, Peitrzak, & Speaker, 1998). Others have cited decreases (Brenner, Simon, Krug, & Lowry, 1999; Kingery, Coggeshall, & Alford, 1998) or have questioned the seriousness and pervasiveness due to inconsistencies in definitions and methodologies in school violence research (Furlong & Morrison, 1994). The U.S. Department of Justice's *Annual Report on School Safety, 1998*, a comprehensive investigation of recent school violence data, deemed the majority of schools as safe places. Data from this report reveal a decline in school crime and a reduction in the percent of students carrying weapons to school; however, the data indicate that a substantial amount of crime against teachers and students is occurring, multiple-victim homicides at school have increased, and students are more fearful at school than in the past. The following statistics portray a startling picture of the violence permeating the boundaries of our schoolyards (Kaufman et al., 1999):

- About 7 to 8 percent of students in grades 9–12 report being threatened or injured with a weapon on school property.
- Nearly 9 percent of students in grades 9–12 report carrying a weapon to school.
- About 15 percent of students in grades 9–12 report being in a physical fight on school property.
- From 1993 to 1997, teachers were victims of 1,771,000 nonfatal crimes at school.
- Of students aged 12 to 19, 9 percent report avoiding one or more places at school because of fear about safety.

Although there is a lack of agreement regarding the current extent of school violence, its presence is undeniably high and must be addressed. Schools are no longer the safe havens of the past. Understanding the nature and scope of school violence is critical as educators and other service providers participate in community collaborations to create safer learning environments for all children. Unfortunately, exposure to school violence constitutes only a small fraction of the many tragic events that affect children's lives. The violence apparent in our nation's schools is reflective of the violence that children face in their homes and communities.

Violence in Our Communities

Many children in America grow up in communities where violence is a common occurrence. All children are exposed to community violence, whether directly or through the media. It is reported that 75 percent to 95 percent of children living in urban settings, especially those in low-income neighborhoods, are direct victims of or witnesses to significant acts of violence in their communities (Fitzpatrick & Boldizar, 1993; Mazza & Reynolds, 1999). Community violence, however, is not limited to these settings. Violence is also occurring at alarming rates in rural and suburban communities (Garbarino, 1999; Osofsky, 1995). Parents in all communities are extremely concerned for their children's safety.

Historically, community violence was viewed as a way to build stronger communities. Goal-oriented in nature, community violence was seen as the backbone for defending neighborhoods or "turfs" and promoting ethnic solidarity. This violence most often occurred in the form of fighting in the neighborhood. Over time, however, community violence changed. Today, although the ethnic composition of perpetrators of violence mirrors the current diverse American population, the cultural goals of ethnic solidarity have dissipated. Further, violent acts in the community more often than not involve "strangers without a face" and have become more lethal. The availability of guns and other weapons may be one explanation for the increased lethality of community violence. In particular, children's access to guns and other weapons has become a national crisis (Potter, 1999).

Community violence also has been customarily an adult-on-adult crime. Today, not only are children witnessing and being victimized by community violence, but they are also committing violent acts against peers, adults, and animals in record numbers. In 1999, U.S. law enforcement agencies arrested an estimated 2.5 million juveniles (Snyder, 2000). Youth with learning disabilities or emotional disturbances were arrested at higher rates than their nondisabled peers (Chesapeake Institute, 1994; SRI International, Center for Education and Human Services, 1997). The types of crimes for which all of these children were arrested include:

- 9 percent of all murder arrests
- 14 percent of all aggravated assault arrests
- 33 percent of all burglary arrests
- 25 percent of all robbery arrests
- 24 percent of all weapons arrests

Although the arrest rate is high, statistics reveal the rate of homicides is decreasing. However, gun-related homicide is still a leading cause of death for urban, African-American males age 15 to 19 (Fox & Zawitz, 2000). Despite the decreasing trend in homicides, the rates and lethality of other interpersonal violence among young people has increased dramatically, especially for young males. For example, children having access to guns and other deadly weapons is directly linked to the increased number of drive-by shootings and violence committed by gangs. Although gang violence has been well documented for more than 200 years, the severity of gang violence has burgeoned and become more pervasive in the school environment. This may be one reason that children are increasingly reporting exposure to community violence (Richters & Martinez, 1993).

Perhaps the most alarming statistic is the time of day when young people commit a violent act in their community. The Office of Juvenile Justice and Delinquency Prevention (OJJDP, 1999) found that violent acts of crime committed by juveniles occur immediately after school hours. They also found that during this time juveniles are more likely to become victims to crimes. Schools and communities must work together to develop ways to prevent this serious problem of community violence and implement best practices to assist children who are increasingly exposed to violence in their homes, schools, and communities.

Common Trends across Home, School, and Community Violence

It became evident by the late 1900s that the escalating violence across environments in American children's lives—that is, child maltreatment, school discipline problems, and neighborhood gangs—has placed them in greater danger on a more continuous basis. Simultaneously, the increased use of weaponry, particularly guns, evidenced in gang violence in neighborhoods and schools and between partners in their homes, has further contributed to children's limited access to safe and nurturing environments. These trends and the increased severity and lethality of violence across all systems compound the crises many children have faced in the past decade. Their involvement in violence in the home, school, and community has served as one means to resolve conflict and create their own sense of safety. However, this is a false sense of safety because their desensitization toward violence against others and their use of weaponry seems to increase their vulnerability and possible victimization. The persistent problems and historical trends central to children's exposure to violence laid the groundwork for programmatic and legislative actions at the local, state, and federal levels; however, few initiatives address the systemic nature of this violence.

LEGISLATION AND FEDERAL INITIATIVES

The promotion of a free and appropriate education for all, violence-free schools, and parental and community involvement have become top priorities for our nation's educational agenda. This is reflected in current legislation and federal initiatives intended to improve results for student success. The incremental changes over time in legislation and pedagogy related to viewing children systemically have been important to policy and practice not only in the field of education but across all health and human sciences.

Special Education

Historically, Public Law 94-142, the Education for all Handicapped Act of 1975, protected the rights of every child to individualized education in order to remove the barriers that make learning difficult. The law did not specify barriers such as child maltreatment, witnessing violence in the home or community, and school violence; however, these problems can serve as much as a barrier to learning as any type of perceptual problem (Gronna & Chin-Chance, 1999; Rudo, Powell, & Dunlap, 1998).

Currently, Public Law 105-17, the Individuals with Disabilities Act Amendments of 1997 (IDEA), acknowledges the importance of addressing behavioral as well as learning problems within the special education population. This reauthorization of PL 94-142 requires educators to conduct functional behavioral assessments and implement behavior intervention plans that include positive behavioral interventions and supports. These mandates are aimed at providing students with disabilities, particularly those who are at risk for or who engage in aggressive and violent behavior, with the necessary skills to handle their anger and aggression in acceptable ways (Hartwig & Ruesch, 2000). Additionally, IDEA places enormous emphasis on increasing the involvement and participation of parents of children with disabilities in order to enhance their children's learning. Although not specific to children with disabilities, increased parental involvement in education is also an aim of the U.S. Department of Education's Goals 2000.

Child Abuse and Neglect

It was not until 1964 that a state law was drafted mandating how and by whom child abuse should be reported and providing immunity from civil liability and/or criminal penalty for the reporters. Currently, every state requires educators to report any suspicion of child abuse to the local authority; however, some states specify only teachers, principals, nurses, and counselors as mandatory reporters, whereas others designate all school personnel. Educators are protected under the Federal Family Educational Rights and Privacy Act of 1974 regarding the release of information from school records in cases where a "health or safety emergency" exists. In most states, child abuse is clearly recognized as a situation in which a child's health or safety is endangered. Further, most states now carry a penalty ranging from professional sanctions to time in jail for mandated reporters who do not make a report. Enforcement of these laws has steadily increased.

Safe and Drug-Free Schools

The seventh goal of Goals 2000 called for the existence of safe, disciplined, and drug-free schools by the end of the century. To assist schools in fulfilling Goal 7, the Safe and Drug-Free Schools and Communities Act of 1994 provided funding and technical assistance to schools for the development of safe school plans. The Clinton administration allocated $300 million to schools via the Safe Schools/Healthy Students Initiative to continue efforts aimed at building safe schools. The National School Safety Center, which disseminates information on school violence and prevention, was established to deal with the increasing problem of school violence and the need for safe school environments. Two further indicators that violence-free schools has become a top priority for our nation's educational agenda have been (1) the nationwide distribution of the U.S. Department of Education's *Early Warning, Timely Response: A Guide to Safe Schools* and its accompanying action guide and (2) the release of the first *Annual Report on School Safety 1998*.

Gun Control

Laws prohibiting the carrying of a concealed or illegal weapon, mandatory licensing of firearms, and a minimum seven-day waiting period for gun purchases are some of the initiatives the federal government has undertaken to prevent community violence. The use of gun locks and gun-free school zones are additional initiatives that have not yet been codified into law but have been proposed for future legislation. Several national centers, such as the Center to Prevent Handgun Violence and the National Center for Injury Prevention and Control, have been established to develop curricula around gun safety and to study the impact of gun-related violence. Some communities have reduced the number of handguns within their borders. For example, the Boston Gun Project promoted legislation to educate youth about the consequences of gun use for settling disputes and restricted their access to firearms. This effort effectively reduced the number of Boston youth killed by a handgun in 1996 (Garbarino, 1999).

THEORETICAL PREMISE

To understand the "whole" child, theories developed since the middle of the twentieth century suggest that all the surrounding systems involved with the child be considered. General Systems Theory (von Bertalanffy, 1956) provided a conceptual framework that paved the way for a paradigmatic shift in thinking from the study of an individual unit to the study of a society. Basic to General Systems Theory, a system is defined as a whole composed of interrelated and interdependent parts, a transactional approach to understanding the nature of an entity in relation to the things it affects and by which it is affected (Katz & Kahn, 1978).

In 1979, Uri Bronfenbrenner made a vast impact in the social science field in his application of systems thinking to the study of children and families (Dunst, Trivette, & Deal, 1994). He proposed an ecological theory of human development focused on the bidirectional relations between the child, family, and other social environments, within which children and parents function in a hierarchy of systems at four levels: the microsystem, mesosystem, exosystem, and macrosystem (see Table 6-1). Ecological systems theory provides educators with a framework for understanding the interrelationship and interdependence of the various systems in which violence occurs, the factors within each system that contribute to violence, its impact on children, and strategies for prevention and intervention.

From a strengths perspective, the ecology of child development necessitates that for a child to develop into a healthy adult, it is essential that the child be loved, nurtured, esteemed, and valued by the family and the systems surrounding the family. Second only to the family, the school is the system with the greatest opportunity to promote the development of competent, caring, and loving children. Noddings (1995b) contends: "We should want more from our educational efforts than adequate academic achievement. . . . We will not achieve even that meager success unless our children believe that they themselves are cared for and learn to care for others" (pp. 675–676). In fact, Noddings asserts that schools have an ethical commitment to address issues of care. Our society, she argues, does not need to create students who are first in the world in math and science, but rather it needs to care for its children—"to reduce violence, to respect honest work of every kind, to reward excellence at every level, to ensure a place for every child and emerging adult in the economic and social world, to produce people who can care competently for their own families and contribute effectively to their communities" (Noddings, 1995a, p. 366). In essence, our country's main educational aim should to foster the growth of competent, caring, loving, and lovable people.

Given the social climate of our times, it is likely that few would refute Noddings's central argument that the creation of "caring" and "cared for" students is critical. In fact, the creation of a caring school community in which all members feel connected, safe, and supported has been touted as one of the key components of a comprehensive plan to prevent school violence (Dwyer & Osher, 2000). We contend that in addition to the traditional responsibilities of the home and school, the development of "caring" and "cared for" students requires collaboration among the many systems of which children are a part. No system can address violence in a singular fashion. Thus, an ethic of care

TABLE 6-1
Systemic Levels of Ecological Systems Theory

- *Microsystem*—a pattern of activities, roles, and interpersonal relations experienced by the developing person in a given face-to-face setting with particular physical and material features, and containing other persons with distinctive characteristics of temperament, personality, and systems of belief. For example, for teachers, the microsystem includes their immediate setting (i.e., the classroom) and the interactions that occur as a result of student and teacher characteristics, job assignment, and class size.
- *Mesosystem*—the linkages and processes taking place between two or more settings containing the developing person, (e.g., the relations between home and school, school and work place, etc.). In other words, a mesosystem is a system of microsystems. For example, for teachers, the mesosystem consists of interrelations among several variables in the teacher workplace, such as collegiality and administrative support.
- *Exosystem*—the linkage and processes taking place between two or more settings, at least one of which does not ordinarily contain the developing person, but in which events occur that influence processes within the immediate setting that does contain that person—for example, for a child, the relation between the home and the parent's workplace and for a parent, the relation between the school and the neighborhood group. For teachers, the exosystem includes the formal and informal social structures that influence the teacher's workplace—for example, socioeconomic level of the community and the nature of the school district.
- *Macrosystem*—the overarching pattern of micro-, meso-, and exosystems characteristic of a given culture, subculture, or other broader social context, with particular reference to the developmentally-instigative belief systems, resources, hazards, lifestyles, opportunity structures, life course options, and patterns of social interchange that are embedded in each of these systems. The macrosystem may be thought of as a societal blueprint for a particular culture, subculture, or other broader social context. For example, for teachers, the macrosystem consists of cultural beliefs and ideologies of the dominant culture as well as economic conditions that impact schools and the decisions of teachers within them.

Sources: Bronfenbrenner (1989), pp. 227–228; Brownell & Smith, (1993), p. 271.

must serve as the foundation upon which all systems operate. The most promising strategies are those that extend beyond the home to include the school and the greater community.

PROFILING CHILDREN EXPOSED TO VIOLENCE

If schools, families, and communities could accurately predict whether a child with disabilities will become violent or a victim of a violent act, much harm could be prevented and concern for these children's exposure to violence would greatly decrease. Unfortunately, there is no single factor or set of early warning signs that specifically identify these children; however, certain risk and protective factors and characteristics have been linked to youth violence and childhood victimization. An understanding of these factors within the varying social systems potentially impacting student cognition and behavior can assist school and agency personnel to more effectively structure prevention and intervention efforts to ameliorate or mediate the occurrence of violence and aggression and to promote success for students with disabilities. School staff can use these indicators in their efforts to identify and refer children requiring special assistance.

Risk Factors

The systemic nature of the risk factors correlated with youth violence and childhood victimization makes it necessary to consider these factors within a multidimensional framework that includes the individual, family, peer group, school, and community (see Table 6-2). This multidimensional approach is fundamental to identifying and assisting children with disabilities who have been or may be exposed to violence. Practitioners and researchers must recognize that in many of these children's lives any number of these factors may coexist and compound the problems they face in their homes, schools, and communities. For example, 25 percent to 41 percent of children with serious emotional and behavioral disturbances nationwide have been found to have two or more disabilities, including learning disabilities and mental retardation (Greenbaum et al., 1996; Wagner, 1995). In another example, children with disabilities living in homes with partner violence are at increased risk for being abused themselves, with the reported degree of overlap between partner abuse and child abuse ranging from 26 percent to 65 percent (Feldman et al., 1995; O'Keefe, 1995). Many studies, however, do not evaluate the children in their samples for the presence of more than one risk factor. Thus, the findings of these studies may to some degree be attributable to these multiple factors and should be regarded with caution.

There are clear similarities between risk factors correlated with youth violence and childhood victimization and characteristics associated with children with disabilities, particularly children with emotional and behavioral disturbances. For example, common characteristics of children with serious emotional disturbances include: predominantly male, overrepresented with culturally and ethnically diverse and low-income, primarily diagnosed with conduct disorders and a second disability, and live in single-parent families (Duchnowski, Johnson, Hall, Kutash, & Friedman, 1993; Rosenblatt & Attkisson, 1993). The cognitive, psychological, and peer group factors of children at risk for youth violence and childhood victimization are also common in children with disabilities. It is then not surprising that children with disabilities have a higher rate of maltreatment victimization and school discipline problems.

Protective Factors

Some children with disabilities in discordant, impoverished, and abusive environments appear to develop stable and healthy personalities and display resilience in the face of life's adversities. Despite the adverse life circumstances surrounding them, these children maintain their sense of self, academic stability, and cultural identity, implying a capacity for successful adaptation, positive functioning, or competence. Resilient children with attention deficit hyperactivity disorder have been found to have higher intelligence and more advanced coping strategies, cognitive-integrative abilities, and problem-solving and social skills (Hechtman, 1991).

Studies investigating familial factors have indicated resilient children more often come from home environments characterized by warmth, affection, emotional support, and defined and feasible structure and limits (Werner, 1990). Block (1971) found resilient children to have parents who are competent, loving, patient, integrated, compatible, and who have shared values. These same factors of caring and nurturance are equally important in the other systems impacting children with disabilities, particularly the school environment as identified by Noddings (1995a).

Other predictors of resilience include the child's perception of the quality of his or her relationship with the family, the presence of alternative caretakers in the home, and the absence of maternal mental health problems (Werner, 1989; Werner & Smith, 1982). The significance of parental values and beliefs has also been studied. Comer (1988) reported that parents' beliefs in opportunities through education help children attain considerable success and competence in their adult lives. This belief served as the basis for public outcries, especially from parents of children with disabilities, to institute laws protecting the rights of all children to a free and appropriate education.

Community factors in resiliency have also been indicated by several studies. Positive outcomes have been associated with high use of support systems by high-risk children (Garmezy, 1985). In addition, positive school experiences, academic and nonacademic, offer children experiences that enhance self-esteem and competence by reinforcing resilience (Brooks, 1991; Zunz, Turner, & Norman, 1993).

The resiliency literature has implications for children exposed to violence, especially for prevention and intervention efforts to assist these children. The relationship between the protective and risk factors linked to youth violence and childhood victimization seems overly apparent. Further study of this relationship is warranted. Additionally, many studies have indicated that community programs that offer support services to children and their families reflective of the factors identified can be enormously beneficial in terms of

TABLE 6-2
**Multidimensional Framework of Psychosocial Risk Factors of Youth
Violence and Childhood Victimization**

Individual
Population Indicators
- Male
- Age 15 to 25
- Ethnic minorities—African American, Hispanic, Native American

Biological Factors
- Low resting heart rate
- Low serotonin levels
- High testosterone levels
- Brain damage
- Minor physical abnormalities
- Pregnancy and delivery complications, such as low birth weight

Cognitive Factors
- Low verbal IQ
- Hostile attribution biases
- Lower levels of moral reasoning, abstract reasoning, and problem solving

Psychological Factors
- Impulsivity/Hyperactivity
- Difficult temperament in infancy
- Risk-taking
- External locus of control
- Poor frustration tolerance levels
- Aggressiveness
- Limited coping skills
- Attention and concentration problems, restlessness
- Early initiation of violent behavior
- Involvement in other forms of antisocial behavior
- Beliefs and attitudes favorable to deviant or antisocial behavior

Family
- Marital and family conflict
- Low levels of parental involvement
- Delinquent siblings
- Frequent changes of residence
- Poor family management practices
- Parent/child separation
- History of criminal behavior and substance abuse
- Low family warmth, cohesion, and bonding

TABLE 6-2 continued

- Inconsistent, erratic, arbitrary discipline practices
- Problematic parent-child interactional patterns
- Favorable parental attitudes toward violence, crime, and substance abuse
- Parental failure to reinforce and model prosocial behavior
- Insufficient parental monitoring and overly harsh or permissive parental discipline
- Intrafamilial violence, such as partner abuse, child abuse/neglect
- Single-parent homes, particularly adolescent males living with mother only

Peer Group
- Affiliation with deviant peers
- Poor peer relations
- Gang membership

School
- Strict and inflexible classroom rules
- Presence of gangs in school
- Teacher hostility
- Ineffective classroom instruction
- Competitive school environment
- Dropping out
- Overcrowded schools and classrooms
- Frequent school transitions
- Truancy
- Lack of classroom management and structure
- Inconsistent enforcement of discipline policy
- Curriculum that does not reflect interests, needs, and culture of students
- Lack of explicitly stated student academic and behavioral expectations
- Low academic achievement, academic failure, and lack of commitment to learning
- Large enrollment leading to student alienation and low bonding to school community
- Exposure to community violence and prejudice
- Availability of firearms, drugs, and alcohol
- Lack of opportunities for education and employment
- Repeated exposure to media violence
- Neighborhood poverty, social disorganization, and criminal activity
- Much transition among residents and low sense of community

Sources: Group for the Advancement of Psychiatry, Committee on Preventive Psychiatry, 1999; Hamburg, 1998; Hawkins, Farrington, & Catalano, 1998; Howard & Jenson, 1999; Kashani, Jones, Bumby, & Thomas, 1999; OJJDP, 2000; Warner, Weist, & Krulak, 1999.

providing protective functions and increasing positive outcomes (Copple, Cline, & Smith, 1987; Price, Cowen, Lorion, & Ramos-McKay, 1988).

Characteristics of Troubled Youth

It is not always possible to predict when a student may engage in aggressive or violent behavior at school; however, administrators, teachers, support staff, students, parents, and agency personnel should be aware of the warning signs that a student is troubled and potentially dangerous. Because these individuals are on the front line, they are often in the best position to identify and assist students who are troubled. Though not meant to serve as a checklist against which to match individual children, the behavioral and emotional indicators listed in Table 6-3 can signal that a student may need help.

Characteristics related to children with special needs help to identify these children's increased risk for committing violent acts or being victimized. Specifically, research on children with Attention Deficit Hyperactivity Disorders (ADHD) indicates that interpersonal and self-regulatory problems in these children potentially place them in harm's way or result in their violence toward others. For example, characteristics of ADHD, such as hyperactivity,

TABLE 6-3
Behavioral and Emotional Indicators of Troubled Youth

- History of tantrums and uncontrollable anger
- Characteristically resorts to name calling, cursing, or abusive language
- Makes violent threats when angry
- Previously carried a weapon to school
- History of serious disciplinary problems at school and in the community
- Low school interest and poor academic performance
- History of drug, alcohol, or other substance abuse or dependency
- Socially withdrawn; has few or no close friends
- Preoccupied with weapons, explosives, or other inflammable devices
- Previously been truant, suspended, or expelled from school
- Cruel to animals
- Little or no supervision and support from parents or other adults
- Witnessed or been a victim of abuse or neglect in the home
- Bullies or intimidates peers or younger children or has been a victim of such persecution
- Tends to blame others for difficulties and problems he or she causes
- Consistently prefers TV shows, movies, music, or reading materials with violent content
- Expresses violence in writings and drawings
- Affiliation with a gang or other antisocial group
- Often depressed and/or has significant mood swings
- Threatened or attempted suicide or other self-injurious behaviors

Sources: Dwyer, Osher, & Warger, 1998; National School Safety Center, 1998.

concentration problems, restlessness, and risk-taking, were found to be strong predictors of later violent behavior (OJJDP, 2000; Williams & Van Dorn, 1999). More specifically, boys with restlessness and concentration problems were five times more likely to be arrested for violence than boys without these behaviors (Klinteberg, Andersson, Magnusson, & Stattin, 1993). In another study, teachers' ratings of male children's concentration and restlessness problems predicted later violent behaviors (Farrington, 1989). Distractability and hyperactivity in children with ADHD has also been shown to precipitate abuse by causing severe conflict or attachment problems (Alexander, 1992; Patterson & Forgatch, 1995). Additionally, children with ADHD exhibiting incautious and impulsive behaviors have increased risk of trauma, especially from child maltreatment (Barkley, Grodzinsky, & DuPaul, 1992).

Studies on children with Oppositional-Defiant Disorder (ODD) have associated these children's aggressive, defiant, and provocative behavior with potential harm toward their peers and their own victimization (Barkley et al., 1992; Ford et al., 2000). For example, these children have been found to be at greater risk for physical and sexual maltreatment than children with other disabilities (Ford et al., 2000).

Teachers, in particular, should also be aware of the characteristics specific to troubled youth who may be inclined toward gang involvement, especially since the lethality of gang violence has increased in our schools and neighborhoods. Hixon (1999) developed a list of warning signs that may be helpful for school staff, as well as for parents and other community members, in their identification and management of children involved in, or potentially involved in, gang activity. Recognizing the following warning signs in students with disabilities is particularly important because these children are often outcasts among their peers and seek ways to belong for which a gang may be the answer:

- Child suddenly has a new set of friends
- Child has new nicknames
- Child shows little or no interest in family/school performance
- Child has late hours or time that is not accounted for
- Child wears specific colors or has a particular style of dress
- Child has tattoos or clothing or other items with insignias or logos

Characteristics of School Violence Victims

Much of the school violence literature focuses on perpetrators of violence, with surprisingly little attention devoted to victims. However, attempts to more fully understand the characteristics of students who fall victim to aggression and violence at school have recently been made (Batsche & Knoff, 1994; Furlong, Chung, Bates, & Morrison, 1995; Morrison, Furlong, & Smith, 1994). Although males represent the majority of perpetrators, they are also more likely than females to be victims of violent incidents. Not surprisingly, rates of victimization are highest in junior high/middle school and lowest in elementary school. In general, students who are victimized at school are socially isolated with few, if any, close friends; are distrusting of others; dislike school and perceive it as unsafe; change residences often; have poorer social support networks with peers and teachers; and appear emotionally and/or physically weak. Often, the actions of these students signal to potential perpetrators that they are insecure, anxious, and will not retaliate, possibly leading to an "easy target" status.

Similarities between many of the characteristics of school violence victims and the characteristics of children with disabilities, especially children with emotional and behavioral disabilities, seem apparent and lead one to wonder if the rate of victimization at school is higher for these children. One of the only studies examining the experience of school victimization for students with special needs involved (1) high school students in general education, (2) students enrolled in a leadership class, and (3) students with behavioral and learning disabilities enrolled in either an "opportunity class" (a half-day self-contained program for students with emotional and behavioral problems at risk for school failure) or a special day class (Morrison et al., 1994). Students were asked to report the types of violence they experienced at school during a one-month period. Results indicated that students were not victimized at random and students in special education classes were more often school violence victims than students in general education classes. Those students who "stood out from the crowd" reported higher rates of victimization than students in general education.

THE IMPACT OF VIOLENCE ON CHILDREN

Children are impacted by many experiences in their homes, schools, and communities, few as devastating as violence. Whereas the effects of family violence on children's development have been documented (see, for example, Rudo et al., 1998), less is known about the consequences of chronic exposure to school or community violence or the impact of multiple forms of violence exposure (O'Keefe, 1997). For children with disabilities, the impact of violence in their homes can exacerbate existing developmental problems. However, the unknowns about the overall impact of violence, whether in the home, at school, or in the community, are even greater for this population because very little research exists specific to this population. What is known about the impact of violence on children, in general, has often been attained from retrospective reporting (using testimonies of adult survivors); however, more recent studies have focused on the effects by studying children.

Current knowledge suggests that children's exposure to all types of violence exacts detrimental individual, social, and economic consequences. These include serious social, psychological, and academic problems and extend to legal, fiscal, and health issues. Many children with disabilities already experience these types of problems; therefore, it is not hard to imagine the increased suffering exposure to violence could have for these children. In general, when children witness acts of interpersonal violence, it often discourages them from engaging in normal home, school, and community activities when they are young and into adulthood (Jenson & Howard, 1999). As many of these children mature and grow older, their exposure to violence is often perpetuated and emulated. Specifically, many children living in violent homes, in homes in which physical punishment is used, or in violent communities have been found to more likely become violent adults and criminal offenders (Garbarino, Dubrow, Kostelny, & Pardo, 1992; Widom, 1989). For children with emotional disturbances, by the time they have been out of school for three to five years, 58 percent have been arrested. Similarly, for children with learning disabilities, 31 percent have been arrested in that time frame (SRI International, Center for Education and Human Services, 1997). As a result of the known consequences, children's exposure to violence has become a major public health problem in our nation.

STRATEGIES AND BEST PRACTICES
FOR SCHOOL PERSONNEL

Whereas many factors contributing to children's exposure to violence occur outside the context of the school, all educators can and must play a part in violence prevention and intervention. However, school personnel cannot address this problem in isolation. We contend that the most effective approaches are comprehensive school-based models that involve collaboration with the home and larger community. Educators, child-serving professionals, families, and policymakers must strive to implement strategies and practices that have been shown to hold promise in effectively preventing and decreasing the incidence and impact of home, school, and community violence.

Educators can pick up cues of possible maltreatment in the home by observing children's behavior at school, observing physical signs, or during routine communications with parents (see Table 6-4). Special education staff should use all these means, but may find talking with their students and regular communication with their students' parents the most effective method because the child's disability may mask behaviors and physical signs associated with the maltreatment.

First and foremost, school personnel should be familiar with school policy regarding child abuse reporting. It is suggested that school staff members who have a suspicion of child maltreatment discuss their observations and infor-

TABLE 6-4
Cues School Personnel Can Observe of Possible Maltreatment in a Student

- Evidence of lack of attention—e.g., malnutrition and/or inappropriate clothing for the environment
- Physical indicators—e.g., skin or bone injuries
- Consistently isolating themselves from their peers and adults
- Closing of the eyes when voices get raised
- Backing away from any physical contact
- Constant sleeping or an inability to pay attention in class
- Sexual behaviors in young children indicating sexual knowledge not ordinarily possessed at that age
- Extreme sexual aggression toward other children

mation with a school team. This team may include outside community resources and parents; therefore, it is imperative that confidentiality be maintained. However, time is of the essence in regard to reporting child abuse or neglect, so a team meeting may not be feasible. Contacting the local authority is the next essential step.

At the same time school personnel are concerning themselves with children who may be maltreated in the home, they are also dealing with the escalating problems of violence in the school. Historically, schools have responded to acts of school violence and other disciplinary incidents by punishing and excluding the offenders. Likewise, there has been an increase in the use of school security measures such as metal detectors and video surveillance. Despite their increased use, such zero tolerance discipline policies have not proven effective in deterring violence (Skiba & Peterson, 2000). Special education is another common response to dealing with individual children who engage in persistent and chronic acts of violence and aggression. The relationship between the receipt of special education services and school violence reduction, however, is yet to be determined. It is known, however, that students with emotional and behavioral disabilities often lack the resources necessary for coping with social challenges, such as conflict resolution or problem solving skills. Therefore, special educators can play a vital role in developing and implementing programs designed to reduce and prevent aggression and violence, such as incorporating social skill classes and anger management discussions into the curriculum.

Proactive approaches to violence reduction stand in stark contrast to the punitive and exclusionary practices often used to discourage the misbehavior of students with disruptive behavior disorders. In fact, it has been suggested that such punitive practices may actually increase misbehavior (Hyman & Perone, 1998). If schools are to break the cycle of violence, current disciplinary practices must give way to a more comprehensive, positive, and proactive model of violence prevention and intervention. A three-tiered approach has emerged providing schools with a framework for building and maintaining a safe school culture (the reader is referred to Dwyer & Osher [2000], for a more detailed discussion of the model). This multilevel system is designed to address the academic and behavioral needs of all children, not just those with the most challenging behaviors.

The assumption underlying the model is that a continuum of effective positive behavior supports is needed to meet the disciplinary challenges of all children in a school (Sugai, Sprague, Horner, & Walker, 2000). That is, schools are comprised of three groups of students, each requiring a different level of intervention. The majority of students (80 to 90 percent) will not exhibit problem behaviors. Universal interventions, which constitute a form of primary prevention, focus on improving the overall level of appropriate behavior for all students. Such interventions might include the direct provision of social skills and problem solving training; creation of clearly-defined schoolwide rules and expectations for student behavior; development of a system to teach and reinforce expected behaviors; and alteration of the school environment to prevent, minimize, or eliminate disruptive and violent behavior, such as increased supervision of specific problematic areas. The development of a schoolwide discipline committee is critical in planning, monitoring, and maintaining school violence prevention efforts.

The establishment of an effective schoolwide foundation will likely result in a significant reduction in student discipline problems; however, not all students will be responsive to universal interventions. About 10 percent to 15 percent of the school population will require targeted interventions. These interventions, which are considered early intervention efforts for students at risk for developing problem behavior, involve support from pupil services personnel such as counselors, social workers, special educators, and school psychologists. Schools will often develop a student support team, or another variously named group of individuals, that works with the teacher, parents, and student to develop interventions to address specific behaviors. Such interventions may, for example, include mentoring, tutoring or other academic support, positive behavioral plans, or the development of a reward system (see Dwyer & Osher [2000], for a comprehensive list of early intervention strategies). For children receiving special education services, these interventions should be incorporated into their Individual Education Plan (IEP) and their behavioral assessment.

There will remain, however, 3 percent to 5 percent of the student body for which targeted interventions are not effective. Students experiencing chronic and intense problem behavior in home, school, and community contexts require more intensive interventions, services, and supports, often extending beyond school resources to include other community agencies. The support team collaborates with professionals from other child-serving agencies, such as mental health, child welfare, and juvenile justice, to provide an individualized array of services and supports to meet the unique needs of a child and family. Intensive interventions may include special education and related services, school-based mental health services, alternative programming and schools, interagency systems of care, and individualized mental health services and supports such as multisystemic therapy (MST) and wraparound planning.

The use of MST and wraparound planning approaches for children with special needs has increased in recent years. As one of the few treatments demonstrating long-term effectiveness with youth who have serious clinical challenges (Henggeler, Melton, & Smith, 1992; Henggeler, Melton, Smith, Schoenwald, & Hanley, 1993), MST seeks to empower primary caregivers with the skills and resources needed to meet the challenges inherent in rearing youth with challenging behaviors and empower youth to cope with difficulties in the home, school, and community. Based on a social-ecological perspective, MST utilizes empirically-validated techniques to change "the known determinants of youth antisocial behavior, including characteristics of the individual youth, family, peer relations, school functioning, and family-neighborhood interactions" (Schoenwald, Brown, & Henggeler, 2000, p. 113).

Wraparound, a rapidly growing ecological approach to serving children and youth with serious emotional and behavioral problems, is defined as "a philosophy of care that includes a definable planning process involving the child and family that results in a unique set of community services and natural supports individualized for that child and family to achieve a positive set of outcomes" (Burns & Goldman, 1999, p. 10). The evidence base for wraparound is emerging with early studies offering preliminary evidence of its effectiveness in improving outcomes for children. Historically, mental health and child welfare agencies have taken the lead in initiating wraparound planning. However, school-based wraparound approaches have increased in recent years with evidence of improved academic and behavioral outcomes (Eber & Nelson, 1997).

Children cannot learn and develop appropriately in environments inundated with fear and violence. A positive school climate that promotes feelings of safety, caring, and support may directly or indirectly affect student learning outcomes and promote positive student behavior and attitudes. For schools to be safe and responsive to the needs of all children, each of the three levels of intervention must be in place and operating effectively. Evidence suggests that schools that adopt a comprehensive violence prevention and intervention program experience improved academics, reduced disciplinary referrals and suspensions, improved school climate conducive to learning, enhanced feelings of safety, increased staff morale, and more efficient use of human and financial resources (Dwyer & Osher, 2000). Perhaps most importantly, safe schools can promote the establishment of caring communities in which students, teachers, parents, and staff build positive relationships. This can be particularly beneficial for students with disabilities who often experience feelings of alienation, distrust, and disengagement. Through the establishment of positive relationships, all members of the school community feel connected to the school, supported in their interpersonal relationships, and engaged in the learning process.

The recommended strategies and practice framework are not a panacea for dealing with violence that occurs in homes, schools, and communities. However, it is clear that what has been tried in the past has not necessarily provided families, schools, and communities with the solutions needed to stop the cycle of violence so prominent in our nation. Of course, any strategy is better than none, but the more collaboration between the home, school, and community, the greater the chance prevention and early intervention efforts will make a difference in decreasing the horrific consequences for children exposed to violence. It must be stressed, however, that teachers and other school personnel may be the only resource accessible to children who are exposed to violent situations in their homes, schools, and communities; therefore, it is imperative they accept the responsibility to understand and take action if something seems amiss. Although this may be uncomfortable for some individuals, there are others in the school environment—school social workers, guidance counselors, nurses, more experienced staff, and administrators—who can help by providing guidance, support, and services. Additionally, talking with a child who is thought to be dealing with or considering violence, visiting with their parents, or consulting with professionals in the community who are familiar with violence prevention and intervention may be the first, and only, solution needed to help a child.

CONCLUSION

Violence is one of the most serious social problems facing our nation today. It has extended into our homes, schools, communities, day cares, and places of employment. The multiple determinants of youth violence as well as the negative impact of violence on the academic, psychological, social, and physical well-being of our children are well documented. Studies examining the effectiveness of youth violence prevention programs are beginning to emerge. Despite this growing body of literature, little attention has been given specifically to the examination of violence exposure and children with disabilities. It is clear, however, that children with disabilities often lack the resources necessary to deal effectively with socially challenging situations. As a result, they may be at increased risk of becoming victims or perpetrators of violence. Educators and other service professionals can play a prominent role in recognizing violence as a significant psychosocial barrier to children's learning and in implementing practices that elicit a caring, nurturing environment conducive to educational progress. Preservice and in-service training on violence-related issues, open avenues of communication between the school and home, and implementation of a continuum of positive behavioral interventions and supports are critical strategies for dealing with the effects of violence on children. These strategies will require schools to collaborate with families and communities, assuring that all systems impacting children take responsibility for their well-being and success.

Further research is needed, not only in relation to violence and children with disabilities but also on the establishment of common terms and definitions of violence across the various systems—home, school, and community. Although literature on children exposed to home, school, and community violence exists, the compartmentalization of these environments in recent studies continues to be perplexing in light of the overlap of much of the information, particularly around characteristics and risk factors. We must recognize the systemic nature of violence in the lives of our children rooted in these three venues and incorporate it into our research, practice, policy, and interpersonal relationships.

NOTE

1. The percents total more than 100% because some children were victims of more than one form of maltreatment.

DISCUSSION QUESTIONS

1. Discuss the importance of systems theory and an ethic of care to understanding and addressing the issue of violence in the lives of children. How can these theories help educators develop the knowledge, skills, and interventions needed to decrease the impact of violence on children with disabilities in their homes, schools, and communities?
2. How might violence exposure serve as a barrier to learning, particularly for children with special needs?
3. What research is needed to further educators' understanding of the impact of violence on children with disabilities?
4. Discuss how common terms and definitions of violence across the various systems could impact policies and services pertaining to children with disabilities exposed to violence.

REFERENCES

Alexander, P. C. (1992). Application of attachment theory to the study of sexual abuse. *Journal of Consulting and Clinical Psychology, 60*, 185–195.
Allen, D. M., & Tarnowski, K. J. (1989). Depressive characteristics of physically abused children. *Journal of Abnormal Child Psychology, 17*, 1–11.

Barahal, R. M., Waterman, J., & Martin, H. P. (1981). The social cognitive development of abused children. *Journal of Consulting and Clinical Psychology, 49*, 508–516.

Barkley, R. A., Grodzinsky, G., & DuPaul, G. (1992). Frontal lobe functions in Attention Deficit Disorder with and without hyperactivity. *Journal of Abnormal Child Psychology, 20*, 163–188.

Batsche, G., & Knoff, H. M. (1994). Bully and victims: Understanding a pervasive problem in the schools. *School Psychology Review, 3*(3), 165–174.

Bell, C. C., & Jenkins, E. J. (1993). Community violence and children in Chicago's southside. *Psychiatry: Interpersonal and Biological Processes, 56*, 46–54.

Block, J. (1971). *Lives through time*. Berkeley, CA: Bancroft Books.

Boney-McCoy, S., & Finkelhor, D. (1995). Psychosocial sequelae of violent victimization in a national youth sample. *Journal of Consulting and Clinical Psychology, 63*, 726–736.

Botash, A. S., & Church, C. C. (1999). Child abuse and disabilities: A medical perspective. *The APSAC Advisor, 12* (1), 10–18.

Bowen, N. K., & Bowen, G. L. (1999). Effects of crime and violence in neighborhoods and schools on the school behavior and performance of adolescents. *Journal of Adolescent Research, 14*(3), 319–342.

Brenner, N. D., Simon, T. R., Krug, E. G., & Lowry, R. (1999). Recent trends in violence-related behaviors among high school students in the United States. *Journal of the American Medical Association, 282*, 440–446.

Briere, J., & Runtz, M. (1990). Differential adult symptomatology associated with three types of child abuse histories. *Child Abuse & Neglect, 14*, 357–364.

Bronfenbrenner, U. (1989). Ecological systems theory. In R. Vasta (Ed.), *Annals of child development: Six theories of child development*. Greenwich, CT: Jai Press, Inc.

Brooks, R. B. (1991). *The self-esteem teacher*. Circle Pines, MN: American Guidance Service.

Browne, A., & Finkelhor, D. (1986). Impact of child sexual abuse: A review of the research. *Psychological Bulletin, 99*, 66–77.

Brownell, M. T., & Smith, S. W. (1993). Understanding special education teacher attrition: A conceptual model and implications for teacher educators. *Teacher Education and Special Education, 16*, 270–282.

Burns, B. J., & Goldman, S. K. (1999). Promising practices in wraparound for children with serious emotional disturbance and their families. *Systems of care:Promising practices in children's mental health, 1998 series, volume IV.* Washington: Center for Effective Collaboration and Practice, American Institutes for Research.

Campbell, C., & Schwarz, D. F. (1996). Prevalence and impact of exposure to interpersonal violence among suburban and urban middle school students. *Pediatrics, 98*, 396–402.

Carlson, B. E. (1984). Children's observations of interparental violence. In A. R. Roberts (Ed.), *Battered women and their families* (pp. 147–167). New York: Springer.

Centers for Disease Control and Prevention. (1993). *The prevention of youth violence: A framework for community action*. Atlanta: U.S. Printing Office.

Chesapeake Institute. (1994). *National agenda for achieving better results for children and youth with serious emotional disturbance*. Washington: U.S. Department of Education, Office of Special Education and Rehabilitative Services, Office of Special Education Programs.

Cicchetti, D. (1987). Developmental psychopathology in infancy. *Journal of Consulting and Clinical Psychology, 55*, 837-845.

Comer, J. (1988). *Maggie's American dream*. New York: New American Library.

Cooley-Quille, M., Turner, S., & Beidel, D. (1995). Assessing community violence: The children's report of exposure to violence. *Journal of the American Academy of Child and Adolescent Psychiatry, 34*, 201–208.

Copple, C. E., Cline, M. G., & Smith, A. N. (1987). *Path to the future: Long-term effects of Head Start in the Philadelphia school district.* Washington: U.S. Department of Health and Human Services.

Curry, G. D., & Decker, S. H. (1998). *Confronting gangs: Crime and community.* Los Angeles: Roxbury Publishing.

Dembo, R., Williams, L., Wothke, W., Schmeidler, J., & Brown, C. H. (1992). The role of family factors, physical abuse, and sexual victimization experiences in high-risk youths' alcohol and other drug use and delinquency: A longitudinal model. *Violence and Victims, 7*(3), 245–266.

Donnerstein, E., Slaby, R., & Eron, L. (1993). The mass media and youth aggression. In L. Eron, J. Gentry, & P. Schlegel (Eds.), *Reason to hope: A psychosocial perspective on violence and youth* (pp. 219–250). Washington: American Psychological Association.

Dryfoos, J. (1998). *Safe passage: Making it through adolescence in a risky society.* New York: Oxford University Press.

Duchnowski, A. J., Johnson, M. K., Hall, K. S., Kutash, K., & Friedman, R. M. (1993). The alternatives to residential treatment study: Initial findings. *Journal of Emotional and Behavioral Disorders, 1*, 17–26.

Dunst, C. J., Trivette, C. M., & Deal, A. G. (1994). *Supporting and strengthening families: Methods, strategies and practices* (Vol. 1). Cambridge, MA: Brookline Books.

DuRant, R. H., Getts, A., Cadenhead, C., Emans, S. J., & Woods, E. R. (1995). Exposure to violence and victimization and depression, hopelessness, and purpose in life among adolescents living in and around public housing. *Developmental and Behavioral Pediatrics, 16*, 233–238.

Dwyer, K., & Osher, D. (2000). *Safeguarding our children: An action guide.* Washington: U.S. Departments of Education and Justice, American Institutes for Research.

Dwyer, K., Osher, D., & Warger, C. (1998). *Early warning, timely response*: A guide to safe schools. Washington: Department of Education.

Eber, L., & Nelson, C. M. (1997). School-based wraparound planning: Integrating services for students with emotional and behavioral needs. *American Journal of Orthopsychiatry, 67*(3), 385–395.

Fantuzzo, J. W. (1990). Behavioral treatment of the victims of child abuse and neglect. *Behavior Modification, 14*, 316–339.

Farrington, D. P. (1989). Early predictors of adolescent aggression and adult violence. *Violence and Victims, 4*, 79–100.

Feldman, R. S., Salzinger, S., Rosario, M., Alvarado, L., Caraballo, L., & Hammer, M. (1995). Parent, teacher, and peer ratings of physically abused and nonmaltreated children's behavior. *Journal of Abnormal Child Psychology, 23*, 317–334.

Fitzpatrick, K. M., & Boldizar, J. P. (1993). The prevalence and consequences of exposure to violence among African American youth. *Journal of the American Academy of Child and Adolescent Psychiatry, 32*, 419–23.

Ford, J. D., Racusin, R., Ellis, C. G., Daviss, W. B., Reiser, J., Fleischer, A., & Thomas, J. (2000). Child maltreatment, other trauma exposure, and posttraumatic symptomatology among children with Oppositional Defiant and Attention Deficit Hyperactivity Disorders. *Child Maltreatment, 5*, 205–217.

Fox, J. A., & Zawitz, M. W. (2000 March). Homicide trends in the United States: 1998 update. *Bureau of Justice Statistics Crime Data Brief.* Washington: U.S. Department of Justice, Office of Justice Programs.

Freeman, L. N., Mokros, H., & Poznanski, E. O. (1993). Violent events reported by normal urban school-aged children: Characteristics and depression correlates. *Journal of the American Academy of Child and Adolescent Psychiatry*, 32, 419–423.

Furlong, M. J., Chung, A., Bates, M., & Morrison, R. L. (1995). Who are the victims of school violence? A comparison of student non-victims and multi-victims. *Education and Treatment of Children*, *18*(3), 282–298.

Furlong, M. J., & Morrison, G. M. (1994). Introduction to miniseries: School violence and safety in perspective. *School Psychology Review*, *23*, 139–150.

Garbarino, J. (1999). *Lost boys: Why our sons turn violent and how can we save them*. New York: Free Press.

Garbarino, J., & Abramowitz, R. H. (1992). Sociocultural risk and opportunity. In J. Garbarino (Ed.), *Children and families in the social environment* (pp. 35–70). New York: Aldine de Gruyter.

Garbarino, J., Dubrow, N., Kostelny, K., & Pardo, C. (1992). *Children in danger: Coping with the consequences of community violence*. San Francisco: Jossey-Bass Publishers.

Garmezy, N. (1985). Stress-resistant children: The search for protective factors. In J. E.Stevenson (Ed.), *Recent research in developmental psychopathology*. Oxford: Pergamon Press.

Gelles, R. J., & Straus, M. A. (1990). *Physical violence in American families: Risk factors and adaptations to violence in 8,145 families*. New Brunswick, NJ: Transaction Press.

Gorski, J. D., & Pilotto, L. (1993). Interpersonal violence among youth: A challenge for school personnel. *Educational Psychology Review*, 5, 35–61.

Gray, H., & Foshee, V. (1997). Adolescent dating violence: Differences between one-sided and mutually violent profiles. *Journal of Interpersonal Violence*, 12, 126–141.

Greenbaum, P. E., Dedrick, R. F., Friedman, R. M., Kutash, K., Brown, E. C., Lardieri, S. P., & Pugh, A. M. (1996). National Adolescent and Child Treatment Study (NACTS): Outcomes for children with serious emotional and behavioral disturbance. *Behavioral Disorders*, 4, 130–146.

Gronna, S. S., & Chin-Chance, S. A. (1999, April). Effects of school safety and school characteristics on Grade 8 achievement: A multilevel analysis. Paper presented at the meeting of the American Educational Research Association, Montreal, Quebec, Canada.

Group for the Advancement of Psychiatry, Committee on Preventive Psychiatry. (1999). Violent behavior in children and youth: Preventive intervention from a psychiatric perspective. *Journal of the American Academy of Child and Adolescent Psychiatry, 38*(3), 235–241.

Hamburg, M. A. (1998). Youth violence is a public health concern. In D. S. Elliott, B. A. Hamburg, & K. R. Williams (Eds.), *Violence in American Schools* (pp. 31–54). Cambridge, U.K.: Cambridge University Press.

Harris, L., and Associates. (1993). *Violence in America's public schools: A survey of the American teacher*. New York: Metropolitan Life Insurance Company.

Hartwig, E. P., & Ruesch, G. M. (2000). Disciplining students in special education. *The Journal of Special Education*, 33, 240–247.

Hawkins, J. D., Farrington, D. P., & Catalano, R. F. (1998). Reducing violence through the schools. In D. S. Elliott, B. A. Hamburg, & K. R. Williams (Eds.), *Violence in American Schools* (pp. 188–216). Cambridge, U.K.: Cambridge University Press.

Hechtman, I. (1991). Resilience and vulnerability in long term outcome of attention deficit hyperactivity disorder. *Canadian Journal of Psychiatry, 36*, 415–421.

Henggeler, S. W., Melton, G. B., & Smith, L. A. (1992). Family preservation using multisystemic therapy: An effective alternative to incarcerating serious juvenile offenders. *Journal of Consulting and Clinical Psychology*, 60, 953–961.

Henggeler, S. W., Melton, G. B., Smith, L. A., Schoenwald, S. K., & Hanley, J. H. (1993). Family preservation using multisystemic treatment: Long-term follow-up to a clinical trial with serious juvenile offenders. *Journal of Child and Family Studies*, 2, 283–293.

Herrenkohl, R. C., Herrenkohl, E. C., Egolf, B. P., & Wu, P. (1991). *The developmental consequences of child abuse: The Lehigh longitudinal study*. Washington: National Center on Child Abuse and Neglect.

Hixon, A. L. (1999). Preventing street gang violence. *American Family Physician*, 59(8), 2121–2124.

Howard, M. O., & Jenson, J. M. (1999). Causes of youth violence. In J. M. Jenson & M. O. Howard (Eds.), *Youth violence: Current research and recent practice innovations* (pp. 19–42). Washington: NASW Press.

Hyman, I. A., & Perone, D. C. (1998). The other side of school violence: Educator policies and practices that may contribute to student misbehavior. *Journal of School Psychology*, 36(1), 7–27.

Jenson, J. M., & Howard, M. O. (1999). Prevalence and patterns of youth violence. In J. M. Jenson & M. O. Howard (Eds.), *Youth violence: Current research and recent practice innovations* (pp. 3–18). Washington: NASW Press.

Jonson-Reid, M., & Barth, R. (1998). *Pathways from child welfare to juvenile incarceration for serious and violent offenses*. Final report to the Office of Juvenile Justice and Delinquency Prevention. Berkeley: University of California at Berkeley, School of Social Welfare, Child Welfare Research Center.

Kashani, J., & Allan, W. (1998). The impact of family violence on children and adolescents. *Developmental and Clinical Psychology and Psychiatry Series*, 37. Thousand Oaks, CA: Sage Publications.

Kashani, J. H., Jones, M. R., Bumby, K. M., & Thomas, L. A. (1999). Youth violence: Psychosocial risk factors, treatment, prevention, and recommendations. *Journal of Emotional and Behavioral Disorders*, 7(4), 200–210.

Katz, D., & Kahn, R. L. (1978). *The social psychology of organizations* (2nd ed.). New York: John Wiley & Sons.

Kaufman, P., Chen, X., Choy, S. P., Ruddy, S. A., Miller, A. K., Chandler, K. A., Chapman, C. D., Rand, M. R., & Klaus, P. (1999). *Indicators of School Crime and Safety, 1999*. Washington: U.S. Departments of Education and Justice.

Kazdin, A. E. (1993). Changes in behavioral problems and prosocial functioning in child treatment. *Journal of Child and Family Studies*, 2, 5–22.

Kazdin, A. E., Moser, J., Colbus, D., & Bell, R. (1985). Depressive symptoms among physically abused and psychiatrically disturbed children. *Journal of Abnormal Psychology*, 94, 298–307.

Kempe, C. H., & Helfer, R. E. (1980). *The battered child* (3rd ed.). Chicago: The University of Chicago Press.

Kingery, P. M., Coggeshall, M. B., & Alford, A. A. (1998). Violence at school: Recent evidence from four national surveys. *Psychology in the Schools*, 35, 247–258.

Klinteberg, B. A., Andersson, T., Magnusson, D., & Stattin, H. (1993). Hyperactive behavior in childhood as related to subsequent alcohol problems and violent offending: A longitudinal study of male subjects. *Personality and Individual Differences*, 15, 381–388.

Laird, M., Eckenrode, J., & Doris, J. (1990). *Maltreatment and the social and academic adjustment of school children: Final report*. Ithaca, NY: Cornell University.

Martinez, P., & Richters, J. E. (1993). The NIMH community violence project: Children's distress symptoms associated with violence exposure. *Psychiatry, 56*, 22–35.

Mazza, J. J., & Reynolds, W. M. (1999). Exposure to violence in inner-city adolescents: Relationships of suicidal ideation, depression, and PTSD symptomatology. *Journal of Abnormal Child Psychology, 27*, 203–214.

Miller, G. E., & Rubin, K. A. (1999, Spring). Victimization of school-age children. *Communique*. Bethesda, MD: National Association of School Psychologists.

Morrison, G. M., Furlong, M. J., & Smith, G. (1994). Factors associated with the experience of school violence among general education, leadership class, opportunity class, and special day class pupils. *Education and Treatment of Children, 17*(3), 356–369.

Moses, A. (1999). Exposure to violence, depression, and hostility in a sample of inner city high school youth. *Journal of Adolescence, 22*, 21–32.

Murphy, E. F. (1981). *2,715 one-line quotations for speakers, writers, and raconteurs.* New York: Crown.

National School Boards Association (NSBA). (1993). *Violence in the schools: How America's school boards are safeguarding our children.* Alexandria, VA: Author.

National School Safety Center. (1998). *Indicators that a student may be troubled.* [online www.NSSC1.org/home.htm]

Noddings, N. (1995a). A morally defensible mission for schools in the 21st century. *Phi Delta Kappan, 76*(5), 365–368.

Noddings, N. (1995b). Teaching themes of care. *Phi Delta Kappan, 76*(9), 675–679.

Nuttall, E., & Kalesnick, J. (1987). Personal violence in the schools: The role of the counselor. *Journal of Counseling and Development*, 65, 372–375.

Office of Juvenile Justice and Delinquency Prevention (1999, November). *Violence after school.* Washington: Government Printing Office.

Office of Juvenile Justice and Delinquency Prevention (2000, April). *Predictors of youth violence.* Washington: Government Printing Office.

O'Keefe, M. (1995). Predictors of child abuse in maritally violent families. *Journal of Interpersonal Violence, 10* (1), 3–25.

O'Keefe, M. (1997). Adolescents' exposure to community and school violence: Prevalence and behavioral correlates. *Journal of Adolescent Health, 20*, 368–376.

Osofsky, J. D. (1995). The effect of exposure to violence on young children. *American Psychologist,* 50, 782–788.

Patterson, G., Debaryshe, B., & Ramsey, E. (1989). A developmental perspective on antisocial behavior. *American Psychologist, 144*, 329–334.

Patterson, G. R., & Forgatch, M. (1995). Predicting future clinical adjustment from treatment outcome and process variables. *Psychological Assessment, 7*, 275–285.

Petersen, G. J., Peitrzak, D., & Speaker, K. M. (1998). The enemy within: A national study on school violence and prevention. *Urban Education, 33*(3), 331–359.

Potter, L. B. (1999). Understanding the incidence and origins of community violence: Toward a comprehensive perspective of violence prevention. In T. P. Gullotta & S. J. McElhaney (Eds.), *Violence in homes and communities: Prevention, intervention, and treatment* (pp. 101–115). Thousand Oaks, CA: Sage Publications.

Price, R. H., Cowen, E. L, Lorion, R. P., & Ramos-McKay, J. (Eds.). (1988). *14 ounces of prevention: A case book for practitioners.* Washington: American Psychological Association.

Richters, J. E., & Martinez, P. (1993). The NIMH community violence project: I. Children as victims and witnesses to violence. *Psychiatry: Interpersonal and Biological Processes, 56*, 46–54.

Rosenblatt, A., & Attkisson, C. C. (1993). *The California AB377 evaluation: Three-year summary*. San Francisco: University of California.

Rudo, Z. H. (1997). Emotional, behavioral, social, and cognitive characteristics of children with serious emotional disturbances: A longitudinal comparison of physically abused versus non-abused children. (Doctoral dissertation, University of South Florida, 1997). *Dissertation Abstracts International, 58* (8), 3088.

Rudo, Z. H., Powell, D. S., & Dunlap, G. (1998). The effects of violence in the home on children's emotional, behavioral, and social functioning: A review of the literature. *Journal of Emotional and Behavioral Disorders, 6*(2), 94–113.

Sampson, R. J., & Lauritsen, J. L. (1994). Violent victimization and offending: Individual-, situational-, and community-level risk factors. In A. J. Reiss & J. A. Roth (Eds.), *Understanding and preventing violence: Volume 3. Social influences* (pp. 1–114). Washington: National Academy Press.

Schene, P. (1987). Is child abuse decreasing? *Journal of Interpersonal Violence, 2,* 225–227.

Schoenwald, S. K., Brown, T. L., & Henggeler, S. W. (2000). Inside multisystemic therapy: Therapist, supervisory, and program practices. *Journal of Emotional and Behavioral Disorders, 8*(2), 113–127.

Schwab-Stone, M. E., Ayers, T. S., & Kasprow, W. (1995). No safe haven: A study of violence exposure in an urban community. *Journal of the American Academy of Child and Adolescent Psychiatry, 34,* 1343–1352.

Schwab-Stone, M., Chen, C., Greenberger, E., Silver, D., Lichtman, J., & Voyce, C. (1999). No safe haven II: The effects of violence exposure on urban youth. *Journal of the American Academy of Child and Adolescent Psychiatry, 38,* 359–367.

Sedlak, A. J., & Broadhurst, D. D. (1996). *Executive summary of the Third National Incidence Study of Child Abuse and Neglect*. Washington: U.S. Government Printing Office.

Shakoor, B. H., & Chalmers, D. (1991). Co-victimization of African-American children who witness violence: Effects on cognitive, emotional, and behavioral development. *Journal of the National Medical Association, 83,* 233–238.

Skiba, R., & Peterson, R. (2000). School discipline at a crossroads: From zero tolerance to early response. *Exceptional Children, 66*(3), 335–347.

Singer, M. I., Anglin, T. M., Song, L. Y., & Lunghofer, L. (1994). Adolescents' exposure to violence and associated symptoms of psychological trauma. *Journal of the American Medical Association, 273,* 477–482.

Snyder, H. N. (2000 December). Juvenile arrests 1999. *Juvenile Justice Bulletin.* Washington: U.S. Department of Justice, Office of Juvenile Justice and Delinquency Prevention.

SRI International, Center for Education and Human Services. (1997). *The national longitudinal transition study: A summary of findings*. Washington: U.S. Department of Education, Office of Special Programs.

Straus, M. A. (1991). Children as witnesses to marital violence: A risk factor for lifelong problems among a nationally representative sample of American men and women. *Children and Violence: Report of the Twenty-third Ross Roundtable on Critical Approaches to Common Pediatric Problems*. Columbus, OH: Ross Laboratories.

Sugai, G., Sprague, J. R., Horner, R. H., & Walker, H. M. (2000). Preventing school violence: The use of office discipline referrals to assess and monitor school-wide discipline interventions. *Journal of Emotional and Behavioral Disorders, 8*(2), 94–101.

Thornberry, T. (1994). *Violent families and youth violence. Fact Sheet #21*. Washington: Office of Juvenile Justice and Delinquency Prevention.

Trickett, P. K. (1993). Maladaptive development of school-aged, physically abused children: Relationships with the child-rearing context. *Journal of Family Psychology, 7* (1), 134–147.

U.S. Department of Health and Human Services (DHHS), National Center on Child Abuse and Neglect (NCCAN). (2000). *Child maltreatment, 1998: Reports from the states to the National Center on Child Abuse and Neglect.* Washington: U.S. Government Printing Office.

U.S. Department of Justice. (1998). *Annual Report on School Safety,* 1998. Washington: Author.

von Bertalanffy, L. (1956). General systems theory. *General Systems.* (Yearbook of the Society for General Systems Theory, pp. 1–10).

Wagner, M. M. (1995). The outcomes of youth with serious emotional disturbance in secondary school and early adulthood: What helps? What hurts? *The Future of Children, 5*(2), 90–112.

Warner, B. S., Weist, M. D., & Krulak, A. (1999). Risk factors for school violence. *Urban Education, 34,* 52–68.

Werner, E. E. (1989). High-risk children in young adulthood: A longitudinal study from birth to 32 years. *American Journal of Orthopsychiatry, 59,* 72–81.

Werner, E. E. (1990). Protective factors and individual resilience. In S. J. Meisels & J. P. Shonkiff (Eds.), *Handbook of early childhood intervention.* New York: Cambridge University Press.

Werner, E. E., & Smith, R. S. (1982). *Vulnerable but invincible: A study of resilient children.* New York: McGraw-Hill.

Widom, C. S. (1989). Does violence beget violence? A critical review of the literature. *Psychological Bulletin, 106*(1), 3–28.

Williams, J. H., & Van Dorn, R. A. (1999). Delinquency, gangs, and youth violence. In J. M. Jenson and M. O. Howard (Eds.), *Youth violence: Current research and recent practice innovations* (pp. 199–225). Washington: National Association of Social Workers Press.

Wolfe, D. A., & Mosk, M. D. (1983). Behavioral comparisons of children from abusive and distressed families. *Journal of Consulting and Clinical Psychology, 51,* 702–708.

Yeatman, G. W., Shaw, C., Barlow, M. J., & Bartlett, G. (1976). Pseudobattering in Vietnamese children. *Pediatrics,* 58, 616.

Zunz, S. J., Turner, S., & Norman, E. (1993). Accentuating the positive: Stressing resilience in school-based substance abuse prevention programs. *Social Work in Education, 15,* 169–176.

7

Informing Professional Issues in Special Education through Disability Studies

Ann Cranston-Gingras and Crystal Roberts Ladwig

Understandings about disability among special education professionals profoundly influence the academic and social environment in which students with disabilities navigate daily. At one extreme may be those who view disability as a defect or flaw residing in the child. Their orientation is toward fixing or changing the child. Alternatively, others may see disability as largely socially constructed, focusing their efforts on changing attitudes and advocating for environmental accommodation. As the beliefs of professionals in special education may fall at either extreme and many points in between, assumptions about disability potentially impact the identity, education, and future of students with disabilities. But how are these beliefs developed? How do textbooks and other materials used in professional preparation programs affect understandings about disability? And perhaps, most critically, from whose perspective are stories about disability being told?

Teacher education texts and scholarly writings about the education of persons with disabilities are abundant. Typically designed for preservice or in-service courses for individuals preparing to teach children with disabilities, these texts and writings most often focus on the characteristics of persons with disabilities and are laden with prognostications about the capabilities and educational potential of these individuals. The most popular and widely used texts often categorize physical, emotional, cognitive, and other human variations by distinct labels such as mental retardation, learning disability, behavior disorder, and physical disability. These labels, their corresponding characteristics, and the methods and strategies developed to address them are the basis of much that has been written for educators about persons with disabilities. According to Jones (1996), this "functional limitations" framework focuses primarily on a student's limitations and strategies for dealing with them and justifying the positions of powerlessness in which students with disabilities are placed. This orientation, reinforced by an emphasis on legislatively mandated categorical eligibility for special education services, is commonly referred to as the medical model of disability and has typically dominated discussions of professional issues in special education teacher education.

Until recently, narrative accounts, lived experiences, and voices of individuals labeled disabled have been absent from the professional teacher education literature, and most notably from textbooks. Beyond the teacher education curriculum and predominantly in fields related to the humanities and social sciences, a different theme in scholarship related to persons with disabilities, namely *disability studies,* has gained momentum and has begun to appear in the special education professional literature (see, for example, Rodis, Garrod, & Boscardin, 2001).

Disability studies is informed primarily by a phenomenological perspective. From the vantage point of individuals with disabilities, it examines the societal forces affecting how people with disabilities are viewed and the effects of those views on the life experiences of persons with disabilities. Significantly, because most of the writing in disability studies has been done by scholars who themselves have disabilities, disability studies encourages professionals in fields such as special education to listen to the voices of people with disabilities. In this chapter, we examine how ideas that have emerged from disability studies can inform discussions of professional issues in special education and propose that content in disability studies be a complement to the perspectives currently included in special education teacher education.

THE AUTHORS

Whether one has to be a person with a disability to engage in professional discourse about disability studies is a question that has been seriously debated. Bragg (1998) contends that "at a bare minimum one has to be in comfortable and committed contact with the community that one writes about" (p. 1). As the authors of this chapter, we feel that for the most part we meet Bragg's minimum criterion. We are also keenly aware of the limits and biases of our perspectives. Interspersed in this chapter, we offer brief accounts from our own personal stories in an attempt to provide glimpses of our identities as individuals whose beliefs and actions have in large part been shaped by our experiences with persons with disabilities. As the first author of this chapter, I (Ann Cranston-Gingras) share the following introductory perspective:

As the sibling, niece and spouse of persons with physical disabilities, I have benefited from a lifetime of familial sharing with the community of persons with disabilities. My childhood memories of day-to-day activity, as well as holidays and celebrations, are filled with images of cherished family members and friends who had visible and significant disabilities. My younger brother, who is now a successful professional, was born with seven broken bones as a result of congenital osteogenesis imperfecta and not expected to live past infancy.

Although he has never walked, and if he could stand, he would be only about three feet tall, he has been the leader among our five siblings. The struggle children of his generation and their parents waged for the right to appropriate education was debated many times in my own living room, and as a young child I witnessed the hope and the fears that educational opportunity for children with significant disabilities brought.

As a teenager and young adult, I worked at a summer camp for children with disabilities, which was part of a national demonstration institute. There, I met fellow college students and professionals who had disabilities. Several have now been friends for decades. When I moved to a new city after college, it turned out a friend from camp had also moved to the same city to work in a hospital for children with disabilities. He introduced me to a coworker who is now my husband. He, too, is a person with a disability. For over twenty years, I have worked in the fields of special education and migrant education, focusing my career on the educational issues affecting individuals who have been marginalized by schools and society.

Though her experiences have been very different, the second author (Crystal Ladwig) also has had close, personal relationships with individuals who have disabilities. These relationships have helped her consider her own identity and her role in relation to people with disabilities:

I first began working in the special education field at the age of 17. At that time, I was not considering a career in education at all. Through this part-time job, however, I quickly began to feel a connection with young children with disabilities and their families. As a child and adolescent, personal experiences had led me to feel isolated. In college, I worked for the local school system in a job that again provided the opportunity to develop relationships with children with disabilities and their families. At the same time, through an organization called Best Buddies, I became friends with a woman with Down syndrome. I soon found myself committed to a career in special education. As a special educator, I now see myself in a number of different roles, including advocate, activist, supporter, educator, and friend.

DISABILITY STUDIES

Medical, psychological, and social theorists have attempted to explain disability form a variety of perspectives and most notably from an outsider's point of view. Closely aligned with other critical perspectives such as feminist theory and ethnic studies, the field of disability studies seeks to address factors influencing the lives of individuals with disabilities from the perspective of the insider. It places "disability in a political, social and cultural context that theorizes and historicizes deafness or blindness or disability in similarly complex ways to how race, class and gender have been theorized" (Davis, 1997, p. 3). Examining disability as lived experience, scholars in disability studies seek to present "an account of the world negotiated from the vantage point of the atypical" (Linton, 1998, p. 5).

Key to an understanding of disability studies is the recognition and understanding of the social construction of disability and the concept of "normal." Davis (1997) places the concept of the norm as first appearing in the English language during the mid-nineteenth century. The construction of the concept of normalcy informs understandings of the concept of disability. Normalcy implies that individuals should fall within a pre-established norm. Any deviation or extreme not falling within the normal range for a trait can effectively create a disability. But how are societal norms determined? Thomson (1997a) argues that norms are merely "a hypothetical set of guidelines for corporeal form and function arising from cultural expectations about how human beings should look and act" (pp. 6–7). Those individuals whose constructed identities define them as "normal" assume positions of authority and power. Such power has been wielded forcibly against individuals with disabilities. Eugenicists grouped together those with "undesirable" traits so that criminal, poor, and disabled became synonymous. Forced sterilization policies attempted to purge from society all individuals deemed unworthy. Institutions housed individuals with disabilities in deplorable living environments under policies that were considered "best practice." For many years, children with certain disabilities were not allowed to attend school, and those who were faced segregation and stigmatization. For a detailed examination of the history of the treatment of individuals with disabilities, one can refer to Davis (1997), Barton and Oliver (1997), and Thomson (1997a).

Disability studies arose as people with disabilities began to politicize themselves and discuss what Barton and Oliver (1997) term the "experience of disablement." The illusory nature of the term "disability" is evident in the Americans with Disabilities Act of 1990 that states that in order to have a disability, one must be "regarded as having such an impairment." Thomson (1997a) defined disability as "the attribution of corporeal deviance—not so much a property of bodies as a product of cultural rules about what bodies should be or do" (p. 6).

Clearly, the notion of disability is subject to social and political construction. Individuals in the deaf community, for example, as well as many individuals with physical disabilities, often do not consider themselves disabled. While persons who are deaf often consider themselves to be in a linguistic minority rather than disabled, other individuals society calls disabled see themselves as normal in their everyday life activities. How others may view them, however, is another issue.

An outcome of including the voices of persons with disabilities in the academic arena is that knowledge of disability, usually relegated to those medical, therapeutic, and educational personnel who work with individuals with disabilities, is entering the realm of cultural studies. This places "disability" in a political, economic, social, and cultural context (Davis, 1997; Thomson, 1997b; Harris & Lewin, 1998). Disability studies examine history, literature, and sociology in a similar fashion as other areas of cultural study including race, class, and gender (Ramirez, 1997). It attempts to critically analyze the concept and construction of "disability" as well as the resulting societal implications (Monaghan, 1998). The goals, therefore, are not understanding and sympathy (Davis, 1997), but a political movement attempting to break down "the barriers that limit people with disabilities from full participation in their communities and in society in general" (Harris & Lewin, 1998, p. 1).

ISSUES OF DISCRIMINATION

Singer (1993) advocates giving parents of newborns with disabilities the opportunity to end their children's lives so that they may focus on the birth of another infant with "better prospects of a happy life" (p. 186). Acknowledging that people with disabilities may object to his proposal because it suggests that their lives are not as worthwhile as those of people without disabilities, Singer adds, "It is surely flying in the face of reality to deny that, on average, this is so" (p. 188). Attitudes and practices such as those suggested by Singer are often justified on utilitarian grounds, placing diminished moral value on individuals with disabilities. As surprising as Singer's proposal may be, his arguments are consistent with those given in the John Hopkins (Diamond, 1977) and Baby Doe (*United States v University Hospital, State of New York at Stony Brook*, 1984) cases in which medical treatment was intentionally withheld from infants with congenital disabilities on the grounds that death for the infant was a better alternative than life with a disability.

> When my brother was born, my parents were told about all the things he would never be able to do and about the burden he would be to his family. They were told not to expect much for his future. They weren't told that he would be a brilliant child with a captivating personality or that his spirit would inspire not only his siblings but people from all walks of life. No one told them that, through his profession, my brother would help countless children with respiratory illnesses and that the parents of those children would be grateful that my parents had not lowered their expectations. (*Ann Cranston-Gingras*)

Absent almost entirely from the conversations about the value of life for individuals with disabilities have been the voices of those in the best position to judge the quality. Writing about what he would say to the obstetrician who, after delivering him, advised his mother to put him in an institution and tell people he had died, Jason Kingsley, an author with Down syndrome, says: "I will tell him that I play the violin, that I make relationships with other people. I make oil paintings. I play the piano. I can sing. I am competing in sports, in the drama group, that I have many friends and I have a full life" (Kingsley & Levitz, 1994, p. 28). Perhaps more than in any other field, professionals in special education consistently demonstrate a commitment to "helping" individuals with disabilities lead "a full life." However, despite our best intentions, discriminatory practices in our field often place students with disabilities on the "cultural periphery" (Kliewer, 1998, p. 3).

> Early in my teaching career, I encountered an unforgettable situation. I accepted a position teaching at a high school in a small school district that had been sending all of its students identified as having mental retardation to a neighboring district with the rationale that they didn't have enough students to support a program. For legal reasons, the specifics of which I never knew, the year I was employed some of the students were being brought back to the district. I was hired to teach a group of students identified as educably mentally handicapped and to arrange mainstreaming opportunities for them. Since I had previously been a high school English teacher, the first teachers I approached to talk about "mainstreaming" were the English teachers. I will never forget how visibly angry one of the veteran teachers was when he said to me, " It ruined my whole summer when I heard those kids were coming here." Those kids, of course, were his kids. They lived in his district. They were his neighbors. Their siblings attended that school. It was their school. (*Ann Cranston-Gingras*)

By focusing on accommodating individual student "problems," educators have placed responsibility for fitting in on the students with disabilities, relieving ourselves from having to face our prejudices and stereotypes about disability. Under inclusion policies, students with special education designations are democratically ushered into schools, but their status often remains that of outsider, their specific learning, physical, and social characteristics seen as justification for alienation. The characteristics of individuals with disabilities are considered pathological and inferior (Thomson, 1997a), giving power and control to those without disabilities. Informed by notions of student difference and deviance, professional discourse focuses on how the child can be changed to blend into the environment. Students with disabilities learn that they need special invitations for normal experiences.

> The elementary school where I taught had three continuous progress (CP) houses. CP houses consisted of four to five classes with three different grade levels in one open pod. Students within these houses received instruction within mixed-age ability groups. When I heard our school was going to open up another CP house, I approached my administration about placing my EMH class within

this setting. The opportunities for inclusion, mainstreaming, and collaboration would be extensive. The administrators supported my idea and agreed to send me, along with other interested teachers, to the required in-service training. As the training date approached, I was informed that my name had been taken off the list of teachers attending the in-service. The explanation given to me was that there were "too many regular education kids that could benefit" from the CP house. Needless to say, my self-contained class remained just that, self-contained. (*Crystal Ladwig*)

Personal accounts of estrangement by individuals with disabilities themselves or from family members can help shift the discourse away from the student with a disability and the disability itself toward individuals in the environment forcing them to confront their own beliefs about every student's worth in school and society. Linton (1996), a scholar in disability studies, notes that "inclusion is not an educational plan to benefit disabled children. It is a model for educating all children equitably" (p. 61). Disability studies pushes issues of bias and discrimination to the forefront. Through a personal account, Olkin (1998), a university professor, provides the following example of how this type of thinking reframes the discourse regarding people with disabilities:

Often at work I've been asked whether I will be attending specific events. The unasked question is, "Do we need to pick a place that's physically accessible?" My response is that it doesn't matter whether I will be attending or not. In either case, the site must be accessible. Irrespective of my attendance, there is a compelling moral reason why a site must be accessible. To bring this point home to faculty, I have asked this question: "Would you hold this function at a site that didn't allow Jews? Would it be relevant to that decision whether someone Jewish was actually in attendance or not?" This question reframes the problem. . . . We now focus on the environment, not on me, the person with a disability. . . . We translate "You can't climb stairs" to "Why isn't there a ramp?" We could focus on the faculty and ask the question: "Why is the faculty holding its meeting in a place that is not accessible?" We could focus on the community and ask: "Why was this building erected without due consideration of accessibility for persons with disabilities?" We could also focus on the sociopolitical arena and ask: "Why do we tolerate discrimination against our citizens?" and "At what cost do we do so?" (p. 110.)

IDENTITY ISSUES

Bogdan and Taylor (1994) suggest that the impact of differences depends largely on how individuals perceive them. Whereas the physical manifestations of a disability are widely considered to originate from within the body, the experience of disability is largely outside the body (Davis, 1998). This is often manifested in barriers to physical access, communication, equality of educational opportunities, and outright prejudice (Barton & Oliver, 1997). For example, individuals without disabilities often do not recognize the impact of their language on the social identity of people with disabilities. We often hear phrases such as the football team that *suffers crippling* defeats or the golfer who has a *handicap* score to make him equal with his peers. Such offensive language becomes part of the everyday vernacular.

Howard (2000) reports that analyses of media portrayals reveal that language and nonverbal expressions work together to construct the identities of those depicted. Davis (1998) observed that many novels portray individuals with disabilities as villains, victims, desexualized, and devitalized. Safran (1998) found similar results in his review of Academy Award winning movies portraying individuals with disabilities. Common representations of individuals with disabilities included sinister, evil, or criminal characters; "super-crip" or overachieving individuals; and pitiable, pathetic, and dependent personalities. Such analyses provide a global perspective of society's images of individuals with disabilities.

Thomson (1999) explains that she chose the term "extraordinary," for her 1997 text, *Extraordinary Bodies*, as a way to "reconceive disability as simply bodily variation rather than lack, excess or abnormality" (p. 51). Thought of this way disability becomes part of the common human experience and identity.

The notion of disability as a socially constructed label pervades the literature in disability studies. This label with its underlying assumptions influences understandings about the identity of individuals with disabilities, not only by society at large but also among people with disabilities themselves. Disability studies prompt an examination of issues regarding the identity of those society labels disabled. Unlike other cultural minorities, individuals with disabilities often do not have role models or elders from whom to glean their identities. Personal narratives and autobiographies offer individuals with disabilities a chance to "say who they are" (Rodis, Garrod, & Boscardin, 2001, p. xiv) contributing to self- and group identity. French (1999) shares her feelings about growing up in a world where she felt misunderstood and the joy she experienced at meeting others with whom she could identify:

> How often these conflicting exchanges occurred I cannot say, but I can still experience the feelings they induced; feelings of isolation, difference and shame. These feelings were made worse by my inability to explain my behavior, even to myself although I always knew that I was right and "they" were wrong. Experiences such as these had an adverse effect on my self-esteem and confidence which only began to abate when, in an abusive boarding school at the age of nine, I met other girls like me. Living our lives together, having them as my friends and knowing they shared my world was nothing short of joy. These deeply rooted friendships are still important; they have buffered my life. (p. 22)

Deficit-oriented perspectives in the literature have often extended beyond individuals with disabilities to their family members as well. Goffman (1963) called this "courtesy stigma" that devalues family members of persons with disabilities. Parent deficit models in education have assigned blame for children's disabilities on parents, placing the professional in an expert role. In contrast, family-centered models informed by disability studies emphasize the importance of familial influence in educational planning and practice. Parents and professionals who examine their conceptions of children with disabilities and how their beliefs about and education for these children differ and how they are similar are taking a positive step toward more effective parent-professional relationships (Danseco, 1997).

Increasingly, parents of children with disabilities are representing their experiences through narratives. In the Epilogue to his book *Life As We Know It*, Berube (1996), a scholar and father of a child with Down syndrome, reflects on his representation of his son James:

> In these pages, I have tried to represent James to the best of my ability. I have done so in the belief that my textual representations of him might make his claims on the world as broadly and as strongly as possible. I know full well that textual representation is only one form of representation. Nothing I write will redraw a political district; nothing I write will change the chemical composition of Jamie's cells. . . . And as he sleeps and as I write, we debate the meaning of words like 'normal,' 'retarded,' 'disability,' and, underwriting all these, 'justice.' My task ethically and aesthetically is to represent James to you with all the fidelity that mere language can afford, the better to enable you to imagine him—and to imagine what he might think of your ability to imagine him. . . . My job, for now, is to represent my son, to set his place at our collective table. But I know I am merely trying my best to prepare for the day he sets his own place. For I have no sweeter dream than to imagine—aesthetically and ethically and parentally—that Jamie will someday be his own advocate, his own author, his own best representative. (pp. 263–264)

IMPLICATIONS FOR THE CURRICULUM

Teacher education programs have included courses on disability for several decades. However, as noted by Linton (1998), and discussed earlier in this chapter, both the structure and the content of the curriculum have been predicated on narrowly conceived notions of disability and void of the significant personal perceptions of individuals with disabilities. In addition, because such courses have been traditionally offered within applied discipline-specific programs, student participation has been limited to program majors. Disability studies afford a vantage point for examining and interpreting exceptionality, not only as part of the teacher preparation curriculum, but also within a liberal arts framework. Dirksen, Bauman, and Drake (1997) have advocated for including perspectives from deaf culture in the teacher education curriculum, and Taylor (1996) argues that principles associated with disability studies should be applied to the study of mental retardation. Beyond the teacher education curriculum, others (Adrian, 1997; Davis and Linton, 1995) have proposed options for inclusion of disability studies within university-wide programs, including the development of an interdisciplinary liberal arts course as part of general education requirements and incorporating disability studies within other liberal arts courses.

At the University of South Florida we have developed a course called Narrative Perspectives on Exceptionality: Cultural and Ethical Issues. The course is required for all special education majors and is offered as an elective exit requirement for students throughout the university. It provides an opportunity for students to interpret exceptionalities through the personal perspectives of individuals with disabilities, their families, and those who play a role in their lives. In addition to narrative accounts written by individuals with disabilities and their families, students also read literary portrayals, both fiction and nonfiction, of individuals with disabilities. Following each reading, students reflect in writing about the perspectives encountered in their reading. These perspectives and the students' reactions to them are used to inform discussions about practices in education and the role of ethics and values in decisions made regarding individuals with disabilities.

CONCLUSION

Individuals with disabilities have been largely excluded from the professional discourse in special education. This has contributed to the construction of cultural stereotypes regarding children with disabilities in school, the estrangement and disempowerment of those the field intends to serve, and the development of inadequate curricula to prepare special education teachers. Disability studies offer an opportunity for authentic representation by individuals most affected by special education policies and practices. Informed by a disability studies perspective, we can rethink professional issues in the field and address issues of discrimination, both intended and unintended.

DISCUSSION QUESTIONS

1. How has the traditional focus on the medical model of disability influenced the teacher education curriculum?
2. In what ways does disability studies reflect a cultural perspective of disability?
3. How is the identity of children with disabilities influenced by school culture?
4. In what ways can disability studies inform the teacher education curriculum and the education of children with disabilities?

REFERENCES

Adrian, S. E. (1997). Disability, society, and ethical issues: A first-year experience for university students. *Intervention in School and Clinic, 32*, 178–184.

Barton, L. & Oliver, M. (1997). Disability studies: past, present and future. Leeds: The Disability Press.

Berube, M. (1996). *Life as we know it.* New York: Vintage Books.

Bogdan, R., & Taylor, S. J. (1994). *The social meaning of mental retardation: Two life stories.* New York: Teachers College.

Bragg, L. (1998). Planet of the normates. *American Anthropologist, 100*, 177–180.

Danseco, E.R. (1997). Parental beliefs on childhood disability: Insights on culture, child development and intervention. *International Journal of Disability, Development, and Education, 44*, 41–52.

Davis, L. (1997). *The disability studies reader.* London: Routledge.

Davis, L. (1998). Who put the *the* in the novel? Identity politics and disability in novel studies. *Novel, 31*(3), 317–334.

Davis, L., & Linton, S. (1995) Introduction: Disability studies. *Radical Teacher, 47*, 2–3.

Diamond, E. (1977). The deformed child's right to life. In D. J. Horan and D. Mall (Eds.), *Death, dying and euthanasia.* Washington: University Publications of America.

Dirksen, H., Bauman, L., & Drake, J. (1997). Silence is not without voice: Including deaf culture within multicultural curricula. In L. Davis (Ed.), *The disability studies reader.* Routledge: London.

French, S. (1999). The wind gets in my way. In M. Corker and S. French (Eds.), *Disability discourse.* Philadelphia: Open University Press.

Goffman, E. (1963). *Stigma: Notes on the management of a spoiled identity.* Harmonsworth: Penguin.

Harris, P., & Lewin, L. (1998). Information package on disability studies [online]. Available: http://eweb.syr.edu/thechp/dspacket.htm#autobiographies.

Howard, J. (2000). Social psychology of identities. *Annual Review of Sociology, 26*, 367–393.

Jones, S. R. (1996). Toward inclusive theory: disability as social construction. *NASPA Journal, 33*, 347–354.

Kingsley, J. and Levitz, M. (1994). *Count us in: Growing up with Down syndrome.* Harvest Books.

Kliewer, C. (1998). *Schooling children with Down syndrome.* New York: Teachers College Press.

Linton, S. (1998). *Claiming disability.* New York: New York University Press.

Monaghan, P. (1998, January 23). Pioneering field of disability studies challenges established approaches and attitudes. *Chronicle of Higher Education.*

Olkin, R. (1998). Psychosocial dimensions of polio and post-polio syndrome. In Lauro S. Halstead (Ed.), *Managing post-polio.* Arlington, VA: ABI Professional Publishers.

Ramirez, A. (1997, December 21). Disability as a field of study? *New York Times.*

Rodis, P., Garrod, A. & Boscardin, M. L. (2001). *Learning Disabilities and Life Stories.* Boston: Allyn and Bacon.

Safran, S. P. (1998). Disability portrayal in film: Reflecting the past, directing the future. *Exceptional Children, 64*(2), 227–238.

Singer, P. (1993). *Practical ethics.* New York: Cambridge University Press.

Taylor, S. (1996). Disability studies and mental retardation. *Disability Studies Quarterly, 16*, 4–13.

Thomson, R. G. (1997a). *Extraordinary bodies: Figuring physical disability in American culture and literature.* New York: Columbia University Press.

Thomson, R. G. (1997b). Integrating disability studies into the existing curriculum: The example of "Women and Literature" at Howard University. In L. Davis (Ed.), *The disability studies reader.* London: Routledge.

Thomson, R.G. (1999). The new disability studies: Inclusion or tolerance? *ADFL Bulletin, 31*, 49–53.

United States v University Hospital, State University of New York at Stony Brook, 729 F. 144 (2nd Cir. 1984).

8

The Teacher Variable: Who Makes Education Special?

James L. Paul and Patricia A. Parrish

Sarah Johnson walks into her fifth-grade classroom at Northridge Elementary School where twenty-six students eagerly await the beginning of school. She is a recent graduate of a well-known teacher education program where she excelled in all of her work. She also is an only child from an upper middle-class family, and her ambition has always been to become a teacher. She had not anticipated teaching in a school where 96 percent of the students are provided free lunch. "Good morning class," she begins, "my name is Ms. Johnson and I am your teacher."

Marvin Snyder is in his late thirties and is wearing khaki pants and an aqua, short-sleeve shirt with a small Dolphins insignia on the front as he walks into his eighth-grade class for students with learning disabilities at Hampton Middle School. He is tall, has a muscular build, and speaks slowly with a deep southern drawl. He has been at Hampton Middle School for six years and has a history of being a strong disciplinarian. Students have heard stories about Mr. Snyder's class. He begins, "Good morning class, my name is Mr. Snyder and I am your teacher."

Brenda Hines is retiring this year. She has had serious medical problems for the last five years, and she has looked forward to having some time with her husband and grandchildren. She has taught second grade at Browning

Elementary School for 34 years and is loved by her students and their parents, and is a source of support and encouragement for the faculty and staff at the school. If there is a special heaven for teachers, all who know her and have ever been taught by her know that she will have a prominent place there. She walks slowly, with slumped posture as she enters the room to find 26 fidgeting students, most with radiant, smiling faces. Mirroring their smiles and visibly filled with joy at being there, she begins, "Good morning class, my name is Mrs. Hines and I am your teacher."

Laurie Henderson is an attractive woman in her early forties, although she looks older. She spends little time in the teachers' lounge and at times she seems aloof and uneasy with others, including her students. She has taught biology and chemistry at Wharton High School for two years. No one except Yolanda Hernandez, the assistant pricnipal, knows any of her personal story. She is in an abusive relationship and sometimes comes to school wearing long-sleeve blouses and excessive makeup to cover bruises on her face. She had missed two weeks of school during her first year at Wharton because she was hospitalized as a result of an attempted suicide. She enters her biology class and, in a soft voice, greets her students, "Good morning class, my name is Mrs. Henderson and I am your teacher."

Marcus Thomas has been teaching at Newton Middle School for four years. He is respected by his colleagues on the faculty and by the administration. His time at Newton has not been without difficulties. Located in a low SES, white neighborhood, some of the parents were less than welcoming of Mr. Thomas, the first African-American teacher in the school. One of his biggest challenges came last year when Billy Martin, the son of a local merchant, had become unmanageable in his class. Mr. Thomas had referred Billy to the school psychologist who interviewed Billy and observed him in class. The psychologist believed him to have a serious behavioral disorder. Mr. Martin, Billy's father, believed the problem was Mr. Thomas. The issues were complex and difficult to address. Mr. Thomas was supported by the principal and his colleagues, but the process had taken a toll. Wearing navy dress pants and a white shirt with a tie, Mr. Thomas enters his new class for the year, "Good morning class, my name is Mr. Thomas and I am your teacher."

WHO ARE THE TEACHERS AND HOW DO WE ASSESS THEIR INFLUENCE?

Who are these people who call themselves "teacher?" They have in common the fact that they occupy the office of "teacher," have completed a program in teacher education, are employed in a place called school, and are authorized to teach students. They vary, however, in gender, race, age, values, and personal life circumstances. Each of them brings a different experience to school and each of them means something different in the classroom.

Long ago most of us lost our innocence about "teacher-proofing" instruction. The teacher not only delivers but, in many respects, is the curriculum. He/she brings values, feelings, and attitudes into the classroom as well as subject-matter knowledge. Students learn content knowledge in the context of a culture and a classroom environment with emotional qualities that vary from teacher to teacher. The variability goes well beyond matters of curriculum or classroom structure, and well beyond whether or not the teacher practices direct instruction or believes in phonics. It involves, for example, the teacher's feelings about children, his/her implicit views of power and how it is exercised in the classroom, his/her views of race, ethnicity, and gender differences, and his/her tacit knowledge of the emotional lives and vulnerabilities of children. It involves the teacher's moral perspectives, his/her beliefs about education, and his/her role as a teacher.

Some interesting questions can be raised when teaching is viewed in this way. What type of lasting impact will each of these teachers have on their students? Which teachers will have the most power in influencing the lives and values of students, and why is that? What type of lasting memories will their students carry with them from these classrooms? In addition to content knowledge, what feelings and attributions of self-value will they carry with them from the hundreds of hours they will spend in these teachers' classrooms? What will the students learn about themselves as poor? female? Latino? Asian? African American? Native American? What will they learn about themselves as having limited intellectual capacity, as being unable to learn at the same levels as other students, or as able to learn faster than others? What will they learn about respect? Equity? Fairness? Cultural history? Should these outcomes be considered as important as academic outcomes?

Outcome accountability in schools focuses on the measurable content-knowledge and academic skills. It does not focus on the qualities of teaching and instructional environments and relationships that, many would argue, are not objectively measurable. The kind of citizens students ultimately become is certainly related to the subject-matter knowledge and academic skills they learn. However, their values, sense of responsibility, caring about social issues, and predisposition to respond to the needs of others, for example, are qualities of character. The recent emphasis on character education in schools reflects a growing recognition of the importance of teachers in impacting the character development of their students (DeVries, Hildebrandt, & Zan, 2000; Halbig, 2000; Krajewski & Bailey, 1999).

CHANGING THE PHILOSOPHICAL LENS AND
SEEING TEACHING DIFFERENTLY

Teacher education programs generally focus on what teachers need to know and to be able to do, not so much on whom they need to be. The teachers' personal values and sensibilities are not central concerns in the teacher education curriculum. The student's ability to learn and to function successfully in the classroom is much more than a matter of measured intelligence or prior learning history. It is embedded in the relationship with the teacher and the culture of the classroom. Personal and professional ethics grounded in principles of equity, fairness, and care, for example, are vital to a teacher's approach to teaching and behavior management. Educational ethnographies (Gordon, 1998; Lipman, 1997; Noblit, 1993) and studies of teacher behavior (Crone, 1995; Ladd, 1999; Short, 1999; Wentzel, 1997) have amply documented the moral and social as well as academic content of teaching and learning in classrooms.

Teacher educators have begun to focus on more than academic skills and mechanistic behavior control strategies (see Fagan and Taylor, chapter 9). They are required, on the one hand, to prepare teachers who are able to teach academic content and skills that are measured in high-stakes tests. On the other hand, they are challenged by critical and feminist scholars, for example, to incorporate deeper understandings of the culture, politics, and moralities of classrooms (Wink, 1997).

Teacher educators are not unaware of the force of personality and values in teaching and the need to be more selective of candidates in preservice teacher education programs. They are not unaware of the need for more supervised teaching and clinical experiences for preservice teachers. However, they are faced with many barriers in making needed changes including, but not limited to, the amount of time allotted to the education and training of teachers, the market demand for teachers exceeding the supply, certification requirements, and the ethical as well as technical difficulties in accounting for variables that are not objectively measurable.

These professional, technical, and political challenges over the last two decades have contributed to an increasingly complex literature in teacher education. What is at issue are the changing ways of seeing and understanding the nature and foundations of teaching and learning. The emergence of alternatives to positivist epistemologies that grounded theories of knowledge in the natural sciences reverberated through the social sciences in the latter half of the twentieth century and, more recently, has problematized traditional understandings of teacher knowledge.

Changes in theories of teaching, learning, and ethics reflect the shift that is challenging the political hegemony of objectivist epistemology. Interestingly, the shift from positivism has not been made to another epistemology.

Rather, there now exists an intellectual environment in which alternative epistemologies, and even perspectives that challenge epistemology as a defensible stance (Rorty, 1989), vie for authoritative voice. Postpositivism and constructivism are the most prominent perspectives now guiding research in education. However, postmodern social theory and other nonpositivist views are part of the intellectual conversation about knowledge.

How, then, do we understand teaching, learning, and the experience of students? Several perspectives with different assumptions about teacher knowledge are being employed to interpret teaching and learning, five of which are: postpositivism (Schein, 1972; Zeichner, 1999), constructivism (Harris & Graham, 1994; Staver, 1998), critical theory (Wink, 1997), narrative theory (Eisner, 1997; Postman, 1996), and postmodern social theory (Elkind, 1997; Heshusius, 1994). Each of these is discussed briefly with examples of the difference the view makes in what we see and understand about teaching and learning. Following this discussion, we describe an existential approach to the study of teaching and learning through the memories of adults. The focus is on how students experience and remember their interactions with teachers.

We believe there are silences about life in the classroom that have been largely unexplored because the student's experience is not observable by an educational anthropologist, for example, and even clinical interviews are limited by the vocabularies and concepts available to children in interpreting and communicating their experiences. We explore the remembered classroom as a venue for student voices to tell untold stories and to reduce the silence. It is a part of knowing something about teaching and learning that is different than what positivist epistemologies have allowed. We believe, and our own research is helping us understand, that variability in student behavior, traditionally explained by essentialists' constructs of disability or disorder, is often much more complex than our theories about learning and behavior have allowed us to see. Our purpose is not to eliminate essentialist arguments. It is, rather, to contribute to the conversation about the experiences of students and the theories employed to explain them.

In studying what is remembered as caring and having a positive impact on one's life or what was experienced as cruel and demeaning and having a destructive impact, we are not interested in the factuality of the memory. The only reality that interests us is the story the person has carried with him/her about being special and cared for, or being mistreated and humiliated by a teacher. The issue is not "good teaching" as reflected in how much a student learned about computation, geography, or science; it is about a child's response to being treated well or cruelly and how this has impacted his or her adult life.

JUSTIFYING REASONS FOR DIFFERENT WAYS OF UNDERSTANDING TEACHING AND LEARNING: ALTERNATIVE EPISTEMOLOGIES

Positivist and Postpositivist Epistemologies

Positivist and postpositivist epistemologies view knowledge as "a formal set of law-like regularities, and the purpose of social science is to predict and control behavior by discovering and explaining these universal laws" (Andrews, 1989, p. 109). Although there are fundamental differences between positivism and postpositivism, they share the assumptions of a preexisting, external, objective reality and are, therefore, discussed together in this context.) Positivism has a realist ontology (Borland, 1990) and an objectivist epistemology (Guba, 1990). While logical positivism of the earlier part of the century is not widely accepted today, positivists and postpositivists do view humans as capable of apprehending objective reality through sensory perceptions (critical realism), however flawed those perceptions may be.

In teacher education, positivist and postpositivist research has led to microteaching, competency-based courses, and interaction analysis (Zeichner, 1999). The goal of such research is to describe pedagogical knowledge that will improve teaching behaviors (Schein, 1972). This approach to teacher education and teacher education research has been dominant during the twentieth century. In the 1970s almost all research in teacher education focused on experimental or quasi-experimental designs with the belief that short-term, measurable changes in teacher behavior would increase student learning, as measured on standardized tests (Zeichner, 1999). This perspective puts teacher behavior, not teacher cognition or teacher affect, at the center of teacher education. Such beliefs have given rise to the attempt to "teacher-proof" the curriculum. In other words if the curriculum and text books associated with it are strong enough, the teacher will be able to follow them without much risk of poor performance and student scores on standardized tests will improve. Again, this belief leads teacher education programs to focus on pedagogical knowledge rather than self-knowledge.

Constructivist Epistemology

The constructivist epistemology focuses on knowledge as created rather than discovered. A basic premise of constructivism is that the self is at the center of knowledge and understanding, and therefore one cannot construct knowledge separately from who she is and what she experiences. Staver (1998) observes that experience is the connection with the world beyond the self.

As a theory of education, constructivism purports that the learner must actively construct knowledge through interactions with her world (Harris & Graham, 1994; Staver, 1998). Therefore, the teacher becomes a facilitator of learning rather than a transmitter of knowledge. From the constructivist perspective, the purpose of teacher education changes from transmission of pedagogical knowledge to the exploration of environmental structure. The teacher in training needs to develop a sense of self so that she can then apply this self-knowledge in facilitating her students' learning. Self-knowledge is critical for teachers who, through their interactions and communications with students, help create the reality in which both teacher and student live.

Critical Epistemology

Critical epistemology subscribes to the critical realist ontology of postpositivism, but to a subjective epistemology (Guba, 1990). Popkewitz (1990) characterizes science as a "matrix of research," including both quantitative and qualitative methods. The purpose of critical theory, according to Andrews (1989), is to conduct "social research . . . to understand a given situation within its historical context to free those researched from whatever claims to restrict understanding and progress" (p. 112). Because situations are explored within their historical contexts, including the present, theory is seen as grounded and emergent (Andrews, 1989). Context and knowledge are inextricably linked, each creating and changing the other.

Power is a central issue in critical science (Popkewitz, 1990). Noblit (1993) discusses the need for teachers to learn to use their power judiciously and to protect the rights of students. While the power differential cannot be completely removed, the teacher can learn to use her power to motivate and to affirm her students rather than to control them (Noblit, 1993).

The goal of critical pedagogy, which is an outgrowth of critical theory, is to generate knowledge that extends past the classroom and into the world. For example, Wink (1997) has outlined a curricular approach designed to help teachers and students recognize social injustice and then to work for change. Teachers in training will need the skills to connect their classrooms to the world, to develop and use experiential learning, and to help students critically evaluate their social and political contexts.

Narrative Epistemology

Narrative epistemology employs a storied approach to research. The stories that are told by researchers can be autobiographical or can describe the lived experiences of others; the key is that the story provides a context and a meaning to what is described. Each unique story helps its writer make sense of her culture and her actions (Bochner, Ellis, & Tillmann-Healy, 1997). The narrative perspective builds knowledge within a subjective epistemology and focuses on the interpretation of the language used in the story. How the story is interpreted can vary from reading to reading.

The self takes a central position in narrative inquiry. Bochner (1994) explains that autobiography is "encouraged and legitimated" (p. 33) in this type of inquiry. Because the researcher is encouraged to interpret and provide meaning to her work, the self also becomes one of the tools of research.

The narrative perspective can be a critical component of teacher education in that the preservice teacher can explore the attitudes and beliefs that helped him choose his career path (Zeichner, 1999). If a preservice teacher is able to explore his past experiences with education, that knowledge may be useful in thinking about how he is inclined to teach and how he is likely to interact with students. The letter writing activity described later in this chapter is an example of the use of narrative to help an individual think about what informs her views of teaching.

Postmodern Epistemology

Postmodern epistemology rejects the belief in a grand theory or meta-narrative (Gary, 1997). This rejection of grand theory goes beyond the subjectivism of constructivist theory. Heshusius (1994) describes constructivist subjectivity as a reaction to the objectivity of modernity. She describes postmodernism as focusing on participatory consciousness, a way of interacting with the world in which the knower and the known enter into a higher level of kinship. The knowledge derived from this level of consciousness is completely individual (Loving, 1997) and recognizes the connection between knowledge and power (Griffiths, 1995).

Postmodern epistemology focuses on the contingency of language. Rorty (1989) describes language as a series of metaphors. Any meaning that can be derived from these metaphors is completely contextual and a function of the social beliefs of its users. Wittgenstein described such language games as the inability of words to describe certain concepts when he stated, "What we cannot speak about we must consign to silence" (Wittgenstein, 1961, p. 151). The contingency of language combined with the anti-foundational stance of postmodernism leads to the deconstruction of language. Loving (1997) explains that "in its purest form, deconstruction theory suggests the *only* meaning of a text comes from the reader's interpretation" [italics in text] (p. 434). Therefore, there is no foundational knowledge that is true for everyone (Griffiths, 1995), but rather each person constructs a personal "reality" based on her individual use of and meaning assigned to the metaphors of language.

The postmodern perspective, especially its focus on the self, has several implications for teacher education. The curricula should celebrate individual experience and not privilege any group. The teacher education curriculum needs to assist teachers in understanding political issues in the classroom and in building common metaphors to enable students to developing a participatory consciousness. These goals of education are incompatible with traditional forms of assessment (Elkind, 1997), so teacher education programs need to provide information regarding alternate forms of assessment, including performance based and portfolio assessments.

THE RECONSTRUCTION OF TEACHING AND LEARNING THROUGH MEMORY

The first author has been studying adult memories of the emotional qualities of the classroom for over a decade. In this study, adults have been assisted in remembering teachers and writing letters to those who stand out in their memories as being especially caring and thoughtful or cruel and hurtful. The letters are written in group settings, and individuals are given an opportunity to share their letter if they choose.

Examining a database of over 800 letters, it is clear that adults have strong emotional memories of their teachers. They reconstruct their emotional memories with the benefit of adult concepts and vocabularies and, in doing so, resurrect early experiences in school that had profound impacts on their lives. They bring a perspective and meaning to those memories they never had as children. While sharing their letters, adults often weep with joy as they remember a teacher who rescued them from the attention of the class in grade three when the welfare worker came to school to interview them, or a teacher who attended the funeral of the father of a fifth grader. Some, even in their 50s and 60s, weep as they remember being humiliated by a teacher in the second grade, or being embarrassed by a physical education teacher in the ninth grade.

Following are two letters written to teachers remembered as caring:

Dear Mr. B,

I am so proud to have been your student in 8th and 9th grade. I remember the very first day of school and Mr. Mayer had left—we all just loved him and we thought no one could compare.

So here I go into my homeroom and you were greeting us as you wrote things on the board.

Lucia and I were talking in Spanish about you—how you looked like a goober and were probably not as nice as Mr. Mayer—when all of the sudden you said to us in Spanish—all you said was Hello my name is—but you warned us that we would never really know how much you knew and understand.

So we should be careful what we said.

You were my homeroom and Bible teacher but more than that you were a friend.

You knew how I was feeling—when my sister got married—you knew I felt alone and abandoned—you gave me the sweetest card.

I remember when you told us that we would do journal writings and I wrote about a special possession—the necklace my grandfather gave me.

You wrote such a wonderful thing back to me.

I remember you and raccoons and how you loved them. And that stuffed animal that you had in class.

I also remember you and Gail and what a lovely wedding you had.

I even used the idea of a taped message of thank you for family and friends at my own wedding.

When you moved to Peru I was so sad but your letters always let me know that your [sic] doing fine and still remember me.

I was so happy to see you a few years ago and share our joys, stories of our lives.

I was glad that you like Darren and you would definitely like Zachary.

The last time I wrote I hadn't switched majors yet you always told me you were proud of me—I think you would like what I am doing.

I'd like to be as kind to my students as you were to me.

You always saw right through me and helped me especially when I was sick and everyone thought I'd end up like Karen Carpenter—you're the one who called my Mom—you went with us to the doctor.

Thank you I truly admire and love you!!! I hope you and Gail and the kids are fine.

Andrew and Beth must be really big—when is the next one coming? Zach is more than enough for right now—I hope to see you again this year!!!
Love,
Odi

Dear Nettie,

I wish I could tell you this in person.

I've enjoyed speaking with you over the years, but now I don't know where you are and wish this could be in person.

Ever since I had you for HR and Eng in 1971–72 you have meant a great deal to me.

You showed your co-workers and students what caring, hard-work and determination meant.

At a time when ESE students weren't ID'd you joyously accepted them in your class.

I remember when you made funny remarks—with other teachers that would have been disastrous but your students adored you and didn't lose interest.

The time you asked me to work with Bubba on Beowulf and wondered why he wasn't motivated...you showed me you really cared about him—and also built me up in that you showed confidence in my abilities.

When the "riots" started—you showed strength, caring, and courage when you herded the students into the safety of your room. I felt very scared, but also very safe and secure.

I'll never forget your words "Beautiful people do beautiful things—thank you beautiful people" when we tricked your arthritis-ridden body out of the class to surprise you with Birthday in May (for your August Birthday).

When you had former students drop in you would suspend class to give your visitor the spotlight—enjoyable for us—as enjoyable as when I became one of those returning students.

I have your book of poetry—read it often and think of you—How I wish I could
sit with you and tell you this in person.
Yolanda

Odi's and Yolanda's memories were quickly called to mind in a group when the focus of attention was on caring teachers. We know from the letters that although many years had passed since they were students in Mr. B. and Nettie's classes, their images and emotional memories were still vivid. They remembered being treated with respect and learning lessons about respecting others, being treated in ways that engendered self-confidence, feeling safe in the presence of danger, and the teacher's gentle good humor.

Odi's and Yolanda's memories were forged in relationships with Mr. B. and Nettie. They experienced an ethic of care and learned something about relationships. They may well tell Mr. B. and Nettie stories to their own children when they teach them lessons about respect.

Not all teachers are remembered as caring. Some are remembered as thoughtless and cruel, as the following letters describe:

Dear Mr. Debeck,

You would have remembered me as one of the three grade eight students who you separated in your grade 8 science class because we came from Bridgeview. I remember the first day of junior high school, how humiliating, how intimidating! What a whirlwind of newness, strangeness and noise. There were only seven of us, a tight knit group of kids from the wrong side of the tracks—terrified of all the others but secretly hopeful that we would be accepted.

We entered your classroom with relief that at least in this block we had 3 of us and we sat down at the science table together. We were quiet, too intimidated by the lab and sparkling science equipment to say anything. We were not causing any trouble.

I had always been a good science student, I loved the subject and was looking forward to Grade 8 science. My past teachers had helped me recognize that I was a gifted student and I saw Gr. 8 science as a way to broaden my science experiences. I looked forward to your classes with anticipation.

When you started the class by calling the role, I was surprised when you appeared to stumble on my name. My surprise turned to anxiety and then fear, when you hesitated over Rick and Lloyd's name too! Horror took over when you called out to the class that the three kids from Bridgeview move to the back of the room—"you can't do this!" I thought to myself, but I numbly stumbled to the back to await your explanation.

As you walked toward us you said that we couldn't do the grade 8 work because our old school didn't have the right equipment.

"You guys couldn't do grade 8 science!" We already knew we were different! It had been reinforced into every facet of our being. Every person that we had dealt with in that school, indicated that we were different in some way or another! Did you know you gave other kids license to treat us differently? Do

you know that end of the day I got beaten up and others were locked in lockers? I vowed then to never let anyone treat me like that again.

Of course, that never really happened and it happened time and time again. But I know that I will never, and have never, separated and isolated students because of who they are and where they come from.

N. B.

This memory did not surface for 20 years—perhaps because the teacher committed suicide at the end of this term and I felt that I could not be critical.

Dear Mr. Hinson,

I am now 26 years old and in the process of becoming a teacher. To teach has been a goal of mind for a long time, and I'm happy I'm finally pursuing it.

It has been about 13 years since I've been in your Algebra class. I deliberately flunked your placement test to advance into the next higher class, because I knew I didn't want to have you as my teacher again.

To sit on your throne as king of Algebra and make up stupid punishments that don't fit the crime is ridiculous. Yes, I was defiant. Think about it though, which would you choose—to look like a fool all day or to be punished and get it over with. If you chew gum you shouldn't be made to sit with gum on you nose for the rest of the class. If you do badly on a test you shouldn't post it on your board or call that person stupid. If someone doesn't feel well, or isn't pretty enough for you, don't call them ugly or say that they're faking it.

Sincerely,

Patricia S. Johnson

P.S. Your class set a record time of office visits for me. It was the most times I've ever done anything bad.

The punishing effects of demeanment and ridicule are lasting. Humiliation breeds anger, contempt, and depression. Teachers have the power to harm children spiritually. Physical abuse is against the law. Emotional abuse is more subtle and difficult to detect. The only evidence may be the hurt feelings of a child and wounds shared years later as an adult in a letter to the teacher.

The significance of the letters is to bring into awareness the power of the teacher and the significance of teacher acts and attitudes. The best of teachers will sometimes have bad days and make mistakes with children. Some teachers, however, are more likely to make mistakes that hurt children or to miss opportunities to nurture children than others. This has two implications for teacher education. First, relatively little attention is given to self, diversity, and ethics in the curriculum of teacher education programs. Helping teachers become aware of the long-term impact of their behavior on the emotional lives of their students should be a part of the teacher education program. Second, teachers carry with them the memories of their own teachers. The four letters shared here were written by student teachers. A teacher's approach to teaching is shaped, for good or for ill, by every teacher who has taught her. Helping teachers to be aware of these formative experiences will give them more insight into their work in the classroom.

CONCLUDING REFLECTIONS

We, the authors, are teachers, and we are very different people—for example, different gender, age, religious background, education, a vocational interests, and family circumstances. We have some things in common. We share an interest in understanding teaching and learning. We share common values of equity, care, and fairness. We share a common interest in understanding variability among students in schools, especially students whose behavior leads to them being identified as having special educational needs. And, we share an interest in teacher education curricula focusing more broadly on the emotional qualities of teachers and their impact on students.

The traditional positivist epistemology of educational research, and the analytic philosophy shaping ideas about the nature and purpose of education, have given way to increasingly complex discourses on teaching and learning. We discussed five of the paradigms now influencing educational research and scholarship. We described the force of objectivist epistemology in unwittingly creating silences by focusing more on empirically demonstrable regularities across settings than on individual experience. We discussed our own research on memories of care and cruelty in classrooms and the implications of enabling student voices to share untold stories that both dignify and vilify the work of teachers. The study of student experience through memory is one means of accessing the sacred spaces (Paul and Smith, 2000) of students where self-appropriated stories of heroes and victims are constructed.

In addition to traditional research on teaching, teacher education curricula should enable student teachers to see the storied domain of student learning that exists beyond the lights of objectivist knowing. Indeed, student teachers' unexplored memories of their own experiences in school serve as a frame of reference for examining and valuing life as it is lived and appropriated in the classroom. We believe a student teacher's knowledge of her own existential story as a student will enable her to see and hear the stories of her students.

DISCUSSION QUESTIONS

1. What are the epistemologies discussed in the chapter? What are the implications of each of these epistemologies for the education of teachers?
2. How do the letters included in this chapter impact your understanding of the long-term effects of teachers' relationship with students?
3. What are the implications of an existential study of memories of teachers for the education of teachers?

REFERENCES

Andrews, S. V. (1989). Changing research perspectives: A critical study of Elliot Eisner. *Journal of Curriculum and Supervision, 4*(2), 106–125.

Bochner, A. (1994). Perspectives on inquiry II: Theories and stories. In M. Knapp & G. R. Miller (Eds.), *Handbook of interpersonal communication* (pp. 21–41). Thousand Oaks, CA: Sage.

Bochner, A., Ellis, C., & Tillmann-Healy, L. (1997). Relationships as stories. In S. Duck (Ed.), *Handbook of personal relationships* (pp. 307–324). New York: John Wiley.

Borland, J. H. (1990). Postpositivist inquiry: Implications of the "new philosophy of science for the field of the education of the gifted. *Gifted Child Quarterly, 34*(4), 161–167.

Crone, L. J. (1995). Further examination of teacher behavior in differentially effective schools: Selection and socialization process. *Journal of Classroom Interaction, 30*(1), 1–9.

DeVries, R., Hildebrandt, C., & Zan, B. (2000). Constructivist early education for moral development. *Early Education and Development, 11*(1), 9–35.

Eisner, E. W. (1997). The new frontier in qualitative research methodology. *Qualitative Inquiry, 3*(3), 259–273.

Elkind, D. (1997). The death of child nature: Education in the postmodern world. *Phi Delta Kappan, 79*(3), 241–245.

Gary, T. (1997). What's the use of theory? *Harvard Educational Review, 67*(1), 75–104.

Gordon, J. A. (1998). Caring through control. *Journal for a Just and Caring Education, 4*(4), 418–440.

Griffiths, M. (1995). Making a difference: Feminism, post-modernism, and the methodology of educational research. *British Educational Research Journal, 21*(2), 219–235.

Guba, E. G. (Ed.). (1990). *The paradigm dialog.* Newbury Park, CA: Sage.

Halbig, W. W. (2000). Breaking the code of silence. *American School Board Journal, 187*(3), 34–36.

Harris, K. R., & Graham, S. (1994). Constructivism: Principles, paradigms, and integration. *The Journal of Special Education, 28*(3), 233–247.

Heshusius, L. (1994). Freeing ourselves from objectivity: Managing subjectivity or turning toward a participatory mode of consciousness? *Educational Researcher, 23*(3), 15–22.

Krajewski, B., & Bailey, E. (1999). Caring with passion: The "core" value. *NASSP Bulletin, 83*(609), 33–39.

Ladd, G. W. (1999). Children's' social and scholastic lives in kindergarten: Related spheres of influence? *Child Development, 70*(6), 1373–1400.

Lipman, P. (1997). Restructuring in context: A case study of teacher participation and the dynamics of ideology, race, and power. *American Educational Research Journal, 34*(1), 3–37.

Loving, C. C. (1997). From the summit of truth to its slippery slopes: Science education's journey through positivist-postmodern territory. *American Educational Research Journal, 34*(3), 421–452.

Noblit, G. W. (1993). Power and caring. *American Educational Research Journal, 30*(1), 23–38.

Paul, J. L., & Smith, T. J. (Eds.). (2000). *Stories out of school: Memories and reflections on care and cruelty in the classroom.* Stamford, CT: Ablex Publishing.

Popkewitz, T. S. (1990). Whose future? Whose past? Notes on critical theory and methodology. In E. G. Guba (Ed.), *The paradigm dialog* (pp. 46–66). Newbury Park, CA: Sage.

Postman, N. (1996). *The end of education* [film]. New York: Vintage.

Rorty, R. (1989). *Contingency, irony, and solidarity.* New York: Cambridge University Press.

Schein, E. H. (1972). *Professional education: Some new directions.* New York: McGraw-Hill.

Short, K. (1999). "Teacher-watching": Examining teacher talk in literature circles. *Language Arts, 76*(5), 377–385.

Staver, J. R. (1998). Constructivism: Sound theory for explicating the practice of science and science teaching. *Journal of Research in Science Teaching, 35*(5), 501–520.

Wentzel, K. R. (1997). Student motivation in middle school: The role of perceived pedagogical caring. *Journal of Educational Psychology, 89*(3), 411–419.

Wink, J. (1997). *Critical pedagogy: Notes from the real world.* New York: Longman.

Wittgenstein, L. (1961). *Tractatus Logico-Philosophicus.* (D. F. Pears & B. F. McGuinness, Trans.). London: Routledge & Kegan Paul.

Zeichner, K. (1999). The new scholarship in teacher education. *Educational Researcher, 28*(9), 4–15.

9

The Reflective Self: Becoming a Special Educator

Patricia Fagan and Ella L. Taylor

"Images of self are critical to the process of becoming a teacher because they constitute the personal context within which new information will be interpreted, and are the stuff of which teaching persona is created" (McLean, 1999).

One of the roles of teacher educators is to develop reflective, ethical, and instructionally competent practitioners who will have the skills to create learning communities in their classrooms. The development of these skills is often predicated upon the establishment of learning communities at the preservice level. A learning community is an interwoven web of relationships including administrators, faculty, staff, and students working together in a spirit of cooperation and care. Our challenge as teacher educators is to learn to identify and understand the lenses through which we reflect upon our relationships with our students. Equally important is how we help our students develop this reflective skill for themselves. This chapter discusses the importance of reflection in teacher education and outlines the progress one special education department has had in establishing a learning community.

THE VALUE OF REFLECTION

Parker Palmer (1998), in his book *The Courage to Teach*, states that "good teachers possess a capacity for connectedness. This connectedness links the elements of teachers' knowledge of themselves, their subjects, and their students" (p. 11). Connectedness can only be developed over time and through deliberate actions. Nel Noddings (2001), in her recent work on care, reinforces Palmer's view on the importance of connectedness.

> As teachers, most of us are primarily concerned with establishing conditions in our classrooms that will call forth the best in our students; conditions that will make "being good" both possible and desirable. These conditions are relational in nature. From the student's perspective, *"How good I can be*, depends to a large extent, on *how you treat me."* (p.13)

Noddings (1993) defines care in terms of relationship and the conditions in which the relationship is embedded, such as a learning community. Care is thus defined in terms of the primary participants in the relationship and the setting in which the participants interact. For example, a classroom in which the teacher and students interact is an environment in which a caring relationship can be established.

An ethic of care, of connectedness with one's students, requires the teacher to be attuned to the nuances of what is being communicated. This includes listening to and hearing the stories students tell, directly or indirectly; observing body language; and attempting to get a sense of what they feel. Noddings (1993) calls this "a special act of receptivity." The connected teacher keeps the interest of his or her student in mind, not just in the current moment, but also how the present interaction may influence the future growth and acceptability of the student. This interest is not limited to a particular student but extends to the whole learning community itself.

> This is necessary because the well being of the entire community depends on the health of the relationships within it. The contribution of the student is vital to the relation; not only does the response of the student sustain teachers in their efforts but it is the essential material by which teachers monitor the quality and effects of their caring, in continuous cycles of attention and response . . . . [The] cared-fors, contribute to the relationship by responding to their teachers . . . . If students show growth as an obvious result of their teacher's efforts, the teacher's caring is completed. . . . Eyes alight with curiosity, honest questions, and passionate debates are all teacher sustaining responses." (Noddings, 1993, p. 48–49).

As Noddings points out, a caring attitude on the part of the teacher is called forth and sustained by supportive, engaged students. Indeed the level of student engagement and support is the measure by which a teacher weighs the success of his or her teaching and often determines the nature of future teacher efforts.

How is this relational balance achieved? As teachers, there is obviously one side of this equation over which we can exercise more control. "Teaching, like any human activity, emerges from one's inwardness, for better or worse" (Palmer, 1998). On considering his own work with both teacher educators and K-12 teachers, Palmer writes:

> As I teach, I project the condition of my soul onto my students, my subject, on our way of being together. The entanglements I experience in the classroom are often no more or less than the convolutions of my inner life. Viewed from this angle, teaching holds a mirror to the soul. If I am willing to look into that mirror and not run from what I see, I have a chance to gain self-knowledge . . . and knowing myself is as crucial to good teaching as knowing my students and my subject." (p. 2)

Without preparing teachers who are skilled in building the relational conditions that call forth the best in their students, our responsibilities as teacher educators are only half met. Developing the reflective skills needed to meet the needs of students is critical in our increasingly diverse society.

LEARNING TO KNOW OURSELVES

"Good teaching," states Palmer (1998), "requires self-knowledge: it is a secret hidden in plain sight." When undergraduates enter our special education department's two-year teacher preparation program at the beginning of their junior year, they arrive expecting to learn the mechanics of teaching content and managing a classroom. These mechanical elements are crucial, but good teaching is so much more than that. Moving ourselves and our students toward "good" teaching has been a multilayered process that has engaged our department for the better part of the past decade.

Our efforts to know and appreciate ourselves, both as individuals involved in the preparation of preservice special education teachers and as a department, involved an ongoing process of reflection about the purpose and value of our work. Initially, this was done in small cohorts known as Collaborative Research Groups (CRGs), which generally consisted of ten to twelve members, including special education faculty, faculty from other departments, and doctoral students (Paul, Berger, Osnes, Martinez, & Morse, 1997).

One of the more productive research groups was the CRG on Policy and Ethics. The group's purpose was to develop an effective training program in ethical decision-making for members of School Advisory Councils (SACs). Though we examined numerous ethical models, including those in business and medicine, it was our conversations with members of the departments of religious studies and philosophy that encouraged us to reflect upon the relational and moral aspects of special education and to extend this reflection to the roles of those who work in the field.

As we struggled with how to develop ethical behavior in others, we found ourselves spending increasing amounts of time considering our own actions, attitudes, and beliefs both as individuals and as a department. Much of this was done through action-research and reflective, recursive discussion over a number of years. Over time, we examined a variety of themes that led to the establishment of another CRG focused on helping preservice teachers see the connection between university coursework and field experiences. Using the departmental mission and belief statements as a guide, this CRG developed a heuristic that encompassed the students' developmental stages, departmental foundational values, and preprofessional standards and benchmarks. Two primary vehicles resulted from these discussions and the development of the heuristic. One is the ongoing development of close, collaborative partnerships with schools where our preservice teachers complete their fieldwork over the course of four semesters. The other, closely linked to the fieldwork, is a series of four professional development seminars. These seminars, also called proseminars, were established as a vehicle through which to address the issues of continuity expressed by the faculty and the foundational values of knowledge, self, diversity, ethics, and collaboration.

Although the foundational values of self, diversity, and ethics could be arrayed in a variety of sequences, we believe that it is important for students to understand themselves before they can address issues of cultural diversity and the myriad ethical considerations inherent within teaching and schools. Understanding one's own values and view of the world is critical for establishing the open communication necessary for a caring, learning community. As Palmer (1998) observes:

> Knowing my students and my subject depends heavily on self-knowledge. When I do not know myself, I cannot know who my students are. I will see them in the shadows of my unexamined life . . . and when I cannot see them clearly, I cannot teach them well. . . . The work to "*know thyself*" is neither selfish nor narcissistic. Whatever self-knowledge we attain as teachers will serve our students and our teaching well. (p. 2)

Additionally, sequencing the professional development seminars to coincide with students' progression through the special education program was necessary. During their first semester, when students have limited access to schools and K–12 students, focusing on issues of self allows them to forge strong connections between their coursework, lived experiences, and each other. Focusing on cultural diversity and building on issues of the self during the second semester allows students to simultaneously examine their own experiences of schooling and focus on the social context of schooling while still having more limited classroom responsibilities. The third semester's emphasis on ethics coincides with the preservice teachers' increased contact with students, parents, and other school personnel. Imbedded within each proseminar are opportunities for students to collaborate and to share knowledge generated through university coursework and field experiences.

Each one-hour proseminar includes eight to twelve students and one or two facilitators who are either faculty or doctoral students. The proseminar facilitator serves in four basic capacities: as a facilitator of the dynamics of the group in becoming a connected learning community, as a mentor who provides emotional and moral support, as an instructor who provides academic content, and as an advocate who helps guide the student through difficult situations. Proseminar facilitators also serve as a liaison between cooperating teachers in the field and the program of study. Beginning with the first semester in the students' professional development program, these seminars meet weekly and continue through the final internship experience. Using a continuity of care model, proseminar groups are kept as intact as possible each semester. Because facilitators remain with the groups, they are able to get to know the students and their abilities. The continuity of this relationship throughout the students' professional program greatly facilitates the final internship's emphasis on the development of professional educators.

On the surface, the plan seems straightforward. The faculty form collaborative relationships with cooperating teachers in the field while developing open and supportive relationships with the preservice teachers. During this process, the preservice teachers ideally develop the ability to form relationships with their own students through their fieldwork and in their future classrooms. However, as Wynne (1991) points out, such a plan requires strong institutional underpinnings that include a high level of communication among faculty and between faculty and preservice teachers. Further, it is vital that new faculty and preservice teachers be quickly socialized into the existing supportive and caring environment. Finally, the importance of collegiality, relationships, trust, dedication, and good humor among faculty, preservice teachers, and other members of the learning community cannot be overemphasized.

THE REFLECTIVE SKILL-BUILDING PROCESS

Trusting collegial relationships are developed over a long and sometimes difficult process. Relationships are labor-intensive. The greatest obstacle that stands between our selves and trusting collegial relationships is fear. Palmer (1998) refers to the "culture of fear" that dominates academic life. This culture encourages us to "distance ourselves from our students and our subjects, to teach and learn at some distance from our own hearts" (p. 35). In the university this distance is often reinforced by the very structures we have put in place to facilitate instruction (Palmer, 1998): the top-down organization of our institutions, the departmentalized organization of our knowledge bases, professional "turf wars" fostered by competition for limited resources including time and financial support, a grading system that pits one student against another, and that expert-driven staple of academic life, the lecture.

> From grade school on, education is a fearful enterprise. As a student, I was in too many classrooms riddled with fear, the fear that leads many children, born with a love of learning, to hate the idea of school. As a teacher, I am at my worst when fear takes the lead in me, whether that means teaching in fear of my students or manipulating their fears of me. Our relations as faculty members are often diminished by fear; fear is nearly universal in the relations of faculty and administration; and fear is a standard management tool in too many administrative kit bags. (p. 36)

Despite our efforts to the contrary, the methods we employ to facilitate our teaching appear to often act as the greatest barriers to the relationships that epitomize the best teaching. We are all, as Palmer (1998) points out, afraid of failing, of having our ignorance exposed or our prejudices challenged, and of looking foolish in front of our peers; "when my students' fears mix with mine, fear multiplies geometrically, and education is paralyzed" (p. 37).

PERSONAL NARRATIVE AND GROUP PROCESS

Preservice teachers preparing to work with all children need to revisit the attitudes, values, and beliefs they bring to the teaching profession. In Sarason's (1993) words "teachers are not empty vessels . . . devoid of knowledge, interests, and experiences ... coming in with no idea how or what a teacher looks like" (p. 150). Adult learners bring with them a lifetime of experiences that informs the way in which they approach their work as teachers (Paul & Smith, 2001). Through the examination of their lived experience they come to understand their existing knowledge base, its importance in their lives as teachers, and their resultant needs for connecting their experience, knowledge, and aspirations. As McLean (1999) points out, giving attention to "the complex and interpersonal dynamics that characterize the whole person of becoming a teacher" (p. 59) is critical for developing reflective, caring teachers.

Because the focus of the first professional development seminar is on understanding self, initial activities include instruments to assess one's personal leadership and effectiveness style, preferred mode of learning in relationship to multiple intelligence theory, and conflict-resolution style. Participants are involved in discussing and writing narratives related to their personal experiences as students in K–12 classrooms, including their recollections of teachers who were caring or cruel and the effect those teachers had upon them. As a result of examining why they want to be teachers, especially special education teachers, students develop a personal philosophy of education and a professional development plan based upon the department's foundational values and preprofessional standards and benchmarks.

Within a variety of assignments during the first semester proseminar, students are asked to share and examine their personal experiences of education. O'Loughlin (1991) notes that "by providing opportunities for students to speak and write about their own autobiographical experiences, teachers affirm students' social and cultural identities" (p. 28). The proseminars are designed to allow students a comfortable and safe place through which to examine their lived experiences in relation to both their growing knowledge base and their peers.

Students note that the proseminar environment is one of comfort and safety. One student commented that "the proseminars provide a more relaxed atmosphere in which we can speak freely about our opinions and ideas." Another preservice teacher noted, "There were so many different personalities within our group. We did not always agree on everything, but we always seemed to find common ground and we respected everyone's viewpoint."

McLean (1999) indicates that the sharing of autobiographical stories is vitally important. It is through this sharing of stories that both students and faculty give meaning to experience. Notes McLean (1999), "This sharing needs to be a process in which both students and professors are engaged as participants" (p. 80). Emphasizing the importance of dialogue and communication, one facilitator observed that within the small group setting "an atmosphere of equality was created in which neither facilitator nor student utilized the hierarchy of power and its inherent privileges to manipulate or dominate the other. Each individual voice was respected for the knowledge and experience it represented. Our collective knowledge was broadened by the sharing of individual lives."

Through the sharing of students' and facilitators' autobiographical stories, a feeling of trust and respect is developed. No one viewpoint comes to be the "correct" viewpoint. Students are empowered to disagree and agree with each other and the facilitators. All voices are recognized as important and contribute to a more complete understanding of the interplay among schooling, learning, and personal experience.

Facilitating the proseminars requires sharing one's own views and values, suspending judgment, tolerating ambiguity, and confronting one's own fears about self-exposure, loss of classroom control, and personal intimacy. Facilitators must be open to different points of view, and be willing to risk sharing ideas, memories, and experiences that stir deep feelings. Through the sharing of these feelings and experiences around schooling by both the facilitator and the students, a bond begins to form that provides the foundation of what Noddings calls a caring relationship. Both facilitators and students are supported in their growth and development as they examine ideas and explore their own values and perceptions.

THE CREATION OF CARING RELATIONSHIPS

In attempting to describe the importance of the small group meetings, one facilitator stated, "Noddings tells us, and I agree, that students need continuity not only of place but also of people when building a caring community. I believe that the proseminar truly allows facilitators and students this opportunity." A student corroborated the facilitator's statement by noting that "the small group helped us develop close relationships that allowed us to open up more."

McLean (1999) contends that the development of reflective teachers "is not a matter of adopting a few new strategies for course requirements or class formats . . . [but] requires fundamental changes in how we think about ourselves and enact our own work" (p. 78). The proseminars provide students a more intimate setting through which to grapple with the challenging tasks of becoming a teacher. Rather than remain one within a large classroom group, each student is afforded the opportunity to become a crucial member of a smaller learning community. As one student stated, "I learned a lot about our group members and I believe we taught each other a lot." Given that, as Maxine Greene (1981) has noted, the process of becoming a teacher is a process of deciding who you will be as a teacher, the opportunity to try on different "selves" in a safe and caring community is critical.

Nowhere is this more evident than in the sharing of personal schooling experiences. It is often within the confines of this activity that the small group of individuals bonds with one another. Students write with raw honesty and passion about the barriers that they have had to surmount to pursue becoming a special education teacher. One student related her middle school experience by sharing the following:

> I attended the Florida School for the Deaf and Blind for my seventh grade year. This was a very unique experience. Making the greatest impact on me was how differently we "blind" students were treated. Based on the fact that we could not see like everyone else, a decision had been made at the outset that our mental capabilities were also impaired. For instance, it was decided that we could not wash our own clothes, find our way around, cook simple foods for ourselves, or comprehend basic academic material. I found this very offensive. Despite my other disabilities, I did have basic living skills! I suppose this was the reason I got into so much trouble with the staff at the school. I was determined to prove to them that I was no less normal than any other child just because I could not see as well.

As their stories unfold, students who may have been perceived as aloof and uninterested, begin to emerge as full persons. Another student, born to an Irish family living and working in Africa, recalls her experiences in an English boarding school after having been raised in African villages.

> As a child in school, whether it be in [the United States] or in the United Kingdom, I felt like an oddity, an alien (which I was in the purest sense of the word), distant from an experience that was expected by others to be wholesome and nourishing. In England I was brutalized for reasons I did not understand. I was raised in [Africa,] a place where what I was, where I came from, and the choices I made were never questioned, were never issues. In the English school system, my Irishness, a heritage that I was very much in touch with, provoked meanness in otherwise good people. My refusal to participate in religious worship at school labeled me as a Catholic although I was not that either. I was born Catholic, but we did not practice.
>
> . . . But here I was, pigeonholed in a box that was too small for me, that limited me, that would have killed me had I not learned to fly from it in my mind without ever leaving it. In English schools I learned the lesson of prejudice and the meaning of the word hatred. I was an Irish African in an English school, and I learned to separate what I was proud to be from where I was, and to hold fast to my sense of worth, freedom and independence"

Another student also writes powerfully of an immigrant experience; facing rejection as an adolescent whose customs, values, and dress did not match those of her new peers. In her struggle to "fit in," she loses her identity, only to find herself again through a life-shaking crisis. An African-American man describes middle school as a "hole in the middle of his education" into which childhood friendships disappeared as issues of race kicked in along with puberty. These friendships emerged again on the athletic field in high school, but the experience remains pivotal to his memories of school.

Placed at the front of the class to accommodate for her visual impairment, a student speaks of her isolation:

> The students in the public school setting were relentless in their teasing. In most of my classes I sat in the front in an effort to see the board. Unfortunately, most of the other kids in the class took this as an opportunity to make jokes, throw things, and constantly pick on me. Because of this, I was a loner for the longest time.

Students also describe the construction of a protective shell that allows them to exist beside but not with their peers.

> [On arriving in America] I revealed little . . . about where I had been, what I had discovered or who I was, for that, I determined, would provide a base on which to judge me—perhaps inaccurately or unfairly. So I kept to myself, I kept my mouth shut, I was the exemplary student from a foreign land whose voice spoke neither Erse nor Pidgin nor thick rural English, but somehow an unfathomable combination of all three. I created no social ties with those who occupied the

classrooms with me, and although I was drawn to the African American students because they brought through their physical appearance a sense of comfort and familiarity to my unsettled soul, I quickly learned they did not view me in the same way.

All who listen to these stories, facilitators and students alike, are humbled by the power of these feelings and experiences expressed. A feeling of communion is developed. "Fear," writes Palmer (1998), "is a powerful feature of both schools and our inner landscape. Specifically I am speaking of the fear of having a live encounter with the 'otherness' in a student, in a colleague, in an idea, or in the voice of our own inner teacher. This results in a disconnect between ourselves and our work as teachers" (p. 37). In these moments of revelation, the groups begin to coalesce as fears are faced and all are forced to rethink how we view each other and our work in special education.

OUTCOMES

There are two perspectives from which we may view our work as educators. On the one hand, the positivist or objectivist point of view, which has long been the traditional approach to understanding social reality in education, purports that "social sciences are essentially the same as natural sciences and are, therefore, concerned with discovering natural and universal laws regulating and determining individual and social behavior" (Cohen and Manion, 1994, p.5). Empirical in nature, this view supports the idea that there is one objective reality, external to ourselves, which holds for everyone in the learning community. However, as suggested by Flew (1984), this raises a number of questions: Whose view is normative? Do human beings respond mechanically to their environments or are they the initiators of their own actions? Are all events, including human actions, predetermined in the sense that they could be predicted, or is the true nature of reality human determination?

The subjectivist view of social reality emphasizes that people differ from inanimate natural phenomena, and indeed, from each other. This view is grounded in the belief that knowledge—about ourselves and others, and about our work as educators—is constructed, "based on experience of an essentially personal nature" (Cohen and Manion, 1994, p. 6). To begin to understand others, we must first understand ourselves and be able to question our personal beliefs.

The proseminar format encourages the study of the world from the perspective of the interacting individual. In reflecting on this humanistic process as she is about to exit the program, one student writes:

As I travel through this [program of study] here at USF, on my way to the degree and credentials that will allow me to impact the heirs to the next millennium, I am struck, not uncomfortably, by the emphasis that is placed in each and every course on thoughts and feelings. Our instructors, it would seem, are not so much interested in reports and reviews as they are in reflections and responses of the mind and the heart and the soul. Is this the new measure of teachers in this day and age, in this culture, in this society where we must educate children not only in academics, but in humanity? If this is indeed true, then I tip my hat to the innovators. I believe that to effectively educate any student, but especially those who are challenged, you must be able to step for a moment into their shoes, to see the world through their eyes, to feel as they do, to appreciate the struggles of their lives, without ever losing sight of your own identity and purpose.

Another student, in her first year, shares what she went through as a child with special needs:

I hope that by reading my experience, future educators and other professionals working with children with exceptionalities might have a clearer insight as to what the child is thinking and going through. Although these are my own thoughts and feelings at the time of the events, I feel the frustrations and feelings expressed are not uncommonly felt by most children with special needs. Although it is impossible to completely know what another person is going through unless you have experienced the same situation, I think it is possible to sympathize or even empathize to the point of understanding. I hope I have helped in that process.

In a meta-analysis of 93 empirical studies relating to teacher preparation, Wideen, Mayer-Smith, and Moon (1998) found that many traditional programs have little impact on preservice teachers' beliefs, but that some programs do. Zeichner and Hoeft (1996) make a similar statement noting that "empirical evidence overwhelmingly supports a view of preservice teacher education as a weak intervention," although some programs "under certain circumstances, are able to have an impact on certain aspects of teacher development" (p. 529). What separates programs that make an impact from those that do not?

According to Wideen et al. (1998), programs that "build upon the beliefs of preservice teachers and feature systematic and consistent long-term support in a collaborative setting" (p. 130) produce the most significant gains. The professional development seminars build upon students' own experiences and encourage them to examine these experiences and their own interpretation of the experiences in a fresh light. This type of reflection impacts students in a significant way. "I have never really taken the time before to evaluate who I am exactly and how the past will affect me in the future," commented one female student. "I think that in my future teaching career it is important to know myself very well. I need to know how that teacher in elementary school or how growing up in a very sheltered environment has influenced me. If I did not understand how the events in my past had an influence on me then I would not be able to compensate for them in my teaching career," she continued.

As Ruddick (1992) has noted, if teachers are to implement reflection and critical examination of their practice, then they must learn these skills within their teacher education program. Becoming a teacher is deciding who to become as a teacher (Greene, 1981). Echoing this belief, one student commented that she learned "that I am not an empty vessel and that it is vital to me to reflect on my past experiences in school to help build and structure me as a new and rising teacher." Observed a facilitator, "I saw growth throughout the semester in students' ability to reflect on experiences and professional practice. They began to ask critical questions and make connections between their life experiences, what they were learning at the university, and what they were seeing in schools."

CONCLUSION

Reflection is an essential component of teaching. It provides the lens through which we all interpret our world, our actions, and our lives. Becoming a teacher requires examining one's inner self and the components that make up who we are. To do so, we must be willing to expose our prejudices, share our experiences, and examine our interpretive lens. Creating an atmosphere in which preservice teachers can undertake this inner examination requires the development of caring relationships between faculty and students. It requires blending roles between teacher and student, developing personal connections, and confronting our fears. Becoming the teacher we want to be requires reflection; facilitating the development of future teachers requires a learning community based upon care. This chapter has outlined the development of a preservice teacher preparation program through the development of a sustained caring, learning community. We believe that explorations of inner knowledge begin to provide the foundation upon which masterful teachers will develop. For as Greene (1981) notes, becoming a teacher is about deciding what teacher to become.

DISCUSSION QUESTIONS

1. Describe how "care" theory was used in the development of the professional seminars.
2. Why is the development of a caring community so important for teacher education?
3. Why is self-reflection so important for teacher education?

NOTE

The authors wish to thank Oonagh Guenkel and Connie Regan for their contributions to this chapter.

REFERENCES

Cohen, L., & Manion, L. (1994). *Research methods in education*. New York: Routledge.

Greene, M. (1981). Contexts, connections, and consequences: The matter of philosophical and psychological foundations. *Journal of Teacher Education, 32*, 31–37.

McLean, S. V. (1999). Becoming a teacher: The person in the process. In R. P. Lipka & T. M. Brinthaupt, (Eds.)., *The Role of Self in Teacher Development* (pp. 55–91). Albany: State University of New York Press.

Noddings, N. (2001) A sympathetic alternative to character education. Unpublished paper, University of South Florida.

Noddings, N. (1993) Caring: A feminist perspective. In K. Strike and P. L. Ternasky (Eds.), *Ethics for professionals in education: Perspectives for preparation and practice*. New York: Teachers College Press.

O'Loughlin, M. (1991). Beyond constructivism: Toward a dialectical model of the problematics of teacher socialization. As cited in McLean, S. V. (1999). Becoming a teacher: The person in the process, in R. P. Lipka & T. M. Brinthaupt, (Eds.), *The role of self in teacher development* (pp. 55–91). Albany: State University of New York Press.

Palmer, P. (1998). *The courage to teach*. San Francisco: Jossey-Bass.

Paul, J., & Smith, T. (2001). *Stories out of school*. Stamford, CT: Ablex Publishers.

Paul, J., Berger, N., Osnes, P., Martinez, Y., and Morse, W. (1997). *Ethics and decision making in local schools*. Baltimore: Paul H. Brookes Publishing Company.

Ruddick, J. (1992). Practitioner research and programs of initial teacher education. In T. Russell & H. Munby (Eds.), *Teachers and teaching: From classroom to reflection* (pp. 156–170). London: Falmer Press.

Sarason, S. B. (1993). *The case for change: Rethinking the preparation of educators*. San Francisco: Jossey-Bass.

Wideen, M., Mayer-Smith, J., & Moon, B. (1998). A critical analysis of the research on learning to teach: Making the case for an ecological perspective on inquiry. *Review of Educational Research, 68* (2), 130–178.

Wynne, E. (1991). Character and academics in the elementary school. In J. Benninga (Ed.), *Moral character and civic education* (pp.139–153). New York: Teachers College Press.

Zeichner, K. M., & Hoeft, K. (1996). Teacher socialization for cultural diversity. In J. Sikula (Ed.), *Handbook of research on teacher education,* 2nd ed. (pp. 525–547).

10

Preparing African American Male Teachers for Urban Special Education Environments

Brenda L. Townsend and Karen M. Harris

The overrepresentation of African American learners in special education classes continues to be problematic. As reported in the U.S. Department of Education's Twentieth Annual Report to Congress (1998), African Americans comprise 16 percent of the school-age population, yet represent 21 percent of special classroom student enrollments. This disproportionate placement is even more dramatic in some special education categories where African Americans are represented at two to three times their percentage in the student population (Harry & Anderson, 1994). Unless these circumstances are seriously addressed, the placement of African American students, especially males, will continue to hold special education practice suspect. That is, schools' ability to appropriately place and program for students of ethnic minority backgrounds will continue to be questioned. While attempts have been made to shed light on this phenomenon, there have been few remedies.

Recent attention has focused on the cultural dissonance that can occur when there is a mismatch between cultural and ethnic backgrounds of school personnel and those of their students (Boykin, 1994; Gay, 1993; Ogbu, 1990). This cultural dissonance has been cited as one factor contributing to disproportionate representation of African American learners in special education (Harry & Anderson, 1994) and gifted classes (Ford, 1998).

In colleges of education across this country, preservice teachers tend to be European American women (King, 1993). In stark contrast, student demographics reflect rapidly increasing enrollments of ethnic minority students. In fact, it is predicted that almost half of the nation's student population will be members of ethnic minority groups by 2020 (Ford, Grantham, & Harris, 1997). Given this population shift, the literature underscores the need to increase the presence of ethnic minorities in the teacher workforce (King, 1993) and particularly in urban schools (O'Keefe, 1999; Pipho, 1998). An assumption is made that teachers of color are more familiar with and therefore less likely to misinterpret ethnic minority students' academic and social behaviors. When describing African American teachers, King (1993) suggested that they engage in "emancipatory pedagogy" or teaching that affirms and responds to their students' cultural and individual needs. An inherent assumption is that teachers from dominant culture backgrounds are more likely to have dissimilar cultural backgrounds and risk cultural misinterpretations.

Teacher shortages in general are of growing concern. Schools are plagued with a dwindling supply of teachers in many disciplines; that situation will worsen due to an aging teacher workforce that will retire en masse by 2006 (O'Keefe, 1999). The teaching supply is so inconsistent with the demand that many urban school districts have developed nontraditional hiring incentives to lure teachers to their districts (Pipho, 1998). Such a forecast is especially dismal in special education, where teachers are more likely to leave the profession early (Draper, 1999). In addition, it is not uncommon for classes for children with emotional/behavior disorders or classes for children with educable mental retardation to be comprised predominantly of African American males who bear little resemblance to their teachers.

This chapter describes one department's teacher preparation initiative to respond to the disproportionate placement of these and other learners by preparing African American men for urban special education teaching careers. To reveal insights gleaned from that initiative, several processes were used. First, participants' journal entries were analyzed. Second, interviews were conducted with a randomly selected sample of African American men who completed the project and are teaching children and youth with behavior disorders in urban schools. Third, the director of the project and first author of this chapter highlighted her observations made throughout the project. The chapter concludes with post-notes relative to the lessons we are learning as we prepare African American men for urban special education teaching careers.

PREPARING INNOVATIVE LEADERS OF TOMORROW (PROJECT PILOT)

A federally funded initiative in the Department of Special Education was developed in 1996 to deliberately respond to issues related to disproportionate special education placement. The project, Preparing Innovative Leaders of Tomorrow (Project PILOT), was designed to recruit and prepare ten

African American men a year for urban teaching careers in the field of emotional/behavior disorders (E/BD). It aimed to go beyond traditional scholarship programs that simply provide financial and academic assistance for students. It is often assumed that underrepresented groups primarily need economic and academic assistance to be successful in college and university settings. The purpose of Project PILOT was to create a comprehensive system of support for African American men to become effective teachers and advocates of children with, and those suspected of having, emotional or behavioral disorders.

To be clear, the intent was not to prepare cadres of African American men to maintain the status quo in special education referral and placement processes. Further, the project was not intended to endorse school practices of overidentifying African American males for special education classrooms. Such dramatic overrepresentation of African American males is an indicator that some students may be inappropriately placed. Instead of aiming to staff those classrooms for students with E/BD, the thinking was that the African American men enrolled in Project PILOT, many of whom who were reared in low-income urban communities, would be aware and understanding of the multiple and often complex factors that contribute to overrepresentation.

Armed with this sensitivity, African American men could be positioned to have a voice in their schools' placement practices. They would be knowledgeable about culturally responsive communication and instructional and management strategies for their own use and that of their colleagues. Thus, in addition to being effective teachers and role models, Project PILOT graduates would be able to advocate for children whom schools have placed at risk for E/BD classes as well as to advocate for children who may need E/BD services that are being overlooked. Another purpose of Project PILOT is to encourage participants to pursue graduate degrees in special education and special education administration so that they can inform policy and practice at local, state, and national levels.

Project PILOT was initiated at the University of South Florida in 1996. Three cohorts of African American men (total of 31) have graduated, and 30 are currently teaching classes for children with E/BD in Florida. This chapter focuses on the first two Project PILOT cohorts. The first cohort was originally composed of 13 men, with all but one graduating as PILOT students. The participants had varying family structures and responsibilities. Two were married with children, four were single with children, five were single with no children, and one was married with no children. As a result of the family demands and responsibilities, two maintained full-time jobs while attending school and seven maintained part-time employment. The average GPA upon enrolling in Project PILOT was 2.66 and the average GPA at graduation was 2.95.

There were 15 men originally enrolled in the second cohort, and 12 graduated. Upon project enrollment, two of them were married with children, one was single with children, and nine were single with no children. When admitted into Project PILOT, their average GPA was 2.66 and it was 2.80 upon graduation.

A comprehensive system of supports was put in place to counter the barriers that have precluded African American men from becoming interested in and matriculating through a special education teacher preparation program. In addition to those barriers, the complexities of teaching and the uniqueness of teaching in urban schools were explored via monthly seminars and journal writing. Based on the literature and personal experiences of students who negotiated their academic and social experiences at predominantly White institutions, nine supports were necessary for a project of this nature.

1. Tuition and book scholarships. Students received a stipend for the fall and spring semesters that covered the costs of tuition and books. If they already received financial assistance covering those costs, the stipend was applied toward living expenses for themselves and/or their families. Students were required to attend university classes full-time during the summer session, but received no scholarship during that time.

2. Project PILOT Advisory Board. An advisory board composed of individuals representing university, public school, and local communities met monthly to guide project activities and to ensure that PILOT students were being prepared in accord with the needs of the communities they represented. Advisory board members represented university faculty, support service staff, local school county administrators and teachers, the African American community, and the students themselves. The advisory board assumed responsibility for interviewing and selecting project participants, monitoring their progress, and exploring avenues for student support, financially and morally.

3. National consultants. As the director of Project PILOT, this coauthor recognized the differing experiences both between herself as an African American woman and the men of Project PILOT, and those differences among the men themselves. Having acknowledged those differences and the fact that because she had not experienced black maleness in dominant culture society, she was in no position to know what their support needs were to plan accordingly. Therefore, she involved two African American men who are national experts in the field of special education and have long advocated on behalf of African American children and youth and have maintained leadership positions in the field.

4. Cohort membership. Cohorts have been used effectively to prepare adult learners for roles in schools and to address diversity-related issues (Barnett, & Caffarella & Daresh, 1992). In the department, students are placed on teams when they begin their special education programs. In that regard, they typically attend classes together. Accordingly, the

Project PILOT students are actually members of a team within a team. In addition to their traditional team member support, they also have their Project member support and move through their classes together. Their cohort membership and class attendance as a team have benefited both the project participants, the other students in our classes, and faculty. Project PILOT students report that, prior to the project, they were typically the "only one" in their community college and university classes. In PILOT, however, they move from that limited presence to becoming a critical mass, as they may have nine or more other African American men in classes with them. Benefits to other students in the college have included their previously having limited contact with African American males and relying primarily on mass media's negative images to form and maintain their attitudes and perceptions of African American men. Although originally there was some resistance to attending class with this critical mass of African American men, there has been a clear shift in attitudes over time on the part of students of dominant culture and the Project PILOT men themselves. Faculty have expressed a phenomenon occurring as a result of the critical mass of PILOT students forcing the professors to examine their university teaching methods. Most eye-opening was coming to grips with the reality that most teaching methods are generally geared for European American women, who until then predominated classes in colleges of education nationally.

5. Monthly student seminars. Despite the changing demographics showing the increase of ethnic minority and poor children, content on urban and multicultural education is not infused in all classes. It was recognized that if project participants were to be successful in urban settings, there is some content unique to those settings that must be addressed in the curriculum. Project participants were required to attend a two-hour-long seminar each month to address various topics relative to teaching in urban settings and interpersonal skills and communication. For example, topics included: nurturing African American students' gifts and talents; exploring African American father-son relationships; and meeting the needs of urban and high-poverty children. Students also needed strategies to enhance their academic and social success in mainstream environments (i.e., university classes, public schools) while positioning them for leadership roles. Therefore, interpersonal skills were honed in the seminars. That is, skills centering on table etiquette and communication skills were included, and local and national experts facilitated those topics.

6. Monthly faculty seminars. University faculty tend to teach in manners similar to the way they were prepared in their teacher-education program. Until recently, multicultural education and urban education content was not focused on in many programs around the country. To

prepare project participants and other students for the realities in contemporary classrooms, there needed to be some ongoing dialogues about diversity-related issues in university and public school classes. As a result of that need, the professional development seminars were held monthly and all faculty and staff in the College of Education were invited to attend. The topics centered on urban special education issues.

7. Field experiences. A relationship was cultivated with a low-income, predominantly African American elementary school to specifically allow the project participants to complete two semester practica experiences. The practica ranged between one and two days a week where the students were placed in a classroom under the supervision of a classroom teacher. Students were there over two semesters, and were able to develop relationships with school faculty, children, and their families.

8. Student journals. To document participants' experiences in their university classes, field experiences, and community settings, they submitted a minimum of two journal entries a month. The entries were semi-structured and simply asked them to record an event that happened, their thoughts and/or feelings, and how they would respond differently the next time. The journals were vehicles for them to begin the self-reflection process and to help inform our teacher education program regarding successful strategies. Journals also assisted in identifying additional ways to respond to their needs, and ultimately the needs of the children and families they would serve.

9. Community-building. There were myriad opportunities for participants to get to know and socially interact with faculty, staff, and their cohort members and their families and significant others. A focus of Project PILOT was on the building of community and the recognition that as full-time students and often employees, those men were often away from their families who provided much support and encouragement. Theme socials were planned and held to include their families and friends and to promote positive interactions with faculty and staff in settings that extended beyond the classroom. The socials also allowed the university and school communities to be exposed to the interests and talents of the project participants.

The impact of Project PILOT is far-reaching. Students began having impact on low-income children and youth in their first year in the project. They were immediately placed at a low-income school that had been designated by the state's Education Commissioner as a "critically-low performing school." Each student was placed in a different classroom in that school during their college junior and senior years. Since the inception of the project, 36 African American men have completed field experiences there.

At that school alone, those men have directly impacted approximately 1,000 students by doing their supervised teaching there. Fifteen men are currently completing their internship in classrooms with a total of approximately 500 students. Ten men have graduated and are teaching in their own classrooms and are directly impacting the lives of at least 500 additional students. In sum total, a minimum of 2,000 students have directly benefited from placing African American men in urban classrooms. As these men have committed to teaching primarily in Hillsborough County in Florida, the impact for local schools is significant.

DATA ON PROJECT PILOT

In order to determine the effects of project PILOT on the educational and professional experiences of the project graduates, a two-tiered research approach was used. The first level involved analyzing the project participants' weekly journal entries for common themes, experiences, and concerns. At the second level, semistructured interviews were conducted with a random sample of five PILOT men to augment the information gleaned from their journal entries. The intent was to gauge their perceptions of their preparation process and their experiences as beginning urban special education teachers.

Journal Themes

Every week during their enrollment in the program, the participants were required to submit two journal entries. Submitted journal entries for all project participants in the first two cohorts were analyzed for topics that were discussed frequently and those that were discussed extensively. Three themes emerged that were discussed frequently in participants' journals: (1) professionalism between students and teachers, (2) classroom behavior management, and (3) Project PILOT experiences. Participants wrote extensively about specific instances in their university classes and the supportive atmosphere created by the Project PILOT staff. Together, the information created a portraiture that can inform future efforts to improve the recruitment and retention of African American males in the special education field.

Many journal entries documented the PILOT participants' frustration with the disrespect shown them by their students in their field experiences. Instances in which the childen used profanity, ignored them, or were defiant left them questioning their placements. They were unprepared for the belligerence demonstrated by a number of the children. They often underscored the importance of developing positive teacher-student relationships. It was observed that teachers often fail to develop some familiarity with the students, their home environment, and the school community. One PILOT graduate wrote about a classroom situation in which a student was continuously acting out and his attempts at traditional behavior strategies were unsuccessful. The PILOT participant talked to the student and learned that the student's father had recently been incarcerated. Obtaining that information enabled the supervising teacher and PILOT participant to develop a plan that was sensitive to the student's needs. The PILOT student teacher realized at that moment the clear connection between school success and family culture.

Behavior management was an area that the PILOT men felt unprepared to effectively address. They believed that their university classes ill-prepared them to manage their students. Compounding their perceived lack of preparation in this area was the constant pressure by colleagues for the PILOT men to act as referees during students' altercations. The men felt that they were targeted because of their "black maleness." In school settings where there were few male teachers and frequently only one black male, they found themselves in the role of "aggressive physical manager." On several occasions, they were called out of their assigned classrooms to handle such disputes. In one instance, a PILOT man was asked to physically restrain a student, despite his protests that he lacked the required training.

Through the process, the participants' journals reflected the knowledge that negative behaviors can be redirected into positive behaviors with some planning and effort. The men expressed renewed energy when they employed alternative methods of action that proved successful. Many used token methods of management and incorporated the activities into the lesson plans. An example was using toy money for tokens and developing activities that required counting money. The men felt that there is a trend for teachers to take the easiest road to achieving peace in the classroom and noted that that road often leaves many by the wayside.

Most memorable of the PILOT project experience as noted in the journal entries was the camaraderie developed among the PILOT men. They often observed that their friendship and brotherhood sustained them during the educational process and their internships. Several remarked that these were people with whom lifelong bonds had been created. They wrote about being inspired by the monthly speakers and felt supported by the intense interest shown by the project PILOT staff. As suggested by Barnett and Caffarella (1992), when cohorts continue to develop relationships among themselves long after their group membership officially ends, that is an indicator of the successful use of cohorts.

Several of the journal entries reported in great detail the instances that highlighted PILOT men's struggles with the demands of a rigorous university curriculum. One participant talked about the challenges he had with balancing his home life with school commitments and the unwavering rules about their attendance at PILOT seminars. At one point his coursework suffered, and he failed a class. The embarrassment he felt along with his sense of failure heightened his resolve to improve his abilities to prioritize his obligations.

A continuous theme of the PILOT seminars centered on their being goal focused without losing their ethnic and individual identities. Several of the speakers connected with the men because of the messages that were espoused. A PILOT man wrote that a speaker "opened thoughts and feelings that I have not remembered for a long time." There was a sense of reconnecting to the dreams and aspirations that had perhaps been buried long ago. Of utmost importance to the PILOT men was having exposure to facilitators who were also African American men.

Interviews with PILOT Men

An interview protocol that addressed key objectives of PILOT and the USF teacher-training program was developed. The interview was designed to target the PILOT graduates' use and knowledge of instructional strategies, behavior management techniques, and cultural responsiveness in their school placements. Five of the 36 participants were randomly selected to be inter-viewed. Three of the interviewees were members of the first graduating cohort and two from the second graduating cohort. Each was a special education teacher in a school where the ethnic minority students comprised over 50 percent of the student population. Their classroom settings varied between self-contained and inclusionary. Most of them had paraprofessionals to assist in the classroom. The interviews were conducted over the telephone and face to face at the university.

Themes that emerged from the interviews mirrored the journal entries. Professionalism, classroom behavior management, and parent accountability emerged as areas of concern among the respondents. Other emergent themes were their PILOT project experiences and their teaching careers.

The PILOT graduates talked about their tenuous relationships with other special and general educators. They began their teaching assignments with the belief that teachers needed to coordinate instructional units and discuss classroom dynamics to form cohesive plans. Unfortunately, their experi-ences did not support their beliefs. Teachers often failed to consult the men about curricular issues but far too often sought them out for disciplinary matters. The PILOT graduates were saddled with the role of behavior specialist, restraining and disciplining students that other teachers could not manage.

The interviews revealed that several of the PILOT men worked at the same school setting. Spread out across the campus, they frequently sought one an-other out for advice and help in dealing with a student or classroom situation. The men had also organized school activities that were well received by the students. Parents that had avoided the school established relationships with the men and visited the school often. Although the PILOT men's camaraderie and school successes were commendable, on occasion they perceived other teachers as jealous of the PILOT men's teaching effectiveness. They believed other teachers were envious of the respect shown them by the students and their classroom management success. The PILOT men discussed keeping those teachers' negative attitudes in perspective, and they vowed to continue making efforts to improve the school environment for the students.

Several of the improvements center on the PILOT men's capacity to establish a learning atmosphere in their classrooms. Consistency, fairness, and realism were mantras of all the men. They talked about the need to be firm about the rules in the classroom and enforce the consequences when appropriate. A failure to execute resulted in a room that was chaotic, as reported by one. Trial and error seemed to be the method by which they developed their management styles. They commented that the teacher-training program could have prepared them better, but they created systems that best suited their personalities and those of their students.

A threefold rationale was proposed by a PILOT man for the current state of the educational system: (1) Parents are not being held accountable for their child's actions, (2) teachers' frustrations are directly related to their lack of training, and (3) schools cannot handle the discipline. The men lamented the lack of parent accountability and involvement. They spoke about students bringing issues from home into classrooms and suggested that teachers are ill prepared to handle the resulting behaviors. Parents, on the other hand, have been through a lot and are often unprepared themselves to handle their life situations. Some parents looked to the PILOT men to fulfill role-model status in their sons' lives. Parents informed the PILOT men that they were helping their children by being Black male role models.

Despite their numerous concerns and lamentations, it was clear that the PILOT men believe they are making a difference in their students' lives. In spite of the negative experiences with fellow teachers, the disrespect shown them by some students, and their own personal challenges, the PILOT participants continue to be committed to serving children with special needs. One gentleman asserted, "What I'm doing is noble. I'm making a positive difference whether I see it or not."

POST-NOTES ON LESSONS LEARNED

Having interacted with, and observed the progress of, three cohorts of Project PILOT men over the course of four years, several lessons come to mind. They are noteworthy for teacher education programs deliberately aiming to prepare African American men for urban special education careers. The lessons focus on cohort membership, professional development, and university-school collaborations.

Cohort Membership

It is imperative that students be recruited as a cohort and progress through their classes and field experiences as an intact cohort, especially on traditionally White campuses or in traditionally White and/or female colleges of education. The critical mass of a cohort of African American men proved invaluable for the participants themselves as well as for our College of Education. Project PILOT participants who might have been silenced in classes where they represented only one or two were given voice and empowered to provide perspectives that might not ordinarily be included in university discussions. Another benefit of their cohort membership was that it afforded the faculty and other students opportunities to witness the diversity within groups based on the varied perspectives articulated by Project PILOT men.

Though the PILOT men found themselves in novel situations in their classes (being empowered and having multiple voices), there must be a balance between that affirmation and their responsibility not to abuse it. An example of abusing that empowerment would be to use their collective voices and presence to silence others. Without considerable discussion and awareness, that could easily happen. There must be structured opportunities for openly addressing those kinds of consequences. The professional development seminars provided excellent forums for holding those sometimes sensitive discussions. Even more important than how those conversations were held were the facilitators. Early in the project, it was most critical to have such discussions led by African American men in higher education—the national consultants or mentors.

Professional Development

Preparing individuals for urban special education teaching careers is a tall and complex order. It is even more complicated when courses continue to be taught in traditional ways. Unfortunately, some teaching strategies continue to be espoused that do not infuse sociocultural considerations and have not been validated for use with children and youth in urban schools. To do so, all faculty (dominant and ethnic minority culture) must commit to ongoing professional development to become more comfortable and knowledgeable around those issues.

In originally planning Project PILOT, I assumed that students would need monthly seminars to address urban special education issues that they may not get in university courses. I discovered that while those topics were necessary and beneficial, equally needed were discussions and activities related to interpersonal growth and development. For example, PILOT men were provided seminars on networking, public speaking, business table etiquette, and exploring their relationships with their own fathers. Seminars should be planned to meet the unique needs of African American men who may have had limited opportunities in the past for professional development and networking.

University-School Collaboration

In addition to faculty taking advantage of opportunities for their own professional growth in urban education, they must also collaborate with each other and communities more to ensure that pre- and in-service teachers are adequately equipped to meet the changing demands of today's student populations. Faculty could develop relationships with schools and communities to enlist the assistance of other "experts" or individuals who are familiar with realistic techniques for positively managing behaviors and connecting with families, and the like. The PILOT men's most serious concern relates to the lack of behavior management strategies in their repertoires. To remedy, instead of a discrete course in behavior management, strategies could be woven throughout teacher preparation programs. For example, a course on reading strategies or art and music could also address behavior management. Another solution could involve aligning university coursework in this area with schools' needs and behavior management training programs. Most importantly, the strategies must be realistic and effective with culturally diverse children and youth.

In a similar vein, field experiences should be consistent with university coursework. The PILOT men's early practicum experiences were in one low-income, predominantly African American elementary school. It was quite helpful to develop relationships with a coordinator at the school who was responsible for their placement and oversight. Missing from that relationship was a way to bridge university coursework with their school experiences. Though participants had two courses that were directly linked to their practica, there was minimal communication with their supervising teachers. Supervising teachers were given course syllabi, and that was the extent of the communication. In that regard, supervising teachers were unaware of what went on in university classes. In response, a university site coordinator or faculty member could meet frequently with the school site coordinator to ensure smooth communication. This has implications for faculty loads where time must be factored in to meet with school personnel.

Strong collaborations with school districts must be developed and maintained for projects like PILOT to be successful. As the PILOT men completed their field experiences, there were a few occasions where their supervising teachers were reluctant to provide them with constructive criticism or feedback. There were times when the PILOT men would not be given such feedback until their midterm or final practicum evaluation. Waiting so late to give feedback creates limited opportunities for addressing those concerns. School personnel must be made to feel more comfortable in giving accurate feedback. University faculty meeting with school supervisors more regularly could heighten their comfort levels.

Another concern expressed by the PILOT men involved the paradox of feeling inadequately prepared in behavior management, yet being heavily recruited by their teacher colleagues to manage children with extreme behavioral difficulties or acting out behaviors. There is a tendency for African American male teachers to be perceived by their colleagues as "great Black hopes" in managing children who look like them. University faculty can assist schools in identifying and understanding this burden and how it gives rise to burnout.

1. Lack of special education background among administrators. The PILOT men also suggested that some of their school administrators lack expertise on special education policies and procedures. PILOT men discussed having either principals or assistant principals who were not trained to address special education issues. One teacher noted that the principal in his school was knowledgeable about special education, but because her schoolwide duties were so broad, she was forced to delegate special education issues to an assistant principal whose knowledge base about special education was limited.

2. Teachers' lack of cultural understandings and competence. It was expressed that many of their teaching colleagues demonstrated a lack of understanding about children's home situations and circumstances. A teacher gave an example of an occasion when a child began acting out frequently and was being written off by other teachers. The PILOT teacher made an effort to get to know that child, beyond the school setting. That teacher established a relationship with him and discovered that the child's parent was incarcerated. That change in the family was causing the student to act out. Once that was understood, the teacher began working on the appropriate behavior.

3. Lack of realistic behavior management strategies. The teachers expressed concern that many behavior management strategies that are taught at the university level may be ineffective with the populations that they are asked to teach. When African American male students have more severe behaviors, the African American men are expected even more than other teachers to be able to manage those children and youth. Several of the teachers said that other teachers bring their "problem" students to them, expecting the PILOT men to intervene. The PILOT teachers noted that in some cases they feel no more equipped than the other teachers do to handle such severe behaviors.

4. Lack of student motivation. The PILOT men consistently reported difficulty getting, and keeping, students motivated to do their best. Their frustration lies in knowing that many of their students are satisfied to do less.

5. Lack of collaboration with regular educators and other special educators. They expressed the desire to develop working relationships with other teachers that will benefit the students in their classes. In the PILOT teachers' perceptions, several factors impede quality working relationships with other teachers. When the PILOT men discussed ways other faculty and staff members related to them, it ranged from idealized images of the PILOT men's ability to manage the behavior of all African American male students. In effect, some school person-

nel believed that because the PILOT students were African American males, they would automatically be competent in managing those students' behaviors. On the other hand, the PILOT men reported that some teachers were envious of the rapport they had with African American students and the respect the students afforded them. Another impediment to collaborative-relationship builders, as noted by several PILOT men, is the flirtatious behavior they perceived on the part of some of the teachers with whom they worked. Those PILOT students noted that it was difficult to develop professional relationships when that occurred.

6. Lack of parent involvement. Most of the PILOT men believed that they had good rapport with the parents of their students, but expressed concern that they were unable to consistently communicate with students' family members. They noted that parents many times would not return their phone calls. The PILOT teachers also wanted family members to take more responsibility for their children's actions.

7. Students look at them as father figures. One student said he got more respect from students outside of his class than those in his class.

8. PILOT helped them better fully understand themselves in order to deal with students better.

9. It was good for non–African Americans to be exposed to PILOT men in university classes.

10. PILOT men empowered through their increased presence as well as the exposure to African American men in higher education.

RECOMMENDATIONS FOR TEACHER EDUCATION PROGRAMS

The interviews of the PILOT men and analyses of their journals throughout their teacher preparation process were revealing. In fact, they hold many implications for teacher education programs. Those teachers recommended that teacher preparation programs provide:

1. More exposure to paperwork in special education. The men wanted more consistent training on ways to manage the mounds of special education paperwork. They noted that training sessions conducted by their school district frequently were confusing as the process for completing paperwork changed frequently. Teacher education programs should link closely with school districts to ensure that guidelines for IEPs and other special education paperwork are consistently articulated to beginning teachers. In addition, teacher preparation should also incorporate strategies for managing time, setting priorities, and managing information and paperwork.

2. More time and emphasis on real-life situations. The beginning teachers suggested that teacher preparation programs should focus more on meeting the needs of children with severe behavior disorders and problems. Several of the teachers noted the difficult tasks of working with students with behaviors such as acting out and aggression.

3. More practicum time built in. Some of the teachers wanted additional practicum time built into the schedules of preservice teachers. Those men began their first practicum, or field experience, during their second semester in the special education program. They spent one day a week in a low-income, predominantly African American school. The following two semesters, they spent two days a week in the same school, and their last semester was spent at another school completing their internship, or student teaching experience.

4. Diversified practicum experiences. It was also suggested that instead of providing experience in one classroom a semester, the field experiences should be diverse within a school to provide students with opportunities to observe teachers other than their supervising teachers. They also wanted opportunities to observe in their cohort members' classrooms.

In sum, teacher preparation in the new millennium is a tall order for any teacher education program. It seems even more complex when the preservice teachers are African American males. The intersection of their ethnicity and gender must be considered when planning recruitment and programming strategies. Whereas the rate at which teachers typically leave the profession is high, it may be even higher among African American male teachers, given the often unrealistic expectations and their desire to "give back" and work with urban, high-poverty children and youth. These findings hold implications for altering teacher education course work and field experiences to respond both to the changing population of pre- and in-service teachers and to the changing faces of the school-aged students and their families who are waiting to be served more appropriately.

DISCUSSION QUESTIONS

1. Why is it important to have special education teachers from culturally diverse backgrounds?
2. What themes arose from the Project PILOT students' journals? Why do you think these themes were predominant?
3. What collaborations must occur in order for initiatives such as Project PILOT to be successful?

REFERENCES

Barnett, B. G., Caffarella, R. S., & Daresh, J. C. (1992) A new slant on leadership preparation. *Educational Leadership, 49*, 72–75.

Boykin, A. W. (1994). Afrocultural expression and its implications for schooling. In E. R. Hollons, J. E. King, & W. C. Hayman (Eds.), *Teaching diverse populations: Formulating a knowledge base* (pp. 225–273). New York: State University of New York Press.

Draper, N. (1999, March 10). Teachers who call it quits cause shortage concern. *Minneapolis Star Tribune,* p. 1B.

Ford, D. Y. (1998) The underrepresentation of minority students in gifted education: Problems and promises in recruitment and retention. *The Journal of Special Education, 32*(1), 4–14.

Ford, D. Y., Grantham, T. C., & Harris, J. J. (1997). The recruitment and retention of minority teachers in gifted education. *Roeper Review, 19*, 213–220.

Gay, G. G. (1993). Building cultural bridges: A bold proposal for teacher education. *Education and Urban Society, 25*(3), 45–51.

Harry, B., & Anderson, M. G. (1994). The disproportionate placement of African American males in special education programs: A critique of the process. *Journal of Negro Education, 63*(4), 602–619.

King, S. H. (1993). The limited presence of African-American teachers. *Review of Educational Research, 63*, 115-149.

Ogbu, J.U. (1990). Literacy and schooling in subordinate cultures: The case of Black Americans. In K. Lomotey (Ed.), *Going to school: The African American experience* (pp. 113–131). Albany: State University of New York Press.

O'Keefe, J. M. (1999). Creative resourcing for Catholic schools: The critical issue of hiring and retaining high-quality teachers. *Momentum, 30*(4), 548.

Pipho, C. (1998). A 'real' teacher shortage. *Phi Delta Kappan, 80*(3),1812.

Townsend, B. L., Thomas, D. D., Witty, J. P., & Lee, R. S. (1996). Diversity and school restructuring: Creating partnerships in a world of difference. *Teacher Education and Special Education, 19*(2), 102–118.

U.S. Department of Education (1998). Twentieth Annual Report to Congress on the Implementation of the Individuals with Disabilities Act. Washington: U.S. Department of Education.

11

Collaborative Professional Development Partnerships

Karen L. Colucci, Betty C. Epanchin, and Kathryn L. Laframboise

In 1998, there were reported 1,037 PDSs in locations across the United States (Abdal-Haqq,1998). Goodlad (1994) observed that "today advocacy of school-university partnerships is de rigeur; not to have one or be part of one could be dangerous to your educational health" (p. 103). The widespread commitment to school-university partnerships to which Goodlad refers grew from a recognition that unless teacher candidates had ecologically valid settings in which to apply their knowledge, their pedagogical understandings were limited. As a number of scholars have noted, the "ivory tower" is not the setting in which teachers can learn to teach.

Concurrent with universities' work to improve teacher education, K–12 schools have engaged in similar efforts to improve the quality of their instruction. Their focus has been to move away from the scientific management that guided the development of modern school bureaucracies and that separate "the role of supervisor from that of worker, creating layers of people whose job it was to plan the work of others. . . . [In such bureaucracies], workers are not supposed to think, just do" (Darling-Hammond, 1997, p. 5). Instead, the schools have been working to create learning communities in which teachers and students are creative and critical thinkers and effective problem solvers.

As these reforms have been advanced, there has been a growing recognition that neither university nor K–12 schools can implement effective reform alone, leading to the support for and growing subscription to school-university partnerships. Although school-university collaborations were part of the educational literature for most of the 20th century, a major emphasis emerged in the 1980s and 1990s. In 1986, the Carnegie Forum on Education and the Economy called for the establishment of clinical schools where new teachers would learn to work in collegial, performance-oriented environments (Levine, 1998).

In 1986, the Holmes Group called for a major restructuring of teacher education in which Professional Development Schools (PDS) play a central role. Specifically, the Holmes Group advocated for connecting colleges of education to the K–12 schools through the PDS in order to make schools better places for practicing teachers to work and learn. The Holmes Group also advocated for connecting the efforts of experienced teachers to renew their professional knowledge and advance themselves as professionals with efforts to improve schools and prepare new teachers.

Levine (1998) maintained that common to the best PDSs is a commitment to a student-centered approach to teaching and learning, the sharing of responsibilities between partnering institutions, the simultaneous renewal of both the school and the university, and a commitment to providing equal opportunity for all participants. Levine also identified what she sees as important assumptions that underlie the PDS:

- There is a knowledge base about teaching that resides among practitioners.
- Knowledge about teaching is created in school settings.
- Teaching and learning are ineluctably tied together; teaching is learning.
- Teachers' learning needs to be contextualized if teachers are to be oriented to continuous learning in practice.
- Teachers' learning needs to be collegial in order to generate more knowledge and to produce comfort with public practice and habits of conferral.
- Teachers' learning needs to be problem-based in order to develop a problem-solving orientation toward practice. (p. 2)

As Levine notes, these assumptions reflect a view that promotes the importance of both students' and adults' learning, which is a major departure from traditional thought that considers teacher education, student learning, and staff development as three separate enterprises. These assumptions also pose teachers as researchers and generators of knowledge—another radically different perspective.

Levine (1992) suggests that teacher candidates need to learn to deal confidently with the uncertainties of practice. She suggests:

It is often the case that teachers, working in isolation, tend to blame themselves for failures that really are the result of an inadequate knowledge base. They believe they ought to be able to do something or ought to know something that is not really possible. Because teachers have little opportunity to work with colleagues and are not trained in collegial settings, they do not know the extent of others' knowledge and ability and, therefore, they maintain unrealistic views of what may be possible. Once they understand that they are working with an inadequate knowledge base, however, they need to know that it is possible to function effectively nevertheless. (p. 18)

Levine suggests that learning in action through inquiry is an important way of coping with the uncertainties of practice.

Though both universities and K-12 schools have been involved in serious reform and renewal, both also face significant challenges in the process. Traditionally, universities have had a privileged position in relation to schools, and there have been "long-standing asymmetries in status, power, and resources" (Little, 1993, p. 129). Universities have traditionally viewed schools as a source for gathering their data, and university faculty have often seen teachers as implementing their research rather than as colleagues in practice. To further complicate this relationship, few teachers regard the work of universities, particularly research in education, as relevant and important to their daily professional lives. For although teachers have long engaged in the problem solving that generates solutions and that is often called "action research" in the current literature, they have recognized a "hiatus between theory and practice" (Guba, 1996, p. ix) that is at least partly caused by the research paradigms of the universities. Much of the research that has been conducted by universities has resulted in statements of general laws and probabilistic implications rather than specific applications to cases, which is exactly the context where teachers are working. Further, schools and universities have dramatically different approaches to their work. As Valli (1999) observed,

In schools, demands for action are too pressing; in universities they are too weak. The historical trajectories of the two institutions parallel the split between theory practice, reflection and action. Praxis, the notion that knowledge should be used for purposeful action and that theory and practice are not separate but tightly interwoven human activities, has been lost in both institutions. (p. 3)

Against this backdrop of change and restructuring in the K–12 schools and in teacher education, we have been working to establish partnerships that will address current needs for teachers who can work effectively in inclusionary classrooms. Winn and Blanton (1997) report:

One of the major challenges regarding inclusion is the need for general and special education to work together to develop curriculum and instruction based on the characteristics of best practices and which, by their nature, are more accommodating to the needs of diverse learners, including those with special needs, than programs traditionally associated with either general and with special education. (p. 5)

The following is a description of the development of one partnership that is working to simultaneously meet the needs of school districts and the university to prepare teacher candidates for work with diverse learners and to retain master teachers in the fields of special and general education. We present seven assumptions upon which we have built this partnership and that are statements of some of the shared values of the partners.

BEGINNING OUR PARTNERSHIPS

Early Collaborations in Special Education

The work of national groups, such as the Carnegie Forum and the Holmes Group, as well as a growing recognition by K–12 schools and universities that in order to improve and meet current needs means fundamentally changing how we do business, led the University of South Florida (USF) to explore new ways of partnering with schools. In the late 1980s, faculty within the Department of Special Education at USF approached the directors of special education in local school districts with the question, How can we work together? Implicit in this question were several assumptions:

1. University programs must be relevant to their local constituencies.
2. Educational reform must be collaboratively planned, implemented, and evaluated.
3. Universities should attend to and focus their research and development efforts on issues generated by and relevant to schools.

As a result of these initial conversations, several collaborative arrangements developed between the Department of Special Education on campus and the two school districts where most of our field-based work occurs. These collaborations have evolved into our current partnership. In Pasco County, a new school was being constructed, and school district and university personnel agreed to support a professional development school located in that county. That initial PDS has led to the creation of several other PDSs. In Hillsborough County, the district had a number of centers for students with disabilities. Very few services for students with disabilities were provided in mainstream classrooms, and district leaders were concerned that services for students with disabilities were not being delivered in the least restrictive alternative environment. In accord with the district's interests and needs, a project was begun to develop strategies for including students with disabilities in general education classrooms. In other school districts in our service area, other collaborative projects also developed. In one district, critical teacher shortages led to a project preparing paraprofessionals to become special education teachers (Epanchin & Wooley-Brown, 1993, 1995), and in other districts, school-based cohorts of students focused on school improvement through the blending of academic and professional development (Smith, Delp, Hamilton, Houck, Ciemniecki, & Archer, 1995; Stoddard, & Danforth, 1995). Each of these projects provided excellent opportunities for learning about working in partnership with school districts.

In the mid-1990s, the department received a federal teacher preparation grant (HO 29G60214) that developed a plan for recruiting school-based leaders as clinical faculty and for more closely connecting students' work on campus and in the field. In this project, teacher candidates were assigned in clusters to partner schools, and site coordinators were identified at each of the partner schools. The site coordinators were responsible for orienting students to the school and for assigning students to classrooms or to activities that had been collaboratively (with the university) identified as beneficial. With time, the role of the site coordinator was expanded to include leading a seminar at the school for the teacher candidates and consulting with colleagues about how to address challenges presented by teacher candidates. The site coordinators met monthly with a few university faculty and the director of special education from the school district. The purposes of these group meetings were to promote the communication and coordination between the on-campus and the field component of the program and to discuss questions or concerns that the group members might have.

The site coordinators were a stable group, and over time trusting relationships developed among the teachers. These meetings became opportunities for teachers to raise concerns about their work with the teacher candidates, and in this safe environment all members analyzed issues and tried to develop strategies for addressing the concerns. The meetings were collegial, and although the director of special education started the meetings and managed the agenda when she was there, members proceeded with their work regardless of who was present at the particular meeting. After the group had been meeting for several years, a focus group was conducted with the members for the purpose of assessing what members thought was worthwhile and how it could be improved. Their comments affirmed the importance of opportunities for continuous professional development and personal learning. Group members valued the opportunities to share and learn from colleagues. As one said, "The monthly meetings are very helpful, vital. We see how others do things and we share our vision. You don't know if people share your vision if you don't talk about it. They helped build mutual respect and trust. We're all struggling for the same goal."

As the site coordinator role was better defined and established, some boundaries between the universities and schools began to blur. One of the first areas in which site coordinators began to overlap with on-campus faculty was the evaluation of teacher candidates. Site coordinators were obviously skilled in identifying students who were having difficulties and also in developing strategies for addressing these difficulties. Another area in which the site coordinators assumed increasing responsibility was the school-based seminars with the preservice interns. These seminars became important resources for the teacher candidates who needed to learn about the school in which they were placed and had numerous questions about their work in the school. The seminars were also settings in which teacher candidates were able to seek assistance in problem solving about how to work with various students and staff within the school and about course assignments that were to be implemented in the field. The demands placed on site coordinators through their new roles caused them to have questions and concerns about supervision, mentoring, and adult learning. University faculty took on a collegial professional development role, different from their traditional role as "expert" or "instructor." As the collaboration grew, roles and responsibilities continued to evolve becoming less distinct as specific functions of either the school district or the university, and a partnership gradually developed.

Early Collaborations in General Education

Simultaneously, the Department of Childhood/Language Arts/Reading Education was also extending its collaboration with the same school districts through work in professional development schools and through a state-supported professional development project designed to prepare schools for implementing continuous progress (multiage groups of students who stay with a team of teachers for several years) and differentiated curriculum (based on a continuous teaching cycle and developmentally appropriate practice). This also strengthened the collaborations between university and school districts and provided faculty in both institutions with more skills and knowledge about how to work in partnerships. The grant included numerous activities and structures that support school reorganization from both top-down and bottom-up directions. Teams of teachers attended two- to four-day retreats at hotels located near model schools where interactive observations of restructured classrooms were made as part of the learning process. Teams were required to have a building administrator as a member of the team. District administrators also participated in the retreat, ensuring that information on the project was owned by all levels in the two districts. After the retreats, role-alike support groups met regularly to further advance the goals of the project, and these groups became involved in developing new retreats as more schools joined the project. Interestingly, an unexpected benefit of the project was the regular interactions among school district personnel from the two counties where our later partnership work would occur.

While much was evolving and changing in the field, there were also changes underway on campus. A faculty committee within the College of Education was advocating for curriculum reform. This group, consistent with the evolving literature on reform and renewal in teacher education, was committed to collaboration with the K–12 schools as well as with the Colleges of Arts and Sciences and Fine Arts, community colleges, and the business community.

THE PDS WITHOUT WALLS PARTNERSHIP

As Winn and Blanton report (1997), inclusion of students with special needs into general education classrooms is becoming more common and teachers are working more collaboratively. In our programs we had talked about the benefits of inclusionary practices and the need for programs to collaborate, but to this point our students rarely saw examples of it at the university. The current partnership was formalized when a federal grant was obtained to specifically extend some of the work of the earlier collaborations. In January 1999 the Departments of Special Education and Childhood/Language Arts/Reading Education began a new partnership grant that would examine the dynamics of partnering with the school districts and find new ways of working with teacher candidates and in-service teachers who would mentor them (H 325P980006). The project, called the PDS without Walls, focused on integrating special and general education preservice training to enhance inclusion in the general education classroom and develop collaborative relationships among special education and general education teacher candidates.

The integration occurs on three levels. First, students in the preservice programs in special education and elementary education are placed in mixed cohorts when they enter the two programs at the beginning of the junior year. Courses that are common to both programs are taken together, starting with an Introduction to Special Education course in the first semester. Course assignments are designed to be carried out collaboratively in field experiences where students are assigned in groups of six—three from special education and three from elementary education. As the students progress through the program, students take program-specific courses and bring those perspectives to the mixed cohort courses, informing each other of the needs, curriculum, and issues of education from the viewpoint of their programs.

Second, site coordinators were identified at each of the school sites where the preservice teachers would be placed in their early field experiences. The site coordinators are teachers, specialists, or school administrators who are hired by the university to coordinate the early field experiences in the school, mentor the students, help them implement their course assignments, and evaluate their performance in the field. The site coordinators meet monthly with other site coordinators and university faculty to discuss the progress of the students, clarify roles, and review and make suggestions about course assignments. Over the past several years, the site coordinators have provided substantial input into the revisions of courses and the organization of the early field experiences.

The third level of integration occurs during the final, full-time internship. Through an application process that included personal statements, evaluation of previous mentoring experiences, administrator recommendations, and interviews, teachers were identified who would participate in an intensive training program (three days of retreat and a series of seminars) for graduate credit and be appointed as clinical faculty at the university. The training activities were also integrated, special education and elementary education as well as teachers from the two participating county school districts. We call the clinical faculty Professional Practice Partners (PPPs) to distinguish them from other cooperating teachers who supervise with a university supervisor making periodic visits. During the semesters when PPPs are assigned interns, they attend a monthly meeting with other PPPs and university faculty and are paid a stipend.

DEVELOPING COMMON UNDERSTANDINGS

As the partnership has evolved, partnership coordinators have identified several principles that appear to be important in determining the outcome or success of the partnership. Discussed next, these seven assumptions appear to be essential in establishing and maintaining a partnership.

Assumption #1: A partnership is different from a collaboration. Partnerships involve changing existing structures to create new and different structures that support the shared work. Partnerships involve formal agreements to work together and share the responsibility of that work. Collaborations involve working together to accomplish a task; whereas partnerships create a new dynamic in defining the working relationships between or among the partners. Collaboratives are valued endeavors among parties committed to a common goal; partnerships are characterized by a shared cost and commitment to the enterprise. Partnerships also are based on agreements among the stakeholders. These understandings among the stakeholders are contractual in nature and have the approval of institutional representatives at the highest levels.

Collaborations may be formal or informal and be developed to achieve mutually agreed upon goals. These goals may be either long term or short term. Our college of education is continuously and simultaneously involved in a number of collaborations and partnerships with the school districts. For example, our arrangements for many of the early field experiences for preservice teachers are collaborative in nature. The understandings are informal—that is, based on frequent communications and developed over time. Moreover, many of these arrangements are made by individuals or programs and individual schools and change or even dissolve as faculty, school administrators, and teachers change. Even though the training of the preservice teachers is considered of critical importance by all involved, the relationships are based on a tradition of working together rather than specific contracts.

On the other hand, our PDSs are partnerships that are based on contracts or statements of mutual agreements negotiated at several levels (school district and university, faculty, teacher unions, etc.). The PDSs involve so many levels of commitment that, even though many aspects continue to evolve as the partners work toward goals, there must be clear agreement about the partners' roles and responsibilities that is validated by the contract. The documents or contracts add permanence to the commitments so that as teachers and administrators change there is a record of the expectations of the partners.

Assumption #2: Effective partnerships are characterized by risks and benefits that are equitable for the partners. In discussing school-university partnerships, Goodlad (1994) suggests that when such relationships are based on "benign intentions" (p. 106), they tend to be fleeting. Likewise, if a partner only focuses on its own needs, ignoring the partner's needs, the partnership is likely to dissolve. If, however, partnerships focus on overlapping self-interests and a common agenda, the likelihood of success and sustainability is increased. As Goodlad notes, "There is greater potential in first seeing in the other partner a source of satisfying one's own needs" (p. 106).

In the PDS without Walls partnership, we are working to negotiate structures that address each partner's needs. Both school districts that work in the partnership have significant needs for quality teachers and both face the pressure of high-stakes testing. Although the partners may have the same or similar needs, their contributions have to be seen as equitable. When partners are not equal in size or resources, there must be a common understanding that balances the contributions and benefits. If one of the partners puts forward more resources, time, or personnel, there are likely to be feelings of inequity. Also if one of the partners derives most of the benefits or the institutions have different levels of commitment, there will be diminished participation in the partnership. For instance, if the K–12 schools see the children's learning as their responsibility and the preparation of preservice teachers as the responsibility of the university, then the teachers and administrators will view their roles with student teachers differently than if they believe that they have ownership in the development of teachers for their profession.

Two related concerns of schools working with interns are the pressures of high-stakes testing and the impact of inexperienced teachers in their classrooms. Some schools, however, see the interns as a wealth of extra help for children. These schools organize and reorganize the activities for the teacher candidates in ways that benefit the children and also provide a wide range of experiences for the preservice teachers. These schools understand that they make valuable contributions to the development of the university students who, in a year or two, will be colleagues in their schools. When the school sees only the risks of working with the teacher candidates as inexperienced teachers and perceives that the benefits all go to the university, which in their view is responsible for the training of the preservice teachers, establishing and sustaining a partnership is extremely problematic. Also when the school or district administrators see the interns as a source for future hires in a competitive market but the teachers believe the risks (i.e., the burden of work) are all theirs, the partners are working at cross-purposes with each other.

Assumption #3: Relationships are the currency of partnerships. Decisions about how to structure and manage a partnership should take into account the nature of the relationships among key persons. Over the years, many faculty at USF have established positive and productive relationships with school personnel through individual projects. These relationships have enabled us to develop the existing partnership. Faculty in the partnership have established relationships with key persons in the school districts enabling them to discuss difficult topics. Inevitably, in forming a partnership there are differences of opinion regarding how things should be done. Trust and commitment to the partnership and to the people in them are essential if the tough issues are to be addressed and resolved (Levine, 1998).

For example, in our partnership, persons from staff development and faculty from the university have often seen issues quite differently. In planning training events, we recently had extended discussions about the place of action research in the professional development of preservice and in-service teachers. The discussion centered on several questions: What is the role of research for teachers? Is it a school or university function? Will teachers find it valuable? Is it a high priority in the limited time and resources available for the training events? Slowly we have worked through clarification of terms and concepts, needs and goals to see how action research is critical to the vitality of the project. The discussions included examining each other's vocabulary, conceptual frameworks, and ways of doing things until we found commonalities that would allow us to understand each others' perspectives.

The relationships on which the partnership is built must also be dynamic. If the partnership is too dependent on individuals, then if those individuals leave the partnership, it is likely to dissolve. We have found, however, that close professional relationships are essential for the members to work through the issues and challenges that are part of our complex work. There must be trust and commitment among the members. In order to strengthen existing relationships while offsetting the attrition that normally occurs, the structures and activities of the partnership must be dynamic and varied so that new members are continually brought into the work and new relationships are continually being formed.

Assumption #4: Partnerships need "dialogue spaces"—time to talk about beliefs and wishes regarding the partnership. This dialogue becomes the foundation for a shared understanding of action and directions. These dialogue spaces need to be as "naturally occurring" as possible. This assumption is closely related to Assumption #3. Relationships develop from these dialogues. With adequate time to discuss issues, people come to understand each other's perceptions and beliefs, and they are able to find common ground upon which they can plan. In order to achieve this goal, we have regular meetings with various groups within the partnership. When there is a meeting to conduct business, there is an agenda with mutually agreed upon time commitments in order to honor the busy schedules of the participants. There is also "down time"—that is, time to make sure that there are some relaxed conversations so that relationships grow and there is a comfort level among the participants who must work together and also confront tough issues and challenges in the partnership.

As we began to grapple with the challenging issues that are inherent in any partnership, it became necessary for all parties to be honest and open in the discussions. We found that if we did not get to the heart of the issues or challenges, any solution we developed together was not effective. However, we found that getting to the heart of the issues and challenges was not easy. It required that we talk seriously about things within each of our systems that might be ineffective or even in conflict with the needs and goals of other partners or stakeholders and were blocking the path of the partnership. We had to bring many issues out into the open and had to trust our partners to work with us through some potentially sensitive issues. We are definitely seeing that it is a powerful exercise in relationship building.

Assumption #5: To successfully build a partnership and address all the challenges inherent in partnerships, work needs to be focused in two directions: top-down and bottom-up. We found over time that when we were not working at all levels of the systems (both university and school district) within the partnership context, problems emerged. Relationships with the service providers (school-based personnel and university faculty) had to be established, and a common understanding of shared goals was crucial. If any of the service providers was not invested in the project and did not see any benefits to its involvement, the project did not move forward.

Equally important was the support of the systems' administrations. We found that a common understanding of shared goals also had to be established at this level. This takes some effort. Administrators have responsibility for oversight of large systems, limiting their available time. However, they must be completely informed about the goals, work, and needs of the partnership and be appropriately consulted about decisions. Additionally, both school districts and universities have complex organizational structures that require careful navigation to make sure that decisions by one branch/department are not offset by differing decisions and actions of separate and often parallel branches and departments in the institutions. A clear picture of how the partnership fits within the broader context of district and university initiatives and goals had to be developed. Administrators are responsible for developing and advancing a vision for the system in which they work. If they perceive that an initiative runs counter to the vision or are unclear as to how it fits within the vision, they will not provide the support needed for success. Support must include recognition of time commitments and work within the other system as valuable and part of the basic work load of those who are working in the partnership. Without administrative support, service providers find it very difficult to sustain their involvement in an initiative no matter how invested they are at the outset.

We also found it beneficial in our work with all levels not to enter the dialogue about the partnership with too many absolutes or structures. Providing initial opportunities through dialogue to develop a shared vision, shared goals, and individual benefits gave the partnership a stronger foundation. Issues around specifics and structures can often squelch a partnership if they are dealt with before a firm foundation of trust and shared goals is laid. We provided opportunities for dialogue by hosting day-long retreats involving school district and university faculty and school district and university administrators. During the retreat, role-alike groups (school faculty, university faculty, school administrators, and university administrators) discussed their vision for the partnership, benefits, and challenges. Opportunities were then provided for cross-role groups to discuss the same areas. It was in the cross-role discussions that clearer understandings and considerations of multiple perspectives began to develop. Simultaneously, a curriculum reform group that operated across all the departments in the college of education was working. They were invited to participate in grant activities while grant faculty were active in the college of education reform committee. The opportunity for partnership members across all levels to engage in discussion proved invaluable as common goals were established and benefits and challenges for all groups as well as structures to carry out the work of the partnership were outlined.

In order to carry out the work of the partnership, new roles were developed and some existing roles were changed. We quickly realized, however, that these evolving roles could use the existing structures of both systems (university and school district). The bureaucracy of universities and school systems make the creation of new structures very daunting and can easily sap the energy from any partnership. Although the purpose of the partnership may be to create new structures (Assumption #1) such as a PDS or new roles for mentor teachers, there are many structures in the systems that can perform specific functions of the partnership, such as communication of information affecting stakeholders through meetings of those groups or curriculum review by the college's curriculum reform group, which was also reaching out to the community. We recognized the importance of using existing structures such as regularly scheduled meetings rather than add new meetings to overcrowded schedules. On the other hand, sometimes one-on-one meetings with administrators provided them information without having to coordinate appointments with several administrators at the same time.

We also worked to institutionalize the new roles to make sure that as individuals left those roles, the work of the partnership would not stop but would be sustained by other individuals stepping in. Many of the new roles in the partnership involved teachers who became teacher educators and mentors. The teachers' mind-set changed over time as they began to examine their own practice in an effort to effectively mentor university students. They began to see the enormous responsibility they held in terms of the positive impact they could have on the teaching profession and took that responsibility seriously. The teachers grew in their role as teacher educators and freely admitted that at first they were quick to judge the university students they were working with and quick to tell them "how things should be done." Over time, however, as they examined adult learning theory and mastered the shift from a teacher of K–12 to that of teacher educator (a shift that occurs back and forth throughout any given day they are working with university students), they began to feel empowered.

The teachers' growing feeling of empowerment uncovered issues within the partnership that had not been considered previously. As they worked with and mentored the university students, they began to identify areas within the university program as well as areas within the schools and the curriculum in which they worked that were problematic. They became torn as to what to do with their critical analyses. They felt that they were not being loyal or "team players" if they openly discussed the problems they had identified in their schools. Equally, they were hesitant to discuss problems they saw with the university program. Teachers historically have not been in positions of power and privilege in the systems in which they work. Loyalty and conformity are rewarded, whereas those who do not follow that line are labeled as troublemakers. It was important to recognize the precarious position in which the teachers had been placed and equally important to help them resolve the issues they faced. We wanted them to understand that it was important to not only identify problems but also to work toward solutions. By doing this they were not only loyal to the systems in which they were working, they were helping to make them better and were supporting the goals of the partnership, improving education outcomes for K–12 students, and improving the teacher education program for preservice teachers.

This example, as well as other experiences we had in our work through the partnership, validated the need for systematic and systemic communication.

Ongoing and frequent opportunities for dialogue with the service providers became an important part of the communication structure of the partnership. We also found that regular communication with administration was critical. Although frequent dialogue with top-level administration was not feasible due to schedules, written updates on partnership activities as well as annual meetings provided opportunities to keep the partnership on track. Monthly meetings with middle-level administration (who make up the management team for the partnership along with university faculty) provide dialogue opportunities to discuss challenges, make plans, and evaluate progress.

Assumption #6: By reconfiguring the way each partner spends time and resources, strengths can be optimized. In the field of education, we are faced with diminishing resources and increased performance expectations. With this pressure, both sides of the partnership recognized the benefits of developing new and successful ways of delivering programs. This type of an undertaking was daunting because it was important for the partnership and its activities to fit within the existing systems. Although we have made many inroads in this area, we still have several challenges to resolve.

Many partnerships, including ours, start with seed money from a grant to establish supporting activities and structures that are not in the current systems. This can be a problem in terms of sustainability unless careful thought is given to reconfiguring or reallocating existing resources to support the partnership when the grant money is gone. When we examined available resources at the university and also in the school districts, we found that some reconfiguring was possible. For example, money that the university had previously spent to pay university faculty to supervise interns could be used to appoint master teachers in the school districts as clinical faculty who would carry out the supervision of interns in their classrooms. Then, to provide training and support for those master teachers in their work with the interns, another reallocation was used. The university tuition vouchers that cooperating teachers normally receive for their work with interns were used to "pay" for a graduate-level course that was developed to give them opportunities to discuss with other mentor teachers and university faculty the challenges of mentoring preservice teachers. The course also provides opportunities for professional development through action research.

From the university standpoint, we wanted to put our resources where they would be most beneficial. We think that an intern's professional development will be facilitated better by our working to develop mentor teachers rather than spending our resources to supervise the interns directly. We found through past experience that supervising interns by visiting/observing them periodically only gave us a partial picture of their development and needs. We depended quite heavily on the cooperating teacher to provide the full picture and provide meaningful and sustained feedback to the intern. One teacher described this relationship metaphorically, "The university supervisor has a snapshot of the intern. We have the video." In the traditional triad relationship of intern teacher, cooperating teacher, and university supervisor, the university supervisor is often extraneous unless there is a problem. Therefore, it seemed more prudent to put resources in the areas that have proven to be effective. We still continue to meet with the interns on campus for seminars during their internship so that they are provided opportunities to discuss with other interns and university faculty the challenges and the successes they have experienced. This provides another level of support for interns as well as an opportunity to remain in contact with university faculty. University faculty also work with the cooperating teachers and interns when serious issues arise; however, we have found that most of the challenges of the mentoring relationship are worked through in the monthly meetings with other mentor teachers and through the network of teachers that is established through these meetings.

District staff development resources were also used in training and developing mentor teachers. The district had identified retention of master teachers as a goal. The partnership provided a way for master teachers to receive recognition (appointment as mentor teachers) and professional development around their interests (utilizing action research and receiving graduate credit for some of their work). By reallocating resources, several partnership goals were addressed.

These are just some examples of reconfiguring resources to optimize strengths and meet the goals of the partnership. As we continue to work in this area, we have come to understand that resources are directed to areas that are deemed of value by a system. If the values of the system(s) are not congruent with the goals of the partnership, problems can arise. For instance, if teacher learning is not valued as much as student learning in a school district, it will be hard to direct resources into developing mentor teachers even though their development will most likely have an impact on K–12 student learning.

Values of systems are often evident in policies. Although administrators may avow certain values, if the policies within the system do not support those values or if in some instances run counter to those values, it becomes difficult if not impossible to uphold them. We think that some of the most challenging conversations that must take place within a partnership involve the values of the partners, and it is important to go beyond stated policies to the underlying values that sustain those policies. These conversations involve the honesty and trust that were discussed previously. They also involve a careful and critical examination of practice. Some areas to consider are values and policies around partnering, research, teacher empowerment, and reward systems.

A system may publicly state they value partnering, but if there are not policies in place that support it, partnerships with that system may not succeed. For example, an established commitment to partnering should be part of the hiring criteria for personnel within the system. Hiring in a new PDS provides opportunities to bring in experienced faculty from other schools and new faculty as well who are committed to the values of the PDS. However, as the partnership continues and there is a normal turnover in the school, new teachers must be brought in with the same values and understandings of the goals of the partnership. This is becoming more difficult as the teacher shortage for both special and general education teachers grows. However, the professional environment of the PDS can then become a recruiting tool to attract energetic and committed teachers. In addition, part of the professional environment needs to be the recognition of partnership activities as part of the basic workload of teachers. Although teachers are primarily responsible for the children in their classrooms, their work with preservice teachers should be seen as essential to the future health of their school and profession.

Valuing of partnering should also be evident in the tenure and promotion criteria of the university, as well as in the load assignments of faculty who spend large amounts of their time in partnership sustaining activities. In the area of research, a broad range of research needs to be evident and considered important to the mission of the university. Faculty who elect to align their research with partnership activities and goals should be rewarded equally with those who do not. On the school district as well as the university side, partnership-initiated research should be viewed as a way to transform and improve practice (Teitel, 1998).

Teacher empowerment values the important role that teachers play within the field of education and within our society. Policies that include them in decision making within a system are crucial. An example described earlier told of teachers within the partnership who recognized a disconnect between university curriculum and field experiences that led us to identify problematic areas in both the school and university systems. If their voices are not trusted and valued, improvement in both systems will be hampered. Resources that are directed to provide opportunities for teachers to engage in dialogue and professional development together are evidence of valuing teacher empowerment.

Assumption #7: There must be multiple opportunities for participants in the partnership to collaborate in meaningful ways. If relationships are the currency of partnerships, active participation in meaningful collaboration is the fuel; it keeps members engaged and interested and propels the partnership forward. Collaborative efforts should be directed at the interests, needs, queries, and goals that each of the partners identifies. Although it is important to establish a foundation for the partnership through multiple opportunities for dialogue, it is equally important to continue that process through action. In other words, "talk" can only take you so far; action plans must be initiated to move forward. These action plans often become the substance of discussions that move communication and understanding to deeper levels.

The implementation of action plans provides for myriad collaborative opportunities and ways to keep the partnership vital. When members of the partnership are actively involved in meeting goals and seeking answers to questions they deem important, the mutual benefit of the partnership is evident and momentum is established. Through our experience with partnerships, we have seen many ways collaboration through action research has taken place. For example, the research interests of university faculty and doctoral students have been aligned with identified questions/challenges raised at school sites. Field-initiated research has been collaboratively conducted to address the questions/challenges identified by the schools. At one school site, there was a large turnover in faculty teaching in inclusive classrooms. Although teachers communicated that they had shared values for co-teaching arrangements with general and special education teachers in inclusive classrooms, the teams of teachers usually asked to "take a break" after two or three years. Because the energy required to start new co-teach teams was extreme, the school worried that the model would not be sustained. A university doctoral student and faculty member worked collaboratively with teachers and administrators at the school site to study the problem through surveys and interviews. The data were analyzed and used to develop and/or change policies and procedures within the school that addressed the issue. As Tractman (1998) suggests, inquiry can be a powerful basis for change or refinement.

Classroom-based research initiated by teachers is another way to transform practice. We found through our partnership work that by supporting teachers in analyzing and investigating their own practice through action research, we were collaboratively meeting several goals of the partnership. For example, the retention of master teachers was being addressed. Barnes (2000), states, "Staff development that incorporates school-based research projects can nourish the values and beliefs that have impelled teachers to work in education in the first place" (p. 42). By providing collaborative staff development for teachers around action research, the teachers receive encouragement and support for delving deeper into their own practice and have a chance to analyze their practice for alignment with values and beliefs they hold. Further, by engaging in action research, teachers are empowered by becoming the problem solvers and are more likely to take ownership of the solutions. Supporting action research also has the potential to positively affect educational outcomes for K–12 students. It holds opportunities for university students who are being mentored by the teachers to engage in inquiry around educational practice, establishing habits of reflective practice in the pre-service teachers. Data gathered from action research to support improved education outcomes for K–12 students as well as university students are a powerful affirmation for partnerships.

Collaborative opportunities within partnerships also emerge as new roles are established. As classroom teachers become teacher educators, they have opportunities to live in both "worlds" of the partnership. Just as athletes who cross-train become stronger and more adaptable, teachers who "cross-train" reach new levels of professional development and empowerment: developing preservice teachers, advising the university curriculum, and aiding in teacher retention. University programs, for example, are improved as the teachers bring an important perspective to collaborative discussions about the programs and engage in university program improvements that more closely align the program with the field. "When teachers engage in the work of supporting student learning, they become curriculum developers and curriculum interpreters" (Teitel, 1998, p. 45). The "worlds" in which they live also become better because of their new expertise and involvement.

One of the most important areas for collaborative action within a partnership is the evaluation of partnership activities and initiatives (Goodlad, 1988). Collaboration in this area facilitates a focus on partnership goals and ensures that resources and efforts are directed and/or redirected to meet those goals. If progress toward shared goals cannot be documented, participants in the partnership may lose interest and the partnership may stagnate.

Evaluation of partnership effectiveness and outcomes must take many forms. Griffin and Pugach (1997) tell us that "evaluation efforts must be ongoing, interactive, both short- and long-term, and employ multiple methods." (p. 268) Existing data collection procedures from both systems can be used in addition to collaboratively collected data. For example, existing procedures in school districts to collect data on K–12 student learning can be used to analyze educational outcomes. Data on university student learning that can be connected to positive education outcomes for K–12 students provides measures of accountability for the partners.

Additionally, the climate of the partnership should be monitored and evaluated. The satisfaction of partnership members, attitude shifts and changes, collaborative behavior, and morale provide a measure of the health of the partnership. If evaluations uncover areas of concern, they should be promptly addressed. Conversely, as successes are identified, they should be celebrated, shared, and documented.

CONCLUSION

At a time of intense scrutiny of programs and institutions that prepare teachers, we need to demonstrate an ability to adapt and develop new ways of working in partnerships that will maximize our successes. Public education is not expanding its resources. The need for preparing and retaining successful teachers is increasingly challenging. In our state, as in many others, the teacher shortage, which has long been a problem for special education, is now also reaching into general education as teachers retire and our school population continues to grow. Our work in partnership with two school districts and between special education and general education has focused on using the resources and energy that already exist within the systems to find more effective, as well as more efficient, ways to prepare teachers and to create a professional environment that will improve teacher retention. Issues that challenge the institutions—that is, K–12 schools and colleges of education—and faculties should be considered within the context of partnering so that we can mutually aid each other in addressing those challenges.

Lessons we have learned through our work with two neighboring school districts who both have long histories of collaborations with the university, but who differ in size, resources, structures, and needs include the following:

- The need to communicate about the essential values, needs, and challenges of the partners is critical for the survival and growth of the partnership.
- Learning how to communicate within the systems of the partnership is essential. This can be especially difficult in large systems with many parallel structures that may be operating independently from the partnership.
- Each of the partners has diverse perspectives on critical issues that frequently lead to creative solutions to challenges that seem unsolvable by one of the partners working alone.
- Resources are decreasing, even as needs increase. Reallocations and innovative uses of resources and faculty time and energy can expand the effectiveness of our work.
- The demands of accountability are expanding, not shrinking. There are many ways to use essential components of our work (for instance, university faculty expertise in research and school district understanding of K–12 student learning outcomes) to present partnership outcomes that are clear indicators of the results of the work.

As we continue to work, we realize that the lessons we are learning should continue to frame our work together. Communication, diverse perspectives, reallocation of resources, and building accountability into our work to demonstrate the outcomes of the partnership become critical components of our work together.

DISCUSSION QUESTIONS

1. Is the distinction between a partnership and collaboration valid?
2. Do you think equity must exist in all areas of a partnership for it to be successful?

3. How might issues of power and privilege within a partnership create challenges to equity?

REFERENCES

Abdal-Haqq, I. (1998, October). Keynote presentation at the National Professional Development School Conference in Baltimore.

Barnes, N. (2000, January). Teachers teaching teachers. *Education Week*, pp. 38–39.

Darling-Hammond, L. (1997). Reforming the teaching profession: A conversation with Linda Darling-Hammond. *The Harvard Education Letter, 13*(3), 4–5.

Epanchin, B., & Wooley-Brown, C. (1993). University-school district collaborative project for preparing paraprofessionals to become special educators. *Teacher Education and Special Education, 16*(2), 110–123.

Epanchin, B., & Wooley-Brown, C. (1995). Sharing the responsibility for educating "homegrown teachers." In J. Paul, H. Rosselli, & D. Evans (Eds.), *Integrating school restructuring and special education reform*. Fort Worth, TX: Harcourt Brace.

Goodlad, J. (1988). School-university partnerships for educational renewal: Rationale and concepts. In K. A. Sirotnik & J. Goodlad (Eds.), *School-university partnerships in action: Concepts, cases, and concerns* (pp. 3–31). New York: Teachers College Press.

Goodlad, J. (1994). *Educational renewal: Better teachers, better schools*. San Francisco: Jossey-Bass.

Griffin, C. C., & Pugach, M. C. (1997). Framing the progress of collaborative teacher education. In L. P. Blanton, C. C Griffin, J. A. Winn, & M. C. Pugach (Eds.), *Teacher education in transition: Collaborative programs to prepare general and special educators* (pp. 249–270). Denver, CO: Love Publishing Co.

Guba, E. G. (1996). Foreward. In E. T. Stringer, *Action research: A handbook for practitioners* (pp. ix-xiii). Thousand Oaks, CA: Sage.

Holmes Group. (1986). *Tomorrow's teachers*. East Lansing, MI: Author.

Levine, M. (1992). *Professional practice schools: Linking teacher education to school reform*. New York: Teachers College Press.

Levine, M. (1998). *Designing standards that work for professional development schools*. Washington: National Council for Accreditation of Teacher Educators.

Little, J. (1993). Teacher's professional development in a climate of educational reform. *Educational Evaluation and Policy Analysis, 15*(2), 129–151.

Smith, L., Delp, W., Hamilton, W., Houck, L., Ciemniecki, R., & Archer, F. (1995). Preparing and initiating a collaborative teacher education program. In J. Paul, H. Rosselli, & D. Evans (Eds.), *Integrating school restructuring and special education reform*. Fort Worth, TX: Harcourt Brace.

Stoddard, K., & Danforth, S. (1995). Empowering teachers to be responsive to individual differences. In J. Paul, H. Rosselli, & D. Evans (Eds.), *Integrating school restructuring and special education reform*. Fort Worth, TX: Harcourt Brace.

Teitel, L. (1998). Professional development schools: A literature review. In M. Levine (Ed.), *Designing standards that work for professional development schools* (pp. 33–80). Washington: National Council for Accreditation of Teacher Education.

Tractman, R. (1998). The NCATE professional development school study: A survey of 28 PDS sites. In M. Levine (Ed.), *Designing standards that work for professional development schools* (pp. 81–110). Washington: National Council for Accreditation of Teacher Education.

Valli, L. (1999). Collaboration: Building bridges to transform cultures: Overview and framework. In D. Byrd & J. McIntyre (Eds.), *Research on professional development schools: Teacher Education Yearbook VII*. Thousand Oaks, CA: Corwin.

Winn, J., & Blanton, L. (1997). The call for collaboration in teacher education. In L. P. Blanton, C. C Griffin, J. A. Winn, & M. C. Pugach (Eds.), *Teacher education in transition: Collaborative programs to prepare general and special educators* (pp. 1–17). Denver: Love Publishing Co.

12

The Use of Educational Technology and Assistive Devices in Special Education

Barbara L. Loeding

For students with disabilities, the ordinary classroom can present monumental barriers. However, special educators have at their disposal a larger array of educational technology and assistive devices than at any other time in recorded history to rectify this situation. Educational technology refers to "any technical method for achieving the purpose of education and is comprised of those methods that facilitate all of the facets of the process we deem education" (Vertrees, Beard, & Pannell, 2001). An assistive technology device is "any item, piece of equipment, or product system, whether acquired commercially off-the-shelf, modified, or customized, that is used to increase, maintain, or improve the functional capabilities of a child with a disability" (P.L. 101-407). Assistive devices may be as simple as a pencil grip to make it easier to hold a pencil, or as complex as software that enables a computer to respond to voice commands. Assistive technology services are "any services that directly assist an individual with a disability in the selection, acquisition, or use of an assistive technology device" (P.L. 101-407). These services may include adapting a toy so that it can be operated by a child with disabilities, teaching a child to use an augmentative communication device, or teaching an individual to use a Braille note-taking device.

Prior to IDEA, assistive devices were usually considered only for students with severe/profound disabilities. According to Decoste (as cited in NCES,1998), educators have expanded their thinking about AT to include referrals for children with mild-to-moderate disabilities. However, not enough educators have the necessary expertise in assistive technology, so the U.S. Department of Education has funded a master's training program (2001–2004) at the University of Wisconsin–Milwaukee to prepare educators and occupational therapists specializing in the use of assistive technology to enhance the educational achievement of students with mild disabilities (http://www.uwm.edu/~edyburn/ctp.html). Legally, according to the 1997 reauthorization of the Individuals with Disabilities Education Act, the IEP teams must consider and indicate on the Individual Educational Program (IEP) whether or not each student receiving special education services is in need of assistive technology (AT) devices and services to access the general education curriculum. An important distinction to make between educational technology and assistive technology is that assistive technology is only considered to meet the needs of students receiving special education, whereas educational technology is being used with all students. For example, electronic books and audiobooks would be considered assistive technology for students who are blind because without them (or another assistive device like a Kurzweil Reading Machine) they wouldn't be able to "read" a conventional book at all; whereas for students without disabilities, electronic books or audiobooks would be considered educational technology that offers another way to read.

In this chapter, we explore the range of technology that is currently available and how it can be used to empower and improve the education of students with varying exceptionalities. Issues related to underutilization of technology and preservice training are explored, such as faculty modeling the use of technology for preservice teachers; instruction regarding selection, use, and integration of appropriate assistive technology; and the importance of preservice teachers continuing their professional development in technology use after graduation. The importance of parent and child involvement in the decision-making process and their training, consideration of the impact of the family's culture and first language in this process, and ethical questions and professional standards related to the use of technology are addressed.

USES OF TECHNOLOGY

Educational technology and assistive devices can be used to assist children in four general ways: (1) to give students a way to access an appropriate education (i.e., compensate for some impairment, empower students to be more independent) so that they can engage in skill building or remediation of skills; (2) to enhance students' educational experience (e.g., improve productivity, make learning more enjoyable); (3) to assess progress; and (4) to manage instruction. Some technology is quite specific to a particular disability, whereas other technology assists students with varying exceptionalities.

Access

To provide access to the curriculum for visual learners, educators may use computer projection equipment to display material on the screen such as PowerPoint presentations, digital photos, Quick Time movies, or to show appropriate software or connect to Web sites on-line. For kinesthetic learners, educators can also convert PowerPoint presentations into handouts of the presentation slides or guided notes for students to write on or fill in during class. For students who find writing to be laborious or impossible, a computer word processor or portable keyboard such as AlphaSmart (www.alphasmart.com) allows students to organize their thoughts in a legible and professional manner. Software, such as Inspiration (Inspiration Software, Inc., 1994), can automatically generate a concept map from an outline (or vice versa) for learners who need this type of organizational support for writing activities. Students who are nonreaders or who are blind utilize screen reading software such as JAWS (Freedom Scientific) or CAST eReader (http://www.cast.org/udl/index.cfm?i=211) to gain access to text via the computer. If the text is not on-line, educators can obtain audio versions of textbooks for their students from The National Library Service for the Blind and Physically Handicapped or Recordings for the Blind and Dyslexic (http://www.rfbd.org/). A handheld device called the Quicktionary Reading Pen allows students to scan a word and read or listen to its pronunciation and definition (http://www.ldresources.com/tools/quicktionary. html). With this device, students with learning disabilities may be able to read independently. For those unable to turn pages of a book, educators, encouraging independence, may introduce students to Web sites where they may read on-line books and access on-line dictionaries (http://www. magickeys.com/books/index.html, http://www.franklin.com, http://www.acs .ucalgary.ca/~dkbrown/stories.html or for books in Spanish http://www .csusm.edu/csbs/). These students may also require mobility aids such as a walker or powered wheelchair or environmental controls to give them the ability to turn lights and other accessories on and off. To enable students with physical impairments to access computers or games, educators can use alternative keyboards, switches, or adapted toys obtained through vendors who specialize in adaptive technology (http://www.aacproducts .org). A large variety of augmentative/alternative communication devices now enable students who cannot communicate verbally to make their needs, thoughts, and preferences known.

Technology to Enhance Educational Experience

Computers can also be used in providing instruction to students (e.g., recording data from experiments, providing computer-based instructional activities, and accessing the Internet). The Internet can connect students with information resources that were unavailable to students in the past, bringing with it a responsibility to teach students how to evaluate the quality of those resources (Bakken & Aloia, 2000). Educators are directed to sites such as the Internet Detective to assist in this process (http://sosig.ac.uk/desire/internet-detective.html).

Technology can promote literacy. The results of a national research study on special educators' use of technology to promote literacy are now available via the Web (http:/www.abledata.com/literacy). In addition, preliminary analysis indicates that children with mild disabilities were more motivated to write and they wrote longer and more descriptive stories using a Web-based literacy learning environment called TELE-Web (Zhao, Englert, Chen, Jones, & Ferdig, 1999).

Technology may also serve to motivate and empower students with emotional impairments (McCandless, 1995). Students as young as seven years old can now create their own behavior plans using software called KidTools (Fitzgerald & Semrau, 2000). This may help them take responsibility for their actions and build an internal locus of control. Video Futures is a project that has demonstrated that seeing oneself as a positive role model on videotape is a powerful tool that can help people learn new skills, improve a new or inconsistent skill, or transition to a new situation (Ben, Caires, Connor, & Dowrick, 1998; Dowrick & Fitzgerald, 1995) by showing them what their life could be like if they behaved like they did in the video all the time. "Self-modeling" tapes are made of the person attempting the targeted skill; then any mistakes, support given, or inappropriate behavior is edited out before the person sees the tape.

The Use of Technology to Assess Progress and Manage Data

Technology can also be used to assist the educator in numerous ways. Recent research supports the use of computer-read-out-loud tests for students who have learning disabilities (Calhoon, Fuchs, & Hamlett, 2000) or for students who are auditory learners, allowing the educator to spend time with other students (as long as reading ability itself is not being tested). Students indicated a preference for the anonymity provided by this computer-read test accommodation. To fairly assess students who rely on sign language, a multimedia assessment such as SHIPS (Loeding & Crittenden, 1993) may be used because it uses digital video segments of an interpreter signing the assessment in ASL and/or English-based signs. Because principles of universal design were used in SHIPS, this particular assessment can meet the needs of students who are blind or have visual or physical impairments, or learning disabilities by having the educator select the appropriate user interface in the setup program.

Educators are using technology to create and score their own curriculum-based assessments, electronic grade-books, and portfolio programs to catalog, monitor, and reflect on student progress (Powers, Thomson, & Metcalf, 2001). Scanners and the huge memory capabilities of modern computers make it possible to scan in photos of children, record them reading a story, and scan in examples of their actual school work so that it can become part of an electronic portfolio that could be saved on a Zip disk or CD-ROM disk. Having either the student or educator share these portfolios with parents helps convey an authentic picture of student progress and develops ownership and empowerment (Powers, Thomson, & Metcalf, 2001). Some schools are making student information available for parents to access on the Web. One example is a school that serves a large number of students from migrant worker homes. When these families move, the parents are given a Web page address so that the new school can access the students' health and academic records, making the transition for the family much smoother. Using computer networks, educators can monitor student homework and provide electronic feedback. With the addition of a small camera, the educator's feedback could be provided in a visual or video e-mail. This allows educators and students who use sign language a way to communicate using their preferred mode of communication. Computer e-mail and word processing programs are used to correspond with parents and professionals. For educators wishing to learn more about the uses of technology, informational Web sites, on-line journals, and tutorials on the Internet can be a convenient way for them to engage in professional development.

Manage Instruction

Technology can also assist special educators in managing activities related to instruction. Software such as Excent, IEP Planner, and Dynamo allow educators to create computerized IEPs, ITPs, and Section 504 plans (http://www.excent.com, http://www.ansim.com, and http://www.gibcoinc. com/). Educators need not reinvent the wheel when it comes to lesson plans. Sites such as Ask ERIC (http://ericir.syr.edu/Virtual/Lessons) or Dr. Smith's Special Educator Web page (http://www.geocities.com/Athens/ Styx/7315/subjects/ Lessonplans.html) can provide educators with a guide on how to write lesson plans and can give them access to a database of over 1,000 lesson plans on various topics. There are numerous grading software programs available today, such as GradeSpeed (from Campusware www. gradespeed.com), that help educators maintain grades for each student and give them quick access to records, such as how to contact the family, when the IEP is due for review, and assessment data for each student.

UNDERUTILIZATION OF TECHNOLOGY

Despite the research that demonstrates the potential benefits of technology for students with disabilities (Behrmann, 1984; Butler, 1985; Esposito &

Campbell, 1987; Garner & Campbell, 1987; Hofmeister & Friedman, 1986; Romski & Sevik, 1988; Todis & Walker, 1993; Todis, 1996), there is evidence that technology is not being utilized to its fullest potential. A survey done by Derer, Polsgrove, and Reith in 1996 concluded that 34 percent of the total population of students with disabilities currently use assistive technology. However, a national survey of assistive device use in students with cognitive impairments found that more than twice the number of students who currently use assistive devices could potentially benefit from them but did not have access to them (Wehmeyer, 1999). Wehmeyer also proposed that if the underutilization is that great with one population, it might indicate that the percentage of those who could benefit from assistive technology is far greater than the 34 percent mentioned earlier.

IMPORTANCE OF PRESERVICE TRAINING IN THE INTEGRATION OF EDUCATIONAL TECHNOLOGY AND ASSISTIVE DEVICES

Perhaps the underutilization of technology relates to the amount and quality of preservice training of our educators. Do all educators of students with exceptionalities need knowledge of educational technology and assistive devices? With the legal responsibility to consider AT for each student receiving ESE services, I would strenuously argue yes. These devices are not only beneficial for students with severe to profound physical impairments. Students with learning disabilities, emotional, cognitive, visual, or hearing impairments can benefit from them greatly. Apparently, more and more states agree because they are adopting high standards for what teacher candidates should know and be able to do with technology, according to the preliminary results from a national policy analysis of state-level technology requirements (DeWert, 1999). The International Society for Technology in Education (ISTE) has developed 23 national performance-based standards for preservice teachers (available on the Web at http://cnets.iste.org/index3.html). The National Research Council, in its 1999 report, has urged every individual to become FIT (fluent with information technology) and delineated the 30 highest priority items to focus on. Becoming computer literate (i.e., developing certain basic skills) is no longer the goal because of the rate at which technology is changing. There is a need to be able to advance along a continuum, learning new skills after the skills and software programs you have mastered have become obsolete (NRC, 1999). Therefore, the concept of fluency indicates a lifelong learning process that goes beyond mere computer literacy.

For educators to effectively utilize technology, they need sufficient training and technical assistance, either through preservice training, continuing education programs, graduate degree programs, or through on-line technical services and training embedded into computer programs. An example of the latter form of support, electronic performance support systems (EPSS), is Tool Resources that has an informational database for educators who are using the software program called KidTools (Fitzgerald & Semrau, 2000). Conferences such as Technology and Media (a division of the Council for Exceptional Children), Closing the Gap, CSUN's Technology and Persons with Disabilities Conference, ISAAC (International Society for Augmentative and Alternative Communication), USSAAC (United States Society for Augmentative and Alternative Communication), RESNA (Rehabilitation Engineering Society of North America), ATIA (Assistive Technology Industry Association), Communication Aids Manufacturer's Association (CAMA) tours, the technology strand and hands-on lab at CEC (Council for Exceptional Children) and state educational technology conferences are ways to keep up to date with new developments in the use of technology.

In addition, there are increasing numbers of Master's degree programs in Assistive Technology, with a few certificate programs as well. CSUN's Assistive Technology Applications Certificate Program and George Mason University's AT Certificate Program both incorporate an on-line component as well as an on-site classroom component (Behnke, 2000; Behrmann, Castelliani, Jeffs, & George, 2000). ATTO (Assistive Technology Training Online) offers myriad AT "virtual workshops" on-line (Mistrett, 2000). RIATT's Competency Certificate Program in AT is a distance education program to be completed entirely from home or office (with e-mail interaction with your professor). St. Norbert College in Wisconsin offers an AT certification program over the course of two summers on campus (Peterson, 2000). This add-on certification program consists of twelve credits and is open to anyone holding Wisconsin certification in special education, SLP, OT or PT. Experts in assistive technology have expressed serious concerns about the appropriateness of on-line only certificate programs because there is evidence that links hands-on training with more effective use of assistive devices (Behnke, 2000; Behrmann, Castelliani, Jeffs, & George, 2000).

Quality indicators of effective assistive technology services have been developed by a consortium of assistive technology specialists from across the country (Bowser, Korsten, Reed & Zabala, 1999; Zabala, Reed, Bowser & Marfilius, 2000). Indicators exist for several different areas: administration's policies and procedures, consideration of student's need for AT, inclusion of AT in the student's IEP, AT assessment, AT implementation, and evaluation of AT effectiveness. These indicators can be used as a guide for planning appropriate preservice education in these areas (http://sac.uky.edu/~jszabala0/QIAT.html).

In addition, many resources now exist for assisting educators in integration of technology into their curriculum. On-line resources such as The PEP Registry (http://www.microweb.com/pepsite), the Children's Software Revue (http://www.childrenssoftware.com), ConnSENSE Letter (http://www. pappanikou.uconn.edu/cdbull.html) and IntelliTools Activity Exchange (http://www.intellitools.com) abound. *Technology @ your fingertips: A Guide to Implementing Technology Solutions for Education Agencies and Institutions* is also available on the Web (http://nces.ed.gov/pubs98/tech/ index.htm). For example, when teaching Social Studies, educators might want students to use the Internet to access *LIFE* magazine's list of the most important 100 people and events of the millenium (http://www.path-finder.com/Life/millennium/people/01.html). For resources in teaching math, a good Web page, available in English and Spanish, is Dave's Math Tables (http://www.sisweb.com/math/tables.htm). It has a real-time chat room with a white board for the educator to use with students who are having trouble with their homework. Publications such as *Assistive Technology in Special Education: Policy and Practice* (Golden, 1998) and *Has Technology Been Considered? A Guide for IEP Teams* (Chambers, 1997) can be useful as well. Both are published by the Council of Administrators of Special Education and the Technology and Media Division of CEC (http://www.cec.sped.org). For educators of low-incidence impairments, such as deaf-blindness, refer to articles such as "Computers in Our Classrooms" (Buckley, 1999–2000).

For preservice educators to become technologically competent, it is important that their professors model the use and integration of technology in their courses. Educators tend to teach as they were taught. Increasing numbers of faculty are using e-mail and list-serves to communicate with their students and facilitate student-to-student communication, incorporating on-line syllabi and chat room components into their Web pages, and are varying their in-class presentations to include PowerPoint, Hyper-Studio, live Internet connections with other college classes and sites, and demonstration of relevant software programs. Now, there are entire college courses, certificate, and degree programs in Special Education being taught on-line (M. Churton, personal communication, January 2000). The University of Washington has created a Web site of resources, tools, templates, support, training, and advice to assist faculty in integration of education technology, (http://depts. washington.edu/catalyst/home.html). Cooperating teachers and university supervisors are using e-mail to communicate with each other and with their interns (Yildirim & Kiraz, 1999). Graduating seniors in teacher education programs at the University of South Florida and other institutions (Rogers, Lodge-Rogers, & Markell, 2001) are beginning to put their teaching portfolios on CD-ROM disks, demonstrating a high level of expertise with technology because there is evidence that administrators prefer electronic teaching portfolios (Tichenor & Sipek, 1999). Course instructors are now requiring the use of technology to an extent never seen before. Students are using the Internet to search for information and making multimedia presentations to their classmates. Professors at Southeast Missouri State University received two grants to purchase laptop computers, projection devices, software, an augmentative communication device, switches, and switch adapters for their preservice educators to use in their field experiences (Anderson and Anderson, 2000). Students were first taught how to operate the hardware and software in their methods courses through demonstration and practice. Not all students elected to take the technology into their field experience classroom, but reports from those who did indicated that their students and cooperating teachers were excited and asked them to bring it again. Preliminary reports indicate that these experiences were successful in improving knowledge and use of technology by preservice teachers (Anderson & Anderson, 2000).

RANGE OF TECHNOLOGY

A mere twenty years ago, educational technology available in classrooms consisted of devices such as overhead and slide projectors, film/filmstrip projectors, Language Masters, and cassette recorders. Today, many schools have facsimile machines, computers with modems, connections to the Internet, CD-ROM drives, videodisc players, scanners, digital cameras, LCD data projectors, PC-compatible, big screen televisions and videoconferencing systems. Classrooms for students with disabilities have various types of assistive technology such as motorized wheelchairs, page turners, communication aids, voice-input software, alternative keyboards, switch-operated toys and devices, presentation software, and specialized software to magnify the screen and/or read the computer screen to a student, and check spelling and grammar of text. Some software contains word prediction capabilities so that as students type, each word is predicted by the program. This feature assists students who fatigue easily by reducing the number of keystrokes needed to type their documents. It is also helpful for students who may recognize the word they want but are not able to spell it properly. By logging all the words a student types, these programs also become better at predicting the words a particular student would use over time. In addition, there are Internet sites that allow people to read books on-line, reducing the motoric requirements to turn pages (e.g., http://magickeys.com/books/index.html), for educators to use.

The future may bring virtual reality helmets and software to teach children with physical impairments how to guide their motorized wheelchairs while traveling on varied terrain (Ira, 1997). Children and youth with behavioral disorders may use virtual reality to learn and practice prosocial skills such as cooperative learning and interactive role-playing (Muscott & Gifford,1994). Research is currently underway to determine whether students with developmental disabilities can learn to use a wearable computer that has a program to guide them through the steps to a simple task (Schweder, 2001). If successful, wearable computers could assist in promoting independence and partial independence in these students. Interactive "picture" or video-phones currently exist but may become more widely used in the future. Special software can be installed in a computer along with a tiny camera so that a person can communicate by voice and image to any other person with the software to receive the communication. Video e-mails can also be sent and do not require the receiver to have the corresponding software. This will increase the ways a person can communicate to include voice and sign. With respect to communication devices, it appears that we may be reaching the logical limit on how small these devices can be with the new handheld devices, but additional features will be incorporated as time goes on. The most exciting development for nonspeaking individuals who haven't been able to use existing communication devices is the emerging technology that allows these persons to use their thoughts to communicate through electrodes that are placed on their head and connected to a computer (Boyd, 1999) (http://www.alssurvivalguide.com/als_news/990324brain_waves_ harnessed _for_commun.htm).

SELECTION OF APPROPRIATE TECHNOLOGY AND PROVISION OF TRAINING

It is critical for educators to involve students and families in the selection process. First, everyone looks at the curriculum the child is expected to study. When a task analysis is completed, the team can consider how the child is going to access the curriculum and engage in the learning tasks to achieve desired outcomes. In some tasks, no technology will be needed. In others, a low-tech solution will be appropriate. In yet others, a high-tech device or a specialized type of software will be needed. It is preferable to select low-tech applications whenever possible, but it is not clear how teams will address pressures to include AT in IEPs. In choosing assistive technology, it is important to consider possible barriers to successful integration such as attitudes to the use of technology and layout of the classroom.

After the selection has been made, the team needs to tie the technology to specific tasks or objectives in the IEP in order to prevent abandonment by educators and/or students (and promote its successful integration). Other strategies that will promote integration are development of a time line and outline for putting supports in place, collection of data on how well the student is using the AT, and assignment of responsibility for certain tasks. One of the early tasks or "supports" may be to ensure that the students, their parents, and their educators consult or receive actual training from other professionals (Struck, 2000). It is essential that future educators realize that the key to effective utilization of technology is training. Students not only need training in the use of the technology, they need time to practice within contexts.

ETHICAL QUESTIONS REGARDING
THE USE OF TECHNOLOGY

Some questions can be more easily resolved than others. For example, should educators assume that the use of technology would automatically improve or facilitate instruction? The answer is no. Although research has been conducted evaluating technology, there remains a need to document the impact and effectiveness of emerging technology and assistive devices. Preservice educators must be taught how to evaluate the desirability and effectiveness of technology. There may be unintended consequences of the use of technology. For example, it is unfortunate that most popular software for children is repeating gender stereotypes, exhibits a lack of diversity (Luke, 1999; Vertrees, Beard, & Pannell, 2001,) and promotes aggression (Vertrees, Beard, & Pannell, 2001). Another unexpected consequence can be reduced creativity because most educational software emphasizes one correct answer as opposed to encouraging imaginative answers (Vertrees, Beard, & Pannell, 2001). Students who use simulation software or technology to make learning easier can develop an expectation of instant proficiency and may become impatient and give up on acquiring a new skill too soon because their sense of real time has been truncated (Vertrees, Beard, & Pannell, 2001). Regarding assistive devices, there is documentation showing that AT has been abandoned in situations where the devices did not improve independent functioning, were too difficult and expensive to repair, were too difficult to use, were unreliable, or required too much assistance from another person (Blackstone, 1992; Phillips, 1992; Phillips & Zhao, 1993). Educators are now addressing the barriers to assistive technology implementation by advocating participatory decision making to increase ownership, designating responsibility, and outlining specific ways to enhance training (Reed, 2001).

Therefore, instructors may wish to emphasize the desired characteristics of software and assistive devices with respect to nonsexist materials, multicultural education (Poole, 1995), perceived consequences, and variables that lead to effective use of that technology. In fact, one of the ISTE standards for preservice teachers is to "identify and use technology resources that affirm diversity" (ISTE, 2000).

A related question is, Are there better ways to spend the money being spent on technology? The purchase of new technology fragments the resources of our institutions. Decisions have to be made by examining the demonstrated merits of each kind of technology. Recent studies have indicated that computers in schools don't necessarily improve academic performance (Struck, 1999). Mixed results have been obtained in studies of the effectiveness of talking storybook programs (Lewis, 1999). These programs were found to be helpful for students with learning disabilities when some degree of structure was imposed on their interactions. Students were not likely to attend to the reading task or gain new skills using the programs independently (Lewis,

1999). Studies such as the one conducted by the National Council on Disability (1993) are encouraging because it indicated that 75 percent of the students were able to remain in the regular education classroom through the use of assistive technology. This study also showed that 45 percent of the students needed fewer special services from the school.

Are we providing enough opportunities for preservice educators to develop the competencies they will need? What do they need to know to teach their students to be technology-literate in the 21st century? A definitive work has been published on this topic by the Mid-Central Regional Education Laboratory (MCREL) that presents standards and benchmarks of what needs to be taught in K–12 schools from various sources. What technology competencies do they need to enhance their own productivity? What do they need to function as a member of an IEP team that must consider whether assistive technology is needed for each student receiving ESE services?

Are we doing enough to prepare our preservice educators for their responsibility to teach students how to evaluate the safety, appropriateness, and quality of resources found on the Internet? ISTE Standards (2000) require preservice teachers to "promote safe and healthy use of technology resources." Students as young as first grade should be taught to ask the question "Is this site appropriate for a person my age?" (Bakken & Aloia, 2000) or "What would my mother say if she saw me looking at this site?" As students grow older, they can be taught to evaluate the quality of the information at each site by determining things such as recency and reliability of the information provided at a site. They can also address the inadvisability of giving out their addresses and phone numbers to people they meet in chatrooms. Professors and educators may find the following Internet site helpful in teaching skills required to evaluate critically the quality of an Internet resource (http://www.sosig.ac.uk/desire/internet-detective.html). There are a growing number of sites dedicated to providing information on how to assist safe and effective exploration of the Internet, such as SafeKids.com, Americalink.sup.org, cyberangels.org, and getnetwise.org. There are also e-learning resource sites such as "inetlibrary" (www.inetlibrary.com) that provide educators and students with access to thousands of Internet sites and online magazines/periodicals that have been reviewed and selected for appropriate content.

Is it ethical to accustom a pre-service educator to the use of new technology that most likely won't be available after graduation? If preservice educators see the value of using technology and become proficient at its use, it is likely that they will advocate for the purchase of that technology after they are hired. Some educators won't wait and will actually purchase the technology themselves to use in their classroom or will solicit donations of technology to their classroom. Hopefully, these educators can serve as role models for other educators and catalysts for change rather than being the target of envy and jealousy from educators who believe that educators are substituting use of technology for solid instructional practices in the classroom. However, future educators should be aware that collaboration may be more difficult as they acquire more technological proficiency and see how their use of technology benefits students because they could become less patient with educators who do not incorporate technology.

Some of the ethical questions that educators are beginning to encounter are these:

(1) Does technology have a "built-in" cultural bias?

Dozier-Henry (1995) raised and answered this question affirmatively, indicating that although the prevailing view of technology is that it is objective and neutral, so beneficial to all people, that relationship-oriented cultures may perceive this "reverence" for technology quite differently/negatively (Dozier-Henry, 1994). To them, the electronic media of Western culture may not serve their learning and knowledge needs (Bhola, 1992) even though information technologies play a central, defining role in Western culture (Dozier-Henry, 1995). There is also a fear that technology may inadvertently serve to make the gap between the rich and poor worse by reinforcing social inequities (Neuman, 1991; Vertrees, Beard, & Panell, 2001) with students who are technologically illiterate relegated to low-level, low-paying jobs when they enter the job market. Dozier-Henry (1995) concludes by imploring the schools to offer access to technology that is "sensitive to the complexities of intercultural exchange and diversity" (p. 15) so that the ranks of the "information poor" do not swell. It is important to notice that what she is not saying is as important as what she is saying. She is not giving educators permission to "excuse" or discourage students from various cultures from developing competencies in the use of technology. Rather, she is encouraging educators to find ways to involve students and their parents in the advances in technology that may benefit their lives without offending them in the process. Two of the ISTE (2000) standards for teachers are to (a) "apply technology resources to enable and empower learners with diverse backgrounds, characteristics, and abilities" and (b) "facilitate equitable access to technology resources for all students." Leaving behind a portion of our society hurts all of us. If students are discouraged from mastering skills in technology, this, in effect, denies access. The learning process can be adapted to the individual instead of making the individual adapt.

(2) Is it ethical to use technology with a student if the family objects to technology?

For example, an Amish family allows their children with disabilities to attend public school, but the parents state that they do not approve of the use of modern technology and do not want their child exposed to it. However, the educators believe that these children would be able to demonstrate more progress, given assistive technology. In order to maintain a cooperative relationship based on trust and mutual respect, the team may choose not to pursue high-tech assistive technology. It may be appropriate for the team to discuss the possibility of the use of low-tech devices or equipment for a particular child. In the process, it is important to have frank and open discussion about the prevalence of technology-use in the classrooms today (even without being specified on the child's IEP). How will the educator avoid the use of overhead transparencies, videos, use of the intercom, and cassette players?

(3) Is it ethical to provide technology and/or assistive devices at school only?

No, if the IEP team has decided that the technology is needed at home in order for the child to achieve their IEP goals (IDEA, 1997), the assistive device must be available to the child at home also. Even a school board may not change the IEP's determination.

(4) Is it ethical to accustom a student with disabilities to the use of technology that most likely won't be available after graduation?

This question may make an incorrect assumption. Recent laws have increased the level of cooperation and involvement between the Department of Vocational Rehabilitation and the public schools (Thomas, 2000). If the student meets the eligibility criteria for DVR, DVR may purchase assistive technology from the school for the graduating student to use in a postsecondary setting or job site or decide to purchase new equipment.

(5) How will we decide if a piece of assistive technology is necessary for appropriate education—or if it is optional, useful, or desirable?

The laws require schools to provide access to appropriate education. Schools are not required to provide children with the most sophisticated or optimal technology that exists as long as the equipment they provide allows the child access to appropriate education. When assessing the needs of a child, the team generally establishes what needs the child has and what devices have features that can match those needs. Parents may request a particular device, but the team must determine whether the child needs all the features of that device or whether a device costing less still can provide for all the needs the child has for an appropriate education. In explaining why a particular device is preferable, it is important that educators know how to be diplomatic. In addition, preservice educators must be taught to carefully evaluate emerging technology because newer isn't automatically better.

Lastly, even if preservice educators graduate with appropriate competencies in the area of technology for today, how will they develop the competencies needed for tomorrow? Technology is changing at such a fast rate that assistive technology just demonstrated for students last semester is now out of date. How are those students going to be aware that there is a better product on the market that will save the school district or parent money and provide more features? As teacher educators, we must instill in our students the need to remain current in all aspects of our professional life. How will the students obtain training on this new device? Some software now comes integrated with help options, training assistance, references, and on-line technical services. The Internet also is a great source of information (see Loeding Web site for a number of links to visit sites for information and tutorials about assistive technology, http://lklnd.usf.edu/USSAAC). Educators can subscribe to on-line listserves such as ACOLUG (Augmentative Communication On-Line User Group) or on-line updates from companies that manufacture assistive devices such as Grapevine (Prentke-Romich Company). Universities are beginning to offer assistive technology certificates for those who wish to come back for further training. School districts are providing training or sending educators to conferences and workshops for training. The Communication Aids Manufacturers' Association (CAMA) and individual vendors offer low-cost training and conferences throughout the country in an attempt to help educators stay up to date.

For perhaps the first time, special educators have at their disposal myriad technological inventions. As computers, the Internet, multimedia presentations, and assistive technology continue to reshape how we instruct students, how they learn, and how they gather information, there are professionals who envision a future where the teaching of traditional academic subjects will increasingly be done via on-line courses (Schank, 2000). We are witnessing a proliferation of on-line college courses and whole degree programs now. This development has already spread to the high school level as well with virtual high schools originating in Arizona, California, Colorado, Florida, Indiana, Kansas, Kentucky, Maryland, Massachusetts, Michigan, Minnesota, Missouri, Nebraska, Nevada, New York, Oregon, Pennsylvania, Utah, West Virginia, Australia, Canada, and other countries as early as 1994 (Carr & Young, 1999; Carr, 1999; Carr, 2000; Chaika, 1999). Some of these high schools have been created by state governments, universities, or consortia, although an equal number are run by private schools or companies. Several (e.g., Colorado and New York) offer courses at the middle-school level. Most are fully accredited, allow students anywhere in the world to register for their courses, and focus mainly on offering Advanced Placement and college preparatory courses. Traditionally, many conventional high schools haven't had enough teachers or money to offer these types of classes, so it is possible that students in poor districts now have opportunities to take advanced classes through virtual high schools (VHS) that they have not had in their own districts. So far, the student body appears to be made up of students needing a course or two to graduate or homebound instruction, students being home-schooled, gifted and talented students, and students whose other commitments preclude a traditional high school schedule (competitive athletes, models, actors, etc.), although one school was specifically for dropouts and students who have been expelled (Colorado) and NovaNET and CompuHigh offer coursework for English-as-Second Language learners. It is not clear to what extent these courses are accessible for students with disabilities. A search of each school's Web site that allowed searches only revealed one site (class.com) that addressed whether their courses were appropriate for students with disabilities. A quote from the Florida On-line High School Web site indicates that "students need to be self-motivated and be able to direct their own learning to fulfill course requirements and achieve individual academic success" (http://fhs.net/FHSWeb. nsf/Home?Open). Some sites ask prospective students to take a quiz to find out if on-line courses are for them (as virtual education is "not for everyone"). At least six virtual high schools (class.com, Indiana, Minnesota, Colorado, and the University of Missouri at Columbia High School) offer or expect to offer (Florida On-Line High School) an entire high school degree program to 6,000 students by the year 2001 (Carr, 1999; Zoldan, 1999; http://fhs. net/FHSWeb.nsf/Home?Open). In Florida, funding for the first on-line K–8 charter school was shot down by the Chairperson of the Education Budget Committee in 2000 (Fleming, 2001, personal communication). This proposal involved students using school-district-provided computers for four hours a day and spending one night per week at a "center" for art, music, physical education, socialization, and supplementary activities (Frisbie, 2000). However, it may only be a matter of time before other school districts offer similar options. There is a commercial site called ChildU.com (Learning Odyssey) that offers an individualized on-line curriculum for students K–8 to supplement their education. As this happens, what will it mean for the exceptional student? Will the role of the educator be reshaped as well? Certainly, a bigger component of their job would be to assist in determining the advisability of on-line education for particular students, determining what assistive technology a student would need to participate in on-line courses and to educate students for whom on-line courses were not appropriate. Will educators see their role as providing things that technology cannot? Will educators focus on personal one-on-one tutoring, teaching students how to work in a group effectively, and teaching crucial interpersonal relationship skills? Will they move from the role of authority figure to advisor? Schank (2000) predicts that, at first, educators will feel disenfranchised by the increasing use of technology but that they will realize they can fill a void by teaching social and interpersonal skills by shifting to the advisor role.

As special educators look forward, it is certain that educational technology and assistive devices will continue to play an important role in leveling the playing field for students with disabilities. In order for technology to have the greatest impact, the field needs educators who are sensitive to the ethical dilemmas and unintended consequences of technology. It is vital that preservice teachers develop competencies in the selection, use, and integration of educational technology and assistive devices and that they demonstrate continual growth in technology knowledge and skills to stay abreast of current and emerging technologies (ISTE, 2000) so that they continue to make informed decisions and appropriate recommendations regarding the use of assistive technology.

DISCUSSION QUESTIONS

1. Compare and contrast educational technology and assistive technology.
2. Name four ways that technology can be used to empower children with special needs. Give an example of technology/assistive technology that can be used for each.
3. What does the law require of teachers with respect to assistive technology?
4. How can technology be used to motivate and empower students with emotional disturbances?

REFERENCES

Anderson, C., & Anderson, K. (2000). Using technology in field experiences for pre-service educators. Presentation at TAM 2000 Conference, Milwaukee, WI, January 21, 2000.

Bakken, J., & Aloia, G. (2000). Teaching students with disabilities to evaluate information from the Internet. Presentation at TAM 2000 Conference, Milwaukee, WI, January 22, 2000.

Behnke, K. (2000). The development of an on-line AT certificate program. Presentation at TAM 2000 Conference, Milwaukee, WI, January 21, 2000.

Behrmann, M. (1984). A brighter future for early learning through high technology. *Pointer, 28,* 23–26.

Behrmann, M., Castelliani, J., Jeffs, T., & George, C. (2000). Assistive technology certificate program at GMU: Tools and training. Presentation at TAM 2000 Conference, Milwaukee, WI., January 21, 2000.

Ben, K., Caires, J., Connor, M., & Dowrick, P. (1998). *Video futures: A new frontier* [videotape]. (Available from The Center for Human Development, 2330 Nichols, Anchorage, Alaska 99508)

Bhola, H. (1992). *Literacy, knowledge, power, and development: Multiple connections* (ERIC Document Reproduction Service No. ED 345 587).

Blackstone, S. (1992). For consumers: Rethinking the basics. *Augmentative Communication News, 5,* 1–3.

Bowser, G., Korsten, J., Reed, P., & Zabala, J. (1999). Quality indicators of effective assistive technology services. *TAM Connector, 11,* 5, 1–5.

Boyd, R. S. (1999, March 23). Brain waves harnessed for communication. Knight Ridder Newspapers.

Buckley, W. (1999–2000). Computers in our classrooms. *Deaf-Blind Perspectives, 7,* 2, 1–7 . [On-line available at www.tr.wou.edu/tr/dbp].

Butler, C. (1985). Effects of powered mobility on self-initiative behavior of very young, locomotor-disabled children. *Developmental Medicine and Child Neurology, 27,* 112.

Calhoon, M. B., Fuchs, L. S. & Hamlett, C. L. (2000). The effects of computer-based test accommodations on mathematics performance assessments for secondary students with learning disabilities. *Learning Disabilities Quarterly, 36,* 271–281.

Carr, S. (1999, December, 12). 2 more universities start diploma-granting virtual high schools. *The Chronicle of Higher Education.*

Carr, S. (2000, April 12) . Virtual high-school programs begin looking for students overseas. *The Chronicle of Higher Education.*

Carr, S., & Young, J. R. (1999, October 22). As distance-learning boom spreads, colleges help set up virtual high schools. *The Chronicle of Higher Education.*

Chaika, G. (1999, March 1). Virtual high schools: The high schools of the future? *Education World* [On-line available at http://www.education-world.com/a_curr/curr119.shtml].

Chambers, A. C. (1997). *Has technology been considered? A guide for IEP teams.* Reston, VA: Council of Administrators of Special Education and Technology and Media Division of the Council for Exceptional Children.

Churton, M. (2000, January). Personal communication.

DeWert, D. P. (1999). The times they are a-changin': A look at technology-related requirements for teacher licensure and certification. *Journal of Computing in Teacher Education, 15,* 2, 4–6.

Dowrick, P. W., & Fitzgerald, K. (1995). Video Feedforward: Strategies for children and adults with Autism and other disabilities. Paper presented at Pathways Conference, Anchorage, Alaska, 1995.

Dozier-Henry, O. (1994). The perspective is in the paradigm: The congruence of worldview and research methodology. Preconference proceedings of the Adult Education Research Association, October1994.

Dozier-Henry, O. (1995). Technology and cultural diversity: An uneasy alliance. *Florida Technology in Education Quarterly, 7,* 2, 11–16.

Esposito, L., & Campbell, P. H. (1987). Computers and severely and physically handicapped individuals. In J. D. Lindsey (Ed.), *Computers and exceptional individuals* (pp. 105–124). Columbus: OH: Charles E. Merrill.

Fitzgerald, G., & Semrau, L. (2000). Enhancing self-management through computer tools. Presentation at TAM 2000 Conference, Milwaukee, WI, January 21, 2000.

Fleming, S. (2001). Personal communication.

Frisbie, S. L., IV. (2000). Cyber tech school a byte closer to reality. *Polk County Times, 5,* 4, 6.

Garner, J. B., & Campbell, P. H. (1987). Technology for persons with severe disabilities: Practical and ethical considerations. *The Journal of Special Education, 21,* 122–132.

Golden, D. (1998). *Assistive technology in special education: Policy and practice.* Albuquerque, NM: Council of Administrators of Special Education.

Goldman, A. (2000). Personal communication.

Hofmeister, A., & Friedman, S. (1986). The application of technology to the education of persons with severe handicaps. In R. Homer, L. Meyer, & B. Fredericks (Eds.), *Education of learners with severe handicaps: Exemplary service strategies* (pp. 351–368). Baltimore: Paul H. Brookes.

Individuals with Disabilities Education Act Amendments of 1997 Pub. L. No. 105-17. 64 Fed. Reg. 12406 (1999).

Ira, V. (1997). Virtual reality and mobility skills. *Exceptional Parent, 28,* 11, 50.

ISTE (2000). ISTE National Educational Technology Standards and Performance Indicators [on-line]. Available: http://cnets.iste.org/index3.html.

Lewis, R. B. (1999). Literacy skills for students with learning disabilities: Are talking storybook programs effective? *Closing the Gap, 18,* 5, pp. 1, 8, 33.

Loeding, B. L., & Crittenden, J. B. (1993). *Self-Help Inter-Personal Skills Assessment for Youth who use sign language* [videodisk version]. Tampa, FL: USF.

Luke, C. (1999). What next? Toddler netizens, Playstation thumb, techno-literacies. *Contemporary Issues in Early Childhood, 1,* 1, 95–100.

McCandless, K. (1995). A troubled teen embraces computer. *TECH-NJ, 7,* 1, 5.

Mistrett, S. (2000). Virtual workshops: Assistive technology training online. Presentation at TAM 2000 Conference, Milwaukee, WI, January 22, 2000.

Muscott, H. S., & Gifford, T. (1994). Virtual reality applications for teaching social skills to students with emotional and behavioral disorders. Presentation at Center on Disabilities Virtual Reality Conference. Northridge, CA.

National Council on Disability (1993). *Study on the financing of assistive technology devices and services for individuals with disabilities: A report to the President and Congress.* March 4, 1993, Washington.

National Research Council. (1999). Being fluent with information technology. Washington: National Academy Press. [On-line, available at http://books.np.edu/html/beingfluent].

NCES. (1998). *Technology @ your fingertips: A guide to implementing technology solutions for education agencies and institutions* (NCES#98293). Washington: National Center for Education Statistics.

Neuman, D. (1991). Technology and equity. *ERIC Digest* (ERIC Document Reproduction Service No. ED 339 400).

Peterson, C. (2000). State certification program in Assistive Technology. Presentation at TAM 2000 Conference, Milwaukee, WI, January 22, 2000.

Phillips, B. (1992). *Perspectives on assistive technology services in vocational rehabilitation: Clients and counselors.* Washington: National Rehabilitation Hospital Assistive Technology/Rehabilitation Engineering Program.

Phillips, B., & Zhao, H. (1993). Predictors of assistive technology abandonment. *Assistive Technology, 5,* 36–45.

Poole, G. (1995). Using technology to meet the needs of multicultural children: What administrators, educators and program directors need to know. *Florida Technology in Education Quarterly, 7,* 2, 58–65.

Powers, D. A., Thomson, W. S., & Metcalf, D. (2001). Electronic portfolios in a K–3 school: Impact on teachers' perceptions of students, instructional behavior and use of technology. Presentation at TAM 2001, Albuequerque, NM, January 12, 2001.

Reed, P. (2001). Assessing students' need for assistive technology. Pre-Conference sessions at TAM 2001 Conference, Albuquerque, NM. January 11, 2001.

Rogers, D. C., Lodge-Rogers, E. L., & Markell, M. A. (2001). Electronic portfolio: A learning by doing grant. Presentation at TAM 2001 Conference, Albuquerque, NM, January 13, 2001.

Romski, M. A., & Sevik, R. A. (1988). Augmentative and alternative communication systems: Considerations for individuals with severe intellectual disabilities. *Augmentative and Alternative Communication, 4,* 83–93.

Schank, R.C. (2000). Futurespective: A vision for education for the 21st century. *T.H.E. Journal, 27,* 6, 42–45.

Schweder, W. (2001). The grilled cheese project: Using multimedia presentation software to create functional software for your classroom. A presentation at TAM 2001 Conference, Albuquerque, NM, January 12, 2001.

Struck, M. (1999). Studies fuel technology debate. *ADVANCE for Speech-Language Pathologists and Audiologists, 9,* 5.

Struck, M. (2000). Assistive technology: A hot topic in schools. *ADVANCE for Speech-Language Pathologists and Audiologists, 10,* 1, 13.

Thomas, T.F. (2000). How to negotiate the DVR maze: DVR rehabilitation and AT. Presentation at TAM 2000 Conference, Milwaukee, WI, January 22, 2000.

Tichenor, M. S., & Sipek, M. (1999). Perspectives of school administrators on electronic portfolios. *Journal of Computing in Teacher Education. 15*, 4, 24–27.

Todis, B. (1996). Tools for the task? Perspectives on assistive technology in educational settings. *Journal of Special Education Technology, 13*, 49–61.

Todis, B., & Walker, H. (1993). User perspective on assistive technology in educational settings. *Focus on Exceptional Children, 26*, 1–16.

Vertrees, D. R., Beard, L. A., & Pannell, E. T. (2001). Educational reform: Ethical choice, educational technology, and special education. Presentation at TAM 2001, Albuquerque, NM, January 13, 2001.

Wehmeyer, M. (1999). Assistive technology and students with mental retardation: Utilization and barriers. *Journal of Special Education Technology, 14*, 1, 48–58.

Yildirim, S., & Kiraz, E. (1999). Obstacles in integrating online communication tools into preservice teacher education: A case study. *Journal of Computing in Teacher Education, 15*, 3, 23–28.

Zabala, J. S., Reed, P., Bowser, G., & Marfilius, S. (2000). Expanding the conversation: An invitation to discuss the development of quality indicators for technology services for students with disabilities. Keynote Address at TAM 2000 Conference, Milwaukee, WI, January 21, 2000.

Zhao, Y., Englert, C. S., Chen, J., Jones, S. C., & Ferdig, R. (1999). *TELE-Web: Developing a Web-based literacy learning environment.* (CIERA Report #1-006), Ann Arbor: University of Michigan.

Zoldan, D. (1999, February 7,). Bold new initiative has high school students studying in cyberspace. *Naples News* [On-line available at http: //www.naplesnews.com].

RESOURCES

http://www.inspiration.com/kidspiration/index2.html Kidspiration is the K–3 version of Inspiration, an outlining, diagraming tool.

13

The Utilization of Distance Learning and Technology for Teaching Children with Disabilities

Michael W. Churton

Revolutionary technological advances in medicine, science, telecommunications, and educational technology have occurred over the past decade. Technologically advanced educational services delivered via distance learning are becoming ubiquitous. Most likely the number of individuals benefiting from broad access to distance learning will increase exponentially. Concurrently, such ongoing special education issues as academic placement, inclusion, and functional curriculum will influence how children with disabilities are identified and schooled. Distance learning and technology will facilitate outcomes to these and other significant issues concerning children with disabilities. Moreover, distance learning and technology will provide alternative means by which children with disabilities can access information and educational services.

The school reform movement of the late 1980s and early 1990s created significant changes in how children with disabilities are schooled (Yell, 1998). Issues such as identification, assessment, curriculum, and parental involvement have played and continue to play a critical role in changing how we teach children with disabilities. Concomitantly, programs that prepare special education teachers have undergone significant changes relative to academic content, requirements, and areas of specialization. Additionally, as a direct result of parental and professional concern and influence, state and federal regulations for children with disabilities have been revised.

The information age of the 1980s has metamorphosed into the electronic, digital age of the 1990s (Oberg, 1998). Educational technology has emerged and evolved to become a critical tool in educating and delivering services to children with disabilities. Chapter 12, "The Use of Technology and Assistive Devices in Special Education," addresses the instructional and technological assistance that has been provided to children with disabilities.

Speech synthesizers, electronic and ergonomic keyboards, the Internet, and a host of other innovations have provided functional assistance to children with disabilities. These inventions are critical tools all children can learn to wield in order to participate in our dynamic world. The digital age provides all children, but especially children with disabilities, opportunities to achieve their full educational, vocational, and personal goals. As children become more technologically capable, their teachers and parents should also develop the attitudes toward technology and technological skills that will best benefit children's education.

Academic performance, school overcrowding, limited fiscal resources, diversity, and professional preparation programs are but a few issues that continue unresolved and that form a rationale for parents and teachers to consider alternative service delivery (Lange & Ysseldyke, 1998). In such a situation, technology provides opportunities for parents and educators to envision alternative forms of schooling for children.

Distance learning is by no means a new practice for accessing information and learning opportunities (Churton, 2000). Distance learning has, however, gained recent attention due to the advances in technology and the declining costs associated with delivering distance education. Technology has provided the conduit by which creative schooling techniques, alternative schooling, and experiential opportunities are initiated. Distance learning technology enables teachers, parents, and children to access information, programs, and creative opportunities that can assist in all children's educational growth and development.

The Telecommunication Act of 1996 includes provisions for ensuring that our public schools and libraries are equipped with the infrastructure necessary to link classrooms to the information highway. Electronic rates (e-rates) generate funding for the establishment of an electronic infrastructure for our schools and libraries. These e-rates are funded in part by a fee applied to monthly telephone bills. E-rates help schools and libraries establish and maintain infrastructure connectivity and permit them to compete in a global society and world market.

Technology and distance learning can assist children by providing access to information and subject matter in a timely, current, and interactive fashion. As a profession, we will depend on the creativity and innovation, and also the willingness, of educators, other professionals, and parents to embrace technology's advantages in aiding the education of children with disabilities. In this chapter, we envision educational opportunities for children with disabilities, created through distance learning and enhanced by technology that provides nontraditional opportunities unrealized but a few years ago.

DISTANCE LEARNING OPPORTUNITIES FOR CHILDREN WITH DISABILITIES

Currently, there exists a variety of educational placement for children with disabilities, including placement supported by distance learning and technology (Donahoe, 1995). Because of technological advancements and declining costs for educational technology, distance learning environments will continue to increase the number of children served (Minoli, 1996). The schooling opportunities we have created to illustrate distance learning capabilities are current at this writing; they are projected to serve increasing numbers of children in public schools, homebound placement, home schooling, and charter and private schools.

Public School Settings

We continue to support children with disabilities being schooled at all levels of the public educational system including elementary, middle, and high school, and in rural and inner-city school settings. Historically, discrete classes for children with disabilities are seldom as well provided for as mainstream classes, either by services or in the competence of the teachers providing services (Putnam, 1993). In contrast, we envision placements that can embrace a distance learning approach to many educational challenges faced by teachers, parents, and students as they struggle to achieve learning outcomes. We see clearly the benefits of providing access to information from every type of educational placement and perspective. The Telecommunication Act of 1996 and a new generation of technologically competent teachers will help supply the foundation for public school access to information, programs, services, and opportunities to enhance the teaching/learning environment.

Homebound Placements

As an educational category for public schools, homebound students are "placed" at home due to acute medical or other conditions that might endanger them if they were placed outside of the home. We see distance learning as a means to enhance educational opportunities for students who cannot or choose not to be served in public schools or other educational placements. Homebound placement differs from home schooling in that the public school continues to provide direct services, and usually only one child of the family is served at home.

Home Schooling

Clearly, home schooling is a growing phenomenon in the United States. Home schooling is a well-networked system of parents, companies, and privately employed teachers providing academic, religious, and/or cultural emphasis on children's education (Kaseman & Kaseman, 1997). We do not see this form of schooling diminishing but rather increasing the total number of children served by distance learning technologies. The Internet and distance learning have provided a wealth of information, academic lessons, materials, and resources for the home schooling movement.

Charter and Private Schools

The current conservative educational and political climate toward schooling encourages spending tax dollars to place children in nonpublic school settings. Many states have already embraced the charter school movement (USDE, 1999), and others are offering public referendums on the use of tax dollars to support private school tuition. The political significance of these schooling options is not the question to be addressed by this chapter. Rather, our focus concerns children with disabilities being schooled in alternative learning environments. From a distance-learning perspective, this situation replicates home schooling or public school placements. Will distance learning improve the learning opportunities for children with disabilities placed in charter and private schools? Probably! However, distance learning will also improve the learning opportunities and outcomes for children with diverse abilities, placed in a variety of educational settings, including those served in public schools.

DISTANCE LEARNING AND ITS IMPLEMENTATION FOR CHILDREN WITH DISABILITIES

Distance learning is defined as either synchronous or asynchronous teaching/learning that occurs when the teacher or educational resources are separated from students either by location or time (Churton, 2000; Moore & Kearsley, 1996). Similarly, *distance education* refers to the process of teaching and learning in which distance and time separate the instructor from students (Keegan, 1993). However, the outcome of distance education includes distance teaching as the instructor or facilitator's responsibility; distance learning remains the responsibility of the student. Distance education, a term often used interchangeably with distance learning, has been delivered through a variety of methods, including print materials and through electronic and/or technological media. Both distance education and distance learning allow those constrained by time and distance or by medical, professional, or social needs to be educated or to educate themselves.

Distance learning can be applied through a synchronous or an asynchronous medium. Synchronous learning refers to experiences, conversations, and communications that occur interactively in real time. Opportunities are available for students and teachers to interact spontaneously across geographical barriers with very minimal temporal delay. Asynchronous learning denotes communication that can occur any time, any place. Time and location are irrelevant. Access is available to teachers and/or students 24 hours a day, 7 days a week. Innovative educators and parents should be able to envision a vast array of creative opportunities for children through both synchronous and asynchronous media.

Distance learning has experienced exponential growth in the past decade due to rapid advances in the technologies that assist in delivering instruction to students at distance sites. Nearly 75 percent of institutions of higher education are offering not only courses through distance learning but entire degree programs on local, national, and international levels (Connick, 1999). The increasing number of distance learning opportunities relates directly to the decreasing costs of technologies that deliver instruction. Today's distance learning opportunities include not only correspondence courses and television and radio broadcasts but also satellite communications, microwave transmissions, interactive videoconferencing through telephony and the Internet, audioconferencing, World Wide Web-based courses, and emerging technologies such as V-SAT (very small aperture transmission).

SATELLITE COMMUNICATIONS

The use of satellites to conduct distance learning activities requires telecommunication equipment and significant expense. Most schools, libraries, and other government facilities have at least downlinks or transponders to receive the telecommunications signal. By 2006, all signals will convert to digital format; this will enhance educational opportunities due to increased channels and lower overall costs.

Microwave Communications

Instruction Television Fixed Systems (ITFS) are local (up to a 25-mile radius), one-way microwave frequencies reserved for educational purposes. ITFS requires television installations equipped to convert signals to those used by a television. For educational purposes, this network operates similarly to satellite transmissions and will also be digitized by 2006.

Satellite and ITFS communication offer a variety of educational opportunities for students and teachers. National and international broadcasts are conducted through the Public Broadcasting Service and other agencies. Instructional lessons can be delivered through these formats. Broadcasts consist of one-way video transmissions with return communications via telephone, fax, or electronic mail (e-mail).

Students and teachers, however, will need to identify the nearest facility that has a transponder to link the telecommunication signal to the site. Most urban areas in the United States will have at least one facility equipped to receive the signal. Rural areas, however, may be harder pressed to identify a facility. Many Chapter I schools have been equipped with downlinks, as have universities, hospitals, and other social and public service agencies.

Interactive Videoconferencing

Using telephony, videoconferencing enables instructors and local and/or remote students or community members to initiate and maintain synchronous interactive two-way video and audio communication in real time. Videoconferencing closely approximates face-to-face communications with similar outcomes. In the near future, the Internet may well be the most cost-effective means of transmitting video data. Videoconferencing provides opportunities to use the World Wide Web and the Internet.

The World Wide Web (WWW) and the Internet

The Internet is a global decentralized system of computers, software, and network connectivity. A World Wide Web site can access tools such as bulletin boards, e-mail, and chat applications for interactive communication among students and teachers. E-mail enables the transmission and reception of electronic messages through cyberspace. Electronic bulletin boards provide a forum by which individuals can post information to a particular WWW page. Chat rooms, synchronous communication options, enable ongoing interactive discussions between two or more individuals. A LISTSERV can deliver an electronic message from one subscriber to every other subscriber simultaneously.

Audioconferencing

An effective distance learning format used throughout education and business communities is the traditional analog telephone. High-quality analog speaker-telephones provide opportunities for interaction among schools, agencies, and programs. Current technology allows for echo-cancellation and automatic audio gain control. These features permit clear, high-quality audio communications.

Table 13-1 identifies a variety of technological formats, summarizing instructional advantages and disadvantages for each format. Technological schooling options offer children with disabilities access to programs that meet individualized educational needs, including the specialized and unique services required to further their academic, social, and vocational pursuits.

EXAMPLES/VIGNETTES

We have created several vignettes that exemplify how children with disabilities can be appropriately served by five separate distance learning technologies. The vignettes are followed by potential distance learning experiences that include at least one of the technologies just outlined. Some children, by virtue of their educational needs and/or the views of their parents, will receive a significant portion of their education through distance learning. Others will benefit from distance learning because they can access information, resources, and services previously unavailable due to location, geography, costs, and/or schedules. The vignettes include:

- Homebound students
- Inner-city schools
- Full-inclusion public school class
- Home schooled students
- Charter and private schools

Although each vignette could use any of the distance learning formats just described and in Table 13-1, we have chosen to illustrate with the formats that seem most appropriate. If other formats serve an educational value, they certainly should be pursued as well. Accessing only one distance learning medium may not use technology, time, or resources in the most appropriate way; a combination of technologies will better serve children with disabilities. We intend only to establish a baseline from which parents and educators can envision the numerous educational advantages and opportunities afforded by accessing information and knowledge through distance learning and associated technologies.

Vignette 1: Homebound Student

Thomas is a 12-year-old male student with a severe asthmatic condition that prevents him from attending his neighborhood public school. The severity of his medical condition also prevents him from engaging in other activities outside his home. Thomas's movements are restricted, and his extensive medication causes debilitating fatigue. He is unable to play with other children or even take a walk in the neighborhood. His home environment has been sanitized to minimize pollutants that might trigger an asthmatic reaction. His parents have customized the family vehicle through chemical treatment of its interior and the addition of a second air-conditioning unit.

Thomas's parents are dedicated to his health and education. They are concerned that his isolation from other children will have a long-term nega-

TABLE 13-1
Distance Learning Formats

Format	Technology	Instruction	Advantages	Disadvantages
Correspondence Courses	Print Technology	Textbooks, reproduction, articles	Flexibility, reading population, minimal skills, minimal costs, textbook-specific, ATAW*	Asynchronous, noninteractive, postal services involved
Audiotapes	Audio recording technology	Inexpensive cassettes, production, distribution. Similar to correspondence and can accompany print materials.	Inexpensive, flexible, supplemental materials, readily accessible equipment, mobile, ATAW	Asynchronous, nonvideo, noninteractive
Videotapes	Video recording technology	Inexpensive videocassettes, production, distribution. Can accompany print materials.	Inexpensive, flexible, accessible equipment, ATAW	Asynchronous, noninteractive
Voicemail	Telephony/Audio recording	Standard communication options for businesses, university, homes	ATAW, individual and group messages, alternative to more computer based technologies	Supplemental, limited messages, phone charges, noninteractive
Electronic Mail	Telephony/ Software	Messages, bulletin boards, listserves available. Approaches interaction but remains asynchronous.	ATAW, files can be attached, students can obtain free accounts	Internet connection costs, computers, modem, software, confidentiality of messages, knowledge of utilization
Computer Assisted Instruction	Computer technology and software	Sequence instructional programs—self directed	ATAW, self-paced and directed	No instructor interaction
CD and DVS	Computer, video, audio technology	Sequenced instruction	ATAW, self-paced, self-directed-DVS can be interactive with CD	No interaction with instructor, computer based, equipment
WWW-Based Courses	Telephony/ Computer/ software	Internet protocol, asynchronous	Access to WWW; complete lessons, interactive through chat rooms, ATAW, examinations on line, multimedia capable.	Networks unreliable, security cannot be guaranteed, increased e-mail connections

TABLE 13-1   continued

Format	Technology	Instruction	Advantages	Disadvantages
Satellite	Telecommunications	FCC regulated, offers broadcast quality to video/audio	One-way video, two-way audio. Multimedia capable, synchronous through audio links, worldwide distribution	Expensive, place-specific, extensive equipment involved. Instructors do not see students.
ITFS	Telecommunications	FCC regulated, offers broadcast quality to video/audio	One-way video, two-way audio. Multimedia capable, interactive through audio links, worldwide distribution	Expensive, place specific, extensive equipment involved. Instructors do not see students.
Audioconferencing	Telephony	Speakerphone and telephone lines; echo cancellation and auto gain control features.	Synchronous through audio. All sites (bridging) can hear each other simultaneously.	No video interaction, telephone charges, distributed materials.
Videoconferencing	Telephony	Codecs and compressed video, digital telephone lines	Synchronous communication. Two-way video and audio. Approximates on-campus classes, interactive and multimedia instruction	Site specific, $7,000 start-up, recurring line charges.
VideoStreaming	Internet protocol	Compressed video across Internet connection	Synchronous communication, multimedia and interactive instruction, computer based	Limited bandwidth, prone to freezing video and audio distortion. Cannot guarantee bandwidth from Internet provider.

*ATAW: anytime anywhere

tive effect on his emotional/social development. Telephone calls to friends do not bridge the peer relationship gap that Thomas is experiencing. His academics are good and progressing beyond grade level in several subjects. He is interested in travel and wants to visit many of the places that he is currently studying.

Distance Learning Services for the Homebound Student. The format we envision Thomas using most effectively is videoconferencing. For one thing, videoconferencing could play a significant role in bringing Thomas closer to his peers. Videoconferencing units placed in his home and the nearby school would allow Thomas to participate actively in classroom activities. Two-way interactive capabilities permit Thomas to communicate and exchange ideas with individuals or small groups in real time.

Because videoconferencing is a worldwide technology, it can enable Thomas to "travel" to other countries. Locations throughout Europe, South America, Asia, and Africa have ISDN telephony. Locating schools with videoconferencing connectivity can be accomplished either through the WWW, AT&T directories, or from some telephone companies. Seeing and hearing students from different countries in real time would certainly begin to address Thomas's educational needs.

Although costs are associated with the long-distance calls required for videoconferencing, a well-planned lesson with time limits could be cost-effective.

Videoconferencing offers other benefits that could contribute to Thomas's overall well-being and development. Because he cannot attend school or social functions, socializing with his peers is severely limited. For Thomas, the week-end is the low point of the week. To alleviate his isolation, friends who have videoconferencing units or who make special arrangements with the school can videoconference to communicate with Thomas. Thomas's parents can also benefit from the videoconferencing system by being able to communicate with Thomas's teachers and administrators in real time without leaving their home. In addition, through tele-medicine, many of Thomas's checkups can be performed "virtually" without the physician leaving the hospital or Thomas leaving his home. Virtual checkups minimize Thomas's exposure to asthma reactants and communicable illnesses. Videoconferencing might also result in wider, better availability of experts to help treat his medical condition.

The World Wide Web can also support Thomas's educational needs. A WWW site for "his" class can link numerous resources for Thomas and the other students. Thomas's personal WWW site will help him link to students around the globe. Chat rooms, bulletin boards, and e-mail all provide a benefit for Thomas to meet his educational and social needs. Interactive communication is also a possibility on the Internet.

Audioconferencing could provide an advantage by allowing more students the opportunity to interact with Thomas in real time. Speaker telephones cost much less than a videoconferencing unit or a computer. Audioconferences with a group of students could provide an educational advantage while minimizing costs.

Vignette 2: Inner City Schools

An inner-city middle school serves mostly children whose family incomes are at or below the poverty line. Ninety percent of the children are from minority backgrounds. The children are bright but challenged by their environment. Many of the school's students with disabilities are served both through regular programs and discrete settings. The school offers little in terms of after-school activities. The technology infrastructure is limited, with only three computers per grade level and no network connection to the Internet. Teachers are talented but lack resources and opportunities to explore beyond the set curriculum. Administrators, although advocates for their teachers and children, are locked into a pattern of attending to details of school operation and not to the broader picture of academic challenges and opportunities.

Distance Learning for Inner City and Rural Programs. This vignette describes a typical inner-city scenario consisting of limited facilities, resources, and thus opportunities. Rural service delivery models suffer from similar limitations in attempting to meet appropriate education requirements. Videoconferencing in both instances will benefit not only children with disabilities but also other children; the entire class will get to see and hear peers, in real time, from other districts, states, and countries.

Specifically, enrichment activities can be provided with videoconferencing even when limited resources, such as itinerant specialization teachers or reading specialists, serve a large number of programs. Videoconferencing would not replace direct services to schools. However, combining time slots and effecting additional locations can increase the efficacy of limited services; one specialist can serve many programs at one time. Foreign language classes can be initiated as can the services—for instance, speech and language—required to meet the unique needs of children with disabilities.

As with other placements, the World Wide Web will play a significant role in optimizing learning experiences for all children in inner-city and rural programs. Specialized services, instruction, and lessons can be placed on the WWW for children with disabilities to access either by themselves or with a facilitator or teacher. Opportunities worldwide can also be accessed through the WWW. Downlinks should be available for Chapter I inner-city schools to access telecommunications, PBS educational programs, and other broadcast services. Rural schools may be able to qualify for services under Chapter I guidelines as well.

Vignette 3: Third Grade Public School Inclusion Class

A third-grade class of 30 students at a local elementary school includes four children with disabilities, one enabled by a motorized wheelchair. This class is a full-inclusion program—that is, the entire class participates full-time in all academic and social activities. Two full-time teachers instruct the class, with the help of an educational aide. All the students are functioning at or above grade level, although some require additional assistance in certain subjects. The children also interact well. Indeed, many lead the way in assisting the children with disabilities. Although most activities are structured so that the inclusive nature of the class does not interfere with class or school functions, activities that require off-campus excursions, such as field trips, raise significant logistical and management obstacles. This situation severely limits the number of field trips the class can take.

Vignette 4: Home Schooling

Several families with children demonstrating mild to moderate disabilities have decided to home school their children. Seven children have an identified disability, including mental retardation, learning disability(ies), or physical disability(ies). Emotional disturbance, although demonstrated by a few of the children, is not a primary disability area. The parents feel that too much of the school day concentrated on areas that did not impact their children's learning or development. This included long bus rides, limited curriculum, lack of support services, and the general attitude of the educators, staff, and other students toward children with disabilities. After exploring several alternatives for their children, these parents decided to establish a home schooling program that would consist of no more than seven children, with parents offering instructional lessons and experiences.

Distance Learning for Inclusion Class, Home Schooling, Charter Schools, and Private Schools. These educational programs are treated together only to illustrate how distance learning can be an advantage in various group settings to children with disabilities. The instructional theories or political premises that underscore the existence and scope of each program are not germane here; distance learning considerations should focus on accessing information and resources necessary to teach children with disabilities and not on the political structures of programs.

Videoconferencing: Because they can be more flexible than public school settings, nontraditional programs can offer children a wide variety of opportunities. As in Vignette 1 about Thomas, schooling in facilities distinct from the oversight and regulations of public schools can provide enhanced educational opportunities through videoconferencing. Video visits to distant museums, zoos, libraries, agencies, and other home schooling or charter school programs broaden educational scope. The Museum of Art in New York, the Smithsonian in Washington, Cumberland Library in Tennessee, the Atlanta Zoo, NASA, and a myriad of others provide quality interactive distance educational programs.

These placements could follow the public high schools' example of using videoconferencing to address low-incidence classes, such as foreign languages. In addition, electronically linking students in different states and countries supports social studies and other academic subjects. The versatility of simultaneous communication with students of different locations, cultures, and languages implements diversity in learning. Videoconferencing can also provide a communication vehicle for collaboration and services by teachers, parents, and administrators at local, national, and international levels. Regardless of educational placement, videoconferencing programs enhance instructional methods and strategies—the better to serve all children.

World Wide Web and the Internet: Internet use for educational purposes has significantly increased during the past 10 years. A variety of instructional opportunities is available, including WWW sites, chat rooms, bulletin boards, and e-mail. An enhanced computer and associated expanded hardware and software with Internet connection are required for effective distance learning. Primarily an asynchronous mode of communication, the Internet and the WWW provide a means for students and teachers to access information anytime, anywhere.

A Web site that serves the class and/or individuals can be developed. Home schooling programs with WWW sites can set up communication links among hundreds of home schooling and associated programs. Lessons, activities, and materials can be posted on the WWW for open Internet access.

Many educational programs and activities are listed on WWW sites. This information can be accessed either through the WWW address or by conducting a search of the Internet using a Web browser. Children and parents can access information placed on the Web from any Internet location, anytime. Many university and community college classes are now offered on the WWW. In fact, college students can earn their General Education Diplomas through WWW-based courses.

Audioconferences: Audioconferencing can, at relatively low cost, link individuals and/or classes in interactive synchronous learning. Using only audio communication, home-schooling programs can exchange information and hold discussions. Public school programs, notorious for limited budgets, can provide creative, exciting opportunities through synchronous audio communication.

Satellite and ITFS: Distance learning, whether using satellite or ITFS communication, offers minimal opportunity for the placement vignettes due to expensive start-up and operating costs. However, most universities, colleges, government agencies, and hospitals have some form of this telecommunication. Can children with disabilities benefit from this type of distance learning? Children whose classes are near a facility using this technology may be able to access it. More mobile placements have a perhaps greater opportunity to access information through satellite or ITFS communication. However, due to the significant costs, unless the broadcast is free or of nominal cost to the public, schooling environments without partnership-facilitated connectivity usually do not have the fiscal resources to participate consistently.

However, with digital transmissions such as "DirecTV" and cable connections, digital satellite communications are not without possibilities for educational purposes beyond the channel allocations required by the Telecommunication Act of 1996.

SUMMARY

The schooling of children with disabilities consists of a wide variety of educational placements, service levels, professional educators, and support personnel. The public schools have long provided the individualized and unique services required for these children to receive a free and appropriate public education (Farber, 1998). Educational trends in the United States suggest that in the near future, children with disabilities may receive some, if not all, of their education in nontraditional settings supported in part by distance learning and associated technologies. Homebound services, home schooling opportunities, inclusion classes, and charter and private schools will all provide educational opportunities for children with disabilities. As distance learning opportunities and programs become more widely available and more affordable, more and more children will receive their schooling in placements other than public school settings.

Distance learning for children with disabilities provides an opportunity to access information, services, and programs that can assist in meeting their specialized and unique educational needs. At times, the most appropriate education may be delivered through a distance learning format either unilaterally or in association with a traditional classroom. The fact that a child has a disability will not, by itself, support the use of distance learning technologies. However, the situation of a child with a disability who cannot access the information and education to meet individualized needs certainly calls for consideration of viable alternatives offered by distance learning.

The evolving development of technologies associated with distance learning will provide the framework to consider effective distance learning programs. As technologies improve and the costs decrease, more and more children, families, and teachers will have the technological and fiscal capabilities of using distance learning formats. Parents and teachers will need to fully understand the benefits and outcomes associated with distance learning in order to utilize these educational services effectively.

Placement decisions for children with disabilities in programs that have distance learning options should be a collective process including parents, school personnel, and children themselves. Distance learning is not an end in itself. Effective distance learning programs require competent, learned teachers and administrators and concerned parents.

Distance learning will not create an educational oasis. At best, it will support the instructional strategies and methods provided by teachers qualified to serve children with disabilities (Cyris,1997). Technologies should not and must not drive the decisions that place children in educational settings. Parents, teachers, and associated support services should collectively decide the most appropriate educational placement for children.

In this chapter, we have attempted to provide a window through which children, parents, teachers, and administrators can view the world of opportunities offered by distance learning and technology. This window of opportunity will offer ever-wider views as technologies improve and cost declines, and the window is open to all. Those who turn away may well lose a valuable resource. Those who choose to see will discover myriad capabilities, programs, and services—all good things for children, especially for those with disabilities. Educational opportunities have never resided totally within public schools, but with today's technology, opportunities for educational growth can be found anytime, anywhere—through distance learning.

DISCUSSION QUESTIONS

1. What implications does distance learning have for providing educational services to children with disabilities in nontraditional settings?
2. What other placements might distance learning technologies provide educational services for children with disabilities?

REFERENCES

Churton, M. (2000). *Faculty primer: A resource for distance learning faculty*. Tampa: University of South Florida.

Connick, G. (Ed.). (1999). *The distance learner's guide*. Western Cooperative for Educational Telecommunication. Upper Saddle River, NJ: Prentice Hall.

Cyris, T. (1997). Teaching and learning at a distance: What it takes to effectively design, deliver, and evaluate programs. *New Directions for Teaching and Learning*. San Francisco: Jossey-Bass.

Donahoe, S. S. (1995). *Using distance learning telecommunications to develop strategies of communications for widely diverse populations* (Clearinghouse No. SP036425). Washington: (Eric Document Reproduction Service No. ED 390 862).

Farber, J. (1998). The third circle on education and distance learning. *Sociological Perspectives, 41*, 4.

Kaseman, L., & Kaseman, S. (1997). Hanging on to what makes home schooling distinctive. *Home Education Newsletter*, November/December, 3.

Keegan, D. (1993). *Theoretical principles of distance education*. London: Routledge.

Lange, C., & Ysseldyke, J. (1998). School choice policies and practices for students with disabilities. *Exceptional Children, 64*, 21.

Minoli, D. (1996). *Distance learning technology and applications*. Boston: Artech House.

Moore, M., & Kearsley, G. (1996). *Distance education: A systems view*. Belmont, CA: Wadsworth Publishing Co.

Oberg, C. (1998). The price of information technology in the future of higher education. Proceedings of Digital Diploma Mills Conference. September. Harvey Mudd College, Claremont, CA.

Parker, A. (1997). A distance education how-to manual: Recommendations for the field. *Educational Technology Review, 8,* 7–10.

Putnam, J. W. (1993). *Cooperative learning and strategies for inclusion: Celebrating diversity in the classroom.* Baltimore: Paul H. Brookes.

Telecommunications Act of 1996, U.S. Congress. Washington: U.S. Government Printing Office.

U.S. Department of Education (1999, May). *The state of charter schools.* Third Year Report. Office of Educational Research and Improvement. Washington: Author.

Yell, M. L. (1998). *The law and special education.* Upper Saddle River, NJ: Prentice Hall, Inc.

14

Charter Schools and Their Impact on Special Education

Myrrha Pammer, Carolyn D. Lavely, and Cathy Wooley-Brown

Until recently, very little attention has been paid to special education issues within the charter school research. In this chapter, the defining features of charter schools, the history of the charter school movement, and the most recent research related to charter schools and students with disabilities are discussed. In particular, the results of three recent national studies on charter schools and students with disabilities are presented. Also discussed are the major special education issues currently facing charter schools and subsequent recommendations for serving students with disabilities.

DEFINING FEATURES OF CHARTER SCHOOLS

Charter schools are legally independent, publicly funded schools that serve children via a contract or charter and a sponsoring entity, usually a local school board or district, but may also include universities, educational service centers, and other agencies. Also, charter schools may not charge tuition, they may not discriminate, and they may not teach religion (Blackman et al., 1997; Meinhard, 1996). Charter schools, in theory, trade rules, regulations, and bureaucracy for greater accountability. Meinhard

(1996) explains that in exchange for deregulation, charter schools are held publicly accountable by the results of the outcomes they specify in their charters and are evaluated on how well they are able to deliver the promised results. This concept of deregulation is an important point for charter advocates because many advocates assume that the presence of fewer regulations will facilitate the development of greater curricular innovation and more specialized schools to serve particular groups of students. These opportunities, therefore, in theory, would attract parents looking for such innovation.

It is important to point out that if the charter is violated or if an adequate number of parents do not choose the school, the school closes (Meinhard, 1996). Therefore, it is critical for the charter school organizers to carefully plan and develop their charters and subsequent goals and objectives. Developers need to draft well-planned mission and vision statements for their school in conjunction with clear-cut goals and objectives and the means to meet these objectives. Developers also need to market and develop their schools appropriately to attract potential parents interested in particular types of services their school has to offer. These principles are especially true for schools attempting to serve students with special needs or at-risk students, particularly if they hope to venture out into the realm of innovative models of teaching and learning and hope to remain viable, as their very existence is heavily dependent upon the achievement of their students.

Charter schools have four principal defining features. The first and perhaps the most critical concept that defines charter schools is that they should provide an education equal or superior to traditional public schools. Second, they should do so with greater accountability than traditional public schools. Such accountability may come in the form of annual evaluations and annual reports, as well as 3- to 5-year contracts (depending upon the state, and in some cases, maybe longer, as in Arizona which enters into 15-year contracts) allowing renewal only after in-depth financial and/or programmatic audits. Third, they should be free from the bureaucracy typically associated with traditional public schools, which will subsequently allow for greater educational innovation. Fourth, such innovation should spawn new models of educational programming and service delivery for traditional public schools and other charter schools (Blackman et al., 1997; Meinhard, 1996; Spring, 1998; Zollers & Ramanathan, 1998).

In addition, many charter schools have smaller class sizes and lower student/teacher ratios than traditional public schools, and it is expected that these features will facilitate an environment that is more conducive to teaching and learning. It is anticipated that these features will facilitate teaching and learning for both regular education students and special education students (Zollers & Ramanathan, 1998).

BACKGROUND OF CHARTER SCHOOLS

Much of recent educational research is focused on school reform efforts and the lack of quality in our public school systems (Spring, 1998). In fact, many researchers and laypersons contend that America's schools are not competitive with schools in other nations, and are in fact "in crisis." "School choice" has been offered as a potential solution to America's educational problems. School choice initiatives include options for parents to enroll their children in private schools, public schools outside of their district of residence, magnet schools, and charter schools. Some researchers and school choice advocates have advocated that competition in the free market will facilitate student achievement, higher-quality schools, and greater accountability (Spring, 1998).

From a relatively slow beginning in a few states, as of September 1997, over 700 charter schools were operating in 23 states and the District of Columbia, and the numbers are growing rapidly (OERI, 1998). Currently, 37 states now have charter legislation, cities can also sponsor charter schools, and there are well over 2,000 charter schools currently in operation. It is anticipated that charter schools created by local educators, parents, community members, schools boards, and other sponsors might provide new models of schooling and place competitive pressures on public schools that will improve our current system. Others remain concerned that charter schools might be "little more than escape valves that relieve pressure for genuine reform of the whole system" or they may even "add to centrifugal forces that threaten to pull public education apart" (OERI, 1998). Although the rapid growth of charter schools affirms widespread enthusiasm for the movement, very little is known about implementation issues or the effects of charter schools on students with disabilities. Moreover, even less is known about why some parents of these groups of children are choosing to enroll them in charter schools. This is a critical question, because the majority of charter schools are serving children who are either disabled or are considered at-risk.

SPECIAL EDUCATION AND CHARTER SCHOOLS

As previously mentioned, two thirds of the nation's charter schools are serving students either considered at-risk or those with special needs. Many states, including California, Colorado, Delaware, Florida, Illinois, North Carolina, Ohio, Rhode Island, and Wisconsin, now have charter legislation specifically stating preferences for serving special education and/or at-risk students (Fiore & Cashman, 1999). Other states, such as Texas, have recently adopted requirements mandating that schools describe how they intend to serve special needs children in their initial applications or contracts. In fact, some states were strongly influenced by a variety of interest groups to include provisions for special education students in order to successfully acquire charter school legislation in the first place. Moreover, because of the political push for charter school developers to continue to develop schools that serve students with special needs, as well as the large number of charter schools (relative to all charters) that currently serve these populations, it is critical to gain an understanding of the factors that lead parents to select them for their children.

NATIONAL STUDIES OF CHARTER SCHOOLS AND STUDENTS WITH DISABILITIES

Three recent national studies have uncovered some compelling phenomena about charter schools serving students with disabilities and the parents who chose to send their children to these schools. Two of these studies found that the main reasons parents of students with disabilities chose charter schools were class size, opportunities for parent involvement, academic programming, and parent dissatisfaction with the previous school (Pammer, M., 2000; Fiore, T., 2000). Parents in these studies reported being "pushed away" from the previous public school and being "pulled toward" the charter school because of opportunities for greater parent involvement in the special education program, as well as greater individualized attention for their children due to smaller class sizes and a more nurturing environment. In particular, the University of South Florida study provided a detailed look at examined parent satisfaction, parent involvement, and marketing strategies to determine why parents of special needs students choose charter schools. An in-depth look at parent dissatisfaction with the former school revealed that parents were dissatisfied with class size, special education, attention to child's needs, curriculum, and choice of teachers and classes in their former, public school. These parents reported being very satisfied with the same features in their charter school, and the only feature for which they provided a neutral response was transportation. Perhaps more interesting was the finding that parent expectations about the charter school experience either matched or surpassed expectations. This study also found that administrator's perceptions about why parents choose charter schools are similar to parents' perceptions (Pammer, 2000). This finding corroborates a related finding by Fiore (2000).

This study also uncovered a key difference in the reasons parents of nonlearning disabled students and parents of learning disabled students choose charter schools. Parents of learning disabled students were less influenced by two features of the charter school: interactions with peers and inclusion. This is an interesting difference in light of the strong inclusion movement over the last 20 years. It appears that for parents of learning disabled students, class size, academics, parent involvement in the IEP process, and other features superseded their feeling about inclusion in their decision to choose the charter school.

In addition, this study also found that the majority of parents of students with disabilities in charter schools were involved in parent activities at the school. Seventy-six percent reported being involved at the charter school, and the most frequently reported activities included IEP meetings and parent/teacher conferences.

In addition to the Pammer and Fiore studies, Project SEARCH was the third national study aimed at special education in charter schools. The project was designed to examine current special education policies and practices in charter schools to develop a set of policy recommendations to assistant states, districts, and individual charter schools develop the capacity to provide special education programs. The project investigated special education in charter schools in seven states: Arizona, California, Colorado, Connecticut, Florida, Minnesota, and North Carolina. The study focused on the challenges associated with being part of an LEA (local education authority or independent school district), and found that there are substantive benefits associated with being part of the LEA for the purposes of special education. However, some problems were reported by developers in these relationships. The major challenge was a conflict between the ideally deregulated nature of charter schools and the often highly regulated nature of special education. Specific benefits schools reported included assistance with transportation and assessment and other large-scale services, but often there is a struggle for local control of basic services between the charter school and the district (Ahearn, McLaughlin, Lange, & Rhim, L., 2000). Additional findings from Project SEARCH are outlined in the following section.

CURRENT SPECIAL EDUCATION ISSUES AND CHALLENGES FACING CHARTER SCHOOLS

In spite of the intention of the originators of the charter school movement to avoid educational regulations, the responsibility to provide education to students with disabilities has become among the more complex challenges facing charter schools. Charter schools are obligated to comply with all state and federal laws and regulations pertaining to the education of students with disabilities. In particular, the rights as delineated in IDEA and Section 504 of the Rehabilitation Act may not be waived. As result, the requirements of these statutes can create special challenges for charter school personnel.

In 1975, Public Law 94-142 mandated that all children with disabilities would receive a free, appropriate public education in the least restrictive environment. In 1990, the Individuals with Disabilities Education Act (IDEA) amended PL 94-142 to include such important legislation as:

1. All children and youth with disabilities, regardless of the severity of their disability, will receive a free, appropriate public education (FAPE) at the expense of the public

2. An Individualized Education Program (IEP) or an Individualized Family Services Plan (IFSP) will be developed for every child or youth found eligible for special education or early intervention services, stating what types of special education and related services each child will receive
3. To the maximum extent appropriate, all children and youth with disabilities will be educated in the regular education environment
4. Parents have the right to participate in every decision related to the identification, evaluation, and placement of their child or youth with a disability
5. Parents must give consent for any initial evaluation, assessment, or placement that may occur, as well as any changes in placement
6. Parents have the right to challenge or appeal any decision related to the identification, evaluation, and placement of their child

In 1997, Congress revised the 1990 version of IDEA. This legislation addresses special education programs in charter schools. It specifically states that the local education agency must serve children with disabilities attending those schools in the same way it serves children with disabilities in other schools, and it must provide funds to those schools in the same way it provides funds to its other schools.

In addition, Section 504 of the Rehabilitation Act prohibits discrimination on the basis of disability by any agency receiving federal funds. This legislation includes school districts and charter schools, because as public agencies, they are mandated to provide an education for children in a nondiscriminatory fashion.

Enmeshed in the complexities of day-to-day compliance with these statutes is the school's status as an LEA or non-LEA. Depending upon the state in which it is located, an individual charter school may legally be another school within an LEA, a program within an LEA, or it can be separate from or partially connected to an existing LEA. This status has major implications for how much responsibility a charter school has for its students with disabilities. According to Ahearn et al. (2000), if a charter school is its own separate LEA, it means that the charter school has responsibility for all students with disabilities in the school. Yet, in some cases, the issue of ultimate responsibility remains unclear, and the designation of an individual charter school as an LEA for purposes of special education can be confusing at best (Ahearn, McLaughlin, Lange, & Rhim, 2000).

With the LEA status debate in mind, there are nine key issues facing charter schools concerning special education service delivery: preparations to serve students with special needs beginning with the application process; facility acquisition and accommodations; policies and procedures for special education; finance; service delivery models; adherence to the mission and vision of the school; accountability and assessment; hiring, training, and licensure of staff; and addressing technical assistance and training (Szabo & Gerber, 1996; Ahearn, McLaughlin, Lange, & Rhim, 2000; Fiore, 2000).

Preparing to serve students with disabilities in charter schools should begin with the charter application process. States such as Ohio, Florida, and others require that a detailed plan for serving students with disabilities is actually outlined in the educational plan before school opens. The charter school contract and application process provide key mechanisms for detailing the responsibilities and obligations of the school to provide special education services. Unfortunately, not all states yet require such a plan, and for some charter developers in these states, special education is an afterthought (Blackman, Curry, Jackson, Lavely, Mann, & Pammer, 1997; and Ahearn, McLaughlin, Lange, & Rhim, 2000). Organizers often ignore the tenets of special education legislation because they believe it is simply "too hard to do right now." They have the misconception that they are not responsible for providing special education programs.

Facilities acquisition and accommodations is another challenge facing charter schools. Insufficient start-up funds and inadequate facilities have troubled many start-up schools (U.S. Department of Education, 1997; Blackman, Curry, Jackson, Lavely, Mann, & Pammer, 1997). This is particularly true for newly created schools that are located in nontraditional places, although some schools have taken creative, innovative steps to resolve facilities problems, such as leasing space in multiple sites, leasing space in previously closed or parochial schools, shopping malls, or commercial space. This severe resource problem can be compounded when these schools attempt to accommodate students with disabilities. As public entities, charter school facilities must be ADA compliant, meaning that they must comply with all state, local, and federal codes for buildings that house students with disabilities. For some schools, this can mean extensive, costly renovations and modifications to their facilities, including everything from raising or lowering sinks to adding ramps and widening hallways.

The development of policies and procedures for implementing special education statutes represents another key issue for charter schools. Charter school boards and administrators need to understand their responsibilities for ensuring FAPE (free and appropriate public education) for a student with a disability in a charter school, as well as procedural policies concerning time lines and methods for reporting data, monetary reimbursements, and service models. There is a general lack of knowledge among charter school operators of the affirmative requirements such as child find, referral, and identification of special education eligible students (Ahearn, McLaughlin, Lange, & Rhim, 2000).

The complicated methods of funding special education is another area that often presents a challenge to charter schools. Funding in charter schools varies by state. For instance, in Colorado, charter schools apply for funding through administrative units based on reimbursable costs, such as teacher salaries (Blackman, Curry, Jackson, Lavely, Mann, & Pammer, 1997). These funds are earmarked for special education only, and they cannot be combined with other funds. The district where the student lives is required to pay tuition charges for the excess costs of educating the child in the charter school. The district can then count the student for state and federal funds.

In the case of Florida, special education dollars are distributed by means of weight factors that are determined by the type and severity of the disability. Charter schools are entitled to receive special education funds per state funding formulas (Blackman, Curry, Jackson, Lavely, Mann, & Pammer, 1997). Moreover, in states where charter schools are autonomous local education agencies, charter schools are only entitled to state and federal dollars. But in states where they are not legally independent, the school district must aid in funding the costs of special education services.

Unfortunately, in most cases, the dollars provided for special education in any of these circumstances are not enough to cover all the costs of educating students with special needs (Zollers & Ramanathan, 1998; Blackman, Curry, Jackson, Lavely, Mann, & Pammer, 1997; & Szabo & Gerber, 1996). This means that charter schools often have to look elsewhere to supplement their budget and defray the costs of special education. Complying with IDEA may be particularly difficult for charter schools because separating from larger school districts results in a major loss of resources (Szabo & Gerber, 1996). Moreover, special education funding is complex and multilayered. As a result, some charter school administrators have little understanding of the sources of funding available to them, let alone how to access such funding. For example, the Project SEARCH study found at least four fiscal models operating for special education within charter schools:

- Charters that are their own LEA are autonomous and legally responsible for all fiscal and programmatic requirements.
- Charters that are a "hybrid" LEA are autonomous and legally responsible for implementing all programmatic requirements by shared fiscal responsibility with an LEA or other administrative entity.
- Charters are a semi-independent program within an LEA and share some programmatic and fiscal responsibility with the LEA or other administrative entity.
- Charters are schools within an LEA; the LEA retains full programmatic and fiscal responsibility for special education in the charter school.

As it turns out, there are financial incentives and disincentives for serving students with disabilities in charter schools. In particular, perceptions of high costs associated with disabled students can lead to counseling out potential students and referring them to the local district because they "have the program the child needs" (Ahearn, McLaughlin, Lange, & Rhim, 2000).

Moreover, the entire financial picture is further complicated by the fact that fiscal responsibility for certain special education services, including transportation, legal services, and other costs, is not well defined for charter school operators in the first place. The financial waters are similarly muddied when a district retains a percentage for administrative overhead, but does not designate what services to charter schools are to be covered by the fee (Ahearn, McLaughlin, Lange, & Rhim, 2000).

A huge issue facing charter schools is whether or not they must provide services to students across the full continuum of services. According to Ahearn et al. (2000), when a charter school is an autonomous LEA, the legal obligation is to make available the full array of services. However, if a child on an IEP moves from the charter school to another placement when the charter school cannot meet his or her needs, it can be unclear. Moreover, the nature and scope of the special education service delivery are directly affected by the charter school's philosophy, curricular orientation, and mission. This can create conflict between goals and objectives for the school and special education requirements. Charter school personnel must also be knowledgeable about the federal and state statutes for the screening, assessment, and placement process. Children suspected of having a disability are entitled to procedural safeguards under IDEA. Awareness of the laws can assist professionals in understanding the entire service delivery system, ensure protection of civil rights, and improve collaboration with other agencies and families. According to McKinney (1996), charter school personnel, especially principals, lack sufficient knowledge of federal and state special education laws and procedures. Without this knowledge, charter school organizers are unable to provide appropriate due process procedures as defined by IDEA (Blackman, Curry, Jackson, Lavely, Mann, & Pammer, 1997).

Moreover, there are multiple levels of accountability, which can be confusing to a charter school. They may include chartering authorities, SEAs, LEAs, and other agencies. Though charter schools may or may not be included in their state's special education monitoring cycle, some say they would welcome early inspection to help them identify potential problem areas before serious problems arise. For many sponsors and state departments of education, monitoring charter school special education practices is a challenge because many states lack adequate resources and staff. Additionally, consequences for special education violations are not often well known or established, leading charter school developers to view the statutes as inconsistent or set up to "trap a charter school" into defeat (Ahearn, McLaughlin, Lange, & Rhim, 2000).

Hiring, training, and licensure of staff also plague charter schools because certified or licensed special education teachers are scarce in general, and staff aren't always receiving much needed professional development related to special education. However, charters in some states, including Ohio and Texas, are partnering with regional special educational service centers to provide training and support for teachers and staff related to intervention assistance team development, IEP development, student identification, assessment, and service delivery models.

The final area of concern is providing adequate technical assistance and support related to special education to charter schools in every state. Some states, such as Florida, California, and Minnesota, are actively providing special education workshops and training opportunities via their state resource centers and other technical assistance organizations. Also, in Texas, regional special education service centers have been developed to specifically serve charter schools, and Ohio charters are successfully partnering with regional special education resource centers that serve all public schools. Yet, much remains to be done. Charter school staff need intense professional development related to how to specifically and adequately deliver special education services. More professional development opportunities need to be made available to staff in other states, and more technical assistance can conceivably be made available via interactive Web sites, direct training workshops, and charter school liaisons (Ahearn, McLaughlin, Lange, & Rhim, 2000).

Because children who may have a disability are protected by IDEA, charter school administrators and staff need to be aware of the proper procedures for assessing and placing students. They also need to be aware of how to implement an active IEP, because they are required to make accommodations and provide services for students with disabilities.

It appears that some charter schools are in fact having difficulty serving students with disabilities. Both McKinney (1996) and Zollers and Ramanathan (1998) found that many charter schools are not serving children with disabilities. Specifically, McKinney found that only 4 percent of the students with disabilities in Arizona charter schools were being served as special education students, and Zollers and Ramanathan cite numerous attempts of Massachusetts for-profit charter schools to actually "counsel their special education students out" of their schools. This article sheds light on the potential extremes that charter developers may take to ensure success in accountability for their schools. Not-for-profits are not immune to such phenomena.

RECOMMENDATIONS AND FUTURE DIRECTIONS

There are many challenges to overcome in meeting the needs of children with special needs in charter schools. However, it is clear that charter schools, as public agencies, are legally mandated and responsible for providing special education and related services in the least restrictive environment. The following is a list of alternative, innovative strategies for dealing with the challenges faced by charter schools:

1. Form a special education task force to ensure that special education is included in the educational plan of the charter application. Use their

expertise to facilitate compliance with the relevant laws and regulations. Include special education and related costs as part of the financial plan.

2. Negotiate contractual agreements with the sponsor and educational service agencies to provide special education and related services where possible.
3. Hire qualified diagnosticians, school psychologists, and other professional staff on a "per case basis" to reduce the cost of the evaluation procedures.
4. In states where funding procedures are complex, hire financial consultants to assist in the procurement of special education revenues.
5. Set as part of the hiring criteria knowledge of special education and related procedures to ensure that teachers are comfortable with and have a working knowledge of children with disabilities.
6. Form consortia of area charter schools to share costs of special education assessment and program implementation.
7. When special education services are not sufficient to meet the needs of a child in the charter school, staff should work with the local school system to obtain an appropriate educational placement for a more severely disabled student. Due process procedures and regulations as outlined in IDEA should be followed.
8. State and local educational agencies should monitor charter schools for compliance with special education regulations, and should be provided clear and explicit directions that are appropriate for small schools. Consequences for non-compliance should be clearly explained before the charter is granted, and consequences should start with intense technical assistance and support before implementing more negative actions.
9. Special education can be implemented in nontraditional ways while still maintaining the spirit as well as the letter of the law. Special education does not have to be a "special place, a special teacher, or a special curriculum." It should be specially designed *instruction* that meets the unique needs of the student. Also, trained paraprofessionals, parents, and other volunteers should be used to provide additional remedial support in the classroom.
10. Charter schools and other charter friendly organizations must lobby their state legislatures to obtain full funding for special education programs and related services.

DISCUSSION QUESTIONS

1. Why are parents of students with disabilities choosing charter schools?
2. In states where charter schools are legally autonomous school districts (LEAs), who has the primary responsibility for providing special edu-

cation services—the charter school, the local public school district, or parents?

3. What are the major issues facing charter schools concerning special education service delivery?

4. What are the financial incentives and disincentives for serving students with disabilities in charter schools?

5. What are some strategies charter schools can use to help overcome challenges in serving their students with special needs?

REFERENCES

Ahearn, E., McLaughlin, M., Lange, C., Rhim, L. (2000). *Project SEARCH: A national study of special education in charter schools synthesis report*. National Association of State Directors of Special Education and US Department of Education.

Blackman, J., Curry, B., Jackson, S., Lavely, C., Mann, K., & Pammer, M. (1997). *Charter schools: Issues and challenges*. Tampa: University of South Florida.

Finn, C., Manno, B., & Bierlein, L. A. (1996). *Charter schools in action: A first look*. Hudson Institute Educational Excellence Network, p. 6-11.

Fiore, T., (2000). *Charter Schools and Students with Disabilities: A National Study*. Office of Educational Research and Improvement of the U. S. Department of Education; Westat; & SRI International.

Fiore, T., & Cashman, E. (1999). *Review of charter school legislation provisions related to students with disabilities*. Westat Policy Review.

McKinney, J.R. (1996). Charter schools: A new barrier for children with disabilities. *Educational Leadership, 54* (2), 22-25.

Meinhard, G. (1996). *Charter schools: Frequently asked questions*, www.teleport. coml%7Ej wooster/chtrfaq.htm.

OERI. (1998). *U.S. Department of Education four-year study of charter schools*.

Pammer, M. (2000). *Why are parents of students with disabilities choosing charter schools?* Richfield, OH: Bell & Howell Publishers.

Spring, J. (1998). *American education*. Boston: McGraw-Hill.

Szabo, J., & Gerber, M. (1996). Special education and the charter school movement. *Special Education Leadership Review, 135-148*.

U.S. Department of Education. (1997, May). *A study of charter schools: First-year report and executive summary*. RPP International & University of Minnesota.

Zollers, N. & Ramanathan, A. (1998). For-profit charter schools and students with disabilities: The sordid side of the business of schooling. *Phi Delta Kappan, 81* (14), 284–289.

15

Reading the History of Special Education

Sherman Dorn

With so much of today's special education determined and shaped by historical imperatives and precedents, close scrutiny can only serve to aid special educators in forming a balanced understanding and evaluation of our profession. (Winzer, 1993, p. xii)

Special education has appeared to be in unprecedented crisis for over a decade (e.g., Fuchs & Fuchs, 1991). In the last few years, the debate about special education has focused on criticisms of the increasing numbers of children classified disabled, segregation from regular education, poor student outcomes, and the minimal numbers of special education students returning to regular classrooms. Despite appearances, however, these controversies are not entirely unprecedented (Dorn, Fuchs, & Fuchs, 1996). The problems of special education are deeply rooted, in two ways. First, special education has always been at the margins of public schools. Conceived in the progressive era as a humanitarian measure and as a way to relieve classroom teachers of bothersome pupils, special education has inherited a "dumping ground" role within public schooling (Franklin, 1989, 1994; Lazerson, 1975, 1982; Sarason & Doris, 1979; Tropea, 1987a, 1987b, 1993). In addition to its dumping ground role, special education has suffered from the general inability of schools to respond successfully to the problems of at-risk children. This failure results from the organizational problems of school systems at large, not just the problems of special education alone. Although schools may take symbolic steps in reaction to perceived social crises, new programs may not address issues in a substantive or systematic manner (Rogers, 1968; Sarason, 1990).

Special education has inherited a burden from school systems' general inability to succeed with at-risk children; therefore, the history of special education is important. There are several other reasons that some use to explain why the history of special education is important. Some argue that special education inherits a legacy of research efforts, research that educators ignore at their peril. According to this view, unless today's reformers know the history of their profession, they can—and probably will—repeat the mistakes of their predecessors. Deno (1994) wrote:

> Even professionals who should know better often fail to read articles more than five or ten years old under the crush of their busy lives. They thus fail to recognize that what is perceived as a bright new idea today was recognized but expressed in other terms, tried and abandoned for good and sufficient reasons years ago, or was simply tried without properly applying the theory proposed and as a result abandoned as an inadequate conception. (pp. 379–380)

At the brass-tacks level, in the classroom, educators should be aware of instructional methods that others have tried repeatedly in the past. Thus, the most obvious of the uses of history is in providing background to and evaluation of specific interventions. One instance of this history was the renewed development of process training in the middle of this century—an approach that was not, in fact, very new at all. Mann wrote *On the Trail of Process* (1979) to argue that process training followed a long legacy of (failed) attempts at process-oriented and faculty psychologies. Unaware of this history, thousands of practitioners invested years of effort in process training. Had they been aware of earlier failures, Mann implies, perhaps much wasted time could have been saved.

In addition, others would note, the history of special education can serve several valuable roles beyond tracing and providing insight into specific techniques in the field. Histories of special education can provide an opportunity for professionals to step back from day-to-day concerns and place their own work in a distanced perspective. This goal is especially important for the vast majority of special educators who entered the profession in the last thirty years:

> Each generation or era tends to see itself as unique and is more aware of discontinuities than of continuities with its history. . . . [Histories are] helpful to people who are so immersed on a daily basis with matters of policy, programs, management, and education that they have difficulty taking distance from what they are doing and how they are thinking. (Sarason & Doris, 1979, p. x)

Histories can also evaluate reform processes themselves. By explicating the path that reforms took, as well as documenting previous practice, histories of special education can provide evidence of what improvement (or lack thereof) has occurred: "There is always the question of progress. In this regard, and in the parlance of the behaviorist, history provides the baseline data" (Scheerenberger, 1983, p. xiii). Finally, history is already used in discussions about the direction of special education. Special educators have argued about the Regular Education Initiative, for example, based on their own understandings of the history of the field (e.g., Kauffman & Pullen, 1989; Reynolds, 1989). Whether teachers and researchers like it or not, they operate with at least an implied picture in their minds, a suggested understanding, of the history of their field.

The understanding of that history, however, is limited by the rather sparse exposure to the history that professionals typically receive in school. In every introductory special education text is at least one obligatory passage on the history of the field as practice, research, and profession. Usually these histories are perfunctory claims of ancestral practices or origins (even if the ancestors were buried in the mists of the mid-20th century). Seasoned practitioners and researchers, being older and perhaps anxious about their own legacy, are more cognizant and respectful of special education's history. Thus, for example, the Council for Exceptional Children (CEC) has a Pioneers Division for retired or otherwise longtime members of the organization, recognizing their implied importance for the development of the field. (Few note that the majority of CEC members now eligible to join the Pioneers Division were born after the organization's establishment in 1922.) Still, one can expect many graduate students in special education to have scant exposure to histories of the field.

Published histories exist, of course. Some of the more well-known monographs include Lane's (1976) biography of Jean-Marc Itard, Gould's (1991) history of beliefs about intelligence, Trent's (1994) history of mental retardation institutions, Sarason and Doris's (1979) and Scheerenberger's (1983, 1987) general histories of mental retardation, Carrier's (1986a) book on the origins of learning disabilities, and Franklin's (1994) history of schools' views of failure in the twentieth century, as well as more specific histories "for the field" such as Kauffman's (1981b) introduction to the first edition of the *Handbook of Special Education* and Winzer's (1993) recent textbook history of special education. Of those ten authors, only one was a trained historian, and six came from either psychology or special education. The historiography (or historical literature) of special education is predominantly an amateur literature, at least as far as training in history is concerned.

To note that most historians of special education are amateur historians is not an insult, by any means. History as an academic discipline (if one counts such canonization by the establishment of departments) is only about a century old, and so one must count all long-dead historians from Thucidydes to Karl Marx as amateurs. The best-selling books in history are consistently about wars and often dominated (as in Civil War history) by authors without doctorates. We are all historians in the sense that we carry around thumbnail versions of history in our head, which are often very important to providing perspective on our daily lives (Becker, 1932). The fact that most historians of special education have not been trained historians reflects who is most interested in the field's past—special educators themselves. What special educators must be aware of, though, is that all histories broadcast the assumptions of their authors, whether professionally trained or not. Almost a century ago, historians in the United States attempted to craft an "objective" history, often obscuring the broader questions at hand (Novick, 1998). What this chapter can provide is an orientation to varying historical assumptions and different views of the world.

The starting point for this chapter is the fact that all histories must answer the question, "What creates and shapes change?" Different answers to that question are the underlying theories historians constantly debate. And, despite conventional wisdom, the devil is both in the detail and in the big picture. The remainder of this chapter focuses on the big pictures in the historiography (or written history) of special education in this fashion, identifying the existing perspectives and their strengths and weaknesses *as theory*. An initial example will illustrate how examining theories of change is different in a significant way from evaluating the accuracy of the detail. Kirk and Johnson (1951) wrote in their textbook *Educating the Retarded Child*:

> After the compulsory education laws were passed in the latter part of 19th-century the schools found more and more mentally retarded children in attendance. Since many of these children were so retarded that they could receive little benefit from the regular school curriculum, teachers, and administrators, and others associated with public-school education realized that some type of special facilities would have to be provided to meet this problem. It was recognized that educating these children who could not learn as fast as the average child was the responsibility of the community and the state. Since the mentally retarded could not benefit sufficiently from the instruction they received in the regular classes, some type of adapted instruction became a necessity. As a result, the first special classes were organized for retarded children at the turn of the century. Marked growth of public-school special classes has followed their initial organization. Only 50 years later, almost one hundred thousand retarded children were in attendance, and there is no reason to suspect that this growth has ceased. (p. v)

One may forget for a moment the question of how accurate this description is factually (and the prediction of future growth was certainly prescient). Instead, the issue here is the implicit social theory of how special education began in public schools: compulsory education created problems for administrators and other educators who invented special education as a way to resolve practical issues in schools. The historical model here is of public officials who create programs to respond to organizational problems. One can find a more explicit description of this model in the works of Galambos (1970), or one could go to de Tocqueville (1851/1998) for a description of the encroaching powers of the bureaucracy. But one must recognize that primary motivation for special education in Kirk and Johnson's view came from school systems' organizational needs.

Even descriptions that appear to be atheoretical are not. They are, at worst, an evasion of judgment. Bryan and Bryan's (1979) textbook *Exceptional Children* provides an example of a history without causation in some passages. They wrote, in reference to nineteenth-century teaching:

> We do not know whether these pioneers failed in their attempts to teach teachers, whether their followers simply were not good students, or whether the educational technology was incorrect from the beginning. *Whatever the cause,* early hopes for educating the handicapped were not realized. As a result, the initial goal of providing day schools for teaching these children was forsaken for full-time residential care. . . . Segregated institutions . . . were reduced to convenient warehouses. (p. 16)(emphasis added)

One should note the use of the passive voice here ("was forsaken" and "were reduced"), without any reference to who was responsible for turning institutions into warehouses. For the authors, who earlier make bold pronouncements about how prehistoric people treated those with disabilities (p. 9), prospective teachers reading this passage need not understand what happened or the relevance for the present. The decline of nineteenth-century care was a tragedy without fault, apparently. That implication is both wrong and dangerous. Neither policy nor practice exists in a vacuum. There are always individuals who make decisions and act. Cause is important in descriptions of history, if for no other reason than that the deletion of cause removes responsibilities for actions and their consequences. Even if an author claims "no elaborate theories" (Scheerenberger, 1983, p. 254), one can usually identify some assumptions, either hidden or explicit, underlying the choice of topics or reasoning behind conclusions. Being aware of key theoretical assumptions, even if unstated, is as important in reading the history of special education as in reading research reports of teaching innovations.

THEMES IN THE WRITTEN HISTORY OF SPECIAL EDUCATION

The following description of themes extracts them from more complex pieces in order to clarify the different assumptions authors may make in describing the history of special education as a research activity, as a structure in schools, and as teacher practice. These motifs generally do not appear undiluted in any piece of writing, but isolating them will make identification easier. The careful reader will note that many of the examples cited here are from short pieces—articles and introductions from textbooks, rather than books—to show that common assumptions about history will show up in almost any discussion of the history of special education. Each section that follows describes the general assumptions of what drives change, includes several examples, and delineates some strengths and weaknesses of each approach for writing (and reading) the history of special education. One overarching claim I hope to substantiate is that no explanation of change either condones or condemns any aspect of special education. Thus, focusing on theoretical assumptions is not the same as hunting for ideology. One can, for example, be convinced that organizational needs have in large part pushed schools to develop special education, but that conclusion does not, by itself, say whether the practice of special education is ethical.

Great Men (and Occasionally Great Women)

Many times, special educators writing the history of the field point to "pioneers" who came before and, presumably, led the way for what has happened to the present. Leo Kanner's 1964 history of mental retardation is a case in point, with the explanation at the end, "We would not be where we are now if it had not been for the early pioneers" (p. 144). He traces the growth of institutions, as many do, to the founding of individual men (or, sometimes, women like Dorothea Dix), bordering on a history of saints (or hagiography) rather than a history of the field. Whether social conditions made institutional developments likely or even possible is not a significant part of Kanner's history or, to take another example, Lieberman's (1982) description of Jean-Marc Itard as a "problem-solver." Even Safford and Safford (1995), while claiming to have written a "history of children rather than services" (p. vii), describe eighteenth- and nineteenth-century developments as being the inspiration of key individuals. The focus on individuals usually assumes that men or women, by themselves, are influencing the world by their ideas, ingenuity, or fortuitous place.

One can see individuals as important for dissenting from the dominant views of the day as well as for concrete accomplishments. Kauffman's (1976) description of nineteenth-century views of children with severe behavior problems (which he has repeated in his textbook; see Kauffman, 1981a, for an example) notes that not everyone before the twentieth century had barbaric views of those with antisocial behavior. He describes moral treatment (which included formal education as one component) as a legitimate practice in its own right and one very different from the later focus on psychodynamics at the turn of the century. He points to the views of specific heroic dissenters (such as Philippe Pinel, Benjamin Rush, and Francis Stribling) as examples of conscientious objectors to the generally poor treatment of individuals with troubling behavior. The implication of discussing dissenting views is that little in history is inevitable, and (more specifically) that choices about the treatment of individuals with disabilities always exist. Showing the ability of individuals either to shape institutions or to disagree with prevailing views is a real strength of focusing on individuals.

A biographical approach can, however, ignore either salient features of one's life or the context of a person's work. The one-page biographies written by Irving for the *Journal of Special Education* in the 1970s demonstrate this weakness. The description of Sir Cyril Burt as "Britain's most eminent educational psychologist" (Irving, 1974, p. 116), for example, never mentioned his theory of innate intelligence, his influence on secondary school examinations in Britain, or the scandals and accusation of fraud that plagued the end of his life (Gould, 1991). One could even, as Lazerson (1975) has, accuse those focusing on individuals as creating a "conventional historical wisdom" of the "humane and path-breaking individuals, and an unwavering faith that further improvements will come with greater scientific knowledge and professional expertise" (Lazerson, 1975, p. 34). Such is not necessarily the case with a biographical approach to history. Gould's *The Mismeasure of Man* (1991) often focuses on individuals, such as Burt, as emblems of periods or as object lessons about scientific fallacies and political motivations for research. Thus, one can have either optimistic or cynical views of key individuals in the past. The central question of a biographical approach is how influential individuals were and what else may have been important in change.

Genealogy of Theory[1]

Some of those who read about the history of special education focus, if not entirely upon the contributions of individuals in the field, on the importance of theory in the intellectual development of special education. In particular, some trace specific theoretical developments through time as the focus of their history of special education. In some cases, this discussion arises in the context of specific intellectual debates. For example, Nelson and Polsgrove (1984) provide an intellectual history of behavior analysis through discussing four strands of behavioral theory. Polloway (1984) describes efficacy studies as a "microcosm of the field" (p. 19). Kauffman (1976, 1981a) describes nineteenth-century moral treatment as a legitimate antecedent to educational approaches to individuals with troubling behavior, in part to illustrate (as previously described) how one can dissent from prevailing views.

Others, however, argue that the intellectual history of special education has been important in shaping institutional and policy history. For example, Winzer (1986) argued that the Enlightenment thought was important to the development of early-nineteenth-century special education. John Locke's argument that people understand the world through the senses influenced, for example, Abbot l'Epee's development of a manual sign language, providing an intellectual "climate" conducive to change (Winzer, 1993, p. 43). Again, one should not confuse this genealogy of ideas with apologies for special education. Wool and Stephens (1978) argued that concepts developed by late-nineteenth-century institutional professionals lay the groundwork for poor conditions for individuals with mental retardation in the late twentieth century. Their evidence? A year-by-year description of journal contents in the field was what they saw as important. Sam Kirk, late in his life, argued that the American Association of Mental Deficiency's redefinition of mental retardation as an IQ below 84 (Heber, 1959, 1961) ruined special education by expanding the scope too far and also allowed elementary teachers to avoid their responsibilities for teaching to a broad range of children ("Special Education Yesterday, Today, and Tomorrow," 1977). The argument of Kirk claims an extraordinary influence for what is, after all, a very technical report. (I would agree that the document was influential. However, one should be keenly aware that Kirk was claiming that a document, by itself, was formative. As illustrated throughout this chapter, other arguments about key factors abound.)

Even postmodernists often assume the importance of ideas in shaping special education as a field and as practice. Iano (1986) argued that the diagnostic-prescriptive approach of special education came from the "natural science-technical" view of education and of positivism. This, he claimed, derived from the fundamental approaches of educational psychology that special education had inherited from the beginning of the twentieth century. Skrtic (1991), too, claimed that the fundamental problem of special education came from the definition of the field and phenomenological inconsistencies in simultaneously trying atheoretical innovations (what he called adhocracy) and also hewing to a strict hard-scientific approach to knowledge.

One can easily understand the appeal of an intellectual history of special education for a variety of reasons. Those trained in the field naturally look to intellectual progenitors for guidance, perspective, or, perhaps, a basis for rebellion. Those accustomed to political and intellectual history (in their own education) may assume that ideas are very important in shaping policy and practice. Researchers may believe, explicitly or implicitly, that what was important to their intellectual development (what they read in graduate school) is more broadly important. Both the importance of ideas by themselves and the ease of tracing them, however, are questionable. Institutions and practices may develop well outside the influence of broader theoretical concepts in the field. Even to the extent that ideas are important, finding which ones were most important may be more problematic than the commonly-written history of special education suggests. Sixty-seven consulting and associate editors of five special education journals surveyed by Patton, Polloway, and Epstein (1989) disagreed on what germinal readings were most important in the field, with the exception of Dunn's (1968) article criticizing separate special education classes for the "mildly retarded." Maybe no canon for special education exists; if not, does an intellectual history?

Specific to the history of technical fields is a tracing of techniques. For clear, identifiable teaching models, such as Direct Instruction, such a genealogy makes sense as intellectual history of a sort. Occasionally, however, the history of the field includes more distant ancestors of methods that exist in the present. The argument, where it exists, is that a technique is not new, either having a reputable ancestry or, as in Mann's (1979) criticism of process training, a disreputable one of consistently fallacious logic. Talbot's (1964) biography of Seguin claimed that his work was important for the cross-categorical methods and reference to normal development, as well as the theory behind it and the founding of specific institutions. Connor echoed this argument about the importance of technique in the preface: "Seguin's cohesive system of education applies to the deaf, the blind, and the retarded as well as to other groups of children" (Talbot, 1964, p. vi). Friend (1988) made similar arguments about the precedents for consultation in mental health and, more specifically, in an early operational use of consultation, the Vermont Consulting Teacher model. She argued that consultation is "a very *natural consequence* of a human services system (that is, public education) that outgrew its direct service capability" (p. 11; emphasis added). In general, the strengths and weaknesses of this approach parallel those of the intellectual history of a field. I note it separately here because occasionally authors focus on a technique as the most important contribution of a person or a group.

Cultural Values

To many, the key factor in determining treatment individuals with disabilities, including the history of special education, has been the values held by a culture at any point in time. Change, according to this model, comes from changed values in the culture as a whole. (One should keep in mind, again, that this is a description of themes identifiable in various writings, and very few writings will have solely a focus on the values of a culture.) Scheerenberger (1983) argued that mental retardation has always existed and that individual cultures treated individuals with mental retardation differently according to the values of that culture. Thus, he argues that the humanizing influence of Christianity in the fourth century led to improvements in the treatment of deviant individuals (p. 19). Similarly, he argues that the 19th century was the "age of progress." Referring to more recent practice, Hoffman (1975) saw a parallel between contemporary hostility to children labeled as disabled and hostility to those in ungraded classrooms in the late 19th century; in both cases, he suggests, general hostility to immigrants and anybody different from wealthier Americans came from the culture at large and shaped special education.

An argument about contemporary special education that assumes an historical model of cultural change (as opposed to cultural constancy) is Reynolds (1989), who argued that "progressive inclusion" in special education (p. 7) came from changes in the values held by American society. Karagiannis, Stainback, and Stainback (1996) argued that the separation of students with disabilities from general education classrooms was part of a larger segregation that was a strategy of social control. Conversely, the growth of inclusion "is a telling signal that schools and society will continue to shift toward increasingly inclusive practices" (p. 25). Both sources assume that changes in practice begin in cultural change.

Social Movements

Especially for the written history of special education since World War II, the influence of social movements has become important. For example, Kauffman (1981b) argued that advocacy, as well as research, shaped the growth and development of special education in the public schools. In particular, Scheerenberger (1983) noted that although the growth in classes for the "trainable mentally retarded" in the 1950s had many causes, parent pressure was the primary pushing factor. Shapiro (1995) claimed that a disability rights movement in general has been a growing force in American society, both within and outside of special education. Again, the focus on an alleged force is not necessarily either a positive or negative judgment. Kauffman and Pullen (1989), for example, warned against a persistent hyperbole about the benefits of reform.

Social history, more broadly speaking than special education, has also focused more on social movements in the last thirty years. The question about social movements as a driving force in history is how important leadership as opposed to "grassroots" decision-making is. Carson's (1981) history of the Student Nonviolent Coordinating Committee focused on the organization both as a grassroots effort and, inevitably, on the struggles of the leadership. Norrell's (1985) study of the civil rights movement and Tuskegee, Alabama, also focused on both the decisions of everyday residents and of those who were on the vanguard of civil rights efforts locally. (Some, of course, became the vanguard as ordinary residents asserting their rights.) Branch's (1988, 1998) biographical project on Martin Luther King reinterprets American political history in the 1950s and 1960s with a civil rights leader as the focus. That work is a "from the bottom up" history, yet it still places a leader in the driver's seat of history. Similar quandaries plague efforts to describe a disability rights movement. For example, Shapiro (1993) places Judy Heumann and other California activists at the center of the disability rights movement, perhaps slighting the importance of local parent activists in the

1950s who may have laid the groundwork for the grudging acceptance of the disability rights movement several decades hence.

Structural Conflict in Society

Some have argued that special education fits best in the context of an explicit struggle over the structure of American society, especially the place of schools in maintaining inequality, such as Bowles and Gintis (1976) suggest. Carrier (1986a) claims that "special education [is] one of the devices schools have used to differentiate and allocate pupils" (p. 10). From that perspective, he argues that the category of learning disabilities developed at first as neurology and then a lower-stigma way to provide services for wealthier children who were not doing well in school. Then, it "colonized" cultural deprivation theory to providing a "natural" explanation of why poor children were not doing as well in school as one might expect. The result, according to Carrier, was that a flexible concept (learning disabilities) served partly to justify unequal results in school.

The obvious strength of the structural argument in special education is that, in fact, special education does have a history of being an open dumping ground for many students, especially those who have been from working-class backgrounds or those whom the dominant culture has viewed as danger-ous or alien in some way (Mercer, 1973; Sarason & Doris, 1979). Two dimensions of special education need explaining, however. First, special education is not the only way that schools separate and potentially stigmatize students. What requires an account, even if one agrees with the underlying assumptions of a structural argument, is not necessarily how schools treat students but why, in particular, special education is one part of that repertoire. Schools track far more students into vocational education than they do into special education (assuming schools track students into special education); why have special education at all if the primary purpose is to deny opportu-nities, and other methods exist?

In addition, if special education has partly served to deny opportunities in its history, it has also served to create opportunities. Here, the social move-ment explanation of history in special education contradicts the explanation of special education as part of a system that reproduces the social structure. In particular, the growth of special education in many places, in part pushed by parent activism in the 1950s and 1960s, happened concurrently with the grow-ing disproportionate placement of African American children in special edu-cation. Was the expansion of special education a boon to children or a bane?

Organizational Development

One can also explain some parts of special education's history by describ-ing it either as a result of bureaucratic entrepreneurialism or as a safety valve for the school system. Polsky (1991), though not writing specifically about special education, is an example of the argument of bureaucratic entrepreneurialism, arguing that the growth of the "therapeutic state" has marginalized poor citizens and simultaneously provided an opportunity for the growth of mental health and welfare agencies. Franklin (1994) suggests that special education has, in part, served the aims of public school leaders in expanding the role of schools beyond what had otherwise been a relatively circumscribed position. Special education, in this interpretation, is an excuse for schools to do more and more, becoming part of the therapeutic state. As described earlier, Kirk and Johnson (1951) put forth essentially an organizational explanation of the invention of special classes in public schools at the turn of the century: Schools responded to the pressures brought by compulsory education by creating a coping mechanism, ungraded classes. Some explain more recent events also as shaped by organizational behavior. Weatherley (1979) and Weatherley and Lipsky (1977) explained the partial implementation of Massachusetts's special education law as the results of the behavior of "street-level bureaucrats" who always have to meet demand based on limited resources. In the case of special education, the street-level bureaucrats are teachers and principals who only partially met the requirements of the law as described and intended by the legislature. Cuban (1996) came to a similar conclusion about the organizational reasons why national special education laws have resulted in partial implementation. Goodman and Bond (1993) argued that the individualized education plan (IEP) shifted from the original idea for contract-like accountability that some leaders of the field like James Gallagher wanted to a much vaguer statement of services. Without intending to, they claim, Congress created paper requirements of the IEP that controlled curriculum by encouraging compartmentalization of skills and permanence of goals and objectives across months and even years of a child's school career.

I emphasize once again that the description of an organization as the driving force in special education history is not a judgment of its value necessarily. Often, the argument over the nature of organizational responses can be convoluted and difficult to sort through. Consider, for example, the origins of special classes in public schools at the beginning of the twentieth century. Kirk and Johnson (1951) suggested that, in accommodating compulsory education, public schools were being humanitarian and beneficent in creating special education. Sarason and Doris (1979), on the other hand, argued that the public schools' response to compulsory education was not primarily humanitarian but one of hostility toward immigrants. Lazerson (1982) claimed that in combining both humanitarian and social control motives, like many other institutions undergoing reform at the time (Rothman, 1980), public schools have inherited a tension that does not serve students well. One may note that all these explanations stem from organizational analyses, yet they contain different judgments about the development of special education.

SOCIAL THEORY IN THE WRITING OF
SPECIAL EDUCATION HISTORY

As I explained previously, the foregoing explanations have done a disservice to some of the authors I have cited earlier by compartmentalizing the theories implicit in the written history of special education. Only rarely can one find a history that relies only on one of the ideas described earlier. For example, Singer and Butler (1987) argued that the implementation of federal special education laws did improve conditions for students with disabilities, but they claimed that law cannot entirely erase inequalities, despite progress. They argued, in essence, that although laws (organizational dynamics in terms of written mandates) were important in the recent history of special education, broader social values (the culture) limited the change. Being aware of different themes can lead to a more thoughtful reading of the written history of special education. This critical reading is important to a reflective professional. For example, prospective special education teachers can interpret the apparently arcane issue of the origins of special education at the turn of the century very differently, and that interpretation may shape their view of the field overall. If special education was the humanitarian response of general education to expanding education through compulsory laws, then the history of special education is fundamentally beneficent. If special education was the hostile response of general education to immigration, however, then the origins of special education may be fundamentally flawed. And if the origins of special education are complex, new teachers may decide that their judgment of special education as a field should be complex. Thus, one's own history of the field is inevitably intertwined with views and judgment of special education as a whole.

Separating Assumptions from Implications

The implication of history for the field may be both disturbing and different from the theory implicit in a description of special education history. For example, Hendrick and MacMillan (1987, 1989) have described the origins of special education in New York City and Los Angeles as an organizational and somewhat hostile response to expanding education and growing diversity in the schools. To that extent, their views fit in with a more critical reading of special education. They claim at the start of the 1989 article: "It is the authors' hope this article will give the readers a heightened sense of how much—and how little—the goals of special education, and the issues surrounding that policy in the public schools, have changed since early in the century" (p. 395). However, what they described as one of their conclusions is not necessarily as hostile to special education as one might assume: They argue that testing was not responsible for the inequities that have existed in special education. Hendrick and MacMillan point out that special education began in both cities before the common examination of schoolchildren using IQ tests. Considering the criticism of IQ tests in the 1970s and 1980s, one can interpret these articles as a partial defense of IQ tests with the argument that problems started before intelligence testing. Sometimes the description or reasoning may contradict the explicit conclusions. Malofeev (1988) claimed that Communist ideology in the Soviet Union dominated the history of special education in the early twentieth century. However, a closer reading of the description in the article suggests a different mechanism. Specifically, Malofeev claimed that central directives from Moscow prompted first the creation of special education schools in the early 1930s and then the dramatic cutback in special education services by the mid to late 1930s. According to Malofeev, central decisions also created the Institute of Defectology in 1929. Thus, within the article is the description of central administrative decision-making that shaped history apart from any constant ideology (or else the pattern of institutional development would have been more consistent, not expanding and contracting in turns).

The issue of the origins of special education at the turn of the century also reveals how, apart from various theories, a conventional wisdom can remain embedded in the historiography of the field despite some clear problems with an interpretation. Three factual problems contradict the thesis that compulsory education in essence created special education. First, enforcement of compulsory education generally followed, rather than preceded, a rise in attendance. School enrollment began to rise in the United States before the turn of the twentieth century and continued to rise well after it (Snyder, 1993). Special classes thus began in public schools in the middle of a rise in attendance, not necessarily connected to compulsory education. (We are unlikely ever to have enough information to decide exactly how much compulsory education laws affected attendance at the turn of the century.) Second, schools were far more willing to accept student failure at the turn of the century than the "compulsory education" explanation assumes. Schools regularly held back students, often many times, with the result that in some school systems the vast majority of students were in the first few grades, regardless of how old they were (Ayres, 1909; Thorndike, 1907). Finally, the development of special education was very inconsistent in the early twentieth century. Some cities, like New York, created large systems of ungraded classrooms, whereas many others did not have any special education until decades later. And overseas, some nations with very high enrollment, low immigration, and very high attendance before compulsory education nonetheless created special education classes at about the same time as American cities with high immigration (Dekker, 1996).

An interpretation of the rise of special education that is consistent with these facts would acknowledge the local nature of special education before the 1970s. The development of special classes in the public schools was more idiosyncratic, even while it dovetailed with other, broader changes, than the existing written history generally recognizes. Key individuals like Elizabeth Farrell, the first supervisor of ungraded schools in New York City, were important not as "pioneers" (in an assumed wilderness) as much as they were entrepreneurs within a few school bureaucracies. They consciously tried to create a network of similarly minded individuals, created professional organizations like the Council for Exceptional Children, and spread their ideas to others who also were entrepreneurs within the public schools. Schools certainly struggled with the diversity of their clientele and the role of public schools in the newly industrialized world, but special education developed only where the bureaucracy allowed energetic individuals to craft special classes as part of public school repertoire for coping with diversity. (The question of which theories this explanation uses is an exercise for the reader.) Why has the compulsory education explanation remained dominant? Perhaps schooling has become such part of the fabric of our everyday life that we assume that the normative laws (statutes that set expectations, such as attendance) are powerful forces for change, even when that claim confuses concurrent events with causation.

Controversy over the history of the field of learning disabilities suggests a different dynamic in the conventional history of the field: how the powerful judgment of special education's history shapes the response to written histories. Sleeter (1986) argued that learning disabilities became established as a field as tougher academic standards during the Cold War forced schools to separate students doing poorly from the mainstream. Kavale and Forness (1987) responded, accurately, that the intellectual history of learning disabilities as a category began before the late 1950s. (They could also have noted that large numbers of students did not enter special education through the learning disabilities label until the 1970s, as well as the nonexistent documentation in Sleeter's article that schools were actually making standards tougher in the early 1960s.) What most vexed Kavale and Forness, however, was the apparent bias in Sleeter, and they called her a neo-Marxist. However, they incorrectly identified her fundamental argument as a structural explanation. To claim that schools invented learning disabilities as an operational category in response to the problems of trying to raise standards is fundamentally an organizational analysis, not a structural one. (Sleeter suggested that the category served to create disadvantages for some students, but her primary argument was that the category was an invented one rather than a discovered one.) Kavale and Forness misunderstood the mechanisms of her argument, perhaps because Sleeter was questioning the rational basis for learning disabilities as a part of special education.

Separating Larger Forces from Individual Agency

Future and present teachers of students with disabilities should not be intimidated by the issues described here. Much of the written history of special education—as well as much of the sociology of special education (e.g., Carrier, 1986a, 1986b; Mercer, 1973; Richardson & Parker, 1993; Sigmon, 1983, 1987; Sleeter, 1986)—tends to emphasize either broad social forces at work or the actions of heroes of the field. Yet most social historians recognize the immense role of individuals in shaping what only seems, in hindsight, as an inevitable wave. Little is inevitable in history, though broader forces shape our actions. Fortunately, teachers do have the capacity to change their own actions and the lives of students. Cuban (1993) writes of classroom innovation as a whole that "many teachers over the past century, faced with large classes, many responsibilities unrelated to teaching, and innumerable social and cultural constraints, took risks in initiating incremental and fundamental changes. Thus, many teachers, as solo practitioners, were indeed leaders in their isolated, self-contained classrooms" (p. 283). Much constrained pedagogical change, in Cuban's view, but teachers still have retained the ability to make important decisions. In addition, educators can use historical perspectives to shape their efforts to change schools as a whole. A comment from an undergraduate several years ago enrolled in my social foundations of education class may be useful in illustrating this point. I discuss the history of schooling in much of the course, but I also talk about sociological theories of schooling and school reform. That semester was the first in which I had assigned Meier's *The Power of Their Ideas* (1995), which describes her philosophy and efforts to craft a set of alternative schools in New York City (collectively known as Central Park East). Meier devoted one chapter to the myth of a golden age in schooling and the dangers of a nostalgic view of the past. One student, on the last day of class, raised Meier's book over her head and said, "Debbie Meier must have taken this class!" She enthusiastically explained her discovery that Meier, a practicing educator, not only was concerned with many of the same issues I raised in the course but had used that perspective to help herself as a teacher and school director. Meier has never been a student of mine, of course, but she is an example of the many educators who keep reading as a professional activity to inform their own reflection. Fundamentally, this student was correct in understanding what I hoped my students would take from the class, especially the history. Meier writes:

> Being clear about history can help. The myths of both past and present have given enormous advantage to the enemies of universal public education and progressive ideas about reform. The opposition has a good story to tell, and we often seem to have none. We apologize, regret, stammer, and give in step by step. Only when we can confidently build our case on the basis of a clearer and truer story will we be prepared to take the offensive again. (p. 83)

Whether or not one agrees with Meier's perspectives on public education should not interfere with one's understanding that, for her, a solid historical perspective has served as a "usable past." (However, one should also see Commager [1967], for his skepticism regarding such uses.)

CONCLUSION

Developing one's own usable past requires going beyond absorbing the written history of special education that readers may have encountered. A critical perspective requires not only attention to the accuracy of detail (though that is certainly important) and comparisons between one's own experiences and the history but also understanding the assumptions writers bring to the history of special education. As that type of focus on theory is important to reading psychology or sociology, it is also important to reading history. The goal of this chapter has not been to destroy various stories about the history of special education but to help readers see beyond the story to what may be hidden explanations about what changes schools. Identifying the implicit social theory—whether focused on "great individuals," the history of an idea, changing cultural values, social movements, structural conflict, or organizational development—can help one understand the histories of special education one encounters. One can then have a truly usable special education past.

NOTES

1. One may discuss the tracing of ideas and techniques as a genealogy, akin to Nietzsche's *The Genealogy of Morals* (1887/1956).

DISCUSSION QUESTIONS

1. Find a short passage in a special education textbook that discusses the history of special education. What themes, described in this chapter, are evident in the text you have chosen?
2. Read through an argumentative essay on special education practice (what is wrong or right with it). Whether or not there is a clear historical argument, identify implicit assumptions about how society—and special education—changes.
3. Ask a special education teacher how the field has changed (or not). What themes does the teacher raise?

REFERENCES

Ayres, L. P. (1909). *Laggards in our schools*. New York: Survey Associates, Inc.
Becker, C. (1932). Everyman his own historian. *American Historical Review, 37*, 221–236.
Bowles, S., & Gintis, H. (1976). *Schooling in capitalist America: Educational reform and the contradictions of economic life*. New York: Basic Books.

Branch, T. (1988). *Parting the waters: America in the King years, 1954–63.* New York: Simon & Schuster.

Branch, T. (1998). *Pillar of fire: America in the King years, 1963–65.* New York: Simon & Schuster.

Bryan, J. H., & Bryan, T. H. (1979). *Exceptional children.* Sherman Oaks, CA: Alfred Publishing.

Carrier, J. G. (1986a). *Learning disability: Social class and the construction of inequality in American education.* New York: Greenwood Press.

Carrier, J. G. (1986b). Sociology and special education: Differentiation and allocation in mass education. *American Journal of Education, 94,* 281–312.

Carson, C. (1981). *In struggle: SNCC and the Black awakening of the 1960s.* Cambridge, MA: Harvard University Press.

Commager, H. S. (1967). *The search for a usable past, and other essays in historiography.* New York: Knopf.

Cuban, L. (1993). *How teachers taught: Constancy and change in American classrooms, 1890–1990* (2nd ed.). New York: Teachers College Press.

Cuban, L. (1996). Myths about changing schools and the case of special education. *Remedial and Special Education, 17*(2), 75–82.

De Tocqueville, A. (1998). *The old regime and the revolution.* Trans A. S. Kahan. Chicago: University of Chicago Press. (First published in 1851.)

Dekker, J. J. H. (1996). An educational regime: Medical doctors, schoolmasters, jurists and the education of retarded and deprived children in the Netherlands around 1900. *History of Education, 25,* 255–268.

Deno, E. (1994). Special education as developmental capital revisited: A quarter century appraisal of means versus ends. *Journal of Special Education, 27,* 375–392.

Dorn, S., Fuchs, D., & Fuchs, L. S. (1996). Historical perspectives on special education reform. *Theory into Practice, 35,* 12–19.

Dunn, L. M. (1968). Special education for the mildly retarded: Is much of it justifiable? *Exceptional Children, 34,* 5–22.

Franklin, B. M. (1989). Progressivism and curriculum differentiation: Special classes in the Atlanta public schools. *History of Education Quarterly, 29,* 571–593.

Franklin, B. M. (1994). *From "backwardness" to "at risk."* Albany: State University of New York Press.

Friend, M. (1988). Putting consultation into context: Historical and contemporary perspectives. *Remedial and Special Education, 9*(6), 7–13.

Fuchs, D., & Fuchs, L. S. (1991). Framing the REI debate: Abolitionists versus conservationists. In J. Lloyd, A. Repp, & N. Singh (Eds.), *The regular education initiative: Alternative perspectives on concepts, issues, and models* (pp. 241–255). DeKalb, IL: Sycamore.

Galambos, L. (1970). The emerging organizational synthesis in modern American history. *Business History Review, 44,* 279–290.

Goodman, J. F., & Bond, L. (1993). The Individualized Education Program: A retrospective critique. *Journal of Special Education, 26,* 408–422.

Gould, S. J. (1991). *The mismeasure of man.* New York: Norton.

Heber, R. (1959). A manual on terminology and classification in mental retardation. *American Journal of Mental Deficiency, 64* (Monogr. Suppl. No. 2) (entire issue).

Heber, R. (1961). Modifications in the manual on terminology and classification in mental retardation. *American Journal of Mental Deficiency, 65,* 499–500.

Hendrick, I. G., & MacMillan, D. L. (1987). Coping with diversity in city school systems: The role of mental testing in shaping special classes for mentally retarded children in Los Angeles, 1900–1930. *Education and Training in Mental Retardation, 22,* 10–17.

Hendrick, I. G., & MacMillan, D. L. (1989). Selecting children for special education in New York City: William Maxwell, Elizabeth Farrell, and the development of ungraded classes, 1900–1920. *Journal of Special Education, 22,* 395–417.

Hoffman, E. (1975). The American public school and the deviant child: The origins of their involvement. *The Journal of Special Education, 9,* 415–423.

Iano, R. P. (1986). The study and development of teaching: With implications for the advancement of special education. *Remedial and Special Education, 7*(5), 50–61.

Irving, P. (1974). Sir Cyril Burt. *Journal of Special Education, 8,* 116.

Kanner, L. (1964). *A history of the care and study of the mentally retarded.* Springfield, IL: C. C. Thomas.

Karagiannis, A., Stainback, S., & Stainback, W. (1996). Historical overview of inclusion. In S. B. Stainback, W. C. Stainback, [others] (Eds.), *Inclusion: A guide for educators* (pp. 17–28). Baltimore: Paul H. Brookes.

Kauffman, J. M. (1976). Nineteenth century views of children's behavior disorders: Historical contributions and continuing issues. *Journal of Special Education, 10,* 335–349.

Kauffman, J. M. (1981a). *Characteristics of children's behavior disorders* (2nd ed.). Columbus, OH: C. E. Merrill.

Kauffman, J. M. (1981b). Introduction: Historical trends and contemporary issues in special education in the United States. In J. M. Kauffman & D. P. Hallahan (Eds.), *Handbook of special education* (1st ed.) (pp. 3–23). Englewood Cliffs, NJ: Prentice-Hall.

Kauffman, J. M., & Pullen, P. L. (1989). An historical perspective: A personal perspective on our history of service to mildly handicapped and at-risk students. *Remedial and Special Education, 10,* 12–14.

Kavale, K. A., & Forness, S. (1987). History, politics, and the general education initiative: Sleeter's reinterpretation of learning disabilities as a case study. *Remedial and Special Education, 8*(5), 6–12.

Kirk, S. A., & Johnson, G. O. (1951). *Educating the retarded child.* Boston: Houghton Mifflin.

Lane, H. L. (1976). *The Wild Boy of Aveyron.* Cambridge, MA: Harvard University Press.

Lazerson, M. (1975). Educational institutions and mental subnormality: Notes on writing a history. In M. J. Begab & S. A. Richardson (Eds.), *The mentally retarded and society: A social science perspective* (pp. 33–52). Baltimore: University Park Press.

Lazerson, M. (1982). The origins of special education. In J. G. Chambers & W. T. Hartman (Eds.), *Special education policies: Their history, implementation, and finance* (pp. 15–47). Philadelphia: Temple University Press.

Lieberman, L. M., Ed. (1982). Itard: The great problem solver. *Journal of Learning Disabilities, 15,* 566–568.

Malofeev, N. N. (1998). Special education in Russia: Historical aspects. *Journal of Learning Disabilities, 31,* 181–185.

Mann, L. (1979). *On the trail of process: A historical perspective on cognitive processes and their training.* New York: Grune & Stratton.

Meier, D. (1995). *The power of their ideas: Lessons for America from a small school in Harlem.* Boston: Beacon Press.

Mercer, J. R. (1973). *Labeling the mentally retarded: Clinical and social system perspectives on mental retardation.* Berkeley: University of California Press.

Nelson, C. M., & Polsgrove, L. (1984). Behavior analysis in special education: White rabbit or white elephant? *Remedial and Special Education, 5*(4), 6–17.

Nietzsche, F. H. (1887/1956). *The genealogy of morals.* Trans. Francis Golffing. New York: Doubleday. (First published in 1887.)

Norrell, R. J. (1985). *Reaping the whirlwind.* New York: Knopf.

Novick, P. (1998). *That noble dream: The objectivity question and the American historical profession.* New York: Cambridge University Press.

Patton, J. R., Polloway, E. A., & Epstein, M. H. (1989). Are there seminal works in special education? *Remedial and Special Education, 10*(3), 54–59.

Polloway, E. A. (1984). The integration of mildly retarded students in the schools: A historical review. *Remedial and Special Education, 5*(4), 18–28.

Polsky, A. J. (1991). *The rise of the therapeutic state.* Princeton, NJ: Princeton University Press.

Reynolds, M. C. (1989). An historical perspective: The delivery of special education to mildly disabled and at-risk students. *Remedial and Special Education, 10,* 7–11.

Richardson, J. G., & Parker, T. L. (1993). The institutional genesis of special education: The American case. *American Journal of Education, 101,* 359–392.

Rogers, D. (1968). *110 Livingston Street: Politics and bureaucracy in the New York City schools.* New York: Random House.

Rothman, D. (1980). *Conscience and convenience: The asylum and its alternatives in progressive America.* Boston: Little, Brown.

Safford, P.L., & Safford, P.J. (1995). *A history of childhood and disability.* New York: Teachers College Press.

Sarason, S. B. (1990). *The predictable failure of educational reform: Can we change course before it's too late?* San Francisco: Jossey-Bass.

Sarason, S. B., & Doris, J. (1979). *Educational handicap, public policy, and social history: A broadened perspective on mental retardation.* New York: The Free Press.

Scheerenberger, R. C. (1983). *History of mental retardation.* Baltimore: Paul H. Brookes.

Scheerenberger, R. C. (1987). *A history of mental retardation: A quarter century of promise.* Baltimore: Paul H. Brookes.

Shapiro, J. P. (1993). *No pity: People with disabilities forging a new civil rights movement.* New York: Times Books.

Sigmon, S. B. (1983). The history and future of educational segregation. *Journal for Special Educators, 19*(4), 1–14.

Sigmon, S. B. (1987). *Radical analysis of special education: Focus on historical development and learning disabilities.* New York: The Falmer Press.

Singer, J., & Butler, J. A. (1987). The Education for All Handicapped Children Act: Schools as agents of social reform. *Harvard Educational Review, 57,* 125–152.

Skrtic, T. (1991). *Behind special education: A critical analysis of professional culture and school organization.* Denver: Love Publishing.

Sleeter, C. E. (1986). Learning disabilities: The social construction of a special education category. *Exceptional Children, 53,* 46–54.

Snyder, T. D., Ed. (1993). *120 years of American education: A statistical portrait.* Washington: National Center for Education Statistics.

Special education yesterday, today and tomorrow: An interview with Frances Connor, Samuel Kirk, and Burton Blatt. (1977). *Exceptional Parent, 7*(4), 9–14.

Talbot, M. E. (1964). *Edouard Seguin: A study of an educational approach to the treatment of mentally defective children.* New York: Bureau of Publica-tions,Teachers College.

Thorndike, E. L. (1907). *The elimination of pupils from school.* U.S. Bureau of Education Bulletin No. 4, Whole No. 379. Washington: Government Printing Office.

Trent, J. W. (1994). *Inventing the feeble mind: A history of mental retardation in the United States.* Berkeley: University of California Press.

Tropea, J. L. (1987a). Bureaucratic order and special children: Urban schools, 1890s–1940s. *History of Education Quarterly, 27,* 29–53.

Tropea, J. L. (1987b). Bureaucratic order and special children: Urban schools, 1950s–1960s. *History of Education Quarterly, 27,* 339–361.

Tropea, J. L. (1993). Structuring risks: The making of urban school order. In R. Wollons (Ed.), *Children at risk in America: History, concepts, and public policy* (pp. 58–88). Albany: State University of New York Press.

Weatherley, R. (1979). *Reforming special education: Policy implementation from state level to street level.* Cambridge: MIT Press.

Weatherley, R., & Lipsky, M. (1977). Street level bureaucrats and institutional innovation: Implementing special education reform. *Harvard Educational Review, 47,* 171–197.

Winzer, M. A. (1986). Early developments in special education: Some aspects of Enlightenment thought. *Remedial and Special Education, 7*(5), 42–49.

Winzer, M. A. (1993). *The history of special education: From isolation to integration.* Washington: Gallaudet University Press.

Wool, D. I., & Stephens, T. M. (1978). Twenty-five years of caring for and treating feeble-minded persons in the United States: A review of the literature from 1874 to 1900. *Journal of Special Education, 12,* 219–229.

Ethics and Special Education

James L. Paul, Peter French, and Ann Cranston-Gingras

Special education is under attack from outside the profession and experiencing considerable dissension from inside. Challenges from outside are concerned with costs and level of accountability. Cost comparisons with other education services have led some to argue that the social benefits do not justify the costs of special education services (Dillon, 1994; Massachusetts Association of School Superintendents, 1997). Dissension inside involves long-standing perspectival differences of opinion on the demonstrable empirical value and the moral justifications for fully integrated versus pull-out service delivery models (Shanker, 1994; Fuchs & Fuchs, 1995; Ferguson & Ferguson, 1998) and, increasingly, differences among researchers about the nature and representation of knowledge.

Ethical issues lurk, sometimes subtly behind and sometimes boldly in front of professional challenges in special education interventions, policies, research, and teacher education. Special educators rely on a complex foundation of justifying reasons for what they do, and how they do it. Everything from how disability is defined to the educational objectives and the knowledge privileged as foundational for practice reflects a priori considerations that are saturated with values and cultural meaning.

It is surprising that a field so replete with such complexities of interests has devoted so little attention to the study and development of applied ethics. In a survey of doctoral programs in special education in 1995 only one required a course in ethics, although most said that ethics content was embedded in the content of different seminars (Paul, Kane, & Kane, 1996). A few respondents suggested that content in ethics was not needed in a Ph.D. program in special education.

We believe that lessons learned in professional psychology with respect to the study of ethics are instructive for special educators. Increasingly, over the past three decades, doctoral programs in psychology have required courses in ethics because the approach of embedding ethics content lacked a foundational perspective, lacked continuity, and, for teaching purposes, relied too much on ethical issues emerging randomly in class discussions and internships. Special education teachers, researchers, teacher educators, and policymakers need more education and training in ethics in order to address current moral dilemmas in assessment, instruction, curriculum, work with families, instructional competence, philosophy of service delivery, funding, and research. The articulation and application of ethical theory needed to support practice and policy development are critical to the future of special education.

Rather than enumerate the myriad ethical issues in special education and ethical theories to address them, we have elected to focus on four major ethical challenges to the field. The first is the need to examine the moral and political story, the narrative, within which special educators make sense of their work. The second is the need for articulating character morality to complement the more familiar choice morality that is used to think about ethical dilemmas in special education. The third is the need to examine special education in the context of a liberal democracy. The fourth is the need to develop an ethical basis for discourse on the nature and representation of knowledge.

THE HISTORY OF SPECIAL EDUCATION: HOW MORAL IS THE STORY?

Are special educators part of a moral story, doing good things for children and families? Or, is it less than that? Are we part of a story in which we, however unwittingly, bring harm to children with disabilities as a function of the roles we play and the cultural meaning of the story we are in? Or, are we in a confused and complex story, intending good yet knowing some special education policies can harm children? One can find in both the professional and popular literature an affirmative response to each question (Johnson, 1969; Fuchs & Fuchs,1995).

All of us would hope to be part of a moral story and would certainly affirm our intention to do good for children and their families. Special educators, after all, tend to be advocates and defenders of the rights of children with disabilities. The thought that we could in any way participate in anything harmful is appalling. Yet, the narrative of special education suggests that we have and that, in some ways, we still do. We do not participate by informed choice, but the effects are the same. Following is a brief discussion of selected issues in the modern history of special education and examples of tensions over the nature of the story.

Special education is viewed in different ways depending on the political and social context. Some have viewed it as a valued set of programs with an empirically validated knowledge base for practice (Carnine 1991) meeting the unmet needs of children in school who would otherwise be unserved in the general education system (Kauffman & Hallahan, 1995; Lieberman, 1992). Others have viewed special education as having served a purpose in the history of education but now defeating the social egalitarian goals of education by keeping some students away from their age peers and the general education curriculum (Gartner & Lipsky, 1987; Pugach & Warger, 1996). Still others have been more harsh, damning it as a racist bureaucracy, stigmatizing and segregating African American boys, and violating the rights of children (Granger & Granger, 1986; Johnson 1969; Grossman 1998), and ineffective at best (Van Doninck, 1983). So what is special education's story?

Special education is a morally and politically complex area of professional education, and it is colored by both heroic advances and, however unintended, shameful misdeeds. Neither those involved in the advances nor those involved in the misdeeds—in reality many are involved in both—necessarily appreciated the moral story they were in at the time. The point here is not to denigrate the field of special education; that has been done amply by its critics. Neither is it simply to tell the story of "the good it has done and is doing." That story has been well told many times and is continuing to be told by leaders in the field. Rather, our purpose is to examine the moral complexity of the story and consider the value of restorying the field in the contexts of the discourses of ethics, politics, and social science in the beginning of the 21st century.

A couple of examples will suffice to illustrate the moral tension in our history. One moment in time involves the institutionalization of persons with mental illness and those with mental retardation. Psychiatric hospitals and centers for persons with developmental disabilities have a strong history of advocates motivated by zeal and righteous indignation because of the lack of care for individuals with disabilities. They were successful in gaining public support and developing institutions that later, in many instances, became monstrosities where people were abused and neglected in what came to be known as "snake pits" and "purgatory" (Blatt & Kaplan, 1966). The revolutionary leaders who built institutions were, so far as we know, good people doing what they believed were good things for persons in need—that is, those with disabilities. The institutions, when built, improved the living circumstances of individuals and their families. Over time, however, they ran their course and fell apart both sociologically and morally (Lightner, 1999; Smith, 1995; Tomes, 1994). Improved by major reforms in the 1960s and 1970s, residential institutions continue to function today and although the quality of care is controlled by strong accountability measures, their value as a system of care continues to be challenged by those who support community-based care (Coates, 1990).

In our young democracy, seeking to address the diversity in the mass immigration into this country at the beginning of the 20th century, there were philosophical and political differences over how to care for individuals with disabilities. The institution builders promoted an ethic of care translated as decent accommodations and treatment in residential facilities. Other forces, however, promoted the social Darwinian perspective of Spencer, articulated so strongly in this country by William Graham Sumner. They were less supportive of providing care for persons with disabilities and more persuaded by the genetic story of nature knowing best and eliminating error in the process of evolution. They believed it unwise to invest economic resources in caring for those not able to thrive with typical care and potentially contribute to society as independent citizens. It was not until after the middle of the 20th century that society began to develop a more egalitarian ethic as evidenced by the demise of eugenics boards and the development of national policies to reduce institutional dependency. These policies, reflecting a new vision of care and education, supported integrated community programs as alternatives to institutionalization, and inclusion in education as an alternative to pull-out programs.

The advocacy initiatives on behalf of persons with disabilities came, for the most part, from family members or friends with disabilities, and from professionals involved in medical, social, or educational services. Strong vocal and politically active disability constituencies were developed, and the social agenda of caregiving for persons with disabilities struck a responsive moral chord. Ultimately, constitutional arguments, especially the right to due process, became pivotal in successful litigation and the development of law and public policy. What did not happen, however, and what has not yet happened in professionalized caregiving in general, is the articulation of the moral agenda of special education, or other specialized caregiving systems, with the prevailing political theory. This issue is discussed in the section on liberal democracy.

Another significant moment in the history of special education came when, in 1968, Lloyd Dunn, one of the leaders in the field of special education, commented on the ineffectiveness of special education programs for children with mild mental retardation:

> I have been honored to be a past president of the Council for Exceptional Children. I have loyally supported and promoted special classes for the educable mentally retarded for most of the last 20 years, but with growing disaffection. In my view, much of our past and present practices are morally and educationally wrong. We have been living at the mercy of general educators who have referred their problem children to us. And we have been generally ill prepared and

ineffective in educating these children. Let us stop being pressured into continuing and expanding a special education program that we know now to be
undesirable for many of the children we are dedicated to serve. (pp. 5–21)

Dunn implored professionals to be morally responsible for the failures:
"The conscience of special educators needs to rub up against morality" (p.
19). By accepting "problem pupils" referred by teachers in general education
classrooms, he argued, we enable these teachers to avoid dealing with individual differences. Emphasizing the moral culpability of special educators,
Dunn added:

> We must face the reality—we are asked to take children others cannot teach, and
> a large percentage of these are from ethnically and/or economically disadvan-
> taged backgrounds. Thus much of special education will continue to be a sham
> of dreams unless we immerse ourselves into the total environment of our children
> from inadequate homes and backgrounds and insist on a comprehensive ecolog-
> ical push—with a quality educational program as part of it. (p. 20).

Dunn's injunction, over 30 years ago, that the conscience of special educators should "rub against morality" presupposes a collective sense of the
morality of the mission of special education. It also anchors the need for a
moral discourse in special education.

Viewed as a moral story, special education is a field in which "the good"
intended by professionals is to improve the educational outcomes for children
with disabilities. That commitment is manifested in implementing research-
based standards of practice and continuing to improve the knowledge foundation for all interventions. Viewed from the perspective of character
morality, special education has been tainted by insensitive and harmful
practices such as racially biased assessments and placement policies. Also,
cruel practices, such as subjecting persons with disabilities to substandard
conditions in institutions, group homes, and the like, and using harsh aver-
sives such as electric shock and isolation as methods to control behavior, have
been part of the history of special education. These conditions certainly
improved over the last half of the 20th century, but we have always known
how to do better than we have done or are doing. Our practices have never
been adequately guided by sound theory or fully informed by available
research; neither have they adequately reflected our values. This seems a
logical conclusion when, for example, empirically validated practices are not
widely implemented (Kauffman, 1999). We could list many reasons, such as
local control of educational policies and the shortage of qualified special
education teachers, for never quite reaching the mark, and they may be valid.
However, a tension between what we know and what we, as professional
educators, researchers, and policymakers, are able to do will always exist.
Differences among reasonable people about the nature of "approved" knowl-

edge and the work to be done will also persist. A moral story for the field should include a valued and respected space for differences and openness to learn alternatives for keeping the tension productive, the voices respectful, and the discourses fair.

As special educators, we are challenged to employ an ethical theory that is morally defensible in the diverse contexts of our work. In the next section, we examine character morality as a complement to choice morality, the philosophy of ethics most commonly discussed in special education, as a way to address ethical questions in the field.

ETHICAL THEORIES

It is very common to imagine ethics as a kind of moral calculus for solving ethical dilemmas. All we need is the right formula, and all of our problems can be resolved. It would be nice if it were really that simple. In the real world, however, life is complex, ambiguous, and often tragic—it does not readily yield to such a calculus. Ethics is not about being right as much as it is about being responsible. We must intend to discover what is right, but we can be mistaken and still be responsible. However, we can do this only if we are prepared to recognize both our own fallibility and our common humanity. (Fasching, 1997, p. 99)

The theory most familiar to special educators in addressing ethical dilemmas might be called "choice morality." In it meaningful choice, and all that involves, is typically viewed as the cornerstone of responsibility. What we will call "choice moralists" (Kekes, 1990) maintain, or simply assume, that a person can only be legitimately held morally responsible for those things he or she did as a result of having chosen to do them. Meaningful choice implies freedom of action. Choices that cannot affect what the chooser actually does would be vacuous, certainly not meaningful choices. Freedom of action is generally taken to entail that the actor has a range of actions that he or she could choose and that the act of choice is crucial to the deeds actually performed by the actor. This idea is typically referred to in the philosophical literature as the Principle of Alternate Possibilities (Fischer, 1986). The notion, as captured in the Principle of Alternate Possibilities, that humans usually are free to do something other than what they actually do is a metaphysical tenet, a cornerstone, of most theories of moral responsibility. Whether it is consistent with the way responsibility is actually ascribed is a matter of much philosophical dispute (Frankfurt, 1988).

Another tenet of choice morality that is directly related to the first is the principle that "ought" implies "can." If a person cannot do something, what sense does it make to say that he or she ought to do it? If it makes no sense to say that he or she ought to do it, how can it make sense to hold him or her responsible for not doing it? When these two tenets are conjoined, a picture of the basic requirements of holding someone morally responsible for his or her actions emerges. If one could not have chosen to do something other than what one did, it makes little or no sense either to say that one ought not to have done it or to hold him or her morally responsible for doing it. In the absence of the freedom to do other than we do and the ability to choose a genuine alternative to the action we in fact perform, there seems to be no point to moral responsibility and little point to moral principles and rules that direct us to do some things rather than others. Understood in this way, the foundations of choice morality appeal to many of our basic intuitions about accountability and responsibility. There can be little doubt that deeply ingrained in our thinking about responsibility is its dependence on, or assumption of, freedom of action. Little wonder that meaningful choice has been so important an idea in moral philosophy and that moral theorists typically conceive of a "moral situation or dilemma" as one in which a person must make a difficult choice, fully aware of the efficacy of choice with respect to action and hence the affecting of outcomes in human relations for good or ill.

A picture of the moral person in choice morality forms around a conception of what J. L. Austin called "the machinery of action" (Austin, 1961). The action that will be evaluated against moral standards may be envisioned as having many parts or stages. These include planning, appreciating, deliberating, choosing, intending, and, of course, actually executing the action. Deliberation leading to choice emerges as central to the picture of the way a moral person acts. The picture takes something like the following form: Our moral person finds himself or herself confronted with a problem in which various alternative actions are possible, he or she deliberates about the problem by weighing the salient moral features of the situation and the results that choosing one possible action rather than another should have. He or she then applies some moral principle, rule, or "calculus" to the problem, determining thereby a morally acceptable action in the circumstances, decides to act accordingly, and so acts. On accounts like that suggested by Putnam (1978), the application of principles, rules, or a calculus stage may be replaced by nonlinear reasoning in the imagination of the moral person. Moral theorists, as different in other ways as Kantians and utilitarians, share such a picture of the centrality of meaningful choice to moral responsibility and moral condemnation. Little wonder that so many moral theorists have struggled with the age-old problem of free will and determinism. If there is no way to make meaningful choice compatible with what appears to be the causal determinism of the world in which we act, the very idea of moral responsibility is in severe jeopardy of losing any sense whatsoever. Or, at least it is on the choice moralist's conception of responsibility. (For a radically different view see Harry Frankfurt [1988] and John Martin Fischer, *The Metaphysics of Free Will* [Blackwell, 1994].)

The idea that the freedom to meaningfully choose one's actions is the crucial element of moral responsibility promotes the idea that the capacity to choose is *the* identifying feature of moral agents, the subjects of morality and ethics. Some choice moralists maintain that if someone is a moral agent by virtue of his or her ability to make meaningful choices, then all moral agents must have equal moral worth because they all evidence that capacity of choice with respect to their actions. They are, then, worth egalitarians. They maintain that moral worth is the baseline of moral personhood; the recognition of the intrinsic value of moral agents, and it is quite distinct from moral merit, which is the gauge of whether a moral agent is a good or a bad person. For many choice moralists, such as Immanuel Kant and John Rawls, the moral worth of a person is in no way related to what that person morally deserves or merits because of his or her behavior. Insofar as moral agents are understood to possess equal moral worth, they are to be treated with equal respect and should have an equal right to pursue their individual conceptions of the good. Kant (1969) encapsulates that idea in his second formulation of the categorical imperative: "Act so that you treat humanity, whether in your own person or in that of another, always as an end and never as a means only" (p. 54). This is a basic statement of worth egalitarianism. It entails that though people may act in ways that raise or lower their moral merit, they always must be treated with respect, as ends. No matter how bad their actions have been, there are things that must never be done to them. For example, we may not inflict "unnecessary pain" (to use Noddings' [1992] term) on them. What makes the inflicting of pain on a person necessary is, however, a major and unsettled question that should, and does, trouble serious choice moralists (French, 2001).

Several authors writing about educational policy and ethics have based their analyses on principle-based ethics (Howe & Miramontes, 1992) or what we are calling choice morality. Howe and Miramontes (1992) have written an important and influential text on the ethics of special education that includes a description of the process of ethical deliberation and special education-oriented cases. Dokecki and Zaner (1986) addressed ethical issues in the field of mental retardation. Paul et al. (1992) examined ethical issues in policy development in developmental disabilities and, in another work (Paul et al., 1997), ethical decision-making in local schools. These are predominantly concerned with moral choices. Others have emphasized employing an ethic of care in the adjudication of competing moral interests (Noddings, 1984, 1992).

Several other texts on education ethics have been written during the past decade that have particular relevance for special education. Nash's (1996) work on "real world ethics" includes a useful perspective and approach to ethical analysis. Starratt (1994) provides an insightful discussion of building ethical schools that offers helpful guidance for those willing to consider the moral culture in a school in thinking about the inclusion of children with disabilities in general education classrooms.

We will not attempt a summary of these or other works, and it is not our purpose to extend the arguments for choice morality. The appeal of choice morality to many of our basic intuitions about moral responsibility is evident and powerful. Within the choice moralist's conception of ethics, the role of the ethical educator is to make and to prepare students to make morally permissible choices while understanding and protecting individual interests. Ascriptions of moral responsibility rest on the determination that actions were freely chosen. Skill in choosing from the moral point of view when operating one's machinery of action is the condition for moral agency and the primary goal of moral education from this perspective.

There are, however, ways other than choice-based theories to conceive of morality and they suggest rather different and fundamental implications for special education. The intuitions about responsibility and moral accountability to which they appeal are radically different from those that make choice morality attractive. One such alternative theory has been called "character morality" (see Kekes, 1990). Character morality, however, should not be confused with the character education movement currently popular in education. The majority of the "character education" programs currently touted in K–12 circles are versions of applied choice morality. Their models are deliberative, dominated by the conception of the moral person as meaningful chooser over a range of possible actions. Nor does character morality as we use the term exhaust what is called virtue ethics. Many, if not most, of the recent virtue theorists are choice moralists. They are distinct from the traditional choice moralists in adopting concepts such as care as more basic than, for example, justice and in eschewing the central role of rules and principles in moral deliberation that typically are found in choice theories. But choice still occupies the key position in their accounts.

As we use the term, character moralists (for example, John Kekes) begin to examine the moral situation at quite a different place than the choice moralists. They claim to be looking at how humans actually behave and the results of that behavior rather than constructing linear deliberation/decision models. They maintain that observation of humans reveals that most human behavior is not deliberatively chosen. It is habitual or the result of ingrained character traits that were not solely, if at all, formed by conscious choices. They note that character traits may, and typically do, have roots in culture, tradition, training, custom, ritual, convention, routine, and folklore. People, more often than not, character moralists will tell us, act "in character." What they then do, whether good or evil, may not be the result of their choices. It is just what they do. To try to fit the pattern of their actions into deliberative linear models (or even nonlinear imagination models such as Putnam suggests) may miss the mark by a rather wide margin in a vast majority of cases. Further, in a realistic sense, when acting in character, it may not be the case that people have genuine alternate possibilities of action in many, possibly most, circumstances. Choice moralists, when such a suggestion is made, may well argue that it is always at least logically possible for people to choose to act in ways other than they do when they act in character. There is always a possible world in which the person could have made a different choice from the one he or she actually made. The character moralist may grant that is true. But, when viewed realistically, the character moralist argues, the possible world may be so remote from the real world that to hang a judgment of moral responsibility on it must seem highly suspect to most ordinary folks. It has the look of a desperate move to save a theory in the face of the facts. When we say that someone really could not have done otherwise under the circumstances, we generally don't mean that it is logically impossible that he or she could not have done something else. We might well mean that it would take quite a different person to behave differently or even to have considered alternate possibilities of action in the circumstances. Choice moralists, following in the footsteps of Aristotle, might alternatively argue that a person's character traits are the result of previous conscious choices made by the person and that the person, by virtue of a causal chain back to those choices, should be held responsible for his or her character and the actions that result from it even though those actions at the time are not directly the result of a choice. Character moralists, however, will respond that only some, perhaps a rather small portion, of a person's character traits may have been developed by the choice method. The others, the great majority, are the result of what Kekes calls "unconscious habituation." There is nothing reflective or deliberative about the acquisition process.

Though not a character moralist, Barbara Herman (2000) has recently expressed views with which the character moralists can agree. She writes:

> For morality to perform its central function of securing routine action, moral concepts and features of character need to be acquired in the ongoing process of moral education so that a morally literate agent is able to recognize and respond to what is morally salient in the routine circumstances she encounters . . . . This is, for the most part, nondeliberative. Like the spatially competent agent's ability to move through ordinary doorways without performing any geometric calculations, the morally literate agent moves among persons without the need to think whether she should or could shove them aside, use their body parts for this or that good cause, or tell the truth when asked for the time of day. (p. 31)

To grasp a crucial difference between choice and character moralists, it is instructive to think of people whose morally indefensible characters were formed and nurtured in cultures that are imbued with racial, cultural, and other forms of bigotry. As examples, think of White American southerners during the slavery period, KKK members and other White racists, witch hunters in Europe and America in the seventeenth century, medieval crusaders, ethnic cleansing Serbs, German Nazis, and a wide variety of others who have been raised in cultures of hate, bigotry, intolerance, fanaticism, and the like. These, of course, are radical, and not very subtle, examples. Others may be more subtle but not less unsavory. Suppose we grant with the character moralist that such people, or at least the vast majority of them, probably do not choose to be racial and ethnic bigots. Their preferences, and so their characters, are not, or are not fully, or at least with respect to their bigotry, matters of choice. And they do not typically deliberate about what they are doing when their actions display those characters, when they, acting in character, do terrible things to other human beings. Shouldn't they be held responsible for the harm they cause? Choice moralists, unless they deny the basic premise that the characters of such people were not the result of conscious or meaningful choices made by those people, that their evil actions "follow from their unchosen vices, . . . are symptomatic of enduring dispositions, and . . . occur when they act naturally and spontaneously, in accordance with vices they have developed but without choosing to develop them" (Kekes, 1990, p. 66), should not hold them morally responsible for their bigoted characters and their actions that express their characters. But character moralists will hold them responsible for those actions despite evidence that they were unchosen, that their actions were the by-product of their characters (see Kekes, 1990 p. 70).

This is not the place to explore how people come to have morally perverse characters. We suspect that they unconsciously adopt them because they are raised in prejudiced, intolerant, and bigoted communities where the vast majority of the members, including those in positions of authority, regularly express and act on a singular set of pernicious views. Certainly, in such an environment the consideration of questions about the veracity and the morality of the dominant views can be virtually unthinkable for most community members. It takes a special person with uncommon insight to raise the appropriate moral concerns. It is also likely that the members of such communities never have actual opportunities to alter the course of their character development, "since doing so would have required of them a sustained effort to act contrary to their own predispositions and to the social context that favored their development in a particular direction" (Kekes, 1990, p. 75). The very virtues that might have stood them in good moral stead and withstood the pressures of their culture are exactly the ones that they lack because they were never encouraged or trained in them. Their cultures, their upbringings, are inhospitable to the sort of critical reflection that might encourage them to question the inbred and ingrained preferences they have, to examine and adopt better moral preferences. Their personal and social identities, as well as their self-appraisals and those they make of others, are grounded in those preferences. But still, even in the face of such an account, our moral intuitions counsel holding such people responsible for the harm they cause, the undeserved pain they inflict, choice or no choice. Character moralists build their theories on those intuitions; on the contention that morality's primary task is to minimize the evil that people do to each other, regardless of whether it was chosen by the perpetrators.

Kekes (1990) writes: "Character morality . . . requires both curbing evil, which makes good lives possible, and the pursuit of good, which gives good lives their content" (p. 145). If the only evil that can be legitimately attacked by moral principles is that which results from meaningful choices of moral agents, because that is the only evil for which people can be held responsible, then morality will be virtually impotent in responding to its primary task. Most of the undeserved harm inflicted on people by those acting in character, Kekes calls it "unchosen evil," will lie outside of the boundaries of moral responsibility. Character morality attempts to bring the control of evil-producing characters under the authority of morality.

To do that, the character moralist must deny that the principle that "ought" implies "can" is the unassailable base of moral responsibility. The character moralist also attacks the worth-egalitarianism of choice morality. Desert, not worth, the character moralist argues, should govern our moral evaluations of people and their actions. For them, people are not equal with respect to their moral worth. Moral worth is a function of moral merit. The ideal of character morality is that people ought to get what they deserve, and desert depends on moral merit and that depends on what people actually do, not on the capacities they are presumed to possess. We may gain or lose moral merit (a point on which the choice and character moralists agree). But, for the character moralist, moral merit and moral worth are identical. Consequently, restraints on the treatment of persons do not necessarily apply across the human board. Those lacking in moral merit because of their behavior do not deserve to be treated as having moral worth equal to those who behave meritoriously.

These tenets of character morality support its contention that people who perform evil deeds might still be held morally accountable if their harm-causing behavior is the result of inculcated character traits. Character traits, though not the result of linear deliberative processes, that evidence themselves in inflicting undeserved harm on people are serious moral flaws. Morality's *raison d'être* must be to identify and address such flaws, which involves holding people responsible for what they do, seeing that people get what they deserve, what they merit, because of their behavior, and trying to effect changes in character so that whatever evil dispositions people may have are resisted during their interactions with others. Doing so may or may not involve developing deliberative skills, but, in any case, it is outcomes that matter.

Perhaps the most basic difference between choice and character morality is that the character moralist maintains that our moral merit depends on the amount of evil we cause and not on whether we choose to do the things that cause evil. Insofar as our characters and our circumstances are typically different, we do not have the same moral merit. Further, because the character moralist equates moral merit with moral worth, we do not all have the same moral worth. Consequently, we do not all deserve the same things. Social institutions, if they are going to minimize evil and contribute to the flourishing of the conditions in which good lives can be lived, must be structured so that the inequality of desert is acknowledged and becomes a fundamental principle of the distribution of goods.

Simply, things ought to be arranged, the character moralist maintains, so that everyone gets what he or she deserves. The world we inhabit, however, is not so arranged. Good people suffer and wicked people prosper. Character moralists take that fact to be indisputable evidence that we must bring moral order to our lives and our institutions. Human institutions need to be constructed that make it more likely that the development of bad character traits, especially those productive of undeserved harm, is discouraged and that people will get what they are due, that the good are rewarded and the wicked punished. To achieve this, those institutions, education being arguably the most important, must concentrate on ensuring that evil character development is not encouraged and on positively altering the traits of those evidencing bad moral characters. The social engineering problem of forming institutions that will achieve the ends of character morality is its major challenge.

One difference between the choice moralist's perspective on the role of education and that of the character moralist is that the former sees education as preparing students to make choices without reference to the content of those choices. That is, the choice moralist sees education as the preparation of students to make choices that will be consistent with the achievement of their individual conceptions of the good, regardless of what those conceptions may be. These are typically referred to as informed or "educated choices." The character moralist is more concerned with the development of traits of character that are compatible with the maintenance of a community in which the inflicting of undeserved harm is minimized and, if the character moralist is also a communitarian democrat, in which a shared conception of the good is promulgated and informs the habits of behavior of the citizens. Although it is not clear what sorts of regimens are morally permissible in character inculcation, it would seem likely that a character moralist would be willing to sanction a wider selection of techniques than one might expect to pass muster with a choice moralist. Inflicting unwarranted pain, of course, would not be allowed, but the character education process in the classroom would have to mirror, in some large measure, the inculcation processes outside the classroom that incubate the character traits being combated. Most of those are assimilated outside of a linear deliberative process. They are "picked up" through experience in a social climate that is hospitable to them and inhospitable to other traits. The task of the character moralist as educator is to create and sustain an environment that rewards morally appropriate character traits and is uncongenial to morally unacceptable ones, while not assuming that choice, or even the capacity to choose, underlies character and character development.

Although character morality and choice morality have been separated in the present discussion in order to examine issues in special education, ethicists recognize the risk of overdrawing the distinction. Similarly, most experienced educators recognize the risk of overdrawing the distinction between character and choice when discussing the goals of teaching, counseling, or therapy. Although interventions focusing on helping students make better choices have certainly been far more efficacious than attempts to change character, the issue here is not the goal of interventions, but rather the moralities of education and care. The negative outcome data on changing character comes from clinical literature in studies of psychopathology, not so much from studies of character formation and education.

SPECIAL EDUCATION AND CHARACTER: SELECTED ISSUES

Leading humanistic special educators and psychologists in the 20th century focused on character morality as well as choice morality. Fritz Redl talked about "massaging numb values." Bill Morse, similarly, argued that special education teachers must be able to care effectively about their students. Nicholas Hobbs wrote eloquently about the requirement that teachers of "disturbed children" be decent adults, able to nurture children. Teachers are models—moral as well as academic. Modeling is important in developing character, but the teacher as a model is part of a larger social ecology within which other models influence the development of character in a student's life.

The education of teachers has not substantially addressed the issue of the nonacademic qualities required of teachers. It is difficult to address because we do not have adequate ways of thinking about counseling adults out of teacher education when we believe, based on their participation in our classes and in internships, that they would not be good models for children. Our approach at the University of South Florida is to assign beginning teacher education students to small cohorts and to have faculty members and doctoral students follow those students throughout their program and into their first year of teaching. The cohorts meet one hour weekly and focus on self, diversity, ethics, and teaching in successive semesters. An important reason for putting these cohorts together in this way is to get to know the students very well from the beginning of their training and to provide guidance to all, including those who need another career. This is done in a time-intensive interpersonal context with safeguards built in to minimize error in counseling students out of the program. Judgment is of course involved; no part of education is amoral. Teacher character and values matter; the teachers who graduate from our program will be judging their students every day. This is not science; it is the activity of an ethics-conscious community of teacher educators, admittedly political, attempting to negotiate among critical moral issues and interests.

Academic subjects hold center stage in discussions of the school reform agenda, not character education. Behavior, as forecast by Dunn, has tended to hold center stage in special education. In part, the absence of substantial attention to ethics in special education is the result of the complexity of the issues. It is also a consequence of the fact that ethics is not a specific and valued part of the teacher education curriculum or of the doctoral curriculum.

Neither general special education nor specific disability-focused textbooks typically address ethics or morality directly. In the area of behavior disorders, the prevailing narratives have been psychodynamic, behavioral, neuropsychological, ecological, or sociological. Behavior is interpreted within these stories or, if you prefer, theories. Professionals are trained and most comfortable thinking, working, and talking within such a conceptual and linguistic context. Ethics, on the other hand, is more difficult. Perhaps, this accounts, at least in part, for there being so little discussion of morality in special education and why these discussions typically end with a tacit acceptance of relativism—"whose morality?" And the discussion of moral responsibility has tended to focus on the ways in which individuals are less than responsible for their behavior due to pathology, social circumstances, or defeating habits. We are cautious in the discussions of ethics and morality for fear of "moralizing" and "passing judgment." Yet, the presumption that those who teach children ought to adopt an amoral stance is untenable.

The development and reinforcement of character traits or virtues ought not to be factored out of a special education program. In fact, it may be crucial to success in the field. The behavior we would change in a student has meaning in his/her moral construction of self and others. The question is not whether special educators are involved in character education; it is whether or not there is awareness of that involvement and willingness to make character education an explicit part of the curriculum.

Another aspect of the issue of character morality has to do with the culture of the classroom and the school. Starratt (1994) has described the process of building an ethical school. Discussions of full inclusion as opposed to pull-out programs could go differently if cast in the context of an ethical school, one in which ethical qualities of character and place were addressed directly in building and nurturing a caring and learning school culture.

There is, however, a rather serious block to the success of a character morality–based educational approach. There is a tension in contemporary Western societies between the way the social/political process actually and theoretically operates and the social climate that character moralists seem inclined to favor.

DEMOCRACY AND SPECIAL EDUCATION

Schools prepare students to participate in a democracy and make informed decisions affecting themselves and those in their community. In our current system of liberal democracy, decisions are generally made based on the will of the majority with the understanding that there is no privileged conception of the good. Within such a system, special education asks for an exception to accommodate the individual needs of the minority of children who bear special education labels, including those who may be incapable of effectively representing their own interests. Needless to say, this position produces ethical dilemmas including the questions of "Who speaks for this minority?" "How can the interests of special education students and their families best be negotiated in our schools and communities?" and "How much can we expect the majority to concede in accommodating this minority?"

In the Western philosophical tradition, reflecting the current dichotomy of conceptions, there are two rather different stories about democracy, liberalism and communitarianism (or Athenian-style democracy). The Athenian model is what Barber (1994) calls a "strong democracy," whereas the liberal democratic conception requires a rather "thin" democratic political structure. Athenian-style democracy is conceptually thick, building political order and structure out of the very meaning of the term "democracy." It is radically participatory for those considered citizens. Government is carried on through institutions designed to facilitate civic participation in agenda-setting, deliberation, and the implementation of policy. The Athenian model is characterized by the transformation of multiple individual conceptions of the good into a commonly held, and rather singular, communal conception of the good toward whose achievement and/or maintenance political processes are directed.

The Athenian conception derives its strength from the fact that the citizens' individual interests are seen to orbit around their shared conception of the good, tending, by exclusion, to produce a homogeneous population. Citizens in the participatory process of governing, in the Athenian-style democracy, formulate the public ends toward which their community strives and thereby defines itself.

Communitarian democracy amateurizes politics and government, creating a community out of a collective. That community transforms the individual while it sustains itself. It educates its citizens to become effective public participants and to appreciate and adopt its values, its shared vision, and its purpose. The sustenance of the "strong" democracy requires the nurturing of an abiding sense of civic responsibility in the members that is developed through training in the arts of citizenship.

Other than sharing some of the basic descriptive terminology of democracy, there is very little in common between the Athenian communitarian democratic ideal and the conception of the liberal democrat that has dominated the political scene in the West for the past three or four centuries. The liberal democrat's roots are firmly planted in the individualism that marks political philosophy in the West since at least the seventeenth century. Liberal democracy embraces individual autonomy, and its politics is the politics of individual interests and interest groups comprised of individuals. The liberal democratic process, for it, is an adversarial encounter of factions, individuals associated into loosely confederated groups that are generally united only with respect to a single issue, likely with quite distinct conceptions of the good, collectively and individually, each seeking majority support. Its basic conception of government is that of decision-making between competing points of view. Though it may seek consensus, it is not interested in the formative project of citizenship. It radically disassociates the public from the private sphere.

The liberal democrat conceives of the decision, whether it be made by the single voter in the booth choosing among a list of candidates or casting a vote as a representative in the halls of the legislature, as the heart and soul of the political process. The vote is what matters, not the discussion of the issue. The majority rules, and its rule is not constrained with respect to the outcomes to be reached, except that it cannot infringe upon the constitutionally established political freedoms of its citizens. This view of liberal democracy, however, generates a paradox, as Amy Gutmann notes, "in the tension between the popular will and the conditions of maintaining the popular will over time." A liberal democrat should oppose any decision of the majority that restricts any of the basic liberties because it would not be democratic to restrict those freedoms, but the same liberal democrat should support the majority's decision because not doing so would be undemocratic. What then should the liberal democrat do if the majority votes, for example, to restrict the freedom to practice religion by excluding from protection any religion that forbids its practitioners from seeking medical treatment for their ill children? So liberal democrats can discover themselves trapped in their own rhetoric once they start using theoretical stratagems to salvage majority rule from its illiberal and undemocratic tendencies.

Communitarian democracy is deliberation-oriented, and it is deliberation over how the social world, the community, is to be formed and sustained. It is crucially involved in persuasion and the critical examination of options. It is what Barry calls decision by discussion of merits. It leads, of course, to the vote, but the vote is not the be-all and end-all of the democratic process, though it embodies the sense of urgency that marks the process as political. The choice-oriented liberal democrat who sees the political process as a combat between various individual and group preferences can only stave off what could easily become an "anarchy of adversary politics" with the principle of majority rule, despite its potential paradoxes. "Majoritarianism," Barber bemoans, "is a tribute to the failure of democracy." That is not really accurate. It is the failure of communitarian democracy to sustain itself in the modern world; it is not the failure of liberal democracy, which is prepared to live with the paradoxes in the name of getting to closure on an issue.

The foundations of liberal democracy are built on the theory of rational choice. Independent rational preference based on one's conception of one's own best interests drives the political and the economic theory. Political arrangements and choices are the result of aggregated individual choices. Compromise, sometimes called the art of politics, is typically understood as the Pareto optimal choice when one cannot maximize one's preferences, where preferences and their orderings are prepolitical and independent of communal relationships and commitments, even unchosen commitments such as those embedded in culture and heritage. The need for compromise arises, of course, when conflicts of interests occur in the social world. Such conflicts are bargainable, but they do not disappear in the compromise. They are set aside as the competing individuals or groups settle for something less than the realization of their interests in total.

The communitarian democrat requires that citizens develop and practice conversational techniques that allow the forging of a common vision and plan of action for the community. Such techniques are not conducive to a pluralistic or diverse citizenry. But that is exactly the sort of citizenry that dominates modern Western democracies. In fact rather narrow bands of conversational proficiency are typical of people in the contemporary world and that works against anything like the communitarian's common vision–oriented ideal.

The communitarian ideal of democracy is, first and foremost, a story of place, a narrative of a people in a place. Commitment to that narrative drives the communal conscience to sustain the institutions of self-government. No such narrative is possible in the pluralistic social world of contemporary Western democracies like the United States. That is not to say that we have no stories or that we have no sense of place. Rather, with the help and urging of the liberal democrat, we have come to the realization, though probably regretfully, that it is impossible to compose a single coherent narrative that would make interpretive sense for most of the people of their current conditions, explain their commonality, and bring order and a sense of place to their lives. There are far too many strands in the story of America for the communitarian storyteller to weave a coherent communal identity to provide the exemplar for the formative project of communitarian democracy. The liberal conception of procedural democracy, on the other hand, requires little by way of narrative, but it has propensity to morph into a Kafkaesque bureaucracy.

For special education, the issue of ethics and political theory is especially important because children with disabilities are a minority. The interests of children are always juxtaposed with majority interests. Principles supporting the allocation of disproportionate resources and the view that individual needs rather than equality should drive educational policy are ethical matters. The political process sustaining the interests of children with disabilities in federal policy is dynamic, and moral perspectives are transient. Attempts in 1980 and 1981 to reduce federal responsibility by not fully funding PL 94-142 is a vivid example.

In a classic study of the American character, Bellah and his colleagues (1985) described the tension between the focus on individuals and community. The scales are tipped, they found, clearly in the direction of individualism. The deep tradition of liberal democracy with a focus on individualism, privacy, and rational choice does not fit the communitarian image typically conjured up when thinking about the "disability community" and the special needs of minorities, including those with disabilities.

The ethical implications of the tension between liberal democratic and communitarian political theories are important for special education. The moral defense of inclusion depends, in part, on the vision we have for the society we hope to be and the purpose of education in supporting that vision. The debates we have about the relative efficacy of different service delivery systems in meeting the needs of children with disabilities in schools are important. The argument that we should not harm children by denying them the best education we know to provide is sound. It becomes more complicated, however, when one is forced to think in a finite fiscal context and the issue is the relative harm distributed among all children. It is also complicated by the kinds of data used to make the efficacy argument. Some aspects of that issue are explored in the next section.

ETHICAL DILEMMAS IN KNOWLEDGE AND REPRESENTATION

One obvious response to whether children with disabilities are better served in special education programs or not is, What do the data show? The empirical case has been debated pro and con (Danforth, 1997; Fuchs & Fuchs, 1998; Carnine, 1991; Gartner & Lipsky, 1987; Stainback & Stainback, 1992; Kauffman, 1999). Although the empirical response is necessarily part of an answer, it is far from sufficient. One has to be concerned about the outcomes to be considered in assessing the success of the program. How are children's lives impacted by the program? Are the social costs less than the gains for the children served?

Although considerable strides have been made in empirically validating practices (Carnine, 1991), the implementation of those practices in local contexts and the specification of meaningful dependent variables continue to challenge researchers in special education. The psychological models driving the specification of variables and the positivist epistemology of most of the research in special education have not led researchers into investigations, for example, of ethics and curriculum, ethics and teaching, or the development of moral community.

This is a complex area. Controversy surrounds claims and counterclaims about the nature and privileging of knowledge. Arguments center on different philosophies of science, with positivism being the traditional and still prevailing paradigm of the mainstream research community in special education, and the politics of knowledge, again with claims and counterclaims about the use or abuse of power in privileging a perspective. The context of this debate has changed dramatically during the past three decades. Different kinds of questions are being raised now, including not just what we know but how we know it (Gallagher, 1998). Do local school cultures and teachers vary so widely that generalizable interventions or procedures are unrealistic? Can an adequate account of a child's success in school be given in objective terms, or is it so embedded in experience and culture that only narrative accounts are meaningful?

These and other epistemological questions have been raised in limited ways within special education over the past decade (Danforth, 1995; Gallagher, 1998; Kauffman, 1999; Reid, Robinson, & Bunsen, 1995). Discussions in the special education literature have been difficult and, at times, even rancorous. Those defending more traditional positivist understandings are concerned about relativism and the practical implications of nonpositivist epistemologies for teaching children with disabilities (Kauffman, 1999; Sasso, 2001). Those challenging positivist positions have different epistemological views as well as concerns about the control and limitations being placed on scholarly debate by journal editors and resistance of federal funding agencies to support nonpositivist research.

The tension between views that seek to keep the faith with established epistemological traditions and those that seek a more pluralistic discourse about knowledge is reflected by contrasting statements about editorial policies in *Behavior Disorders* and *Mental Retardation*. Kauffman and Brigham (1999), editors of *Behavior Disorders*, wrote:

> Our conceptual orientation, like that of our predecessors, is scientific and positivistic. We believe this orientation best serves not only the profession but also the children and families for whom we advocate . . . . We will . . . do our utmost to discriminate legitimate from nonlegitimate claims to knowledge . . . . In our view, the field will progress most assuredly (and we believe that progress is both possible and desirable) by noting how scientific understanding is built by the slow, often painstaking accretion of reliable and replicable findings, often beginning with the homeliest of topics and questions.

Taylor (2000), editor of *Mental Retardation*, wrote:

> The role of journal editors in our field is not to silence new voices—or theories, methodologies, and modes of exposition, for that matter—but to allow opportunities for reasoned argument, discussion, and debate. If, indeed, we can believe in progress, this is how it can occur.

The sociology and politics of knowledge are well illustrated by the contrast of these two editorial policies. We are not suggesting that either position is unethical. Rather, we are raising the question about how best to construct ethical arguments about the control of knowledge. Each position is stated in good faith and predicated on different understandings of knowledge. Critical theorists worry about the privileging of the positivist voice in the *Behavior Disorders* policy. Positivists may worry about the quality, and even the legitimacy of the view of knowledge reflected in the open position of the *Mental Retardation* policy.

There is an extensive literature on epistemology in the social sciences that has appeared during the last two decades. The differences reflected in the two policy statements are consistent with differences found in that literature.

The at times adversarial debates in special education have not, however, been so much about epistemological issues such as objectivity or the existence of an observer-independent reality, although these are points of disagreement, but of the rights of ideologically minority voices. The tensions are about control and fairness in the exercise of professional duties of editors in the illustrations provided here. We do not have legitimate ways to adjudicate these issues, and rancorous differences have emerged among good people. (This is not a problem found only in special education. It is a problem in the multiple discourse communities in the social sciences.)

Notwithstanding the strong convictions about epistemology held by different members of the professional special education community, the issues cut deep into the conversation about the ethical defense of philosophies of research. Scheurich and Young (1997) reference scholars of color (Banks, 1993; 1995; Gordon, Miller, & Rollock, 1990; Stanfield, 1985; 1993, 1994) who have suggested that the "popular" epistemologies used in educational research—positivism, postpositivism, neorealism, interpretivism, constructivism, critical theory, and postmodernism/poststructuralism—may be racially biased. They have argued that epistemologies, not our use of them, are racist. They point out that epistemological debates focus on issues such as quantitative versus qualitative research (e.g., Cizek, 1995), objectivity versus subjectivity (e.g., Heshusius, 1994), validity (e.g., Lenzo, 1995; Moss, 1994), or paradigmatic issues in general (e.g., Bereiter, 1994; Delandshere & Petrosky, 1994; Gage, 1989), but they do not address the issue of race. Scheurich and Young (1997) argue that the lack of response to the charge of epistemological racism is a function of researchers not understanding "how race is a critically significant epistemological problem in educational research" (p. 4).

Although a significant problem in social science research in general, this issue has particular relevance to special education where the story has included racist practices in the assessment and placement of children with disabilities. Claims of objectivity do not remove researchers from culpability. The research knowledge base for practice is no better than the moral integrity of the research enterprise. The implication of epistemological racism has profound ethical implications in special education where African American males are placed disproportionately in special education services. To the extent that the social science tools we use to know and to legitimize our knowledge are racist, then we have institutionalized the systematic negation of legitimate interests of minorities.

Working in an applied area, special educators are interested in understanding the needs and improving the lives of children with disabilities. As in general education, there is more interest in established and, as possible, empirically validated practices—what to do and how to do it—than in philosophical deliberations about the moral justifications for practice. Professional preparation programs at all levels, typically, give relatively little attention to moral foundations of practice.

The same is true in graduate education, whether in educating teachers or researchers. The focus in training researchers, for example, is on methods of inquiry with little or no attention given to the epistemological foundations of research or the ethics, politics, or sociology of knowledge. The result is that discussions of practice or research tend to focus on methods based on experience and/or research, while philosophical discussions of the justifying reasons for those methods—moral or epistemological—can be rather thin at best or even incoherent.

While special education was growing up in the last half of the 20th century, radical changes were occurring in the physical and social sciences and in technology. As special education researchers and policymakers were developing and extending the knowledge bases for practice and policy, the philosophy of science was changing and creating a complex conversation about the nature of knowledge. The traditional positivism that had guided many of the social sciences, and certainly had a pervasive influence on special education philosophy and research in the form of behaviorism, has been severely challenged by philosophers of science (Popper, 1974). By the end of the century, the conventional positivist-based assumptions about objectivity and certainty had changed and alternative understandings of knowledge occupied a prominent position in the scholarship of different social sciences and humanities. The "new" discourses on research in the social sciences and humanities have focused more on topics such as the nature and power of language (Rorty, 1989), the assumptions about common realities, the connection of observers and observations, ethics, and meaning (Foucault, 1972; Rorty, 1989; Gadamer, 1976; Goodman 1978).

Changes in the philosophies of social science contributed to a loss of consensus in understanding and interpreting education research, and multiple discourse emerged as reflected in the literature in the 1990s (Cizek, 1995; Danforth, 1995; Garrison, 1994; Heshusius, 1994; Skrtic, 1991; Iano, 1986). Having grown out of psychology and medicine, special education researchers were concerned with the learning and behavioral characteristics of children and interventions to address their needs. Notwithstanding, some important work dating back to the 1980s (Iano, 1986; Heshusius, 1989) and 1990s (Skrtic, 1991) challenging the dominant philosophy of research in special education, most special education researchers, especially in the fields of behavior disorders and learning disabilities, have generally maintained a strong commitment to a positivist epistemology (Kauffman, 1999; Sasso, 2001).

Special education researchers, guided by a well-developed and robust philosophy of behavior, generated a substantial knowledge base of technologies for defining and engineering change in behavior. The behavioral philosophy served the field well in the late 1960s, 1970s, and into the 1980s (and some would argue that it continues to serve the field well). With public schools assuming responsibility for educating all children, behavior modification procedures could be taught to teachers in a reasonable amount of time, and many of the procedures were effective in managing the behavior of children in schools and in mental health settings.

Special education is not a discipline and, as it grew to a multibillion dollar service industry, it became predictably self-referenced and lost the relationship with disciplines such as psychology that had guided much of its earlier work (Paul et al., 1997). One consequence of this history is that the changing epistemological perspectives in the social sciences have not been reflected in mainstream special education research.

The general question is not whether these advances, and the epistemology guiding them, are valid and useful. Rather, a more basic question is whether there is a justifiable reason for limiting research and scholarship in special education to a positivist perspective. Ethical issues are relevant in the manner in which the freedom of scholarship is supported or curtailed; they are also relevant in defending principles, including principles of scholarship.

The ethical issue in the politics of knowledge is complicated by the fluid state of arguments about knowledge in the social sciences. The resolution should occur in informed communities of scholars who are sensitive to the limits on what we know at the present time and appreciate the need for an open ethical discourse to enable us to learn from those who hold a different view.

CONCLUDING PERSPECTIVE

Since the development of the modern field of special education in the middle of the 20th century, the pressure of identifying and providing an appropriate education for children with disabilities has occupied the full attention of special educators. It is unfortunate that, in this context, "special education training programs regarding collegial relationships, research projects, and policy-making processes have given only superficial attention to how we might best resolve our ethical problems" (Howe & Miramontes, 1992, p. xiii).

The growth of special education as a useful and valued set of programs has been limited by several realities. Facts are blunted by fictions about disabilities, the vision of education as science or as art has been clouded by philosophical differences among educators, and the research agenda has been thwarted by a lack of consensus on a philosophy of inquiry. Accountability measures burden practitioners with excessive paper, and policymakers continue to be conflicted in justifying the escalating costs in view of the perceived social benefit of special education practices.

The absence of training and research in ethics has been a regrettable omission. However efficacious the interventions, however credible the research, and however informed the policies, the education of children with disabilities is a morally complex set of activities with many ethical challenges.

Our teacher education and doctoral programs should prepare teachers and potential leaders in the field to understand and respect the complexities of different epistemological traditions and to engage in ethical as well as technical analysis of issues in research and practice. These are policy issues that should engage the interests and imaginations of special education as a field and not be limited to the preferences of a few.

Special education is in a place unlike any in its history, attacked in the media, condemned by unaccountable assertions of inefficacy or, worse, unethical practices. For all we know about the power of the context in shaping behavior, we must take care in interpreting current signals about the professional standing of special education.

We are in an age of deep transformation when disciplinary boundaries are frayed and traditions are coming to terms with competing understandings of knowledge and different moral visions of education. Neither a bunker mentality designed to protect hard-won gains nor a position that gives equal standing to all views, irrespective of ethical and epistemological content, is going to serve the interest of the field in the future. The maturity of the professional discourse found in *American Psychologist* or in the AERA journals would seem appropriate models. These journals, clearly anchored in established discipline-based traditions, include diverse views and the scholarly work of different discourse communities.

Three issues stand out as among the most critical to sustaining the work of special educators. First, it is essential that we recognize the implications of the minority status of students with disabilities in a liberal democracy. The tension between the conservative and liberal understandings of the society's obligation to provide appropriate education and care for all citizens is a central issue in the formation of public policy. Modern day special education began in the 1960s when advocacy for minorities (African Americans, women, children, persons with disabilities, and others) had strong footing in the cultural zeitgeist of the era. The minority status was, in fact, a positive feature that legitimized the advocacy movement on their behalf. Things have changed. The rights of those less able to compete and those with gifts less likely to be acknowledged in the competitive marketplace of public education must now be defended on new terms. The present environment pits teachers against teachers, schools against schools, and children against children in competing for public resources. The present political context is fraught with hazzards for those who need special supports to succeed, including students with disabilities.

Second, the inclusion of all children in regular education programs is an ethical as well as empirical matter. The determination of the ethical interest of the child is a matter that must be considered in the presence of information about how and where the child's needs are best met. Whereas the educational policy issue turns on a consideration of the rights and interests of all children, the understanding of rights and interests is constrained by the educational imagination of the policymakers. Those who make policies and those who implement them function in social contexts in which their judgments are confounded by political forces that have moral meaning. Examples include preoccupation with high-stakes testing, mythologies about disability, unchallenged and uninformed mind-sets about what education is and how it occurs, race, gender, and class-biased models of what a classroom and a school should look like. The inclusion debate is a major special education policy issue with significant ethical implications, but it is not a special education issue alone. The ethical issues are, perhaps, most dramatically evident in the practical interface of special and general education where children being "included" live their lives. The qualities of their lives are directly impacted by the outcomes of debates that can overlook the real dependent variables that are essential to the social, emotional, and spiritual well-being of children.

Third, the debate about what counts for knowledge must be open and respectful. The issues are of vital interest to the field and, more importantly, to the children served by special educators. Andrews et al. (2000) distinguished between incremental reformers and substantial reconceptualists in special education. Incremental reformers emphasize the positive known features of special education and support a systematic improvement of practice through established approaches. Substantial reconceptualists take more of a critical perspective and see more serious problems in the knowledge and ethical foundations of special education. They support more fundamental changes in the field. Andrews and his colleagues, including the first author of the present article, advocate bridging the divide. They comment:

> We need to push ahead with traditional and nontraditional research for improving knowledge and practice about enhancing individual student capacity and promoting a caring school culture in which the lines between student categories meld. Our shared goal is the welfare of students with disabilities and all children. (p. 267)

They acknowledge the challenge and affirm an optimism that the field can bridge the divide. The present authors share the hope that the divide can be bridged with respectful appreciation of different points of view and an affirmation of the values of a diverse academic community of special educators.

Multiple discourses are required to instantiate the complexities of ethics and knowledge in special education, but neither essentialist dogma nor relativist ideology is likely to spawn sites of mutual respect and understanding. Both the art and social science of educating all children must occupy prominent places at tables where the moral vision of care and education as well as the instrumental efficacy of instructional practices and schooling are imagined and formed. Perspectival differences between individuals or groups who hold positions at variance with others, no matter how well-established and anchored in precedent or interesting and different, need not be divisive nor defeat legitimate professional purposes. The lack of knowledge among the wisest of us and the lack of humility among those of us most audacious have left all of us without a shared vision of leadership that connects us to the common moral purpose of improving the lives of children with disabilities and their families. Special education is not lacking intellectual capital; however, the press of the discontinuity between the outcomes of practice and the promises of the law has created urgency in defending the entire project of educational support for children with disabilities. Struggles over control of voice have, in some instances, created a culture of rancor and cynicism. Hope for a rapprochement that enables productive scholarship and advancement of the field rests, in part, on the courage and good will as well as the perspicacity of leaders who influence doctoral education programs, research funding priorities, and journal policies.

DISCUSSION QUESTIONS

1. Discuss how understandings about sociopolitical contexts can affect the view of special education.
2. Explain the basic premise of choice morality and how it may be operationalized in decisions regarding special education.
3. Discuss the theory of character morality in relation to the intended and unintended evil that has taken place in the field of special education. How might a choice moralist view things differently?
4. Discuss the place of special education in a liberal democracy and how the communitarian ideal of democracy can inform discussion of professional issues in the field.
5. Discuss factors that have contributed to a call for developing an ethical basis for discourse on the nature and representation of knowledge in the field of special education.

NOTE

The authors wish to acknowledge the thoughtful feedback on this work we received from Betty Epanchin, James Gallagher, Kenneth Howe, William Morse, Nel Noddings, Wayne Sailor, Tom Skrtic, Brenda Townsend, and Daphne Thomas. The chapter was substantially improved with the feedback we used, and areas that still need improvement are likely those where we did not incorporate the views of our critics.

REFERENCES

Andrews, J., Carnine, D., Coutinho, M., Edgar, E., Forness, S., Fuchs, L., Jordan, D., Kauffman, J., Patton, J., Paul, J., Rosell, J., Rueda, R., Schiller, E., Skrtic, T., & Wong, J. (2000). Perspective: Bridging the special education divide. *Remedial and Special Education, 21,* 258–267.
Austin, J. L. (1961). *Philosophical papers.* Oxford: Clarendon Press.

Baers, C.W. (1908). *A mind that found itself; An autobiography.* New York: Longmans, Green.

Banks, J. A. (1993). The canon debate, knowledge construction, and multicultural education. *Educational Researcher, 22*(5), 4–14.

Banks, J. A. (1995). The historical reconstruction of knowledge about race: Implications for transformative learning. *Educational Researcher, 24,* 15–25.

Bellah, R. N., et al. (1985). *Habits of the heart: Individualism and commitment in American life.* Berkeley: University of California Press.

Bereiter, C. (1994). Constructivism, socioculturalism, and Popper's world 3. *Educational Researcher, 23* (7), 21–23.

Blatt, B., & Kaplan, F. (1966). *Christmas in purgatory: A photographic essay on mental retardation.* Boston: Allyn & Bacon.

Carnine, D. (1991). Direct instruction applied to mathematics for the general education classroom. In J. W. Lloyd, N. N. Singh, & A. C. Repp (Eds.), *The Regular Education Initiative: Alternative perspectives on concepts, issues, and models* (pp. 163–176). Sycamore, IL: Sycamore.

Cizek, G. J. (1995). Crunchy granola and the hegemony of the narrative. *Educational Researcher, 24* (2), 26–28.

Coates, R. (1990). *A street is not a home.* Buffalo, NY: Prometheus.

Danforth, S. (1995). Toward a critical theory approach to lives considered emotionally disturbed. *Behavioral Disorders, 20*(2), 136–143.

Danforth, S. (1997). On what basis hope? Modern progress and postmodern possibilities. *Mental Retardation, 35,* 83–106.

Delandshere, G., & Petrosky, A. J. (1994). Capturing teachers' knowledge: Performance assessment. *Educational Researcher, 23* (5), 11–18.

Deshler, D. D., & Schumaker, J. B. (1986). Learning strategies: An instructional alternative for low-achieving adolescents. *Exceptional Children, 52,* 583–590.

Detterman, D.K. & Thompson, L.A. (1997). What is so special about special education? *American Psychologist, 52,* 1082–1090.

Dillon, S. (1994, April 7). Special education soaks up New York's school resources. *New York Times,* p. 18.

Dokecki, P. R., & Zaner, R. M. (Eds.). (1986). *Ethics of dealing with persons with severe handicaps.* Baltimore: Paul H. Brookes.

Dunn, L. (1968). Special education for the mildly retarded—Is much of it justifiable? *Exceptional Children, 35,* 5–24.

Elkind, D. (1997). The death of child nature: Education in the postmodern world. *Phi Delta Kappan, 79,* 241–245.

Fasching, D. (1997). Beyond values: Story, character, and public policy in American schools. In J. Paul, et al., *Ethics and decision making in local schools: Inclusion, policy and reform.* Baltimore: Paul H. Brookes.

Ferguson, P. M., & Ferguson, D. L. (1988). The future of inclusive educational practice: Constructive tension and the potential for reflective reform. *Childhood Education, 74*(5), 302–308.

Fischer, J. M. (1986). *Moral responsibility.* Ithaca, NY: Cornell University Press.

Foucault, M. (1972). *The archaeology of knowledge* (A. Sheridan Smith, Trans.). New York: Pantheon Books.

Frankfurt, H. (1988). *The importance of what we care about.* Cambridge: Cambridge University Press

French, P. (2001). *The virtues of vengeance.* Lawrence, KS: University Press of Kansas.

Fuchs, D., & Fuchs, L. S. (1995). Counterpoint: Special education: Ineffective? Immoral? *Exceptional Children, 61*(3), 303–305.

Gadamer, H. (1976). *Philosophical hermeneutics* (D. E. Linge, Trans.). Berkeley, CA: University of California Press.

Gage, N. L. (1989). The paradigm wars and their aftermath: A historical sketch of research on teaching since 1989. *Educational Researcher, 18*(7), 4–10.

Gallagher, D. J. (1998). The scientific knowledge base of special education: Do we know what we think we know? *Exceptional Children, 64*(4), 493–502.

Garrison, J. (1994). Realism, Deweyan pragmatism, and educational research. *Educational Researcher, 23*(1), 5–14.

Gartner, A., & Lipsky, D. K. (1987). Beyond special education: Toward a quality system for all students. *Harvard Educational Review, 57*(4), 367–395.

Goodman, N. (1978). *Ways of worldmaking.* Indianapolis: Hackett.

Gordon, E. W., Miller, F., & Rollock, D. (1990). Coping with communicentric bias in knowledge production in the social sciences. *Educational Researcher, 19*(30), 14–19.

Granger, L., & Granger, B. (1986). *The magic feather: The truth about special education.* New York: Dutton.

Grossman, H. (1998). *Ending discrimination in special education.* Springfield, IL: Charles C. Thomas.

Herman, B. (2000). *Morality and everyday life, Proceedings of the American Philosophical Association, 74,* 2, 29–45.

Heshusius, L. (1989). The Newtonian mechanistic paradigm, special education and countours of alternatives: An overview. *Journal of Learning Disabilities, 22,* 403–415.

Heshusius, L. (1994). Freeing ourselves from objectivity: Managing subjectivity or turning toward a participatory mode of consciousness? *Educational Researcher, 23*(3), 15–22.

Howe, K. R. (1996). Educational ethics, social justice and children with disabilites. In C. Christensen & R. Rizvi (Eds.), *Disability and the dilemmas of education and justice.* Philadelphia: Open University Press.

Howe, K. R., & Miramontes, O. B. (1992). *The ethics of special education.* New York: Teachers College Press.

Iano, R. P. (1986). The study and development of teaching: With implications for the advancement of special education. *Remedial and Special Education, 7,* 50–61.

Johnson, J. L. (1969). Special education and the inner city: A challenge for the future or another means for cooling the mark out? *Journal of Special Education, 3*(3), 241–251.

Kant, E. (1969). *Foundations of the metaphysics of morals* (second section), trans. Lewis White Beck. Indianapolis: Bobbs-Merrill.

Kauffman, J. M. (1999). Commentary: Today's special education and its message for tomorrow. *Journal of Special Education, 32*(4), 244–254.

Kauffman, J. M., & Hallahan, D. P. (1995). *The illusion of full inclusion: A comprehensive critique of a current special education bandwagon.* Austin, TX: Pro-ed.

Kekes, J. (1990). *Facing evil.* Princeton, NJ: Princeton University Press.

Lenzo, K. (1995). Validity and self-reflexivity meet poststructuralism: Scientific ethos and the transgressive self. *Educational Researcher, 24*(4), 17–23.

Lieberman, L. M. (1992). Preserving special education for those who need it. In W. Stainback and S. Stainback (Eds.), *Controversial issues confronting special education.* Boston: Allyn and Bacon.

Lightner, D. (1999). *Asylum, prison and poorhouse.* Carbondale: Southern Illinois University Press.

Massachusetts Association of School Superintendents (1997). *The impact of special education on educational reform.* Boston, MA.

Moss, P. A. (1994). Can there be validity without reliability? *Educational Researcher,* *23*(2), 5–12.

Nash, R. J. (1996). *Real World Ethics frameworks for educations and human service professionals.* New York: Teachers College Press.

Noblit, G., Paul, J., & Schlechty, P. The social and political construction of emotional disturbance. In J. Paul, & B. Epanchin. (1991). *Educating emotionally disturbed children and youth: Theories and practices for teachers.* New York: Macmillan Publishing Co.

Noddings, N. (1984). *Caring: A feminine approach to ethics and moral education,* Berkley, CA: University of California Press.

Noddings, N. (1992). *The challenge to care in schools: An alternative approach to education.* New York: Teachers College Press.

Paul, J. L., Churton, M., Rosselli-Kostoryz, H., Morse, W. C., Marfo, K., Lavely, C., & Thomas, D. (Eds.). (1997). *Foundations of special education: Basic knowledge informing research and practice in special education.* Pacific Grove, CA: Brooks/Cole.

Paul, J., Kane, M., & Kane, R. (1996). *Survey of doctoral programs in special education.* Unpublished manuscript, University of South Florida at Tampa.

Poplin, M. S. (1987). Self-imposed blindness: The scientific method in education. *Remedial and Special Education, 8* (6), 31–37.

Popper, K. (1974). Autobiography. In P. A. Schilpp (Ed.), *The Philosophy of Karl Popper.* La Salle: Open Court.

Pugach, M. C. & Warger, C. L. (1996). *Curriculum trends, special education and reform.* New York: Teachers College Press.

Putnam, H. (1978). *Meaning and the moral sciences.* London: Routledge.

Ramey, C. T., & Ramey, S. L. (1998). In defense of special education. *American Psychologist,* p. 1159.

Reid, D. K., Robinson, S. J., & Bunsen, T. (1995). Empiricism and beyond. *Remedial and Special Education, 16*(3), 131–141.

Rorty, R. (1989). *Contingency, irony and solidarity.* New York: Cambridge University Press.

Sasso, G. M. (2001). The retreat from inquiry and knowledge in special education. *Journal of Special Education, 34*(4), 178–193.

Scheurich, J. J., & Young, M. D. (1997, May). Coloring epistemologies: Are our research epistemologies racially biased? *Educational Researcher, 26*(4), 4–16.

Segall, M.H., Lonner, W.J. & Berry, J.W. (1998). Cross-cultural psychology as a scholarly discipline. On the flowering of culture in behavioral research. *American Psychologist. 53,* 1101–1110.

Seligman, M.E.P.(1998). Positive social science. *APA Monitor. 29,* 4.

Shanker, A. (1994). Full inclusion is neither free nor appropriate. *Educational Leadership, 52*(4), 18–21.

Skrtic, T. M. (1991). *Behind special education: A critical analysis of professional culture and school organization.* Denver, CO: Love.

Smith, J. (1995). *Pieces of purgatory.* Belmont, CA: Wadsworth.

Stainback, W., & Stainback, S. (1992). *Controversial issues confronting special education: Divergent perspectives.* Needham Heights, MA: Allyn and Bacon.

Stanfield, J. H., II. (1985). The ethnocentric basis of social science knowledge production. *Review of Research in Education, 12,* 387–415.

Stanfield, J. H., II. (1993). Epistemological considerations. In J. H. Stanfield, II, & R. M. Dennis (Eds.), *Race and ethnicity in research methods* (pp. 16–36). Newbury Park, CA: Sage.

Stanfield, J. H., II. (1994). Ethnic modeling in qualitative research. In N. K. Denzin & Y. S. Lincoln (Eds.), *Handbook of qualitative inquiry* (175–188). Newbury Park, CA: Sage.

Starratt, R. (1994). *Building an ethical school: A practical response to the moral crisis in schools*. Washington: The Falmer Press.

Symons, F. J., & Warren, S. F. (1998). Straw men and strange logic: Issues and pseudo-issues in special education. *American Psychologist,* 1160–1161.

Taylor, S. J. (2000). Two perspectives on Foucault and postmodernism. *Mental Retardation, 38*(4), 363.

Tomes, N. (1994). *The art of asylum keeping*. Philadelphia: University of Pennsylvania Press.

Van Doninck, B. (1983). Special education resource programs. *Special Education in Canada, 57*(1), 4–5, 7–9.

Westheimer, J., & Kahne, J. (1998). Education for action: Preparing youth for participatory democracy. In W. Ayers, J. A. Hunt, & T. Quinn (Eds.), *Teaching for social justice*. New York: Teachers College Press.

Zuboff, A. (1995). Morality as what one really desires. *Midwest Studies in Philosophy, 20.*

Index

('i' indicates an illustration; 't' indicates a table)

About the Contributors

ANN CRANSTON-GINGRAS is an associate professor at the University of South Florida. She is the Director of the Center for Migrant Education and the Principal Investigator and Director of the federally funded High School Equivalency program for Youth from Migrant Farmworker Families. Dr. Cranston-Gingras conducts research and publishes in the areas of migrant education and special education with an emphasis on social justice and policy issues. She is a past president of the National Migrant Education HEP/CAMP Association. Dr. Cranston-Gingras is the co-author of a text, *Teaching Learners with Diverse Abilities* (1998).

MICHAEL W. CHURTON is the director of distance learning international development and research in educational outreach at the University of South Florida. He is also a tenured professor and on the doctoral faculty in the department of special education. He has served as graduate coordinator and as department chairperson of special education at Appalachian State University. He formerly directed the Greater Tampa Bay Special Education Consortium and was instrumental in establishing a distance-learning program among the partnership schools. He developed a comprehensive distance-learning faculty and course support unit at USF and now leads the distance learning efforts for international development and research. His publications include a textbook on methods in special education and numerous articles on special education and distance learning.

KAREN L. COLUCCI is a visiting assistant professor at the University of South Florida. She is currently the coordinator of the Professional Development School without Walls partnership between the Special Education and Elementary Education departments at USF and two local school districts. She is also the co-director of the National Clearinghouse for Special Education Teaching Cases. Her research interests include teacher education and the development and use of teaching cases for teacher education programs.

SHERMAN DORN is an historian of education at the University of South Florida. He is the author of *Creating the Dropout: An Institutional and Social History of School Failure* (Praeger, 1996) and is currently writing a history of special education in the urban South since 1940.

BETTY C. EPANCHIN is a professor in special education whose research and professional interests focus on teacher education and the education of students with emotional and behavioral disabilities. Before she joined the faculty at the University of South Florida, she held a joint appointment at the University of North Carolina at Chapel Hill and Wright School, a residential school for students with emotional disabilities. She has taught in an elementary school and directed the educational program of a residential school for students with emotional disabilities, grades pre-K through high school. She also worked as a school psychologist and a child and family therapist in a psychiatric hospital.

PATRICIA FAGAN is a visiting assistant professor in the Department of Special Education at the University of South Florida, and Project Director for the USF Regional Comprehensive System of Personnel Development. In addition to teaching responsibilities, Dr. Fagan has served as coordinator of a collaborative research group on ethics and policy. As a Francis Eldvidge Doctoral Fellow at the Ethics Center at USF, she conducted and promoted research on the impact of ethics and character education on at-risk students, and coordinated the Commitment to Character pilot program in local schools.

PETER FRENCH is the Lincoln Chair in Ethics and the director of the Lincoln Center for Applied Ethics at Arizona State University. He was the Cole Chair in Ethics, director of the Ethics Center, and chair of the Department of Philosophy of the University of South Florida. He was Lennox Distinguished Professor of the humanities and professor of philosophy at Trinity University in San Antonio, Texas, and has taught at Northern Arizona University, the University of Minnesota, and Dalhousie University in Nova Scotia, and has served as Exxon Distinguished Research Professor in the Center for the Study of Values at the University of Delaware. He is the author of sixteen books, of which the most recent is *The Virtues of Vengeance* (2001).

JAMES J. GALLAGHER is a Kenan Professor of education at the University of North Carolina at Chapel Hill. He has worked in the field of education of exceptional children for over 40 years. He has served as U.S. Associate Commissioner for Education and as Deputy Assistant Secretary for Planning, Research, and Evaluation for the U.S. Office of Education, and was the first director of the Bureau of Education for the Handicapped. Dr. Gallagher served for seventeen years as director of the Frank Porter Graham Child Development Center at the University of North Carolina at Chapel Hill, an interdisciplinary research institution with an emphasis on the early education of young children from economically disadvantaged circumstances. He has served as president of the World Council for Gifted and Talented, president of the Council for Exceptional Children (CEC), and is past president of the National Association for Gifted Children (NAGC). He is co-author with Samuel Kirk and Nick Anastasiow of a textbook on educating exceptional children and co-author with his daughter, Dr. Shelagh Gallagher, of *Teaching the Gifted Child.*

KAREN M. HARRIS is completing her doctoral work at the University of South Florida in special education with an emphasis in child and family policy. Her areas of research interest include school reform and restructuring, urban education, and systems of care.

HAROLD HODGKINSON is the director of the Center for Demographic Policy. He is the author of 12 books and over 200 articles, for which he has been honored by the American Education Press Association. He has been editor of several journals, including *Harvard Educational Review* and *Journal of Higher Education.* His professional activities include writing, lecturing and producing demographic reports for states, cities, businesses and nonprofit groups.

KATHRYN L. LAFRAMBOISE is an associate professor in the Department of Childhood/Language Arts/Reading Education at the University of South Florida. She is co-principal investigator for the Professional Development School without Walls grant from the U.S. Department of Education, a collaboration between the Departments of Special Education and of Elementary Education at the College of Education at USF and two school districts, Pasco County Public Schools and Hillsborough County Schools.

CAROLYN D. LAVELY has served at the University of South Florida in various capacities: Coordinator of Mental Retardation, Coordinator of Specific Learning Disabilities, Director of Diagnostic and Remedial Projects for Children with Learning Disabilities, and as the Department Chair of Special Education. Currently, Dr. Lavely is the director of two institutes in the College of Education, the Institute for At-Risk Infants, Children, and Youth and their Families and the Institute for Instructional Research and Practice. Grants and contracts for these two institutes have resulted in $70 million in external funding for USF. Dr. Lavely is the author, co-author, or co-editor of several books and book chapters, 30 technical reports, over 50 refereed and invited articles, and various surveys, proposals, pamphlets, and handbooks.

BARBARA L. LOEDING is an associate professor at the University of South Florida, where she is in charge of the special education program on a regional campus (Lakeland). While on sabbatical she served as visiting associate professor at DePaul University (Chicago) in the School of Computer Science, Telecommunications, and Information Systems, and was part of their ASL Synthesizer research team. She has been engaged in research and publication in the areas of the use of assistive technology in special education, design of accessible software and Web pages, and augmentative/alternative communication.

NEL NODDINGS is Lee L. Jacks Professor of education, emerita, at Stanford University. She is past president of the Philosophy of Education Society and of the John Dewey Society. She is the author of more than 170 articles and chapters on various topics ranging from the ethics of care to mathematical problem solving, and of twelve books, of which her latest are *Starting at Home: Caring and Social Policy* (University of California Press) and *Educating Moral People: A Caring Alternative to Character Education* (Teachers College Press), both published in 2002. Dr. Noddings is the recipient of several awards, among them the Anne Rowe Award for contributions to the education of women (Harvard University), the Willystine Goodsell Award (AERA), a Lifetime Achievement Award from AERA (Div. B), and the Excellence in Education Award (Pi Lambda Theta).

MYRRHA PAMMER has a background in school reform, school choice, and special education. Dr. Pammer is currently the executive director of the Education Resource Center, where she provides technical assistance to public charter schools, private schools, and traditional public schools in Ohio. Dr. Pammer has taught both graduate and undergraduate courses in special education, school psychology, and behavior disorders.

PATRICIA A. PARRISH is the coordinator of interns and field placements at Saint Leo University. She has worked with students developing both typically and atypically in private and public educational settings. Her research interests include caring in student-teacher relationships and how beginning teachers nurture these relationships with students. Additionally, she is interested in teacher retention and how the teacher education curriculum can enhance teacher satisfaction.

JAMES L. PAUL was formerly a professor of special education at the University of North Carolina at Chapel Hill. He served as chair of the Division of Special Education in the School of Education at UNC for seven years and Acting Dean for one year. He came to the University of South Florida in December 1988 as Chair of the Department of Special Education and served in that capacity until 1996. Dr. Paul served for one year as a visiting scholar at Harvard and for one year at Stanford University. He has written or edited 25 books and over 75 articles and chapters. His writing and research have focused on emotional and behavioral disorders, learning disabilities, special education policy, families, and ethics. His current research and writing are in the areas of narrative, ethics, and philosophies of research.

CRYSTAL ROBERTS LADWIG is on the faculty at the University of Florida. She is currently working with the Autism Inclusion Project, focusing on individualized interventions for young children with autism who are included and who have significant behavior and/or social challenges. She is also completing a study of parents of young children with special needs regarding the transition from early intervention to preschool.

VESTENA ROBBINS currently serves as program evaluation coordinator for the Bridges Project, a federally funded school mental health initiative in Eastern Kentucky, and is an adjunct professor in the department of psychology at Eastern Kentucky University. Dr. Robbins is President-Elect of the Kentucky Council for Children with Behavior Disorders and serves on the Kentucky School Mental Health Coalition. Her areas of interest include systems of care for children and youth with emotional and behavioral disorders, school mental health, and positive behavioral supports.

ZENA H. RUDO is a program associate in policy research at the Southwest Educational Development Laboratory (SEDL) in Austin, Texas. Before joining SEDL, Dr. Rudo was an assistant professor at the University of South Florida in Tampa. She has extensive clinical, administrative, and research experience in the fields of family violence, special education, home/school/community collaboration, and education policy. She is the author of numerous articles and educational curricula and has presented nationally and internationally in her specialty fields.

DENISE SMITH is an assistant professor at Indiana University, South Bend, in the Department of Special Education. Before receiving her doctorate from the University of South Florida, she worked as a special education teacher for children with mild disabilities. Her current research interests include school violence and teacher reflection.

ELLA L. TAYLOR is a visiting assistant professor at the University of South Florida. She is currently the coordinator of the online master's degree program in gifted education and the virtual varying exceptionalities program. Her research interests include gifted education, teacher education and distance technology.

BRENDA L. TOWNSEND is an associate professor in the Department of Special Education at the University of South Florida. In 1995, she developed Project PILOT, the first of several initiatives that prepare African American men for urban special education teaching careers. As a result of that initiative, 31 African American men have graduated and are teaching children with special needs. She also directs the Chrysalis Program, which targets African American women, Hispanic men and women, and European American males to teach urban children with special needs. She co-authored a constructuve behavior management text and has written several book chapters on schooling issues related to African American children.

ANN P. TURNBULL is the co-director of the Beach Center on Disability and a professor in the Department of Special Education at The University of Kansas. She has been the principal investigator on more than 20 federally funded research grants and has written 12 books, including three leading textbooks in the field of special education. She has also written more than 175 articles, chapters, and monographs. In 1999, she was selected by a national consortium of seven organizations within the mental retardation field as one of 36 individuals who have made the most significant contribution to enhancing quality of life for individuals with mental retardation across the 20th century. She is the parent of three children, one of whom is an adult son with cognitive and mental health disabilities. She actively participates in the national and international family support movement.

H. R. TURNBULL is co-director of the Beach Center on Disability and a professor of special education and Courtesy Professor of Law. He has written eight books and over 200 articles, chapters, and monographs; has generated approximately $16 million in research and training grants at KU over 20 years; testified before Congress; written briefs in Supreme Court cases; and has carried out more than 200 technical assistance activities at the national, state, and local levels. He has been a senior officer or committee chairman in the American Association on Mental Retardation, The Arc, TASH, American Bar Association Committee on Disability Law, and Bazelon Center for Mental Disability Law. He has received leadership citations from the American Association on Mental Retardation and the Council for Exceptional Children, among others. He is also the parent of a son with multiple disabilities.

CATHY WOOLEY-BROWN is currently the Florida state coordinator for charter schools and directs the Florida Charter School Resource Center. She was previously the administrator of instructional services and the director of exceptional student education with Polk County Schools. Dr. Wooley-Brown has been a teacher, program supervisor, and administrator. She developed innovative teacher education programs in cooperation with the University of South Florida.